IoT Data Analytics using Python

Learn how to use Python to collect, analyze, and visualize IoT data

M S Hariharan

www.bpbonline.com

FIRST EDITION 2024
Reprint 2025

ISBN: 978-93-55515-759

Distributors:

BPB PUBLICATIONS
20, Ansari Road, Darya Ganj
New Delhi-110002
Ph: 23254990/23254991

DECCAN AGENCIES
4-3-329, Bank Street,
Hyderabad-500195
Ph: 24756967/24756400

MICRO MEDIA
Shop No. 5, Mahendra Chambers,
150 DN Rd. Next to Capital Cinema,
V.T. (C.S.T.) Station, MUMBAI-400 001
Ph: 22078296/22078297

BPB BOOK CENTRE
376 Old Lajpat Rai Market,
Delhi-110006
Ph: 23861747

To View Complete
BPB Publications Catalogue
Scan the QR Code:

Published by Manish Jain for BPB Publications, 20 Ansari Road, Darya Ganj, New Delhi-110002 and Printed by him at Repro India Ltd., Rewari

www.bpbonline.com

Dedicated to

My beloved mother, A.C. Kavery

and

My sister ***Uma*** *and niece* ***Pavithra***

About the Author

M S Hariharan, is a seasoned professional in the field of IT with over 25 years of experience. He holds a Masters in Data Science from Liverpool John Moores University, UK. Throughout his career, he has specialized in areas such as digital transformation, system integration, and automation.

Currently, he serves as the Principal Director at LTIMindtree, where he leads the development of the NxT Data platform , focusing on building innovative products. Prior to joining LTIMindtree, he spent six years leading Digital Transformation initiatives at AstraZeneca, contributing to their success in implementing effective solutions. Additionally, he also held the position of Lead Solution Architect in Hewlett-Packard Software Professional Services for more than 8 years.

His diverse experience and expertise has allowed him to contribute to numerous projects and drive impactful transformations within the industry. He is passionate about leveraging technology to drive business growth and optimize operations.

About the Reviewers

- **Niharika Panda** is a distinguished expert in the realm of the Internet of Things (IoT), IoT communication protocols, wireless sensor networks, and machine learning. With a profound skillset and a trail of accomplishments, Niharika has significantly contributed to the advancement of these fields. She is proficient in Python programming and applies her coding prowess in Machine Learning and data analysis for IoT protocols. Throughout her journey, Niharika has garnered remarkable achievements and certifications. She has successfully completed certifications in Python from prestigious platforms like Coursera, and in the realm of IoT, she holds certificates from NPTEL provided by IIT Kharagpur and Lema Labs, IIT Madras. Niharika holds a B.Tech in Information Technology and a M.Tech in Computer Science and Engineering and is currently pursuing a Ph.D. in the field of Internet of Things and Data Science at Amrita School of Computing, Bengaluru. This extensive educational background demonstrates her commitment to continuous learning and staying at the forefront of technological advancements.

- **Kumar Shashank** is a knowledgeable and discerning expert in the field of Data Science and Machine Learning. With an extensive background encompassing six years of industry experience, including three years as a dedicated Data Scientist, his insights carry significant weight. His expertise covers a wide range of BI and reporting tools, as well as mastery of ML/AI algorithms, IIoT, SQL, and Python with essential libraries like Sklearn, TensorFlow, Numpy, Pandas, Matplotlib, and Seaborn.

  He brings a critical eye to the evaluation of technical books, analyzing the clarity, depth, practicality of the content and its relevance to the industry standards. His impartial assessments provide valuable guidance to aspiring data scientists and ML practitioners, ensuring they invest their time in books that truly enrich their knowledge. With excellent communication skills and a collaborative mindset, Shashank's contributions extend beyond written critiques, making them a respected authority in the field and a valuable asset to the technical community.

Acknowledgement

I would like to express my deepest gratitude to the individuals who have provided their unwavering support during the creation of this book. First and foremost, I would like to thank my mother for her constant encouragement and my sister and niece for their unwavering support. Without their presence and encouragement, this book would not have been possible. It saddens me that my mother is not here to witness the publication of this book, but her spirit lives on in my work.

I am immensely grateful for the knowledge and experiences gained from my current and previous organizations. In particular, I would like to extend my heartfelt appreciation to my current organization, LTIMindtree, for providing me with the wonderful opportunity to delve into the development and implementation of IoT Data Analytics. Their support and guidance have been invaluable.

I would also like to extend my heartfelt thanks to Mr. Mahesh Mahajan, my mentor and leader, for his guidance and mentorship throughout this journey. His expertise and encouragement have been instrumental in shaping this book.

To all those who have provided their hidden support, whether through words of encouragement, feedback, or moral support, I extend my heartfelt thanks. Your contributions have made a significant impact on the completion of this book.

Once again, I extend my deepest appreciation to everyone who has played a part in making this book a reality. Thank you for your continued support and belief in my work.

Preface

Welcome to the world of IoT data analytics, a realm where Python developers can unlock the full potential of the Internet of Things (IoT) and harness the power of advanced analytics. In this book, **IoT Data Analytics using Python** we embark on an enlightening journey to equip Python developers with the skills and knowledge necessary to excel in the realm of IoT data analytics. Throughout this book, we will be using real-world datasets, providing practical insights and hands-on experience that bridge the gap between theory and application. Additionally, this book is also well suited for anyone wanting to learn Python as they embark on their journey into IoT data analytics. Join us as we explore the intersection of Python programming and IoT data analytics, paving the way for innovative solutions and data-driven decision-making.

Chapter 1: Necessity of Analytics Across IoT - In this chapter, we explore the essentials of IoT analytics, the impact of the Internet of Things and the Industry Internet of Things, and the revolution brought about by Industry 4.0. We delve into the critical role of IoT data analytics in driving digital transformation and discuss the components of a data pipeline for analytics. Python is introduced as the go-to language for IoT Data Analytics.

Chapter 2: Up and Running with Data Analytics Fundamentals - This chapter serves as a comprehensive guide to Data Analytics fundamentals. We explore various data analysis methods and techniques, enabling Python developers to perform data analysis using different frameworks. From the SEMMA, KDD, and CRISP-DM frameworks to industry-specific frameworks, we provide a solid foundation for analytical endeavors.

Chapter 3: Setting Up IoT Analytics Environment - In this chapter, we delve into the practical aspects of setting up an IoT Data Analytics environment. We discuss the rationale behind choosing Python as the language of choice and guide readers through the installation and configuration of essential tools such as Python IDE, Apache Kafka, MQTT, and PostgresSQL. Python packages are also explored, along with Python basics, data analysis, wrangling, and visualization.

Chapter 4: Managing Data Pipeline and Cleaning - This chapter delves into the crucial task of managing data pipelines and ensuring data cleanliness. We explore different types of IoT data formats and equip you with the necessary skills to handle diverse data formats efficiently. Delving into real-time data streaming, data pipeline management, and the concept of IoT Dataflow, we empower the reader to build robust and scalable data pipelines. Furthermore, we unveil the world of IoT simulators and guide you through their implementation using

Python. With a focus on data cleansing and transformation, we provide you with the tools and techniques to ensure data accuracy and quality.

Chapter 5: Designing Data Lake and Executing Data Transformation - This chapter introduces the concept of designing a data lake and executing data transformation. We uncover the intricacies of data lakes, their role in managing real-time IoT data streaming, and building effective data architectures. Additionally, we emphasize the importance of building Key Performance Indicators (KPIs) and metrics objectives for extracting meaningful insights from IoT data. We will use Python to implement a simple and effective data lake.

Chapter 6: Implementing Descriptive Analytics Using Pandas - This chapter focuses on implementing descriptive analytics using the powerful Pandas library. We explore techniques for descriptive data analysis and time series analysis, enabling Python developers to uncover patterns and trends in time-stamped IoT datasets. Testing methods for time series data are also discussed.

Chapter 7: Time Series Forecasting and Predictions - This chapter takes us into the realm of time series forecasting and predictions. We explore techniques such as data smoothing, lag identification, and autocorrelation, empowering Python developers to make accurate predictions. Python libraries such as Tsfresh and AutoTS are introduced for advanced feature extraction and high-accuracy forecasting. Additionally, we showcase storing wind turbine predictions and constructing an Analytical Base Table (ABT) for efficient analysis.

Chapter 8: Monitoring and Preventive Maintenance - In this chapter, we delve into the critical aspects of monitoring and preventive maintenance in the IoT landscape. We explore condition monitoring, Condition-Based Maintenance (CBM), corrective maintenance, preventive maintenance, and predictive maintenance. The chapter also covers text mining product manuals and automating the creation of maintenance tickets, optimizing maintenance processes.

Chapter 9: Model Deployment on Edge Devices - This chapter takes us on a journey of model deployment on edge devices. We introduce edge computing and analytics, simulators for IoT systems, and provide a step-by-step guide to installing and configuring edge devices and FastAPI. Model building, reuse, and deployment on edge devices are explored, along with the concepts of continuous learning and adaptive learning.

Chapter 10: Understanding Edge Computing with MicroPython - This chapter unravels the intricacies of understanding edge computing with MicroPython. We explore the concepts of edge computing, edge analytics, and the edge platform. Data flow from edge to cloud and diverse use cases for edge analytics are discussed. With a focus on MicroPython, developers can invoke machine learning models and leverage the power of edge computing.

Chapter 11: IoT Analytics for Self-driving Vehicles - In this final chapter, we present a compelling case study that showcases the application of IoT Data Analytics in the context of self-driving vehicles. By leveraging the CRISP-DM framework, we dive deep into the business aspects of self-driving vehicles and demonstrate how to perform end-to-end IoT Data Analytics using Python.

Throughout this book, our aim is to provide Python developers with a comprehensive understanding of IoT Data Analytics and its practical application across industries and use cases. Whether you are a Python developer looking to enhance your skills or someone seeking to learn Python through the lens of IoT Data Analytics, this book will serve as a valuable resource.

Code Bundle and Coloured Images

Please follow the link to download the
Code Bundle and the ***Coloured Images*** of the book:

https://rebrand.ly/a3237f

The code bundle for the book is also hosted on GitHub at **https://github.com/bpbpublications/IoT-Data-Analytics-using-Python**. In case there's an update to the code, it will be updated on the existing GitHub repository.

We have code bundles from our rich catalogue of books and videos available at **https://github.com/bpbpublications**. Check them out!

Errata

We take immense pride in our work at BPB Publications and follow best practices to ensure the accuracy of our content to provide with an indulging reading experience to our subscribers. Our readers are our mirrors, and we use their inputs to reflect and improve upon human errors, if any, that may have occurred during the publishing processes involved. To let us maintain the quality and help us reach out to any readers who might be having difficulties due to any unforeseen errors, please write to us at :

errata@bpbonline.com

Your support, suggestions and feedbacks are highly appreciated by the BPB Publications' Family.

Piracy

If you come across any illegal copies of our works in any form on the internet, we would be grateful if you would provide us with the location address or website name. Please contact us at **business@bpbonline.com** with a link to the material.

If you are interested in becoming an author

If there is a topic that you have expertise in, and you are interested in either writing or contributing to a book, please visit **www.bpbonline.com**. We have worked with thousands of developers and tech professionals, just like you, to help them share their insights with the global tech community. You can make a general application, apply for a specific hot topic that we are recruiting an author for, or submit your own idea.

Reviews

Please leave a review. Once you have read and used this book, why not leave a review on the site that you purchased it from? Potential readers can then see and use your unbiased opinion to make purchase decisions. We at BPB can understand what you think about our products, and our authors can see your feedback on their book. Thank you!

For more information about BPB, please visit **www.bpbonline.com**.

Join our book's Discord space

Join the book's Discord Workspace for Latest updates, Offers, Tech happenings around the world, New Release and Sessions with the Authors:

https://discord.bpbonline.com

Table of Contents

Chapter 1

Necessity of Analytics Across IoT

Introduction

This chapter covers the basic concepts of **Internet of Things** (**IoT**) and how the industry 4.0 revolution impacts our life, economy, and technology advancements. It focuses on how the IoT industry is connected to Industry 4.0 revolution and the role it plays in industry automation. We will investigate important use cases that solve key business problems in industries such as manufacturing, construction, Oil and gas, railroad, pharmaceutical, and other infrastructure developments. We will cover applications for IoT Data Analytics in **Environment, Social, and Governance** (**ESG**), where we will discuss how IoT Data Analytics can help fight global warming and help us achieve carbon emission reduction. In the smart city use cases, we will discuss how the automation of infrastructure and water distribution is improving our lives. In the case of medical and Health Sciences, and pharmaceuticals, we will discuss how it is helping patients, doctors, drug manufacturers, and hospitals to manage their processes more efficiently to help save lives. We will also touch upon other industries and areas where IoT Data Analytics is helping our society in a better way.

Structure

In this chapter, we will cover the following topics:

- Internet of Things and Industrial Internet of Things
- Industrial Revolution and Industry 4.0

- IoT Data Analytics
- IoT Data Analytics for Digital Transformation
- Hardware Devices for IoT Data Analytics
- Data Pipeline for Analytics
- Python: The Go-to Language for IoT Analytics

Objectives

By the end of this chapter, you will be able to understand the basic concepts of IoT, Industry IoT, various equipment used in the industry IoT, and IoT Data Analytics. You will learn about industrial use cases for IoT Data Analytics and IoT hardware devices for analytics. In the last part of the chapter, you will learn about the data pipeline for analytics and the programming language for IoT Data Analytics.

Internet of Things and Industrial Internet of Things

The **Industrial Internet of Things (IIoT)** is revolutionizing various industries by enabling efficient data monitoring and analysis. For instance, consider the application of IIoT in the wind turbine industry. Wind turbines are equipped with advanced sensors that continuously collect data on various parameters, such as wind speed, temperature, and turbine performance. These sensors generate a constant stream of data that provides valuable insights into the turbine's behavior and efficiency.

However, due to the massive volume of data generated, it becomes impractical to store all this information locally within the turbine. Instead, the data is transmitted to the cloud through the internet. In the cloud, this data is processed, analyzed, and stored in vast databases that have virtually unlimited storage capabilities. Engineers and technicians can access this data remotely and in real-time, enabling them to monitor the turbines' performance, detect anomalies, and identify potential maintenance needs.

Similarly, we can provide multiple use cases and examples from other industries such as self-driving vehicles, smart cities, smart buildings, and many others on the impact of IIoT. These industries leverage IIoT technologies to collect and analyze data from various sources, enabling them to optimize operations, enhance efficiency, and improve overall performance. IIoT is a powerful tool that empowers industries to make data-driven decisions, improve productivity, and drive innovation.

Before diving into our main objective of analytics in the IoT world, let us quickly understand some of IoT's basic concepts and background:

- **Demand for IoT and Analytics**: There are several predictions regarding how IoT and IoT Data Analytics will grow in the coming years. *Gartner*, leading research, and advisory company, predicts that the number of connected IoT devices worldwide will reach over 20 billion by 2025, a significant increase from the 8 billion devices recorded in 2018. In addition, another report by Gartner forecasts that by 2030, a staggering 90% of all data will be generated by IoT devices. As a result, the market for IoT Data Analytics is expected to continue to grow, as organizations aim to extract value from the massive amount of data generated by these devices. Another report from the McKinsey Global Institute predicts that by 2026, there will be a need for more than 4 million data and analytics professionals worldwide. This includes those with skills in IoT Data Analytics. This highlights the significance of learning IoT Data Analytics, as it is becoming an increasingly vital area of expertise in the field. With this projection, there is a growing opportunity for professionals with the necessary skills in IoT Data Analytics. Therefore, acquiring proficiency in this area is essential to meet the rising demand and reap the benefits of a rapidly growing industry.

- **Definition of Internet of Things:** In simple terms, any devices or physical objects that connect to the external environment via sensors to generate and transfer data via networks for further usage. Here, we used various terms such as devices and sensors, in the preceding definition. Let us go through each of the terms to understand their role in IoT implementation:
- **Devices:** Any physical object with multiple sensors to serve a purpose is called a device. In our previous example, the wind turbine is a device. The following are multiple devices serving different purposes:
    - **Energy management systems:** The device with sensors to manage and control power usage. Air condition control systems or smart sensors to turn on the lights based on human movement are examples of energy management systems.
    - **Industrial control systems:** The systems used to produce material in the manufacturing assembly. It controls the production process and contains when to switch on the machines.
    - **Vehicle tracking systems:** The device to track the movement of vehicles in the supply chain business. This helps in optimizing routes and managing the delivery of materials.
    - **Process control systems:** The devices used in process-centric industries such as Pharmaceutical or Chemical, where processing is critical for the product and safety.
- **Sensors**: Any physical object which deducts the external environment conditions and changes by measuring them constantly. The following are examples of sensors:
    - **Motion sensors:** The sensors which monitor the environment for any movement of the object to trigger an action, such as turning on/off the lights, or triggering an alarm when an object is detected.
    - **Proximity sensors:** The sensors which monitor the presence of objects near to specific location to trigger an action, such as opening a door when a person is near the door.

- **Pressure sensors:** Pressure sensors are used for detecting pressure in a system like a boiler or steam engine to trigger an action based on the level of pressure detected. We can set thresholds to trigger an alarm if the pressure is too much for the system. This will prevent accidents due to unexpected pressure levels in industrial boilers.
- **Humidity sensors:** These sensors can monitor the humidity level of the air and can trigger an action based on the surrounding humidity levels, such as turning on/off the air conditioning system.

There are many devices and sensors which can help automate the generation of useful information about the environment or system to manage the expected outcome. We will go through various IoT devices and sensors in the later part of this book to understand their role in different industries.

Industrial Revolution and Industry 4.0

The **Industrial Revolution** is used for elaborating the history of our advancements in the industries such as manufacturing, automobile, travel, and transportation. To understand the full context of the industrial revolution, let us go through its history, in brief, to understand the significance of the present industrial revolution and how IoT and related technologies are transforming economies and our lives in general.

First Industrial Revolution

The first industrial revolution started in the 18th century and matured in the early 19th century. It is also called the Agricultural Revolution. The advancement in the production of goods using machines to reduce hard labor is the major contribution of the first industrial revolution. The invention and development of steam engines to transform the transportation industry, mechanical spinning jenny, and power loom to transform the textile industry are a few examples. Then advancement in the production of coal, Iron, mines, and other materials are the key contribution of this Industry 1.0. The great progress in human civilization and expansion of urbanization happened because of the large production of goods using new machines invented during this period. This resulted in new factories, city expansion, economic growth, and further science and technology advancement. The first industrial revolution paved a new way for human civilization and further advancement of science.

Second Industrial Revolution

The second industrial revolution started as a continuation of the first revolution in the 19th century and continued in full momentum until the 20th century. During this period, major technological changes happened which came to be known as the period of technological revolution. With the discovery of new energy sources such as natural gas and petroleum, there was a significant shift in the coal industries that replaced major energy consumption. The inventions such as the telephone and telegraph become a paradigm shift in communication and information sharing. There emerged a major industry that revolutionized our transportation called the **automotive industry**. Along with these industries, there are significant progress made in the chemical, textile, and material industries due to the discovery of petroleum and natural gas. Humanity made huge progress in this period regarding transportation, communication, and social and economic conditions.

Third Industrial Revolution

The digital revolution started at the start of the current century that changed the speed and mode of communication. The emergence of computers, the internet, and mobile technology marked a new era in human civilization. In general, the third industrial revolution expanded inventions and discoveries in every aspect of technology, industry, and society. We re-defined the existing industries that were part of previous revolutions and created new ones. This has transformed productivity, the economy, and social condition with significant automation in every industry. A remarkable shift happened in the telephone, information, and communication industries with the adoption of computers, the internet, and mobile phones. With the growth of **Information and Communication Technology (ICT)**, our social and economic conditions are radically changed. The emergence of mobile devices and internet technology marked a new phase in the technological revolution, leading to the development of smart technologies such as the Internet of Things, robotics, and artificial intelligence. These advancements in technology have paved the way for the current industrial revolution and continue to drive innovation in the digital landscape.

Fourth Industrial Revolution

The **Fourth Industrial Revolution (Industry 4.0)** is the current and ongoing progress in developing new digital technologies. Thanks to the discovery of digital and ICT industries in the early 20th century, we are now progressing with digital adoptions with Artificial Intelligence, Robotics, and the Internet of Things. The revolution impacted every aspect of human lives by adopting digital and smart technologies. We see a change in mobile devices and the integration of technologies in every aspect of our lives. This significant surge in technology adoption required us to expand our storage and processing of information. This enabled us to create new technologies such as Cloud Computing and Big Data. The storing and processing of large data have become an aftereffect of the wide adoption of digital technologies. This created new and advanced existing industries such as autonomous vehicles, smart cities, gene therapy, personalized medicines, advancements in robotics, and so on.

Another major contribution of the Industrial Revolution is in the field of nanotechnologies with the invention of nanomaterials and biodegradable plastics. These industries are making us advanced in our social and economic conditions and our environment sustainable.

IoT and Data Analytics plays a key role in Industry 4.0 as the demand for gathering and analyzing data from IoT devices is growing rapidly. Every industry is shifting to make their day-to-day process automated with the enablement of digital technologies. The need for expansion in terms of scale and quality dictates the need for adopting IoT and Analytics. Making advancements in this area are key to progress into the next industrial revolution of fully automated technologies which minimize human intervention in many aspects of industrial production.

IoT Data Analytics

Introduction to IoT Data Analytics: IoT Data Analytics is the process of acquiring, transforming, storing, analyzing, and visualizing data from IoT devices and sensors. The main objective of IoT Data Analytics is to extract insights from the data to enable business users to perform informed decisions and actions. We know from the previous section that IoT devices and sensors monitor the external environment to generate data at frequent time of interval. Because of this, we can see that the data generated by IoT devices and networks are in a large amount. Performing analysis on this large amount of data can benefit the business in optimizing their operations, improving the business outcome that leads to more profitability and expansion. New business models can be derived from the analysis of the large data. Before diving deeper into **IoT Data Analytics**, let us explore the key processes and technologies associated with it.

- **Data generation:** IoT devices, sensors and the network of devices monitor the environment based on the configured parameters and generate data continuously. These devices or sensors are tiny in nature with low storage and energy in the environment, which are required to operate. Hence, they may not have significant storage or processor facility within these IoT devices to perform the required data operations of collecting, storing, and transformation. Based on the preceding constrain in environment, we need a process for collecting data.

- **Data Collection:** In this step data is collected from the IoT devices, sensors and networks using push or pull method. Either the IoT devices send the data via push, or the server sends a request for collecting data via the pull method. There are various protocols used for the communication and transmission of data. Most frequently used protocols are, **Message Queuing Telemetry Transport** (**MQTT**), **Hypertext Transfer Protocol** (**HTTP**), **Constrained Application Protocol** (**CoAP**), and **Advanced Message Queuing Protocol** (**AMQP**). We will learn more about these protocols in the upcoming section.

- **Data storage:** The collected data needs to be stored in a secured, optimized, efficient way where extraction of data is possible anytime. The most common way for storing the data from the IoT devices will be on a centralized database. The location of these databases can be in the **Local Network (LAN)** or the cloud **Wide Area Network** (**WAN**). The cloud is the most used method for the operation since it is scalable, secured, efficient, and cost-effective. The choice of databases varies depending on application and analytics requirements. The most common databases are relational databases such as *Postgres* or *MySQL*. Since the data generated from the IoT devices are of time series in nature as the data generated is in frequent interval. Hence, time series relational databases could be a more suitable choice here. The time series databases such as

TimescaleDB, and *InfluxDB* are also used for this purpose. The relational and time series database has its advantages and disadvantages. When low latency is required, we may need to think of *NoSQL* databases such as *MongoDB* or *Cassandra*. There are cloud provider databases that come with these flavors of relational or *NoSQL*. The *Amazon's DynamoDB* or *RDS*, *Azure's Cosmos DB* or *PostgreSQL*, *Google's Cloud Firestore*, *Cloud Bigtable*, or *Cloud SQL* are examples of the cloud provider's databases.

- **Data transformation or pre-processing:** Most of the time, the data collected from the IoT devices require pre-processing steps. The pre-processing includes, cleaning the data which are not useful and transforming the data when format and unit of the data come in different variations. Python is the most used programming language for performing data pre-processing. Sometimes, we may need to use Apache Spark when parallel processing of large data is required. We will go through this in detail in the upcoming chapters of the book.
- **Data analysis:** In IoT Data Analytics, the crucial and central step is data analysis, where data stored in a database holds no significance unless analyzed for obtaining valuable insights. To gain insights into IoT data, several statistical and probability-based methods are employed. The standard tools used for applying these methods are Python or R programming languages, with Python being the focus of the upcoming chapters. The subsequent part of this chapter will elaborate on why Python is preferred.
- **Insights and actions:** These are the ultimate objectives of any data analysis solution. The data analysis performed in the previous steps is necessary to present the results of the analysis in a simpler, more elegant, and more understandable manner, enabling business and non-technical users to make informed decisions. There are times when the system automatically takes actions on behalf of the business users based on insights. Machine learning algorithms and models are employed for such predictions.
- **Challenges of IoT Data Analytics:** There are many challenges in handling data from IoT devices. We must understand these challenges to address them appropriately. They are:
    - **Data volume:** The IoT devices generate data every second or minute. This poses a problem in handling significantly large volumes of data. To handle the significant volume of data generated by IoT devices, it is necessary to invest in large storage capacities and powerful processors. Cloud-based storage solutions can be employed to store and manage the vast amount of data efficiently. Additionally, implementing data compression techniques and data archiving strategies can help optimize storage usage and reduce costs.
    - **Data velocity:** The frequency of data generated by the IoT devices creates challenges in terms of processing the data promptly and performing real-time analysis on the data. Real-time analysis of IoT data requires efficient processing techniques and solutions. Stream processing frameworks such as Apache Kafka and Apache Flink can be utilized to process and analyze data as it arrives in real-time. These frameworks enable parallel processing and distributed computing,

allowing for timely insights and decision-making. In the later part of this chapter, we will discuss more about how Python and Kafka helps in processing large volume of real-time data.

- **Data variety:** In IoT Data Analytics, the data produced by IoT devices differ based on several factors, including the provider **Original Equipment Manufacturer (OEM)** of the IoT device and sensors. Consequently, the data's format and meaning vary significantly. Managing this variety of data is a critical challenge when conducting analytics on IoT data. Managing the variety of data produced by different IoT devices and sensors requires effective data pre-processing. Python offers various libraries and tools for data cleaning, normalization, and transformation. By applying data pre-processing techniques, the diverse formats, and meanings of IoT data can be standardized and made consistent for analytics.

- **Data quality:** Due to the very nature of the IoT devices, the data quality issues are inherent of IoT data. There are several reasons for this:
  - **Loss of network signal:** The placement and location of IoT devices are constrained by the nature of the equipment to which they are attached. When IoT devices are connected to moving vehicles, they may stop sending data in real-time due to signal loss when traveling to remote areas with poor network coverage. Data packet loss due to poor network signals is a common occurrence in the IoT environment. To address this issue, measures can be taken to mitigate network signal loss and intermittent device failures. Implementing redundancy in network connections and using signal boosters or repeaters can help ensure consistent data transmission. Regular maintenance and monitoring of IoT devices can prevent failures, while robust anomaly detection techniques can identify and handle missing or corrupted data.
  - **Intermittent device failure:** IoT devices are often deployed in locations where they are exposed to severe weather conditions. For instance, they can generate excess heat when placed near industrial equipment in factories, or they might endure heavy rain and other natural calamities in agricultural projects. Consequently, IoT devices are prone to damage or malfunction, requiring regular maintenance. During these breakdowns, they fail to provide the necessary data for continuous analysis, resulting in significant data anomalies. Managing missing data becomes crucial in such scenarios, necessitating data cleaning and anomaly detection techniques to address this challenge.
  - **OEM upgrade:** It is a frequent occurrence for the supplier of IoT devices to handle upgrades sporadically, as they are managing multiple customers. This can result in sudden changes in the data format and meaning, caused by driver upgrades. Failure to regularly verify and rectify such data formats can lead to the accumulation of a significant amount of bad data, rendering them unusable for analysis purposes. Collaborating with OEM providers and establishing clear communication channels can help address sudden changes in data format and meaning. Regular verification and validation of data formats can ensure compatibility and consistency.

  - **Lack of industry standards:** There are no industry standards for the OEM providers to send the data from the IoT devices in the pre-defined format. We might need to deal with multiple data formats even for the same equipment. The inconsistency in the data format creates noise and anomalies in the data. Standardization efforts within the industry can drive the adoption of common data formats and promote interoperability.

- **Data security and privacy:** IoT devices can generate information about a person, location, health condition, and other sensitive information. It leads to breach of privacy when an unintended person views the data. Hence, it is important to perform necessary data encryption and compression while transmitting data from IoT device to the cloud or external systems. Implementing robust encryption and authentication mechanisms can protect IoT data during transmission and storage. Data anonymization techniques, such as masking personally identifiable information, can safeguard privacy. Compliance with data protection regulations, such as GDPR, ensures responsible handling of sensitive information.

- **Location based data:** The precise geographical positioning of equipment monitored by sensors is a critical requirement for supply chain and fleet management IoT implementations. The **Global Positioning System** (**GPS**), which transmits data via corresponding sensors, may experience connectivity issues with the gateway due to signal loss, resulting in significant data quality problems. Consequently, we may be unable to accurately determine the vehicle's location, leading to substantial business impacts such as delivery delays, spoilage of perishable products, customer penalties, and more. Managing such data loss through statistical methods is essential to mitigate these impacts. Additionally, implementing redundancy and failover mechanisms can help address this challenge.

- **Integration with other systems:** IoT data alone may not provide sufficient insights unless combined with data from other systems, such as **Enterprise Resource Planning** (**ERP**), inventory, supply chain, accounting, and worker management. Master data, including information about suppliers, vendors, operators, and shift details, is necessary to contextualize IoT data for advanced analysis. These relational data points are crucial for IoT data to fulfill its purpose in data analysis. To integrate IoT data with other systems like ERP, inventory, and supply chain management, it is necessary to establish data integration protocols and leverage APIs for seamless data exchange. Data synchronization and consistency checks are essential to maintain the accuracy and reliability of integrated IoT data.

IoT Data Analytics for Digital Transformation

In various industries, the adoption of IoT technologies and computing advancements is driving digital transformation. These technologies are used to automate processes and reduce the need for human intervention, especially in industries facing workforce shortages due to aging populations and increased consumption.

As the number of connected devices grows, so does the need for IoT Data Analytics to make sense of the resulting data.

Let us explore how Data Analytics, in conjunction with IoT sensors, is revolutionizing manufacturing, construction, mining, agriculture, ESG, and the creation of Smart Cities:

- **Manufacturing:** In the manufacturing industry, IoT sensors generate vast amount of data from equipments, production processes, and supply chain operations. Data Analytics plays a crucial role in extracting valuable insights from this data. Advanced analytics techniques, such as machine learning and Predictive Analytics, can be applied to identify patterns, optimize production processes, and detect anomalies in real-time. By leveraging IoT sensor data analytics, manufacturers can achieve predictive maintenance, improve product quality, and enhance overall operational efficiency.

- **Construction:** In the construction industry, IoT sensors are deployed in various areas such as equipments, vehicles, and building infrastructure. These sensors capture data related to equipment performance, energy usage, worker safety, and environmental conditions. Data Analytics enables construction companies to analyze this sensor data and gain actionable insights. For example, predictive analytics can identify potential equipment failures before they occur, allowing proactive maintenance. Furthermore, by analyzing worker behavior data, construction firms can enhance safety protocols and identify areas for process improvement, resulting in cost savings and better project outcomes.

- **Mining:** In the mining industry, IoT sensors are employed in mining equipments, vehicles, and environmental monitoring systems. These sensors collect data on equipment health, energy consumption, air quality, and worker safety. Data Analytics empowers mining companies to analyze this sensor data and optimize operations. Predictive maintenance models can be built to identify equipment failures in advance, minimizing downtime and reducing maintenance costs. Environmental sensor data, combined with advanced analytics, can enable proactive monitoring, and help mitigate the impact of mining activities on the environment.

- **Agriculture:** In the agricultural sector, IoT sensors are used to monitor soil moisture, temperature, humidity, and crop health. This sensor data, when combined with Data Analytics, offers valuable insights for precision farming. By analyzing historical and real-time sensor data, farmers can make data-driven decisions regarding irrigation scheduling, fertilizer application, and pest control. Predictive analytics models can forecast crop yields, identify disease outbreaks, and optimize resource utilization. These insights help farmers improve productivity, conserve resources, and maximize crop yields.

- **Environment, Social, and Governance (ESG):** IoT sensors play a significant role in supporting ESG initiatives within organizations. They collect data on energy consumption, emissions, waste management, and other sustainability-related parameters. Data Analytics enables companies to analyze this sensor data and track their environmental performance. By leveraging advanced analytics techniques, organizations can identify opportunities to reduce energy usage, optimize waste management practices, and improve overall sustainability. This data-driven approach allows companies to meet regulatory requirements, enhance their ESG performance, and communicate transparently with stakeholders.

- **Smart Cities:** IoT sensors are integral to building Smart Cities by collecting data on various aspects such as transportation, energy usage, waste management, air quality, and public safety. Data Analytics enables city authorities to process and analyze this sensor data to make informed decisions. For example, traffic sensor data can be analyzed to optimize traffic flow and reduce congestion. Environmental sensor data can help monitor air quality and trigger alerts for pollution incidents. By applying advanced analytics techniques, such as anomaly detection and predictive modeling, cities can improve resource allocation, enhance citizen services, and create more sustainable urban environments.

In conclusion, Data Analytics plays a crucial role in leveraging IoT sensor data across industries. By applying advanced analytics techniques to this data, organizations can gain valuable insights, optimize operations, enhance sustainability, and make data-driven decisions. The combination of IoT sensors and Data Analytics enables industries to achieve digital transformation, improve efficiency, and address complex challenges effectively.

Hardware Devices for IoT Data Analytics

In the previous part of this chapter, we covered the fundamentals of IoT Data Analytics and explored various business scenarios and use cases across different industries like manufacturing, construction, mining, healthcare, pharmaceuticals, and more.

Now, let us focus on the specific hardware device requirements for performing IoT Data Analytics, with a focus on the wind turbine, self-driving vehicle, and manufacturing industries. These industries face unique challenges that necessitate specialized hardware devices for effective IoT Data Analytics.

In the wind turbine industry, IoT devices are connected to turbines located in remote areas. These devices often encounter intermittent network issues as the turbines rotate and move to capture wind energy. Relying solely on cloud data for analysis becomes challenging, and real-time insights and decisions are crucial. Deploying hardware devices near the turbines enables the implementation of machine learning models for tasks like predictive maintenance, allowing real-time predictions to be made in the field.

Similarly, self-driving vehicles incorporate IoT devices to collect real-time data on various parameters. These devices can face network connectivity challenges in areas with poor signal coverage or while navigating through tunnels or underground parking lots. Depending solely on cloud-based analysis for decision-making becomes impractical. To enable instant response and decision-making, machine learning models for collision avoidance and traffic prediction need to be deployed near the IoT devices in the vehicles.

In the manufacturing industry, IoT devices are connected to machinery such as assembly lines, robots, and conveyors to monitor performance and optimize production processes. Due to the complexity of manufacturing environments and the constant movement of equipment, network issues can arise, affecting data transfer to the cloud. Relying solely on cloud-based analysis for all manufacturing operations is not feasible, and real-time insights and decision-making become critical. Deploying hardware devices near the IoT devices on the factory floor allows for predictive maintenance and efficient process optimization.

In addition to these industry-specific challenges, there are several other reasons for performing Data Analytics near the data source (technically called IoT Edge Computing and Analytics), which we will explore further:

- **Network issues**: IoT devices deployed in remote locations often experience network outages and signal loss, making cloud-based analysis and data transfer impractical.
- **Bandwidth issues**: IoT devices in remote locations require higher network bandwidth, but limited data transfer rates hinder cloud-based analysis and reliability.
- **Low latency requirement**: Real-time analysis and quick action often require low data latency, which can be challenging to achieve with network bandwidth limitations.
- **Security and privacy**: IoT-generated data may contain sensitive and private information, making local analysis near the devices more secure and privacy-compliant.
- **Cost saving**: Centralized data transfer and storage for massive volumes of IoT-generated data can be costly. Performing analysis and taking action locally near the IoT devices offers a more cost-effective solution.

By understanding the unique challenges faced by these industries and considering the specific hardware device requirements, organizations can effectively leverage IoT Data Analytics to optimize operations, make data-driven decisions, and overcome the challenges specific to their respective industries.

Now, let us look at the various computing and data processing hardware for IoT Edge Analytics:

- **Raspberry Pi:** This is the most economical single-board computer to perform IoT Data Analytics near the devices. This can help collect data from the IoT Sensors, perform required data pre-processing, and perform data analysis and predictions. This device has Debian based operating system designed for Raspberry Pi. It supports operating systems such as *Ubuntu*, *Kali Linux*, and *Windows 10* IoT Core, specifically designed for IoT devices. This minicomputer supports a Python environment for data analysis and machine learning implementations.
- **Arduino:** This open-source microcontroller electronics platform has simple in-built hardware and software. It is mainly used for microcontroller programming. It supports C++ programming with its own **Integrated Development Environment** (**IDE**). The Arduino hardware and platform are unsuitable for high-volume data analysis and machine-learning applications. It does not support a full python execution environment. But it supports integration with the python environment via a python library called *PySerial*. Lightweight IoT operations can be performed using this device.

- **NVIDIA Jetson:** This device is the most used IoT Data Analytics solution for performing complex analytical and machine learning tasks. The NVIDIA Jetson is a series of embedded computing boards that provides processing power for high-performance requirements. Compared to Raspberry Pi, the Jetson device is costlier since the computing power it supports is higher than Raspberry Pi. The Jetson boards support a Python programming environment with many python libraries and packages, including pandas, NumPy and sci-kit-learn. In addition to the standard Python libraries, the Jetson platform provides powerful GPU processing NVIDIA CUDA libraries. This is very useful for video, image, and audio processing on the edge device.
- **Intel Edison:** This is a small computer called computer-on-module that provides good computation for performing IoT data analysis and machine learning. This device comes with an Intel Atom processor and runs on a Linux operating system. The device supports a python programming environment where we can analyze data and deploy machine learning models. In addition to computing power, this device supports various network connectivity options such as USB, Wi-Fi, and Bluetooth. These connectivity options are very helpful in transferring data or pushing/pull of machine learning models from the cloud. Based on the features, this device is a more powerful, flexible platform for IoT Data Analytics.
- **Intel NUC:** The **Intel Next Unit of Computing** (**NUC**) is a small form-factor computer embedded with an Intel processor and comes with a different processor and memory configuration. This device supports Windows and Linux operating systems with full Python programming language capability for performing IoT Data Analytics and machine learning. Most of the Python libraries, such as Pandas, NumPy, and sci-kit-learn are supported well on this platform. In addition to this, we can run Python IDEs like Jupyter notebook for data analysis. This is one of the best devices for performing end-to-end edge analytics, from collecting data from IoT Sensors to processing and analyzing data. Due to its full range of support with powerful computing configuration, it is one of the preferred devices for IoT Edge Analytics.
- **BeagleBone:** This single-board computer performs a wide range of IoT Edge Analytics. This device runs on the Linux operating system and supports full Python programming language capabilities and libraries. The BeagleBone can be used for IoT Data Analytics and machine learning. It supports various Python IDEs, such as Jupyter Notebook, for data analysis. This is the most powerful, flexible, cost-effective IoT Edge Analytics device. End-to-end IoT Edge Analytics can be performed using this device. The device supports collecting data from IoT Sensors, performing necessary data processing, powerful data analysis capability and machine learning model deployment. Since the cost of the BeagleBone is less when compared to Intel and NVIDIA, it is the most preferred choice for a low-budget implementation.
- **Particle Photon/Electron:** This is a series of microcontroller boards with external connectivity support via Wi-Fi. But due to the processing limitation, it does not support Python programming language for IoT Data Analytics. The device supports C++ and

JavaScript for basic data operations from the IoT sensors. Suppose we need to use this device for IoT Edge Analytics. In that case, the only possible way is to connect to the local computer via Wi-Fi to let the processing happen in the computer. Otherwise, it needs more processing capacity to support any major data analysis.

- **Adafruit Feather:** This is a series of compact development boards with microcontrollers, sensors, Wi-Fi, BLE, and LTE connectivity. It supports Arduino **Integrated Development Environment (IDE)**. The Arduino IDE supports C++ and Arduino programming language. Since its limited processing capacity, it does not support Python programming language. Hence, it is not suitable for performing end-to-end IoT Data Analytics without some external computer. Like the Particle Photon Series, this device requires connecting to a local computer via Wi-Fi or BLE to perform IoT Data Analytics.

Data Pipeline for Analytics

The following figure shows the end-to-end flow of the IoT data pipeline. This helps us understand IoT Data Analysts' role in various data pipeline stages. In the subsequent chapters, we will be building a data pipeline for a practical business scenario, so it is important for the readers to under the flow of standard data pipeline.

The following *Figure 1.1* depicts data pipeline flow:

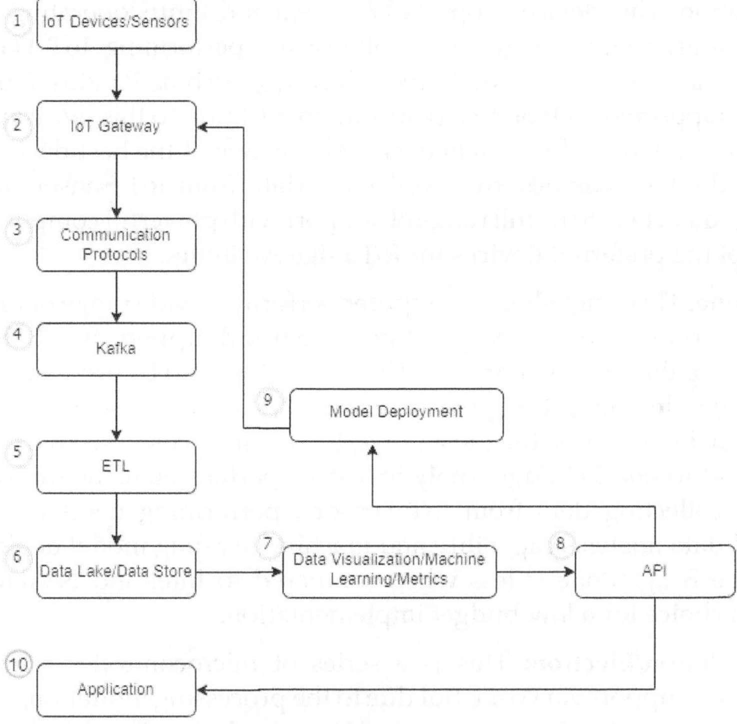

Figure 1.1: *Data Pipeline flow*

The following points explains the process of data pipeline flow:

- **IoT device/sensors:** IoT devices use sensors to monitor and control environmental conditions such as temperature, humidity, pressure, air quality, chemical presence, power, voltage, vibration, RPM, Weight, and so on. Depending on the configuration setup, the device generates data every few seconds or every few minutes.
- **IoT Gateway**: The IoT Gateway is installed near the IoT devices for local data transmission. Since IoT Devices are sensors that cannot store a large amount of data for a longer duration due to storage and battery/power constraint, it needs to constantly transmit the data to the nearest Gateway devices. The IoT Gateway devices will have more storage, power, and network connectivity to send the aggregated data to the cloud or central data stores.
- **Communication protocols**: The protocols such as HTTP, MQTT, AMQT, CoAP, CANBUS, and MODBUS are the widely used protocol for sending data from the IoT Devices/Gateway to the cloud. Each protocol is used for different purposes. Here is a quick summary of each protocol and its main role in data transmission and communication:
    - **HyperText Transfer Protocol (HTTP)**: It is a widely used protocol on the application layer. This is used for transmitting data over the internet. The HTTP protocol uses a request and response model, where an IoT Device/Gateway sends an HTTP request, and the data consumer in the cloud returns an HTTP response.
    - **Message Queuing Telemetry Transport (MQTT)**: It is a lightweight publish and subscribe protocol for data transmission and communication between IoT Devices/Gateway and the cloud. In MQTT, the IoT device will play the role of a publisher, and the data consumer on the cloud will play a role of a subscriber. It is also called a broker. The IoT device/gateway sends data to the data consumer on the cloud by publishing a message on a specific topic. The data consumer receives the message and stores it under a unique topic. Usually, the MQTT is used for the IoT solution where low latency is required for a higher transmission speed. This protocol works well in an environment that has a low-bandwidth network. Due to these advantages, MQTT is the most popular protocol for IoT solutions.
    - **Advanced Message Queuing Protocol (AMQP):** It is the most secure and reliable protocol for data transmission from IoT Devices to the cloud. This is a messaging protocol that is used for communication between IoT Devices to cloud servers as well.
    - **Constrained Application Protocol (CoAP):** It is a protocol that works in constrained devices where the IoT Devices have limited memory and low power, and low processing capability. Since it is a lightweight protocol, this is well suited for IoT solutions where device memory, battery, and network bandwidth are limited.
    - **Controller Area Network Bus (CANBUS):** It is a highly reliable and secured protocol commonly used in the automotive industry. This protocol is usually

used for communication from moving vehicles via **Electronic Control Units (ECUs)**. Hence, this protocol is widely used in Industrial IoT Solutions.

- MODBUS is a communication protocol that operates on a master and slave concept. It is widely utilized for connecting manufacturing control equipment, including **Programmable Logic Controllers (PLCs)** and **Human-machine interfaces (HMIs)**. In manufacturing industries, PLCs are responsible for machinery control, while HMIs facilitate data transmission from systems like **Supervisory Control and Data Acquisition (SCADA)**. The MODBUS protocol provides a reliable and robust means of communication, enabling the transmission of data from control units to the cloud. However, due to its weak security layer, it is crucial to implement additional security measures to ensure secure data transmission.

- **Kafka:** The data from the IoT devices must be stored and processed quickly without any major delay. Since the data volume coming from the IoT devices are huge, we need a scalable and reliable data consumer. Apache Kafka is the widely used data processor and consumer in the IoT solutions for high-throughput, low-latency, reliable data pipelines. The IoT Devices/Gateway can send the data to Kafka via a unique topic. The Topic in Kafka can publish the data to external access via the same topic. The publishing data on the topic is called producer in Kafka. Once the data is produced for a topic, the same can be consumed by the Kafka consumers. The consumers are data readers in Kafka, which subscribe to a topic to read and process the data to the databases. In the later chapter, we will cover more about the installation, configuration, and setting up of a data pipeline using Kafka.

- **ETL:** In the previous step, the data from IoT Devices are received and stored in a topic. The IoT devices' data cannot be directly stored in the database for insights. Various data cleaning and transformation steps are required before storing them in a database. An **Extract, Transform, and Load (ETL)** or **Extract, Load, and Transform (ELT)** process is required to make the data useful for analysis. Let us go through each step in the ETL or ELT process:

  - **Extract:** This is the process of extracting the data from the Kafka topic. The IoT data transmitted to the Kafka topic is stored in Kafka. We need to write a topic consumer to extract the data from the Kafka topic. This consumer can be written in Python. We will be covering this step in the later chapter in more detail.

  - **Transform:** The data received from the IoT Device will have various formats and may contain information in a non-tabular JSON format. We need the data to be transformed to insert them into a SQL table. Also, the data sent from the IoT Devices are often in different formats. For example, some IoT Device providers (OEMs) will send the DateTime format as DDMMYYYY HH:MM: SS, and some providers will send the datetime format as MMDDYYYY HH:MM:SS. We need to make the necessary transformation to store the data in the same SQL table for data analysis, leading to better data quality and correct insights. Similarly, significant transformation processing is required to clean up and format the data before storing it in the database. The entire transformation process can be performed using Python. We will cover the transformation process with practical implementation in the later chapter.

- **Load:** This is a simple step of connecting to the destination database to insert transformed data.

The ELT process is similar to ETL, except that in the case of ELT, we will extract data from Kafka and then store the data in as-is format in a *NoSQL* database. Then we will transform the data to store it in *SQL* for analysis. We may need to store the as-is data in a *NoSQL* database because the data received from the IoT devices will have an unstructured format such as JSON. It is highly efficient to store it in a *NoSQL* database like *MongoDB* instead of *SQL* for later processing. The ELT process can be implemented using Python, like ETL.

- **Data Lake/Data Store:** The Data Lake is the centralized data storage using multiple databases or data stores. The data lake aims to store the data in a modular fashion to make the availability of data more efficient. Like a water lake, the data lake is designed with multiple data streams or pipelines to land the data in different layers. These layers are also called zones. Let us go through commonly used zones in most of the data lakes:
    - **RAW zone:** This is where as-is data from the IoT devices are stored. No transformation is performed on the data.
    - **Trusted zone:** This is where data is cleaned for usage. The data cleaning and data transformation performed in the data on this zone are generic in nature. We will not perform specific transformation for business use cases in this zone.
    - **Transformed or curated zone:** The data transformation is performed for specific use cases in this zone. For example, units like kilometers or miles are transformed for specific use cases and stored in this zone. In some countries, the calculation of equipment's distance travel needs to be in kilometers, and in others, it needs to be in miles. To perform this kind of transformation on the fly may be too costlier from the performance point of view. So, we must transform data for a specific use case and store it in this zone to avoid on-the-fly data transformations.
    - **Metric zone:** We perform required business metrics on the data to store the results for quick reporting. For example, equipment performance, such as the total distance traveled in a day for a truck in the construction industry, requires calculation. Performing such calculations on the fly is not feasible for performance and latency reasons. Hundreds of **Key Performance Indicators (KPIs)** are calculated and stored for the dashboard, reporting purposes for the visibility of business users.
    - **Analytical zone:** This is the zone where the data is stored for data analytics, such as forecasting, machine learning, predictive maintenance, and so on. The **Analytics Base Table** (**ABT**) is a fully transformed, combined, and curated table where the data can be directly used for performing analytics quickly. Usually, in IoT Data Analytics, the data that comes from IoT devices alone is not sufficient to perform any major analysis In most cases it is required to be integrated and correlated

with the data from ERP and other systems. These systems provide other business information such as worker details, finance, and cost-related information, details about the materials, inventory information on the stocks, supply chain information, and so on. These details are required to correlate with data from IoT devices to provide meaningful insights. To perform such tasks, we must build an ABT.

- **Data visualization / Machine Learning / Metrics:** The data stored in the databases or data lake will be more useful if it is analyzed for insights. The insights from the data analysis need to be presented to the business users in a graphical, simple, and pictorial way to make the insights powerful and easy to understand. The data visualization can be performed using python with its rich library support.
- Other than data visualization, the important reason for storing the data in the database is to provide insights on future business behavior based on past behavior. This helps the business to take appropriate action. For example, forecasting the raw material requirement will help the business users to place the order in advance. There are various use cases for forecasting and predictive intelligence. We will cover the details in the later chapters.
- In the Industrial IoT solution, one of the keys asks from the business is to predict the equipment failure to prevent such failure in future. This use case is called preventive maintenance. This can be achieved only through implementing machine learning models. We will be using Python for this purpose to demonstrate various preventive maintenance use cases:
- **API:** To enable the sharing of data stored in multiple data lake zones with external applications and IoT Edge Devices, an API layer must be implemented. This layer is necessary for securely, reliably, and structurally sharing the data. In the following sections, we will explore the use of Python FastAPI to demonstrate the capabilities of the API layer.
- **Model deployment:** For real-time prediction and action, the machine learning models created for the IoT solution must be deployed on the Edge. Python can be used for this deployment, and we will delve into this topic in later chapters.
- **Application:** To facilitate timely and accurate decision-making, the data stored in databases must be made available to business users through various means such as dashboards, reports, and text. To accomplish this, a presentation layer must be constructed that enables users to view the data in a more appealing format, allowing for greater utility in performing prior steps in the data processing pipeline. To achieve this, a **User Interface** (**UI**) must be designed and integrated with the API layer to present the data in a more meaningful way. An alternative approach would be to leverage Business Intelligence tools for presenting insights.

Python: The Go-to Language for Analytics

Python is the most widely used programming language and tool for most of the data analytics implementations. It is widely used for IoT Data Analytics solutions. Here are the major reasons for the wide adoption of Python:

- **Easy to learn and implement**: Python is a simple, readable, and structured language where it is easy to use, understandable and modular.
- **Flexible and powerful**: Python supports almost all the platform and operating systems which are commonly used in the market. It supports operating system and platforms such as Windows, Linux, and Unix. The python program written for one platform can be ported to other platform quickly without making many changes.
- **Compatibility**: IoT devices require that the programming language used in the solution be compatible with multiple platforms. Python is the most versatile language for IoT solutions, as it supports platforms such as Raspberry Pi, Linux, Unix, and Windows.
- **Performance**: Python is one of the fastest efficient languages which can handle significantly large volume of data easily. Any analytical solution may require handling data in large size from few GBs to petabyte. Especially the IoT Data Analytics require handling huge volume of data from IoT devices and other integrated systems. Python is the preferred choice when it comes to handle large amount of data. Python can be used for IoT Edge Analytics with C/C++ extension. The performance is the key requirement when it comes to IoT Edge Analytics. Since the requirement for any IoT Edge Analytics is to provide insights and action in real-time, we must have a highly performing language to serve the need. Python with the C/C++ extension is becoming popular in the IoT Edge Analytics implementations.
- **Cost-effective**: Thanks to the open-source community, Python and majority of libraries, packages, tools, and pre-built models are free to use for any implementations. This makes Python is the most preferred choice since every customer is conscious of cost. The research and development projects are also using Python since it is free of cost.
- **Scalability**: The flexible and powerful architecture of Python makes it easy to scale for any large implementations. It is important that the code once written should be kept from being modified for large volume of data in the later stage. Python is by nature scalable language which can handle large volume of data. Hence it is more suitable for IoT Data Analytics as the data from IoT Devices and sensors grows every minute.
- **Rich libraries and tools**: Python have large number of libraries that supports quick implementation of any IoT Data Analytics solution. It has libraries, packages, and tools for data ingestion to data transformation to data visualization and machine learning. It will be difficult for anyone to manage and maintain solutions which has multiple technologies and tools. So, with the rich library to support each stage of the data pipeline implementation, Python is the most preferred language for any IoT Data Analytics solution. Here are the libraries, packages and tools that are widely used for any IoT Data Analytics implementations:
    - **Numeric and basic mathematics libraries:** NumPy, SciPy and SymPy
    - **Data handling libraries**: Pandas, PyMongo, psycopg2, sqlite3
    - **API integratons**: Flask, FastAPI, requests
    - **Data visualization**: Matplotlib, Seaborn, Plotly, ggplot

- **Data analysis:** Statsmodels, Scikit-learn, PySpark
- **Machine learning:** Scikit-learn, TensorFlow, PyTorch, Keras, XGBoost, CatBoost, LightGBM
- **UI framework:** Django, Flask, CherryPy
- **IoT:** Paho-mqtt , PySerial, Requests, Flask
- **Prebuilt Models:** Python has several pre-build models such as spaCy, BioBERT, CheXNet, OpenAI GPT-3

In summary, Python is the go-to language for any data analysis, AI, IoT, IIoT implementations. In our subsequent part of the book, we will go through each stage of the data pipeline to understand how Python is the preferred programming language for IoT Data Analytics.

Conclusion

In this chapter, we covered the basic concepts of IoT and IIoT, and how they are used in digital transformation and Industry 4.0 to automate and optimize business processes. We learned about the challenges of IoT Data Analytics, include handling large data volumes, ensuring data quality, and addressing security concerns. We also learned how to handle these challenges using Python and IoT edge devices. We discussed about various industrial use cases for IoT Data Analytics, including manufacturing, construction, mining, agriculture, ESG, pharmaceuticals, life sciences, and smart cities. Hardware devices for Edge Analytics and end-to-end data pipelines for IoT Data Analytics. The reasons why Python is the preferred language for IoT Data Analytics implementation.

In the next chapter, we will learn about data analytics fundamentals and different methods of data analysis such as descriptive, predictive, and prescriptive and how to apply them to IoT Data Analytics in Industrial IoT use cases. We will learn about different frameworks like SEMMA, KDD, and CRISP-DM, for approaching data analytics requirements with practical example from manufacturing Industry. Finally we will learn other frameworks for data analytics development.

Points to Remember

- The industrial revolution's advancements in automation and data collection technologies laid the foundation for IoT, which, in turn, created vast amounts of data that can be analyzed to gain valuable insights using IoT Data Analytics.
- Data generation, data collection, data storage, data transformation, data analysis, Insights and actions are the major steps in the IoT Data Analytics.
- Data volume, velocity, variety, quality, security, privacy, geo-location, and integration requirements are the key challenges faced in any IoT Data Analytics.

- IoT Data Analytics is a versatile solution that can effectively tackle numerous business challenges across a wide range of industries, including manufacturing, construction, mining, ESG, agriculture, pharmaceutical and life sciences, as well as smart city initiatives.
- IoT Edge Computing and Analytics is a solution that effectively addresses a range of challenges encountered in IoT Data Analytics, including network connectivity, bandwidth constraints, latency, security, privacy, and cost optimization.
- A wide range of edge computing devices are available to meet various requirements for IoT Edge Analytics, including popular options such as Raspberry Pi, Arduino, NVIDIA Jetson, Intel Edison, Intel NUC, BeagleBone, Particle Photon/Electron, and Adafruit Feather. It is important to note that each device offers different computing speeds, storage capacities, and platform supportability for Python.
- The purpose of a data pipeline flow is to manage data from the edge to the user. The full data pipeline flow of any IoT data is covered, starting with IoT sensors, and ending with a data lake, analytical layer, and visualization layer.
- Python is the most preferred language when it comes to IoT Data Analytics due to its performance, compatibility, flexibility, scalability, rich libraries, and communities. It is cost effective since the entire Python and the libraries are open source.

CHAPTER 2

Up and Running with Data Analytics Fundamentals

Introduction

In this chapter, you will learn about the basic concepts of data analysis.

The first section of the chapter will cover various methods and techniques for implementing data analysis requirements. We will cover descriptive, predictive, and prescriptive data analysis methods. Within each of these methods, we will cover various algorithms and techniques. While learning about different methods and techniques of data analysis, you will learn how to apply the same to IoT Data Analytics with practical examples.

In the next section of the chapter, we will cover frameworks for approaching data analysis projects. Learning the methods and techniques alone will not be useful if you do not know how to approach them in a structured manner. This section of the chapter will help you with multiple frameworks for approaching any data analysis implementations. We will cover important frameworks used widely in the industry with practical examples from Industrial IoT use cases. We will be covering **Sample, Explore, Modify, Model, and Assess** (**SEMMA**), **Knowledge Discovery in Databases** (**KDD**), and **CRoss Industry Standard Process for Data Mining** (**CRISP-DM**) frameworks mainly due to their wide usage. Other industry frameworks are explained for your familiarity. This chapter will prepare you for performing end-to-end data analysis for IoT and Industrial IoT use cases.

Structure

In this chapter, we will cover the following topics:

- Data Analysis Methods and Frameworks
- How to Perform Data Analysis
  - o SEMMA Process Framework
  - o KDD Process Framework
  - o CRISP-DM Framework
- Other Frameworks`

Objectives

By the end of this chapter, you will be able to understand the basic concepts of data analytics, various widely used methodologies, and frameworks for data analysis. You will learn about descriptive, predictive, and prescriptive data analytics methods and techniques. You will also learn how to apply widely used SEMMA, KDD, and CRISP-DM frameworks to industrial use cases for IoT Data Analytics. Finally, you will learn about other frameworks available in the industry.

Data Analysis Methods and Frameworks

Data analysis is a method and technique of finding insights from the data to empower us to make informed decisions. The insights we obtain from the data can help us to optimize business processes, save costs, preserve our environment, predict behaviors, forecast future needs, understand current challenges, and act accordingly. These are the few noteworthy values we can obtain from applying data analysis methods to the data we collect. The data analysis can be performed on data collected from IoT devices and external systems such as ERP, inventory, supply chain, and HR. We may often need to combine data from various sources to perform the required analysis.

Various methods for performing data analysis use statistical, probability, and other mathematical theories. The method we choose depends on the underlying data and the goals we set for the task. Let us go through each data analysis method and how it can be applied to IoT Data Analytics.

Descriptive Analytics

This is the most rudimentary method in the data analysis approach. Though it is a fundamental step, it is critical in any data analysis project. When you receive a dataset, the first step in understanding the dataset is the key to the successful subsequent analysis. Descriptive Analytics is the best method to perform a fundamental dataset analysis. We can gain a basic understanding of the dataset to decide whether the dataset is useful for the business objectives. It is helpful in understanding the quality of the dataset.

Descriptive Analytics helps us to summarize and describe the data through standard statistical measurement techniques:

- **Measurement of central tendency:** The central tendency helps us understand the trends and patterns in data. Basic statistical methods such as the mean, median, and mode can be used to understand how the data is distributed.
- **Measurement of the variability of data:** We must understand the variability of data. This helps us understand outliers, specific patterns, and spread in the data. The statistics methods variance, standard deviation, and range can be used for this purpose.
- **Understanding the distribution of data:** The distribution of data can help us understand how to approach the dataset for data cleansing and further analysis. The frequency distribution uses a tabular form of data display to understand how the data is distributed by category or interval. The frequency distribution helps us understand underlying patterns and outliers in the data. This gives us insights into how to use the dataset for further analysis. It provides us with the data cleansing requirements, such as removing outliers and noise in data. Data visualization is very important to understand **Skewness** and **Kurtosis** in the data. The Skewness tells us about the symmetry and inclination of the data. The Kurtosis measures data distribution around the mean about normal distribution.

  The histogram is a very useful visualization technique for understanding the data's patterns, intervals, and outliers. The box plot presentation can help us with outliers, distribution of data by quartile, and skewness in data.
- **Understanding relations in data**: The analysis mentioned in the preceding section methods are usually called univariate analysis. This is because we are analyzing the data by each variable independently and do not worry about the relationship among different variables within the same dataset. Analyzing the relationship between variables helps us understand more about the dataset. The approach to analyzing the relationships and patterns from these relationships are called multivariate analysis. Scatter plots, correlation, and regression analysis are the methods used for performing multi-variate analysis to uncover the relations and patterns in the dataset.

Since the methods used for performing most of the descriptive analysis are statistics, it is called inferential statistical analysis. The objective is to infer data to gain insights.

We have seen in the previous chapter various use cases of **Industrial IoT (IIOT)**. Let us take one example from those use cases to understand how useful descriptive analysis is on IoT data. Equipment utilization, energy consumption, and various equipment parameters must be monitored and reported in the manufacturing industry for improved business performance.

Let us go through how descriptive analysis can help IoT Data Analytics with an example:

- By applying the method of descriptive analytics to the data collected from IoT sensors that monitor the engine on/off, it is possible to perform a basic pattern analysis. This analysis can reveal patterns of equipment utilization and identify any unusual idle time. Such information is valuable to equipment supervisors and production planning teams, as it enables them to take appropriate measures to optimize equipment usage and minimize inefficiencies.
- Monitoring equipment parameters are critical for maintaining the good health of the equipment in manufacturing and various other industries. This can be achieved by measuring variability using descriptive analytics methods (standard deviation and variance). For example, the pressure sensors from the IoT sensors will provide data about the pressure of the industry-grade boilers. Performing a simple descriptive analysis can help us find abnormal pressure readings and inform the factory supervisors immediately for appropriate action.
- Performing a simple correlation analysis or plotting a scatter plot on machinery's energy and heat parameters can help prevent equipment failures due to inconsistent power supply. Simple correlation or multi-variate analysis are popular descriptive analytic methods for achieving this.
- Descriptive analytics can be utilized to optimize energy consumption. By summarizing energy parameters from equipment data, it's possible to identify patterns of average usage by hour or day. This can help factory supervisors pinpoint instances of higher energy consumption and take necessary actions to optimize energy usage.

Similarly, there are various problems we can solve using a simple descriptive analysis for other industries. In every industry, descriptive analytics can be applied to the data generated by the IoT sensors to understand underlying patterns, trends, and correlations to gain more insights from the data. The possibilities and opportunities are enormous.

In addition to the preceding application, descriptive analytics plays a significant role in data cleaning and transformation tasks in data analytics projects. A histogram or box plot can identify outliers and anomalies in the dataset. The outliers can be removed based on the result of this analysis. The data from the IoT devices will have a different unit, and scaling or transforming the data is required for any useful analysis. To perform the data scaling, a simple descriptive method can be applied to transform the necessary data with a mean of 0 and a standard deviation of 1. The mean 0 and standard deviation 1 will ensure consistent data scaling for the variables. One significant challenge we encounter when dealing with IoT datasets is the presence of missing values. In the IoT environment, data loss due to signal is unavoidable and requires to be handled in the dataset. The missing values can be handled using descriptive analytics methods. A simple heatmap can be plotted to visualize the missing data pattern. We can then perform necessary data imputation techniques such as mean imputation, median imputation, and zero imputation.

Predictive Analytics

Predictive Analytics is a crucial method for foreseeing future events through statistical and probabilistic techniques. Its applications span across various domains within Industrial IoT, including supply chain management, inventory control, sales, and marketing.

Before delving into the application of predictive analytics in Industrial IoT solutions, let's explore the various techniques available. These methods enable us to predict and forecast future events based on historical data.

IoT sensor-generated data often exhibits the characteristics of a time series dataset, where variables are recorded at regular intervals. To better understand predictive analytics in this context, let's first delve into the fundamental concepts of time series analysis.

Time Series Analysis

Time series analysis is a statistical method that relies on data generated at regular intervals and recorded with timestamps. It plays a crucial role in understanding the behaviors, trends, underlying patterns, and anomalies within variables over time. In the context of predictive analytics, time series analysis enables us to forecast future events within a specific time frame based on historical data.

The time series analysis mainly has the following methods:

- **Decomposition:** This method helps us analyze seasonality, residuals, and trends in the time series data. IoT sensors fixed in the agricultural land can help us with data on soil moisture, temperature, and humidity condition to predict the need of water quantity requirement for irrigation over different seasons like winter, summer, and rainy. Another application of the time series analysis on the IIoT is to predict the raw material requirement over the other seasons. For example, in a flu season, the drug manufacturer can increase the production quantity of their anti-biotic drugs based on historical data from the supply chain data.
- **Moving averages:** Time series data often exhibit granularity, making it challenging to understand and predict patterns. Moving averages are effective smoothing methods that extract seasonal and periodic trends over longer intervals. To evaluate the accuracy of predictions, we can use an error matrix, also known as a confusion matrix, which breaks down prediction outcomes. The error matrix includes metrics like **True Positives (TP)**, **True Negatives (TN)**, **False Positives (FP)**, and **False Negatives (FN)**. The evaluation measures derived from the error matrix include:
    - **Accuracy (ACC):** The overall correctness of predictions, calculated as (TP + TN) / (TP + TN + FP + FN).
    - **Precision (P):** The proportion of correctly predicted positive instances out of all instances predicted as positive, calculated as TP / (TP + FP).

- **Recall (R):** The proportion of correctly predicted positive instances out of all actual positive instances, calculated as TP / (TP + FN).
- **F1 score (F1):** The harmonic mean of precision and recall, providing a balanced measure, calculated as 2 * (P * R) / (P + R).

- **Autoregressive Integrated Moving Average (ARIMA)**: ARIMA is a widely used statistical method for forecasting future behavior based on past observations and residual errors. It consists of three main components: **Autoregression** (**AR**), **Integration** (I), and **Moving Average** (**MA**). ARIMA models are extensively employed in the industrial IoT domain for predicting equipment failures, optimizing energy management, and forecasting demand. The evaluation of ARIMA models can be done using metrics like **Mean Absolute Error** (**MAE**), **Mean Squared Error** (**MSE**), and **Root Mean Squared Error** (**RMSE**).
- **Exponential smoothing:** Exponential smoothing is a statistical method used to improve data predictability. Unlike other smoothing methods, exponential smoothing employs a weighted average of past data, with recent data given higher weightage than older data. By using this technique, the model can control trends and seasonal variations that may impact the data. By assigning more weight to recent data and less weight to older data, the exponential smoothing method helps to smoothen the data for better prediction. There are many important applications for exponential smoothing in Industrial IoT use cases. Forecasting material demand based on the production line's capacity and predicting equipment maintenance requirements are some of the key use cases in the manufacturing and construction industries. To evaluate the accuracy of predictions, we can use metrics like MAE, MSE, and RMSE, which quantify the difference between predicted and actual values.

Machine Learning Algorithms

Machine Learning is part of Artificial Intelligence that focuses on applying statistical and probabilistic methods to build a model from the data. The computer can learn from the new data to optimize its performance without being explicitly instructed beforehand. There are various types of machine learning; here are the major types of machine learning:

- **Supervised learning**: In this type of machine learning, the data is labeled for the target variable with the actual values. The model built on the labeled data is expected to predict the value of the target variable in the unseen new data. There are several algorithms used for this supervised learning method. The widely used algorithms are linear regression, logistic regression, k-nearest neighbors, and decision trees. In IoT Data Analytics, the supervised learning method is widely used for predicting equipment failures, energy usage, and predictive maintenance. To evaluate the performance of supervised learning models, we can utilize the error matrix and associated evaluation measures like accuracy, precision, recall, and F1 score.
- **Unsupervised learning:** In this type of machine learning, the input data for the machine learning model is not labeled. The system needs to train on understanding the

underlying patterns, grouping, distribution, and trends in the data. The most widely used unsupervised algorithms are k-means clustering, hierarchical clustering, and Principal component analysis. The important applications of unsupervised learning in IoT Data Analytics are for finding anomalies in the data. For example, an unsupervised model can be built to find anomalies in the temperature or vibration of the equipment to predict future failure and prevent production loss. Evaluation measures for unsupervised learning models can include metrics like Silhouette Coefficient, *Davies-Bouldin* Index, and *Calinski-Harabasz* Index.

- **Reinforcement learning:** Reinforcement learning involves determining actions based on previous actions and learning from unknown data. It is particularly useful when dealing with rapidly changing and high-volume data streams. Reinforcement learning finds applications in robotics, autonomous vehicles, predictive maintenance, and adaptive control systems. The evaluation of reinforcement learning models typically involves measuring their performance against predefined reward functions or by comparing their performance with baseline models.
- **Graph analysis:** Graph analysis focuses on analyzing relationships and connections between different variables to perform predictive analysis. It is beneficial for IoT use cases involving multiple sensor inputs and their relationships in equipment operations. Evaluation of graph analysis models can be done using metrics such as accuracy, precision, recall, and F1 score, depending on the specific predictive task.
- **Artificial Neural Networks (ANN):** Artificial Neural Networks are a class of machine learning models inspired by the structure and functioning of biological neural networks. ANN models consist of interconnected nodes called neurons that process and transmit information. They are capable of learning complex patterns and relationships from large amounts of data. ANN finds extensive applications in Industrial IoT for tasks such as predictive maintenance, anomaly detection, and image recognition. Evaluation of ANN models typically involve metrics like accuracy, precision, recall, F1 score, and loss functions such as **Mean Squared Error** (**MSE**) or Cross-Entropy Loss.
- **Deep Learning:** Deep Learning is a subset of machine learning that utilizes deep neural networks with multiple layers to learn hierarchical representations of data. Deep Learning models excel at handling unstructured and high-dimensional data, making them well-suited for tasks such as Natural Language Processing, computer vision, and speech recognition. In the context of Industrial IoT, Deep Learning can be applied to various use cases, including predictive maintenance, quality control, and energy optimization. Evaluation of Deep Learning models involves similar metrics as ANN, such as accuracy, precision, recall, F1 score, and appropriate loss functions.

By leveraging the power of these machine learning algorithms, businesses can unlock valuable insights from their IoT data, enabling informed decision-making, operational efficiency, and improve overall performance. Proper evaluation and selection of the most suitable algorithm for a specific IoT use case are crucial for achieving accurate and reliable predictions.

Prescriptive Analytics

It is a method of analysis using historical data and mathematical models to provide recommendations for decision-makers. For example, the prescriptive analytical models can help optimize production lines in the manufacturing industry by looking at the historical data with different mathematical models and recommending production quantity, equipment to be used, and workers to be assigned. There are multiple prescriptive analytical methods and techniques available. Here are the major methods and types of Prescriptive analytics:

- **Rule-based systems:** As the name indicates, it is a simple method to perform prescriptive analytics using a set of rules to provide decision recommendations by governing data. The subject matter experts can define the rules or learn them automatically from the data using machine learning algorithms. For example, in the manufacturing industry, a rule can be set for controlling the operation of a boiler by setting a rule to monitor a certain threshold of the pressure from the boiler. If the threshold crosses the limit, it can automatically trigger the action to shut down the boiler. Another simple example is turning on the air conditioning system if the room temperature exceeds 30 degrees Celsius.

- **Simulation modeling:** This is a very useful method of Prescriptive Analytics where the systems, process, and business scenarios are simulated using a computer to find their behaviors, patterns, and failures for different simulated scenarios. For example, the production process, equipment behaviors, and raw material supply in the manufacturing industry can be simulated with various conditions. We can re-design the entire production process based on the simulated scenario and the outcome. This will be very helpful for setting up a new production line and factory setup. Simulating existing production lines helps the business to identify bottlenecks in the current setup and optimize the same for a new setup.

- **Decision analysis:** This is a mathematical model like the simulation model discussed in the preceding section, except that we focus on modeling complex decisions and their potential outcomes for different scenarios here. The main objective of this model is to identify decision problems and various possible outcome from the decision. The model takes all past decisions and their consequences to provide a possible outcome for future decisions under various conditions. For instance, in the manufacturing industry, IoT sensors offer valuable insights into equipment utilization. When we combine this data with essential factors like raw material availability and production planning, we can uncover different planning scenarios that can greatly impact production output. This approach enables informed decision-making and optimization of production requirements to meet various scenarios and demands.

- **Mathematical optimization:** This mathematical model uses different optimization algorithms for formulating a problem and finding the optimal solution. Different optimization algorithms are used to implement this model, such as integer programming, linear and non-linear programming, constraint programming, and dynamic programming:

- **Integer programming:** As the name indicates, integer programming uses only integer type variables for optimization, such as the number of units produced, the number of workers involved in the shift, and the number of equipment used. This is useful for optimizing production lines in the manufacturing industry.
- **Linear programming:** In this model, linear equations play a major role; hence, the object and constraint variables must be linearly related. For example, the linear model can optimize the production capacity by looking at the linear relationship between equipment used, units produced, and the number of production lines for comparison.
- **Non-linear programming:** Unlike linear programming, the optimization is applied using variables that are related in a non-linear way. For example, in the production line of the manufacturing industry, energy consumption and equipment utilization are not linearly related as we cannot keep increasing energy input for more equipment utilization. But we can apply non-linear optimization to save energy.
- **Constraint programming:** In this mathematical model, the object variable will be subject to a set of constraints to find the optimized outcome. This method is used when linear and non-linear programming cannot achieve the required optimization. The model uses both linear, and non-linear variables and their complex relationships. In the manufacturing industry, this model can be applied for allocating raw materials to the production line based on various constraints like the availability of equipment and workers for expected production output.
- **Dynamic programming:** This mathematical modeling technique is used for solving complex decision problems by breaking the decision process problems into multiple stages or subprocess levels to optimize each stage of the decisions to reach the required optimization for the end objective of the decision-making process. This can be used in production optimization in the manufacturing industry by breaking down the production process into multiple smaller processes and optimizing each process individually. In the end, it helps in optimizing the production line.

- **Game Theory:** Game Theory is a mathematical framework that helps in analyzing situations where the outcome of a decision depends on the actions of multiple decision-makers. The theory helps identify the optimal decision strategy for each decision-maker, considering the actions of the others. In Prescriptive Analytics, game theory is used to model complex decision-making scenarios involving multiple parties with competing interests. By modeling such scenarios, businesses can gain insights into the behavior of stakeholders and predict the outcomes of various strategies. In the manufacturing industry, several production lines require raw materials from a limited inventory store. However, due to limited stock, it is impossible to supply the raw materials to all production lines. Instead, the raw materials must be optimized for the production line that is building a high-demand model of the product. In this scenario,

Game Theory can be used to prioritize raw material sourcing and route the materials to the appropriate production line based on market demand. The goal is to optimize the strategy for prioritizing raw material sourcing to ensure that the high-demand model is produced efficiently.

- **Heuristics:** This is a simple and effective method to build a model for the decision-making process. Unlike the other mathematical models explained in the preceding sections, Heuristics does not rely on mathematical models or algorithms. It is a simple rule-based model combined with expert guidelines to solve complex problems. The industry's best practices and guidelines, along with the expertise, can help build a heuristics model to enable the decision-making process for the business. Production processes, guidelines, and expert input in the manufacturing industry, along with the data from inventory, supply chain, and equipment performance, can help optimize production capacity.

In summary, data analytics methods are the building block for any data analysis solution. Many methods are critical to the achievement of data analytics goals for Industrial IoT. Descriptive, Predictive, and Prescriptive are the key methods for most IoT use cases. We will go through some of these methods in the upcoming chapters.

How to Perform Data Analysis

In the previous section, you learned about various data analytics methods and techniques. These methods are essential for conducting analyses on the provided datasets. However, failing to follow a structured approach to analysis can not only waste time and resources but also jeopardize the organization's investments, yielding no positive outcomes. There are several frameworks available to help structure data analysis tasks, each with its own set of advantages and disadvantages. In this section, we will focus on industry-standard frameworks commonly used in data analysis projects, specifically in the context of IoT Data Analytics.

SEMMA Process Framework

SEMMA is one of the simple and effective frameworks for data analysis. It stands for **Sample, Explore, Modify, Model, and Assess**. The framework helps the data analyst perform the data analysis task in a structured and iterative way. The framework process ensures that the result is consistent, verified, effective, and accurate.

Let us go through a business scenario of Industrial IoT in the manufacturing industry to learn how to apply the SEMMA framework to achieve the objectives:

- **Business scenario:** In the manufacturing industry, the business wants to optimize the utilization of the production equipment based on the data generated from the IoT sensors of that equipment.
- **Sample:** This step takes sample data, which are sub-set of the entire dataset and can represent the dataset characteristics. In the business scenario of optimizing production

equipment utilization, this step involves selecting a random sample of the IoT sensor data from the production equipment. Since the dataset is of time series, we could select a certain period from the main dataset. Let us say that if the main dataset contains the last three years of data, we could take three months for our sample. The percentage of the sample can vary on the use case and the quality of data.

- **Explore:** The next step in the process is to explore the data to investigate patterns, anomalies, missing values, outliers, and correlation among variables. In our example, this could mean looking at the equipment data to see any abnormal readings from the sensors, any patterns on equipment's energy usage, engine on/off, vibration levels, and heat generated by the equipment. Exploring the relationship between how vibration and heat are related, could help us find the pattern in the equipment's engine off-value. The engine off reading could indicate equipment failure due to higher heat generated by the equipment due to vibrations. We can advise equipment maintenance requirements with these insights to avoid sudden failures.
- **Modify:** This part of the process is to modify the data for transformation requirements to create new features for analysis. There are several ways to transform the data, such as aggregating the data, combining multiple variables, splitting one variable into multiple variables, and removing outliers. In our example, the equipment's average heat and normal vibration can be combined to create a new feature that indicates 0 and 1 for equipment under normal or abnormal conditions. The newly created feature can help us further analyze equipment failures in various parts of the day and the output from the equipment. The finding can help us to re-configure the equipment for optimization.
- **Model:** This is the important step in building models using statistical or machine learning methods. In our example, production output data and equipment data from the IoT sensors can be used for building regression models to understand how each equipment's performance impacts the overall production output. This helps us in planning and scheduling equipment maintenance.
- **Assess:** This is the last step in the process, where we assess the model, we built in the preceding sections. The assessment includes the model's accuracy, performance, consistency, reliability and usability. In our example, the model we built for planning and scheduled maintenance can be evaluated for its performance, accuracy, reliability and usefulness.

KDD Process Framework

Knowledge Discovery in Databases (KDD) is a simple framework for extracting insights and valuable information from the dataset. The dataset could be large, with many variables and other complex relationships. Here are the steps involved in the process:

- **Data selection:** In this step, the process is to select data from the database which are relevant and meaningful. The selection process involves multiple sub-steps, such as defining the scope of the analysis, size of the data, variables required, and records such as the last three months period.

- **Data cleaning:** This is where we will clean up data with missing values, outliers, and inconsistencies.
- **Data transformation:** In this step, we perform necessary data transforming to make the data relevant for analysis. This may involve a conversation of data from text to numeric, categorical to numeric, scaling the data, or creating new features using aggregation or combining other variables.
- **Data mining:** This is the important step in the process where we perform data mining. The data mining can be done using various algorithms and techniques to extract insights, patterns, relationships, and behaviors in the data. Several methods and techniques can be used for this purpose, including clustering, decision tree, or association rule mining.
- **Pattern evaluation:** This is the final step in the KDD process, which is to evaluate the insights, patterns, relationships, and behaviors found in the data. The evaluation can be performed using various visualization techniques or different testing methods.

The KDD can be applied to various Industrial IoT use cases. For example, in the manufacturing industry, we will have a large volume of data from the IoT sensors on production equipment about their engine on/off status, heat, vibration, and pressure. This data can be analyzed using the KDD framework to gain insights into the equipment's performance and how it impacts the overall production capacity. This can be achieved by analyzing equipment's on/off conditions about its heat, vibration, and pressure parameters. This gives us insights into equipment health to prevent failures, plan maintenance, and improve production capacity.

CRISP-DM Framework

Cross-Industry Standard Process for Data Mining (**CRISP-DM**) is one of the important and widely used frameworks for performing data analysis. This is the most matured and end-to-end process, with a structured approach to data analysis tasks. The CRISP-DM process consists of the following six steps:

1. **Business understanding**: The initial and crucial stage of the process is the business understanding step. It involves defining the business goals and objectives while gaining a clear understanding of the problem statement. This step includes identifying the stakeholders and understanding their roles, strategies, and pertinent information. For instance, let us consider the example of Industrial IoT in the manufacturing industry. During this step, the stakeholders are identified, and the business goals are determined, such as enhancing production capacity, increasing equipment utilization, and decreasing costs. The objectives are defined, such as agreeing to a 5% improvement in production capacity, a 10% improvement in equipment utilization, and a 20% reduction in overall costs.

2. **Data understanding**: This is the most critical step in data analysis. We can have goals and objectives and understand the problem statements. But suppose we do not have the necessary data to meet the data analysis criteria, such as data volume, quality, relevant variables, and their relationships. In that case, it is not possible to meet the objectives. Hence in this critical step, the data is collected and analyzed for relevancy, volume, quality, and limitations. We may need to go back to step one again to redefine business goals and objectives based on data availability and its limitations.

   In the example of the manufacturing industry, the data from the IoT sensors, ERP, and other external systems are collected for performing initial analysis to gain insights into the datasets. The IoT sensors provide data about equipment conditions and performance. The ERP and other systems provide information about raw material stocks, product inventory status, and worker details. We perform the necessary analysis to gain insights into the data to map the goals and objectives defined in the previous step.

3. **Data preparation**: Data cleanup and necessary transformations are performed in this step. This will make the final dataset ready for analysis.

   In our manufacturing example, the data collected from IoT sensors and other systems require cleanup, scaling, and transformation. For example, IoT sensors may provide empty packets due to signal loss or bandwidth issues. We need to clean up this data to address the quality issues. In the same way, we need to scale the data from the IoT sensors as each device may send a different unit of temperature, vibration, or pressure of the equipment. Finally, we need to perform the transformation on the data like an engine on/off status from Yes/No to 1/0. Other such data cleanup and transformation are required on the data collected from other external systems.

4. **Modeling**: This is the important step in the process where the data is analyzed, and various modeling methods and techniques are implemented. The machine learning and mathematical modeling techniques depend on the problem statement, business objective, and dataset content.

   In our manufacturing example, predictive, prescriptive models are built to optimize the production process, predict equipment failures, and forecast raw material requirements.

5. **Evaluation**: In this step, the performance, accuracy, reliability, and consistency of the model we built is evaluated. The model perform should meet the business goals and success criteria defined in the first step.

   For example, in the manufacturing use case, we evaluate the models built for optimizing production process, predicting equipment failures, and forecasting raw material requirements. We can evaluate model performance using the preceding criteria.

6. **Deployment**: This is the final step in the process, the model built is being put to real use. The stakeholders are communicated on the results, and the continuous improvement process is defined. The model we built can be used for taking business decision, providing recommendations, predicting future event, or optimizing business processes.

In our manufacturing use case example, we will look at the objectives set in the first step to check whether the models perform as per the expectations. In our case, the objectives are set as, 5% improvement in the production capacity, 10% improvement in the equipment's utilization and overall cost reduction of 20%. If the model we built can prevent the failure of equipment by scheduling maintenance in advance, then it could achieve 5% improvement in the production capacity, likewise, the equipment utilization will improve by 10% if we optimize equipment configuration based on vibration and heat analysis of equipment data and its output. Finally, 20% can be reduced by optimizing equipment utilization, re-configuring the equipment, and forecasting raw material requirements.

Other Frameworks

The following are the other frameworks to perform data analysis:

- **Acquire, Describe, Analyze, Present, and Transform (ADAPT)**: Acquire, Describe, Analyze, Present, and Transform is the framework widely used for scientific research and business intelligence projects. In this framework, more focus is given to acquiring and transforming important data before analyzing and showing results.
- **Prepare, Investigate, Predict, Evaluate, and Line (PIPELINE)**: Prepare, Investigate, Predict, Evaluate, and Line up for the next iteration is the framework widely used for machine learning and predictive modeling tasks. The following are the key steps in this framework: Preparing data, investigating data for quality, patterns, and relationships, building a prediction model, and evaluating the model for accuracy, performance, and reliability. Finally, refine the model for better results.
- **Six Sigma**: Six Sigma is a data and process-driven methodology to improve quality and outcomes. They are widely used in the manufacturing industries for achieving high quality goals.
- **AGILE**: AGILE is a software development framework used for data analysis. The important contribution of AGILE is to build a solution quickly in a smaller iterative style. The success of AGILE depends on the collaboration between data engineers, data analysts, software developers, business users, and stakeholders.
- **OSEMN**: **Obtain, Scrub, Explore, Model, iNterpret** is an end-to-end framework for data analysis. This model focuses less on data collection and clean-up and more on exploration, modeling, and visualization. This framework is very effective in data science projects where data engineers have already performed data collection and much of the clean-up.
- **SPADE**: **Synthetic Performance Assessment for Data-IntEnsive Systems** is a framework used for analyzing the performance of data-intensive systems, as the name suggests. The framework covers data collection, data clean-up, building models for prediction using different simulation techniques, and identifying performance bottlenecks in various situations.

- **WQS: Web Quality Score** is a framework that mainly analyzes the website's performance and quality. As part of the framework, data collected from the website on performance, content quality, navigation time, and user experience are analyzed for optimization.
- **R-PAS: Revised Psychopathology Assessment Scale** is a framework mainly used for analyzing patients' data for psychopathology symptoms. The framework focuses on collecting data on patients' symptoms, behaviors, responses, and attention to perform analysis for diagnoses and treatment approaches. The patient's data in this framework is collected via interview and rating of answers. The classification system called **Diagnostic and Statistical Manual of Mental Disorders; 5th edition (DSM-5)** is applied here.

Conclusion

In this chapter, we covered some of the important topics for performing data analysis tasks. You have learned about various data analysis methods and techniques, such as Descriptive, Predictive, and Prescriptive Analytics. We covered how these methods and techniques can be applied to IoT Data Analytics with a practical example from the Industrial IoT and manufacturing industry. Then in the subsequent section, we covered the frameworks for approaching data analytics projects with examples from Industrial IoT and the manufacturing industry. The frameworks like SEMMA, KDD, and CRISP-DM are widely used in the industry for performing data analysis tasks. We also covered some noteworthy frameworks. Though these frameworks are not widely used, it is important to know about them.

Learning about the data analysis methods, techniques, and frameworks will set a strong foundation to start your IoT Data Analytics journey. They provide a clear view of how to approach business problems and what methods to use for the given problem.

In the next chapter, you will learn about basic installation and configuration of necessary software and tools such as Python and **Integrated Development Environment (IDE)**, Apache Kafka, Apache Jmeter, MQTT Broker and PostgresSQL. We will also learn details of Python packages used for performing data collection, simulation, cleaning, transformation and analysis. Basics of Python programming languages with practical examples using IoT dataset and data analysis and data visualization using Python.

Points to Remember

- Data analysis methods and techniques: Descriptive, Predictive, and Prescriptive Analytics.
- Descriptive Analytics involves analyzing historical data to identify patterns, trends, and insights.

- Predictive Analytics uses statistical and machine learning techniques to make predictions about future events or behavior.
- Prescriptive Analytics combines historical data, predictive models, and optimization techniques to recommend specific actions to take to achieve a desired outcome.
- Descriptive Analytics in the manufacturing industry uses IoT Data Analytics to gain insights into operational efficiency, machine utilization, and product quality based on historical data.
- Predictive Analytics in the manufacturing industry uses IoT Data Analytics to forecast maintenance requirements, predict equipment failures, and optimize supply chain processes.
- Prescriptive Analytics in the manufacturing industry uses IoT Data Analytics to optimize production processes, reduce waste, and minimize downtime by recommending specific actions based on real-time data.
- SEMMA framework is used in the manufacturing industry to identify patterns and relationships in IoT data, perform exploratory data analysis, and develop predictive models to optimize production processes.
- KDD framework is used in the manufacturing industry to preprocess IoT data, select relevant features, mine the data for patterns, and validate the results to support decision-making.
- CRISP-DM framework is used in the manufacturing industry to define business goals and objectives, understand the problem statement, prepare, and preprocess the IoT data, build and validate predictive models, and deploy and monitor the results to improve operational efficiency and reduce costs.
- There are many other frameworks available for performing data analysis such as ADAPT, PIPELINE, Six Sigma, AGILE, OSEMN, SPADE, WQS, and R-PAS.

Join our book's Discord space

Join the book's Discord Workspace for Latest updates, Offers, Tech happenings around the world, New Release and Sessions with the Authors:

https://discord.bpbonline.com

CHAPTER 3
Setting Up IoT Analytics Environment

Introduction

In this chapter, we will set up the required environment for performing IoT Data Analytics in the subsequent chapters. You will learn the Python programming language from basic string, numeric, and mathematical operations to data analysis tasks. Practicing all the examples given here will prepare you for the rest of the IoT Data Analytics examples we will cover in the upcoming chapters. We will install and configure the necessary tools and databases to create a data pipeline. This will help you learn about *Kafka* and *PostgresDB*, which are essential for setting up a data pipeline for our IoT Data Analytics purpose. Furthermore, we will simulate various Industrial IoT equipment data. This data will come from IoT sensors and gateway devices in the real world. Hence, simulating the data is necessary to understand how the equipment data from the IoT devices can be consumed and stored in the databases. The same data will be used for analytics and machine learning purposes.

Structure

In this chapter, we will cover the following topics:

- Why Python Language
- Installation and Configuration of Python IDE
- Installation and Configuration of Apache Kafka

- Installation and Configuration of MQTT
- Installation and Configuration of PostgresSQL
- Important Python Packages
- Basics of Python Language with Examples
- Data Analysis using Python
- Data Wrangling with Python
- Data Visualization using Python

Objectives

You will be equipped with the information necessary to set up the crucial software and tools needed for IoT Data Analytics by the end of this chapter. This will need knowing how to set up PostgresSQL, Kafka and MQTT as well as installing and configuring a Python environment using Anaconda. You will also get a foundational understanding of data analysis and programming in Python. Finally, this chapter will equip you with the core Python programming abilities required to perform data analytics and machine learning activities on IoT data in the following chapters. It will also prepare you to set up all the software and tools required for IoT Data Analytics.

Why Python Language

In *Chapter 1, Necessity of Analytics Across IoT*, we discussed why Python is the most popular language for data analysis. After exploring the methods and techniques required for IoT Data Analytics, it is evident that Python is the ideal language for programming. The SEMMA, KDD, and CRISP-DM frameworks cover all the essential steps for implementing IoT Data Analytics. Python is advantageous for covering all the phases of each framework mentioned in this chapter. Let us examine why Python is the best option for each of these steps in these frameworks and the methods and techniques we discussed in *Chapter 2, Up and Running with Data Analytics Fundamentals*:

- **Data collection:** The initial step in any data analysis task is to collect data from various sources. In IoT Data Analytics, data must be acquired from IoT devices that generate data via the sensors embedded in equipment. These devices can be used in manufacturing, construction, mining, pharmaceuticals, ESG, agriculture, and smart cities. Python supports most of the protocols required to acquire data from IoT devices, such as MQTT, AMQT, HTTP, CoAP, TCP/IP, Modbus, and CANbus. Libraries such as paho-mqtt, requests, pika, asyncio, aiocoap, pymodbus, python-can, and modules like socket can be used to acquire data from any of these protocols. Python is the language with the most support for a variety of protocols required for data acquisition from IoT devices used in most industries.

- **Data cleaning and transformation:** The data received from IoT devices is likely to be in different formats, making it difficult to use. Python has extensive libraries for data cleanup and transformation that make this task easier. Libraries like NumPy, Pandas, Dask, PySpark, and OpenCV provide more efficient methods to perform this task.
- **Data analysis**: In *Chapter 2, Up and Running with Data Analytics Fundamentals,* we learned about various data analysis methods used for IoT Data Analytics, such as Descriptive, Predictive, and Prescriptive. Python is the best language for performing all these types of analysis. For Descriptive Analysis, we have extensive libraries like NumPy, SciPy, Pandas, Statsmodels, and scikit-learn for performing detailed analysis to gain insights from IoT data. For Predictive Analysis, we have several libraries like NumPy, SciPy, Pandas, Statsmodels, scikit-learn, TensorFlow, Keras, LightGBM, and XGBoost that can help perform predictive analysis using various algorithms and methods. For Prescriptive analysis, we have several libraries like SimPy, Pyomo, PyKnow, Pyke, FuzzyWuzzy, PuLP, Gurobi, Pyomo.Constraints, DynaPy, Nashpy, Axelrod, PyEconometrics, Gambit, QuantEcon, and SymPy can help us implement mathematical models such as Rule-based systems, simulation modeling, decision analysis, mathematical optimization, and game theory.
- **Data visualization:** Python offers several data visualization libraries that can display more intuitive and colorful representations of insights. These libraries include Matplotlib, Seaborn, ggplot, Plotly, Altair, Bokeh, Dash, and ReportLab.
- **Evaluation**: Python comes with a wide range of libraries that evaluate the models built in the earlier steps. The scikit-learn, TensorFlow, Keras, PyTorch, CatBoost, XGBoost, and LightGBM libraries have their own module to support model evaluation and accuracy.
- **Deployment and continuous learning:** It is crucial to have a pipeline for deployment and continuous correction of the models built. This can be easily achieved in Python compared to other languages using MLflow and KubeFlow libraries. From the preceding discussion of Python libraries in every phase of IoT Data Analytics implementation, Python is the language of choice for data analysis projects. Python is not only easy to use, but also powerful, flexible, portable, and versatile.

Installation and Configuration of Python IDE

Anaconda is one of the widely used integrated development environments for Python. It has the required tools, development environment, and packages for data analysis and machine learning. For executing IoT Data Analytics examples given in this chapter requires you to install this.

The following are the steps to install and configure Anaconda:

1. Go to the Anaconda website **https://www.anaconda.com/products/distribution** and download the latest version of Anaconda, as per your operating system, as shown in *Figure 3.1:*

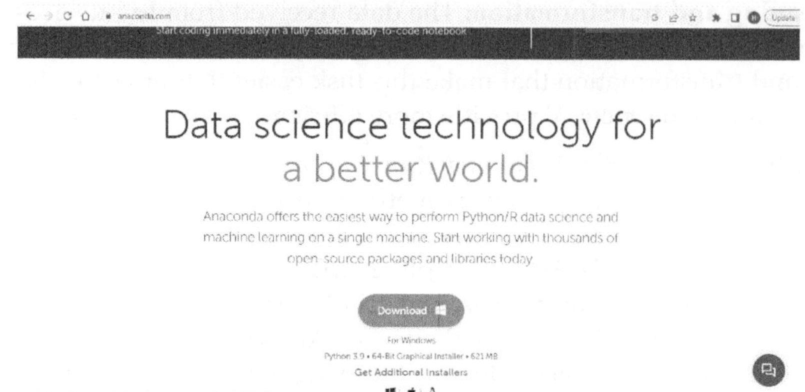

***Figure 3.1:** Download Anaconda*

2. After the **Download**, start the installation by clicking on the downloaded package.
3. Click **Continue** to go to the next step.
4. On the Readme step, click **Continue** to go to the next step.
5. Select **Accept** on the License and Terms of use and click **Continue** to go to the next step.
6. Make sure you have enough space in the computer (at least 500 MB) to select the location where you want to install and click **Next** to go to the next step. Refer to *Figure 3.2*:

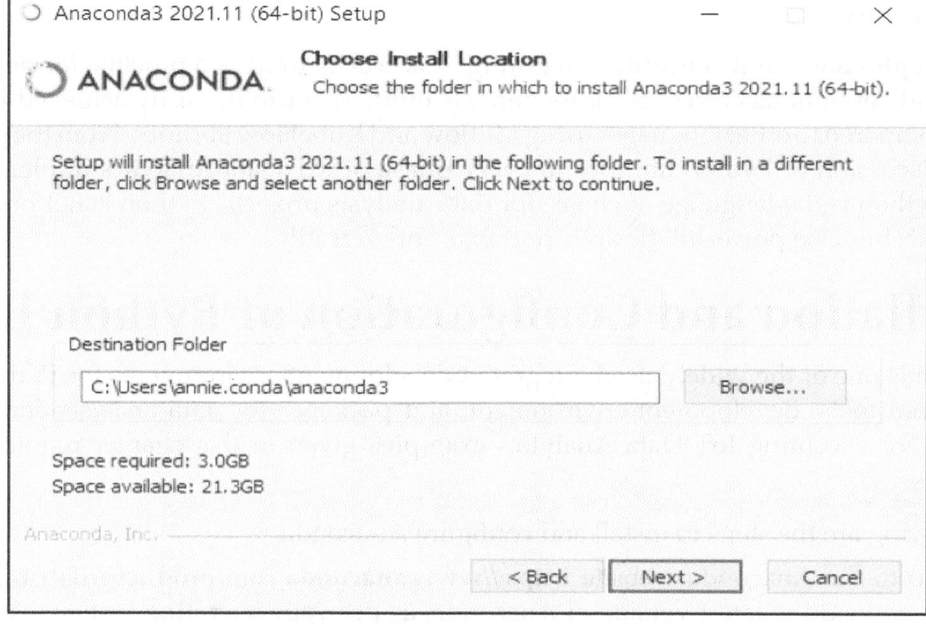

***Figure 3.2:** Installation of Anaconda*

7. Click **Install.** This will take a few minutes. Refer to *Figure 3.3*:

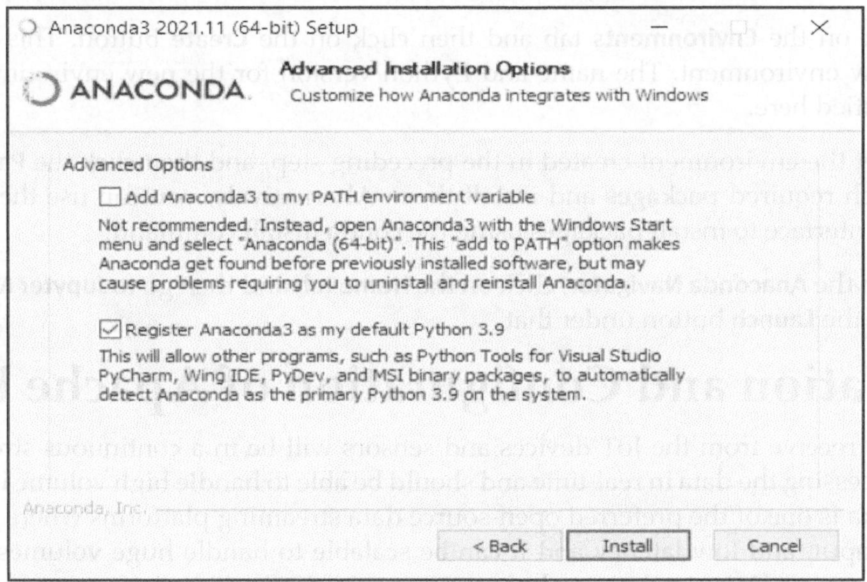

Figure 3.3: Selecting Anaconda3 default option

8. Select the option **Register Anaconda3 as my default Python 3.9** from the preceding screenshot.
9. Click **Finish** to complete the installation. Refer to *Figure 3.4*:

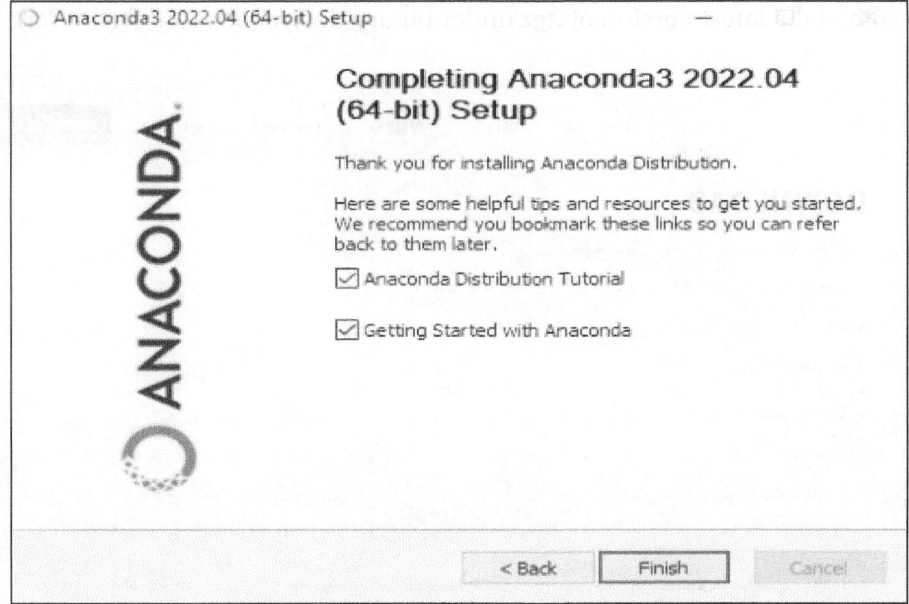

Figure 3.4: Finishing Installation of Anaconda

10. Launch the **Anaconda Navigator**.
11. Click on the **Environments** tab and then click on the **Create** button. This will create a new environment. The name and Python version for the new environment can be specified here.
12. Select the environment created in the preceding step, and then click the **Packages** tab. Search required packages and install them. Alternatively, you can use the command line interface to install packages using the conda install command.
13. From the **Anaconda Navigator**, click on the **Home** tab and then go to **Jupyter Notebook** to click the **Launch** button under that.

Installation and Configuration of Apache Kafka

The data we receive from the IoT devices and sensors will be in a continuous stream which requires processing the data in real-time and should be able to handle high volume in less time. Apache Kafka is one of the preferred open-source data streaming platforms where it supports high throughput, and low latency and it can be scalable to handle huge volumes of data in parallel. In any IoT Data Analytics solution, we require Kafka-like platforms to handle real-time data streaming. Both Microsoft Azure and AWS uses their own product to handle data streaming. Cloud providers offer their own data service products. For instance, Azure Event Hub and AWS Kinesis are widely used options in this category.

The following are the steps for downloading, installing, and configuring Apache Kafka:

1. Go to the official website of **Apache Kafka** (**https://kafka.apache.org/downloads**) and **Download** the latest version of **.tgz** under binary downloads (see *Figure 3.5*):

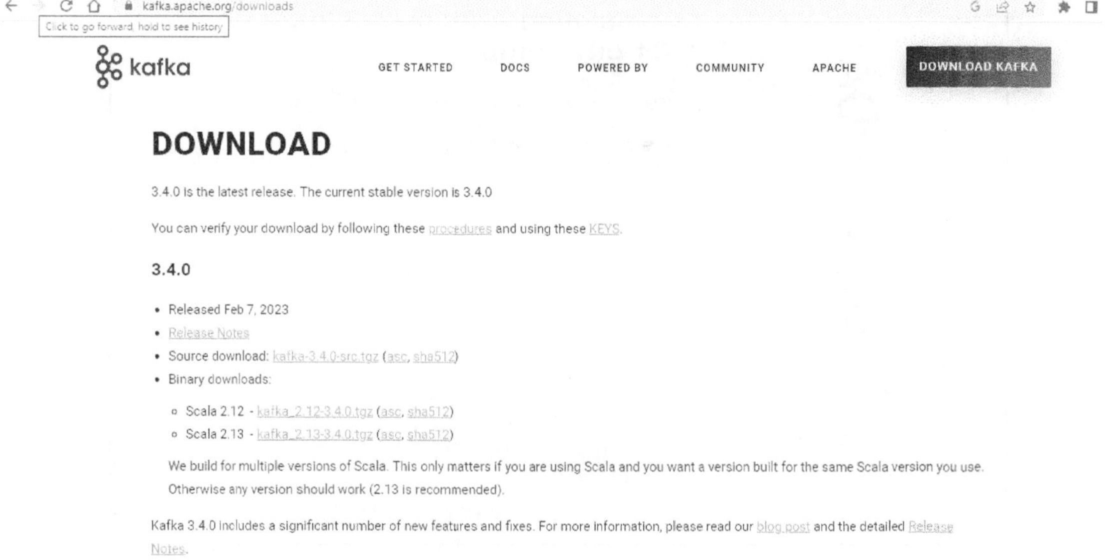

Figure 3.5: Installation of Kafka

2. After the successful download, extract the **.tgz** file to your desired location.
3. Apache Kafka requires Java installation on your computer. If you do not have Java installed already, you can download the latest version of Java from the official website (**https://java.com/en/download/**).
4. Both **`JAVA_HOME`** and **`PATH`** environment variables need to be set for the computer to know the location of your Java installation. Set the **`JAVA_HOME`** to the location where you have installed Java and add the bin folder location of Java to the **`PATH`** environment variable.
5. Apache Kafka uses ZooKeeper for managing clusters. The first step in starting Apache Kafka is to start the ZooKeeper server. From your command line utility, go to the bin folder of the Apache Kafka installation and run the following command: **`zookeeper-server-start.bat config/zookeeper.properties`**.
6. After the successful start of ZooKeeper, start the Apache Kafka server. From a new command line window, go to the Apache Kafka installation bin folder. Execute the following command: **`kafka-server-start.bat config/server.properties.`**
7. **Apache Kafka** uses publish and subscribe methods for receiving and processing a stream of data. Each stream can be defined as a separate topic that is uniquely named for processing data of a particular stream. Create a topic by running the following command from the command line window: **`kafka-topics.bat --create --bootstrap-server localhost:9092 --replication-factor 1 --partitions 1 --topic new_topic.`**
8. Here **`localhost`** is the computer IP Address where your Apache Kafka is installed. The **`new_topic`** is the unique name of the topic to receive a particular data stream. We will discuss more on this in the upcoming chapter.
9. After the successful creation of the topic, the data can be published via Apache Kafka producer. To produce messages (data) to a topic, execute the following command from your command line window: **`kafka-console-producer.bat --bootstrap-server localhost:9092 --topic new_topic.`** Now, the producer is ready to publish the data on the mentioned topic to all consumers to consume the data.
10. To read and process the data published in a topic, we need a consumer, execute the following command: **`kafka-console-consumer.bat --bootstrap-server localhost:9092 --topic new_topic --from-beginning`**. This command reads all data sent by the producer via a unique topic, from the beginning.

Installation and Configuration of MQTT

In *Chapter 1, Necessity of Analytics across IoT*, we discussed how IoT sensors and devices use various protocols to send data to the cloud for IoT Data Analytics. In this chapter, we will utilize the MQTT protocol to simulate IoT data, which is widely used for data transmission in the IoT world. Understanding the MQTT protocol is essential for your IoT Data Analytics journey.

Message Queuing Telemetry Transport (MQTT) is a lightweight messaging protocol that operates on a publish-subscribe model. It is commonly used for IoT data transmission and data simulation for IoT Data Analytics, especially when actual sensor data is unavailable at the start of a project. We will use an open-source MQTT broker, Mosquitto, to simulate data.

The following are the steps to install, configure, and validate Mosquitto:

1. Download the **Mosquitto MQTT** broker from the official website (**https://mosquitto.org/download/**). The installation procedure may vary depending on your computer's operating system. If you use Mac OS, you can install Mosquitto using the **brew install mosquito** command. Refer to *Figure 3.6*:

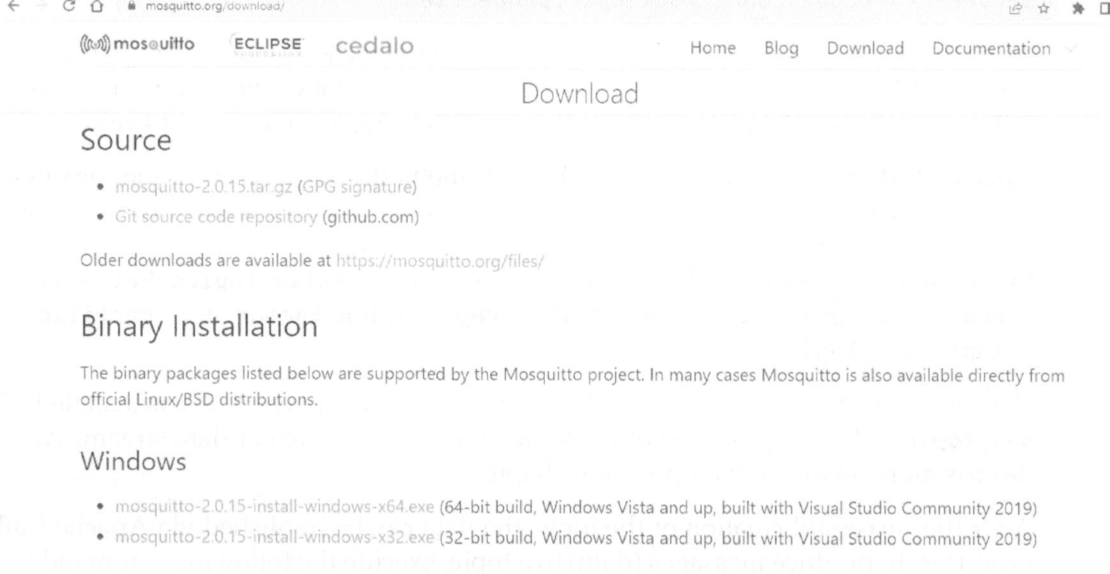

Figure 3.6: Installation of Mosquitto MQTT broker

2. Once the download is complete, run the **.exe** file and follow the installation steps.
3. After installation, open the Command line utility as an administrator.
4. Navigate to the **Mosquitto** installation directory and execute the **mosquitto -v** command to start the **Mosquitto** broker without any issues.
5. The **Mosquitto** broker is now ready for data publication and subscription. To listen to the **iot_sensor** topic, open a new command line window and run the **mosquitto_sub -h localhost -t iot_sensor** command.
6. To publish data for this topic, use another command line window and execute the **mosquitto_pub -h localhost -t iot_sensor -m '{"temperature": 25, "humidity":**

50, "pressure": 1000} command. This will publish data for the specified topic and values.

7. Verify that the subscription window of the command line is displaying the published data. This validates the successful installation. We will cover simulating complex and high-volume IoT data using Python programming and the MQTT library in the upcoming chapters.

Installation and Configuration of PostgresSQL

PostgreSQL is an open-source database that supports a large volume of data and is one of the best choices for storing and processing IoT data for Analytics. It supports multiple data formats like JSON and XML which are required for storing IoT sensor data. It has various built-in functions for storing, extracting, and analyzing large volumes of data. The examples given in this book are written using **postgresSQL**.

The following are the detailed step-by-step instructions to install PostgreSQL on Windows. The steps may differ for other operating system:

1. **PostgresSQL** can be downloaded from the official website. Go to the website (**https://www.enterprisedb.com/downloads/postgres-postgresql-downloads**) and click the package to download.
2. Start the installation process by double-clicking the downloaded file. Choose your installation location and follow the other instructions.
3. Make sure that you select the **PostgreSQL Server** component when the prompt asks you to choose the components to be installed.
4. After the successful installation, the database setup is required.
5. Go to the location where **PostgresSQL** is installed on your computer and open the **pgAdmin** tool.
6. In the **pgAdmin** screen, right-click on the node called **Servers** and choose **Create | Server....**
7. Provide a name for the server as **IoTAnalytics** and switch to the **Connection** tab.
8. Provide the default username as **postgres** and the password as blank, log in to the PostgreSQL server.
9. Go to the **Maintenance DB** tab and choose a database you want to connect.
10. Click on the **Save** button to create the server.
11. The installation of **PostgresSQL** can be verified using a simple command from the **pgAdmin** tool as follows:

a. In the **pgAdmin** screen, open the Servers node and choose the server you just created.

b. Similarly, open the Databases node and select the database you want to connect.

c. Click the **SQL** button from the toolbar. This will open the SQL editor.

d. Enter the following SQL command:

```
SELECT version();
```

12. Click on the **Execute** button to execute the command.

13. You should be able to see the version of the database server if the installation is successful.

Important Python Packages Used

This book uses various **Python** packages for IoT Data Analytics. To install these packages, use the command **pip install <package_name>** in the Python installation environment or **conda install <package_name>**. You can install the required packages through the Anaconda interface by clicking on the Packages tab and searching for the package.

Creating a separate virtual environment is a better way to manage packages and their dependencies. A virtual environment helps in isolating the **Python** environment for each project, preventing version issues and package conflicts.

The following packages are used in this book:

- **NumPy:** Used frequently for handling mathematical, array, list, matrices, and other complex structure operations.
- **Pandas:** Used for data analysis, data processing, and data transformation tasks on structured data such as series and dataframes.
- **paho-mqtt:** Used for MQTT-related tasks in Python, including publishing and subscribing to a MQTT topic for pushing and pulling data from the MQTT broker.
- **PyKafka:** Used for managing Apache Kafka-related tasks, such as creating Kafka topics, producing data for a topic, and consuming data from a specific topic.
- **psycopg2:** Used for handling all PostgresSQL database operations, including connecting to databases, executing queries, and handling transactions such as insert, update, and delete.
- **Matplotlib:** Used to visualize data in the form of charts and graphs to gain insights from the data.
- **Seaborn:** Built on top of Matplotlib, providing a rich and custom-designed interface for creating visualizations.

- **Faker:** Used for data simulation purposes, generating realistic data such as IoT sensor data, energy consumptions, credit card spending, and location for data simulation.
- **Scikit-learn:** Widely used for performing machine learning tasks, containing machine learning functions for performing data analysis and model building using both supervised and unsupervised methods, and functions for model training and evaluation.
- **TensorFlow:** An open-source library for performing machine learning and deep learning in Python, containing functions to build and train neural networks for large datasets, and performing various mathematical operations on large datasets.
- **Prophet:** Used for time series forecasting, building models using time series data, visualizations, and making predictions.
- **SciPy:** used for mathematical operations and scientific computing in Python, containing functions for performing linear algebra, signal processing, and building optimization models.
- **PuLP:** Used for performing linear and integer programming in Python, helping to define and solve various optimization problems as part of Prescriptive Analytics.
- **Pyomo:** Used for building optimization models using various mathematical methods, defining, and solving optimization problems as part of Prescriptive Analytics.

Basics of Python Language with Examples

Data types are an essential aspect of programming languages. In Python, there are several built-in data types that you can use to store and manipulate different kinds of data. Some of the commonly used data types in Python include integer, float, string, Boolean, list, tuple, dictionary and set. They define the type of data a variable can hold. Unlike some other programming `languages` like C or C++, Python dynamically determines the variable type based on the value assigned to it. For instance, if we assign the value **`5`** to a variable called **`x`**, Python will automatically determine the data type as an integer (**`int`**). Similarly, if we assign the string value **`test`** to a variable named **`a`** Python will recognize it as a string. However, assigning conflicting values to the same variable in subsequent lines of code can lead to errors in dynamic type determination. For instance, if we assign the value **`5`** to the variable **`x`** and later assign the string value **`test`** to the same **`x`**, Python will assign the string value to the variable **`x`**, leading to errors. Thus, it is crucial to maintain consistency while handling variables in Python. To illustrate, let us practice using variables and data types in Python.

The integer data type is represented as **`int`** in Python. The following is an example of how we can use integer variables for numeric operations:

```
1. a = 10 # defining variable with initial assignment automatically as-
   signs its data type dynamically.
2. b = 5 # another Integer variable declaration
```

```
c = a + b # We can perform any mathemactial operations. Adding both variable values here.
print("Addition: ", c) # print is the function we will often use for printing the results to the current computer window.
d = a * b # Multiplication operation
print("Multiplication: ", d)
e = a/b # Division operation
print("Division: ", e)
f = a ** b # Exponentiation
print("Exponentiation: ", f)
g = a % b #Modulus
print("Modulus: ", g)
h = a // b #floor division
print("Floor Division: ", h)
```

- **Float:** Floats are used for assigning decimal points to the number variables. The following is the same Python program used in the preceding section. But this time we assign decimal values to the variables:

```
a = 10.5# defining variable with initial assignment automatically assigns its data type dynamically.
b = 5.5# another Integer variable declaration
c = a + b # We can perform any mathemactial operations. Adding both variable values here.
print("Addition: ", c) # print is the function we will often use for printing the results to the current computer window.
d = a * b # Multiplication operation
print("Multiplication: ", d)
e = a/b # Division operation
print("Division: ", e)
f = a ** b # Exponentiation
print("Exponentiation: ", f)
g = a % b #Modulus
print("Modulus: ", g)
h = a // b #floor division
print("Floor Division: ", h)
```

- **String:** In Python **str** is used for the re-presenting String data type. Let us look at some examples of how to use strings in Python:

```
str1 = "Hello, I live in an AI world!" # Creating a string variable
str2 = "I am Robot!" # Creating another string variable
print("Concatenation of two string :", str1 + " "+ str2)
print("Accessing specific characters in a string: ", str1[0]) # Output will be H
print("str1[-1]: ", str1[-1]) # Output: !
print("Extracting substring using slicing with starting position and length of extraction", str1[0:5]) # Output: Hello
print("Slicing string from 7th character onwards: ", str1[7:]) # Output: I live in an AI world!
print("String Repetition: ", str1 * 2) # Hello, I live in an AI world!Hello, I live in an AI world!
print("Finding length of the string: ", len(str1)) # Output: 29, includes space between letters.
print("Making the string to all lower case: ", str1.lower()) # Output: hello, i live in an ai world!
print("Making the string to all upper case: ", str1.upper()) # Output: HELLO, I LIVE IN AN AI WORLD!
print("Making initial letter capitalized: ", str1.capitalize()) # Output: Hello, i live in an ai world!
print("Counting specific letter in a string 'n': ", str1.count('n')) # Output: 2
print("Find 'AI': ", str1.find('AI')) # Output: 20
print("Replace 'AI' with 'Artificial Intelligence': ", str1.replace('AI', 'Artificial Intelligence')) # Output: Hello, I live in an Artificial Intelligence world!
```

- **Boolean:** The bool data type in Python is used for storing either **True** or **False**. The following is an example of Boolean data type operations:

```
# Define two variables and assign boolean values to it
a = True
b = False
print(a) # True
print(b) # False
print(not a)# Output: False, which is opposite of 'a' value
```

```
print(not b) # Output: True, which is opposite of ‘ b’ value
print(a and a) # Output: True, which is True and True is True
print(a and b) # Output: False, which is True and False is False
print(b and b) # Output: False, which is False and False is False
print(a and not b) # Output: True, which is True and True (opposite of False) is True
print(b  and not a) # Output: False, which is False and False (opposite of False) is False
print(a or a) # Output: True, which is True or True is True
print(a or b) # Output: True, which is True or False is True
print(b or b) # Output: False, which is False or False is False
# We can use comparison operators to obtain boolean values
print(5 == 5) # Output:  True
print(5 <= 5) # Output: True
print(5 != 5) # Output: False
print(5 < 10) # Output: True
print(5 >= 10) # Output: False
print(5 > 10) # Output: False
```

In IoT Data Analytics, we need to perform various conversions and transformations. Let us go through one simple example of conversion using Python operators. The following Python program converts the temperature value given in **Celsius** to **Fahrenheit** using arithmetic operators:

```
# Celsius to Fahrenheit conversion
celsius = 105
fahrenheit = (celsius * 9/5) + 32 # Conversion formula to convert Celsius to Fahrenheit
print("Converted temperature in Fahrenheit: ", fahrenheit)
# Liters to gallons conversion
liters = 100
gallons = liters * 0.264172
print("Converted liters to gallons: ", gallons)
```

You will learn more about the data conversions in the upcoming sections and chapters.

Control structures: There are various control statements available in Python to control the execution of the program. Examples of control statements include **if**, **elif**, **else** statements, **for**, and **while** loops.

The following is an example of a conditional statement. In the following example, we use sensor data of humidity level and check for different levels to advise action:

```
# Define sensor data on humidity Level of the environment
humidityLevel = 30.0
# Check the humidity Level using conditional statements and prompt message accordingly
if humidityLevel > 70.0:
    print("Humidity level of the environment is too high, turn on your dehumidifier.")
elif humidityLevel < 40.0:
    print("Humidity level of the environment is too low, turn on your humidifier.")
else:
    print("Humidity of the environment is within normal level.")
```

In the preceding example, we used **`if`**, **`elif,`** and **`else`** statements. The execution of the print statement depends on the value of the **`humidityLevel`** variable. Try changing the value of the **`humidityLevel`** variable to 80, 50, and 20 respectively, and execute the program for each change to see how the conditional statements are executed based on **`if`**, **`elif`**, and **`else`** conditions.

The looping statement is to execute a specific part of the program repeatedly. The repetition can be in fixed numbers or can be based on certain conditions. The following is an example of the **`for`** loop statement:

```
number_of_data = 25 #No of times we need the Loop to run
sensor_data = 0 #Initial value of the data
increment_by = 2 #Increment by adding 2 to the initial value
for i in range(number_of_data):
    sensor_data += increment_by
    print("Generated sensor data:", sensor_data)
```

- **Nested Loops**: The following is an example of a nested loop where we generate sensor data for multiple sensors:

```
number_of_data = 25
sensor_data = 1
# Generate IoT simulation data for multiple sensors with
for id in range(number_of_data):
    for val in range(number_of_data):
```

```
        sensor_id = "sensor_" + str(id) # Assign sensor ID
        sensor_val = sensor_data + val #generate sensor value
        # Print the generated sensor id and values
        print(f"Sensor {sensor_id}: Sensor Value = {sensor_val} ")
```

- **While Loop for data simulation:** The following is an example of a **while** loop that can generate IoT sensor data:

```
# Simulating IoT data for a manufcaturing equipment using while loop
i = 0
while i <= 25:
    # Simulate machine floor humidity, machine temperature and valve pressure from IoT sensors
    floor_humidity = 50 + i * 2
    machine_temperature = 25 + i
    valve_pressure = 150 + i * 10
    #print the results
    print("Floor Humidity: {}%, Temperature: {}°C, Valve Pressure: {}kPa".format(floor_humidity, machine_temperature, valve_pressure))
    i += 1
```

- **Lists, tuples and dictionaries:** Lists are collections of data stored in order. A tuple is like a list except that it is immutable. The values in the tuple cannot be changed once it is created. Dictionaries are similar to list but stores the data in key-value pair.

  The following is an example of a list using IoT sensor data. It explains how to access an element of a list, adding, and removing an element from a list:

```
# Simple program to learn how to handle list using IoT sensor data
# Define some IoT sensor data as lists
machine_vibration = [0.1, 0.2, 0.3,0.4,0.5]
machine_pressure = [150, 155, 160, 165, 170]
# Print the data
print("Machine Vibration:", machine_vibration)
print("Machine Pressure:", machine_pressure)
# Accessing specific elements of a list using index value
print("Reading first element of Machine Vibration:", machine_vibra-
```

```
tion[0])
print("Reading first element of Machine Pressure:", machine_pressure[0])
# Modifying specific element of a list using index value
machine_vibration[0] = 0.150
machine_pressure[0] = 152.5
print("Modified Machine Vibration:", machine_vibration)
print("Modified Machine Pressure:", machine_pressure)
# Adding an element to a list using append function
machine_vibration.append(0.6)
machine_pressure.append(180)
print("New Machine Vibration:", machine_vibration)
print("New Machine Pressure:", machine_pressure)
# Removing an element from a list using pop function
machine_vibration.pop(0)
machine_pressure.pop(0)
print("After removing first element from Machine Vibration:", machine_vibration)
print("After removing first element from Machine Pressure:", machine_pressure)
```

Let us now go through how we can use the dictionary in Python. As mentioned in the preceding section, the dictionary is a collection of data in key-value pairs. Each key is associated with a value, and they are separated by commas for each pair. The entire dictionary is contained in a curly brace **{}**. The following is an example of how to handle a dictionary in Python:

```
# Generate a simple IoT sensor data
floor_humidity = 40
machine_temperature = 30.5
valve_pressure = 100.5
# Creating a dictionary to store the IoT sensor data
machine_data = {
    "floor_humidity": floor_humidity,
    "machine_temperature": machine_temperature,
    "valve_pressure": valve_pressure
```

```
}
# Print the contents of the dictionary
print(machine_data)
# Access a specific value from the dictionary
print("Machine Temperature:", machine_data["machine_temperature"])
# Add a new key-value pair to the dictionary
machine_data["vibration"] = 0.5
print(machine_data)
# Update a value in the dictionary
machine_data["machine_temperature"] = 25.5
print(machine_data)
# Delete a key-value pair from the dictionary using del command
del machine_data["valve_pressure"]
print(machine_data)
```

A tuple is a collection of data similar to a list. But usually, it is represented for fixed data as it is immutable. In Python, a tuple is created using parentheses `()` and each value in the tuple is separated by a comma. The following is an example of a tuple in Python:

```
# Define specific latitude and longitude values in a tuple
location_lat_long = (51.507351, -0.127758)
# Here is how we can access individual values in the tuple
latitude = location_lat_long[0]
longitude = location_lat_long[1]
print("Latitude:", latitude)
print("Longitude:", longitude)
# We can concatenate two tuples
location_lat_long2 = (51.879650, -0.417560)
location_lat_long3 = location_lat_long + location_lat_long2
print("Merged locations:", location_lat_long3)
# We can expand tuple using multiplications with an integer
multiplied_location = location_lat_long * 3
print("Multiplied location:", multiplied_location)
# We can Unpack a tuple into multiple separate variables
lat_val, lon_val = location_lat_long
```

```
print("Unpacked latitude value:", lat_val)
print("Unpacked longitude value:", lon_val)
# Finding the length of a tuple is easy with len function
print("Length of merged location is:", len(location_lat_long))
# Try to change a value in the tuple. Since it is immutable, this will throw error Attempting to change a value in the tuple will raise an error
location[0] = 42.3601
```

- **File handling:** Data handling is a crucial aspect of any data analysis project. Storing data in flat files for later analysis is a common requirement. Python provides an extensive list of libraries and functions for file operations, enabling it to handle different file types and effectively process vast amounts of data. In this part of the section, we will discuss some fundamental file operations in Python.

  We can use the built-in function **open()** for reading and writing files. The following example shows how to create a new file named **mydata.txt** and write data to it:

```
# Open the file to write data
with open('mydata.txt','w') as f:
    # Using write function to write some content
    f.write('sensor01, 01,02,03,04')
```

  In the preceding example, we create the file **mydata.txt** for writing using the **w** mode. This will write the content **sensor01, 01,02,03,04** on the file using the **write()** method.

  Now, we will see how to open the file to read the content:

```
# Open the file for reading the content
with open('mydata.txt', 'r') as f:
    # Use the read function to read the content of the file
    contents = f.read()
    # Print the content
    print(contents)
```

In the preceding example, we opened the file **mydata.txt** for reading. The **r** mode ensures that the file is opened only in read mode and closed automatically after the reading is complete. The **read()** method is used for reading the **content** and storing it in the variable called **contents**. Finally, the content is displayed on the screen using the **print** function.

We can update the file with new content or update the existing content. The following is an example for appending new content to the existing file:

```
1. # Appending the file with new line content using append mode
2. with open('mydata.txt', 'a') as f:
3.     # Use a function called write to add new line to the file
4.     f.write('\nsensor02,50,60,70,80')
```

In the preceding program, we used an append (**a**) mode to open the file for appending the content. The **write** function is used for writing the content **\n sensor02,50,60,70,80'** to the file in a new line.

Modules, Packages, Libraries, and Framework: To work with Python it is important to learn about the structure of Python programming language. The following figure shows a high-level view of how Python is structured:

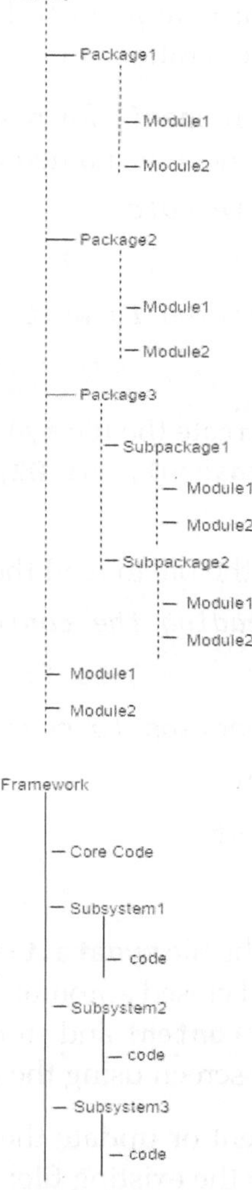

Figure 3.7: Python Structure

Using the preceding figure, we can understand how Python is structured. A library is usually at the top layer with multiple packages in it. Each of the packages may have multiple modules or sub-packages, which contain more modules or sub-packages. In some of the libraries, individual modules may exist directly under the library.

Unlike libraries, a Python framework is a collection of code that provides the necessary building blocks and structure for building applications. The core code contains the essential structure of the framework, but, on the other hand, the subsystems contain pre-written code for common tasks, such as handling new connections, requests, or tasks for building user interfaces.

Let us investigate each of the structures individually:

- **Modules:** A module is a basic and smallest unit of Python that is built for reusability. A module can contain variables, classes, and functions. The aim of building a module is to reuse the code for reducing development time and storage costs. It helps in maintaining code efficiently. Some of the widely used built-in modules in Python are math, random, and os.

  The following are examples of modules that are widely used:

  - Example of complex mathematical operation using the built-in math module:

    ```
    import math
    result = math.sin(0.85)
    print(f"The sin of 0.85 is: {result}")
    ```

  - Random number generation between a range of numbers using the built-in random module:

    ```
    import random
    result = random.randint(1, 100)
    print(f"A random number between 1 and 100 is: {result}")
    ```

  - Operating system-related operations can be performed using the **os** module:

    ```
    import os
    result = os.getcwd()
    print(f"The current working directory of your computer is: {result}")
    ```

  We can create user-defined modules similar to built-in modules. The following is an example of a user-defined module:

  - Create a new text file with the extension **.py**

    The following defines a function as shown in the file you have created in the preceding section:

    ```
    #add two numbers and return the sum.
    def add(num1, num2):
        return num1 + num2
    ```

    Save the **.py** file in your current working directory with the name **myutil.py**.

- o The module is created with a user-defined function to add two given numbers. Let us import the module to call it a function.

  The following is the program to call the module and invoke the function from the module:

```
#Importing user defined module and calling the function.
import myutil
print(myutil.add(10,20)); # this will call the user-defined function in the module myutil and print the result in the screen.
```

- o The function we created within the **myutil** module is called a user-defined function. User-defined functions can be created to simplify complexity and increase reusability, unlike built-in functions that are typically part of packages or modules we import. The user-defined functions can be created in a separate module or within the same program as the following:

```
def calculate_average_temperature(sensor_data):
    """
    This user-defined function returns the average temperature from a given list of sensor data.
    """
    total = 0
    count = 0
    for temperature in sensor_data:
        total += temperature # add temperature to the total
        count += 1
    return total / count # return the average temperature to the calling program
#call the user-defined function to get average temperature
temperature_list = [20.5, 30.0, 25.0, 21.0, 25.0, 28.0, 30.5]
average_temp = calculate_average_temperature(temperature_list) #calling the user-defined function
print(f"Average temperature: {average_temp:.1f}°C")
```

- **Packages:** Packages are created by organizing related modules in a directory structure. The purpose of a Package is to group related functionality and provide an efficient method to reuse code across different programs. Some of the widely used packages are **NumPy**, and **Pandas**.
- **Libraries:** The packages and modules are grouped together as a library to serve related functionalities to the invoking programs. Libraries can be built for solving specific problem or serve domain specific purposes, such as data processing, data analysis,

web development, or scientific computing. Most widely used libraries are **Scikit-learn, Matplotlib, TensorFlow,** and **BeautifulSoup**

- **Frameworks:** Building an application in Python is easier and faster with frameworks. The framework in Python is a collection of code that provides all required structure for building applications. Frameworks are pre-written code for performing common tasks, such as handling building web applications, user interfaces, and handling requests. The frameworks provide necessary building blocks for organizing and building applications. Most widely used frameworks are Flask, FastAPI, Django, CherryPy.

In summary, Python is structured as libraries, packages, and frameworks to make it a flexible and easy-to-use language. While many of these terms are used interchangeably, each one has a different purpose and contexts.

Data Analysis using Python

In this section, you will learn the basics of data analysis using Python. A more detailed approach will be covered in the upcoming chapters. There are many packages and libraries which are available in Python to perform data analysis. Some of the key libraries for data analysis in Python are: NumPy, Pandas, Matplotlib, Seaborn, SciPy and Scikit-learn.

It is essential that you become familiar with some of these key libraries, as we will use them frequently for various data analysis tasks.

Introduction to NumPy: `NumPy` is a powerful Python library that is extensively used for numerical computing and data analysis. With its wide range of functions, NumPy enables users to perform complex array and mathematical operations, including mean, median, standard deviation, variance, and more. Additionally, it supports linear algebra operations such as matrix operations, solving linear equations, and computing eigenvalues and eigenvectors. Moreover, `NumPy` offers numerous statistical functions for tasks like finding data distribution, patterns, percentiles, and hypothesis testing. In this section, we will explore some examples of `NumPy` and its application for IoT Data Analytics.

The following code generates random sensor data with `NumPy`:

```
#Using numpy to generate 1000 random numbers with values 0 and 1
import numpy as np
rand_sensor_data = np.random.rand(1000)
print(rand_sensor_data[:10]) #print the first 10 numbers from the generated list
#perform some basic statistical analysis on the random data
mean = np.mean(rand_sensor_data)
std_dev = np.std(rand_sensor_data)
variance = np.var(rand_sensor_data)
```

```
print("type is: ", type(rand_sensor_data))
# Print the result of statistical analsysis
print("Statistical Mean of the random sensor data:", mean)
print("Standard deviation of the random sensor data:", std_dev)
print("Variance in the random sensor data:", variance)
```

The preceding program generates 1000 random sensor data between 0 and 1 using **NumPy**'s random module, and then prints the first 10 readings. Then it uses **NumPy**'s mean, std, and var functions to compute the mean, standard deviation, and variance of the data respectively.

We can use various data filtering techniques. The following is an example of filtering randomly generated sensor data with **NumPy**:

```
import numpy as np
rand_sensor_data = np.random.rand(1000)
# Filtering the generated sensor data which has readings above 0.5
filtered_sensor_data = rand_sensor_data[rand_sensor_data <= 0.5]
# Let us look at the length of the filtered data along with the originally generated sensor
print("Sensor data before applying any filtering:", len(rand_sensor_data))
print("Sensor data after applying filtering:", len(filtered_sensor_data))
```

We can use **NumPy** to implement a simple predictive maintenance use case. The following example shows certain vibration threshold is set for machine failure, once the vibration crosses the threshold, we print the machine failure prompt:

```
import numpy as np
# Define a sample sensor data array with vibration and temperature readings
sensor_data = np.array([[10, 23], [11, 24], [12, 26], [13, 25], [14, 28]])
# Define a failure threshold for the vibration readings
vibration_threshold = 12
# Create a new array indicating whether each reading is normal or indicates a failure
failures = np.where(sensor_data[:,0] > vibration_threshold, 1, 0)
# Print a message for potential failure of machine
print('Machine may breakdown as the vibration level crossed the threshold:', failures)
```

In the preceding sections, we went through some basic concepts of Python programming. Now, let us go through some advanced analytical concepts Before we proceed further, let us create a dataset using data simulation techniques covered so far. We will be using the same data set for performing further analysis. So, it is important that you execute the following program with a complete understanding of the concept explained:

```
import numpy as np
import datetime #This package has all datetime processing functions
import pandas as pd
# Set the random seed for reproducibility
np.random.seed(42)
# Define the number of data points to generate
num_rows = 1440 # This will generate 2000 rows of data
# Define the start and end dates for the data generation. This is required for time series analysis.
start_date = datetime.datetime(2023, 1, 1) #
end_date = datetime.datetime(2023, 1, 2)
# We simulate an IIOT equipment, wind turbine, for our simulation. Define the turbine parameters and their normal ranges
temperature_mean = 80
temperature_stddev = 10
pressure_mean = 300
pressure_stddev = 50
wind_speed_mean = 10
wind_speed_stddev = 5
rpm_mean = 1500
rpm_stddev = 250
energy_output_mean = 50
energy_output_stddev = 10
# Generate the data
timestamps = np.arange(start_date, end_date, dtype='datetime64[m]')
temperature = np.random.normal(temperature_mean, temperature_stddev, num_rows)
pressure = np.random.normal(pressure_mean, pressure_stddev, num_rows)
wind_speed = np.random.normal(wind_speed_mean, wind_speed_stddev, num_rows)
```

```
rpm = np.random.normal(rpm_mean, rpm_stddev, num_rows)
energy_output = np.random.normal(energy_output_mean, energy_output_stddev, num_rows)
# Combine the data into a single array
#data = np.column_stack((timestamps, temperature, pressure, wind_speed, rpm, energy_output))
# Save the data to a CSV file
data = pd.DataFrame({'timestamps': timestamps, 'temperature': temperature, 'pressure': pressure, 'wind_speed': wind_speed, 'rpm': rpm, 'energy_output': energy_output})
# Save the data to a CSV file using pandas and function 'to_csv'
data.to_csv('wind_turbine.csv', index=False)
```

The wind turbine is an equipment which produces electricity from the wind. The kinetic energy of the wind converts into mechanical energy, then into electrical energy. The rotor blades (fan-like blades) capture the wind energy to operate the generator for converting mechanical energy into electrical energy and the same is stored in a battery.

The amount of electricity generated from wind turbine equipment depends on various factors such as the size of the blades, wind speed, and location of the wind turbine. So, it is important that we capture various parameters of the wind turbine to perform analysis on forecasting the energy, improving its utilization, and operating efficiently during the windy season to produce maximum output with minimum failures and breakdowns. The data simulation with the parameters such as wind speed, rpm, temperature, pressure, and energy output is important for us to perform the required data analysis. We will use simulated data in the next part of the section to demonstrate various data analysis methods using Python.

The following is another example of a Python program that simulates IoT data for a wind turbine. But this time we will include outliers, scaling issues, duplicate values, empty values, and missing values intentionally to try out various data cleaning and transformation methods later part of the section:

```
import numpy as np
import datetime #This package has all datetime processing functions
import pandas as pd
from scipy import stats
# Set the random seed for reproducibility
np.random.seed(42)
# Define the number of data points to generate
num_rows = 1440 # This will generate 1440 rows of data
```

```
# Define the start and end dates for the data generation. This is required for time series analysis.
start_date = datetime.datetime(2023, 1, 1) #
end_date = datetime.datetime(2023, 1, 2)
# We simulate an IIOT equipment, wind turbine, for our simulation. Define the turbine parameters and their normal ranges
temperature_mean = 80
temperature_stddev = 10
pressure_mean = 30000
pressure_stddev = 5000
wind_speed_mean = 10
wind_speed_stddev = 5
rpm_mean = 1500
rpm_stddev = 250
energy_output_mean = 50
energy_output_stddev = 10

# Generate the data
timestamps = np.arange(start_date, end_date, dtype='datetime64[m]')
temperature = np.random.normal(temperature_mean, temperature_stddev, num_rows)
pressure = np.random.normal(pressure_mean, pressure_stddev, num_rows)/ 100 # Scale pressure by a factor of 100
wind_speed = np.random.normal(wind_speed_mean, wind_speed_stddev, num_rows)
rpm = np.random.normal(rpm_mean, rpm_stddev, num_rows)
# Create a linear relationship between wind speed and energy output with a coefficient of 0.3
energy_output = energy_output_mean + 0.3 * (wind_speed -
wind_speed_mean) + np.random.normal(0, energy_output_stddev, num_rows)
# Introduce missing values by randomly setting 10% of the energy output values to NaN
energy_output_mask = np.random.rand(num_rows) < 0.1
energy_output[energy_output_mask] = np.nan
```

```
# Introduce outliers by randomly setting 20% of the rpm values to be greater than 3 standard deviations from the mean
rpm_outliers = np.random.rand(num_rows) < 0.2
rpm[rpm_outliers] = np.random.normal(loc=3, scale=1,
size=rpm_outliers.sum()) * rpm_stddev + rpm_mean
# Create duplicate rows by randomly selecting 10% of the data points and replicating them
duplicates = np.random.choice(num_rows, int(num_rows * 0.1), replace=False)
timestamps = np.concatenate([timestamps, timestamps[duplicates]])
temperature = np.concatenate([temperature, temperature[duplicates]])
pressure = np.concatenate([pressure, pressure[duplicates]])
wind_speed = np.concatenate([wind_speed, wind_speed[duplicates]])
rpm = np.concatenate([rpm, rpm[duplicates]])
energy_output = np.concatenate([energy_output, energy_output[duplicates]])
# Combine the data into a single array
data_wind_turbine = pd.DataFrame({'timestamps': timestamps,
'temperature': temperature, 'pressure': pressure, 'wind_speed':
wind_speed, 'rpm': rpm, 'energy_output': energy_output})
# Save the data to a file
data_wind_turbine.to_csv('wind_turbine_with_issues.csv', index=False)
```

The program above is designed to simulate wind turbine data, similar to the previous example. However, it is important to note that wind turbines installed in any location may face a range of challenges. These challenges include issues such as loss of signal while transmitting data to the cloud or blade and motor failure, which can lead to malfunctions or reduced energy production. Hence, we need to perform necessary data cleaning, transformation, scaling, imputation, and outlier corrections to make the dataset ready for proper analysis. We will be learning all these techniques using the preceding dataset in the upcoming part of the section.

Data manipulation with Pandas: It is the most widely used powerful Python library for working with data. This topic covers the basics of Pandas, including loading data, cleaning, and transforming data, and performing basic statistical analysis.

Reading in the data: It is the simplest way to read in the **`wind_turbine.csv`** file is to use the **`read_csv`** function from Pandas. This will automatically parse the timestamp column as a **`DateTime`** object. Here is how to do it:

```
1. import pandas as pd
2. turbine_data = pd.read_csv('wind_turbine.csv', parse_
   dates=["timestamps"])
3. print(turbine_data)
```

Selecting a single column: To select a single column from the **wind_turbine DataFrame**, you can use the square bracket notation with the column name as the index. The following is how to select the **wind_speed** column:

```
1. import pandas as pd
2. turbine_data = pd.read_csv('wind_turbine.csv', parse_
   dates=["timestamps"])
3. wind_speed = turbine_data["wind_speed"]
4. print(wind_speed)
```

Filtering the data: To filter the **wind_turbine DataFrame** based on a condition, you can use the square bracket notation with a boolean condition as the index. The following code is how to filter the data to include rows where the wind speed is greater than **15**:

```
1. import pandas as pd
2. turbine_data = pd.read_csv('wind_turbine.csv', parse_
   dates=["timestamps"])
3. high_wind_speed = turbine_data[turbine_data["wind_speed"] > 15]
4. print(high_wind_speed)
```

Aggregating the data: To calculate summary statistics for groups of rows in the **wind_turbine** DataFrame, you can use the **groupby** method. The following code is how to calculate the average **wind speed** and **energy output** for each **hour** of the day:

```
1. import pandas as pd
2. turbine_data = pd.read_csv('wind_turbine.csv', parse_
   dates=["timestamps"])
3. hourly_data = turbine_data.groupby(turbine_data["timestamps"].dt.hour).
   mean()
4. print(hourly_data[["wind_speed", "energy_output"]])
```

Merging two DataFrames: If you have data in two separate **DataFrames** that you want to combine based on a common column, you can use the merge method. The following code is how to create a new DataFrame that combines the **wind_turbine** with a separate **wind_turbine_data_issues** based on the **timestamps** column:

```
1. import pandas as pd
2. turbine_data = pd.read_csv('wind_turbine.csv', parse_
   dates=["timestamps"])
```

```
turbine_data_with_issues = pd.read_csv('wind_turbine_with_issues.csv', parse_dates=["timestamps"])
combined_data = pd.merge(turbine_data, turbine_data_with_issues, on="timestamps")
print(combined_data)
```

The following is an example of a program that reads in the **wind_turbine.csv** file generated from the previous example and performs some basic data analysis using the Pandas library:

```
import pandas as pd
# Read in the turbine data from the CSV file
turbine_data = pd.read_csv('wind_turbine.csv', parse_dates=["timestamps"])
# Print some basic statistics about the data
print("Basic statistics about the data:")
print(turbine_data.describe())
# Calculate the average energy output for each hour of the day
turbine_data["hour"] = turbine_data["timestamps"].dt.hour
hourly_energy_output = turbine_data.groupby("hour")["energy_output"].mean()
# Print the hourly energy output values
print("\nHourly energy output:")
print(hourly_energy_output)
# Calculate the correlation between wind speed and energy output
correlation = turbine_data["wind_speed"].corr(turbine_data["energy_output"])
# Print the correlation value
print("\nCorrelation between wind speed and energy output:")
print(correlation)
```

The preceding code shows how to perform basic statistical analysis. The describe function shows basic statistics about the data. The code demonstrates how to create a new derived feature. We created a new column called **hour** using **timesstamps** column with hourly data extracted using **dt.hour** attribute. The code demonstrates how to use **groupby** function to calculate **energy_output** by each hour of the day. Finally, we calculated the correlation between **wind_speed** and **energy_output**.

So far, we have learned about some of the basic concepts of data analysis using NumPy and Pandas packages. We will now learn how to perform time series analysis. The time series analysis is an important method for IoT Data Analytics as the IoT data generated by the sensors will be in the form of time series.

Time Series Analysis with Pandas: This topic covers the basics of time-series analysis with Pandas, including working with time-indexed data, resampling data, and performing basic time-series analysis.

Here we demonstrate a few simple time series analyses using Numpy and Pandas libraries, without any visualization libraries. The visualization and more detailed time series analysis are reserved in the later part of the book.

The following is a program to calculate summary statistics:

```
import pandas as pd
import numpy as np
# Load data into a pandas DataFrame
df = pd.read_csv('wind_turbine.csv', parse_dates=['timestamps'], index_col='timestamps')
# Calculate summary statistics
print("Minimum power:", np.min(df['energy_output']))
print("Maximum power:", np.max(df['energy_output']))
print("Mean power:", np.mean(df['energy_output']))
print("Standard deviation of power:", np.std(df['energy_output']))
print("Correlation between wind speed and energy:", np.corrcoef(df['wind_speed'], df['energy_output'])[0, 1])
```

In the preceding program, we used **min, max, mean, std,** and **corrcoef** functions of Numpy to calculate basic statistics like **Minimum, max,** and **mean** value of **energy_output**. Then we calculated the standard deviation in **energy_ouput** and finally, we look at the correlation coefficient between **wind_speed** and **energy_ouput**. The correlation coefficient will help us understand the relationship between **wind_speed** and **energy_ouput** to see whether the increase in **wind_speed** produces more energy output or less or they are not having any influence at all.

The following is an example of how to calculate the moving average:

```
import pandas as pd
import numpy as np
# Load data into a pandas DataFrame
df = pd.read_csv('wind_turbine.csv', parse_dates=['timestamps'], index_col='timestamps')
# Calculate the moving average with a window size of 7 days
moving_avg = df['energy_output'].rolling(window='7D').mean()
# Print the moving average for the first 10 rows
print(moving_avg.head(10))
```

The preceding program calculates how **energy_ouput** value is moving in a time window of **7** days using rolling method. This will help us understand average energy produced by the wind turbine in last **7 days window** and how it is progressing. This will help us to see the performance of the wind turbine for forecasting energy output from a particular wind turbine.

The following is an example to calculate exponential moving average:

```
1. import pandas as pd
2. import numpy as np
3. # Load data into a pandas DataFrame
4. df = pd.read_csv('wind_turbine.csv', parse_dates=['timestamps'], index_
   col='timestamps')
5. # Calculate the exponential moving average with a span of 7 days
6. exp_moving_avg = df['energy_output'].ewm(span=7).mean()
7. # Print the exponential moving average for the first 10 rows
8. print(exp_moving_avg.head(10))
```

The preceding program calculates the exponential moving average using the **ewm** method. It is similar to the moving average method used in the previous example, except that it uses exponential method to make the average calculation more sensitive to recent changes in data. This will be more useful for short-term analysis and forecasting.

The following is an example on how to calculate autocorrelation with lag of 1 day:

```
1. import pandas as pd
2. import numpy as np
3. # Load data into a pandas DataFrame
4. df = pd.read_csv('wind_turbine.csv', parse_dates=['timestamps'], index_
   col='timestamps')
5. # Calculate autocorrelation with a lag of 1 day
6. autocorr = np.corrcoef(df['energy_output'][1:], df['energy_output'][:-
   1])[0, 1]
7. # Print the autocorrelation
8. print("Autocorrelation (lag=1):", autocorr)
```

The preceding example calculates the correlation of **energy_ouput** with a lag of **1** day using Numpy function **corrcoef**. The idea is to measure the **autocorrelation** of **energy_output** with its past values. It is useful for finding patterns or trends in time series data. A high **autocorrelation** value indicates that past values are highly correlated with current values while a low value indicates a little correlation between past and current values. The energy output from the turbine is based on several factors such as wind speed, wind direction, motor operation, and so on. The trend analysis will be helpful in identifying seasonal changes in wind speed or performance of the wind turbine in comparison to past hours or days.

Data Wrangling with Python

Data Wrangling also referred to as data munging, is the process of preparing, transforming, and cleaning data to analyze it effectively. This step is typically the first one in the data analysis process and involves several key activities.

One of the most significant issues in handling datasets is dealing with missing values. There are a variety of reasons why datasets may contain missing values. In IoT Data Analytics, missing values are an inevitable problem that must be addressed. This is since IoT sensors may stop working for short periods of time due to signal loss or device malfunction, resulting in missing data for those periods. As a result, it is critical to know how to handle missing values.

There are several techniques for handling missing values, including mean or median imputation, mode imputation, similar value imputation, K-Nearest Neighbor imputation, and regression imputation.

The following is an example of mean imputation:

```
import pandas as pd
import numpy as np
# Load the wind turbine data into a pandas dataframe
df_wind_turbine = pd.read_csv('wind_turbine_with_issues.csv')
print(df_wind_turbine.isnull().sum())
# Replace using mean
mean = df_wind_turbine['energy_output'].mean()
df_wind_turbine['energy_output'].fillna(mean, inplace=True)
print(df_wind_turbine.isnull().sum())
```

This program uses the **Pandas** library to **Load the wind turbine data**. We simulated with some missing value for the energy output column, into a **dataframe**. It imputes the missing values in the **energy_output** column using the mean value of the column.

Handling scaling issues: Scaling issues in data analysis refer to situations where the range of values of different variables in a dataset is significantly different. These differences in scale can cause problems in data analysis, such as the misinterpretation of correlation or regression coefficients, or the biasing of machine learning algorithms towards variables with larger scales. There are many reasons for the scaling issues such as:

- Variables measured in different units (for example: meters, kilograms, and dollars) can have vastly different ranges of values, making direct comparisons difficult.
- Variables measured on different measurement scales (for example: ordinal, interval, and ratio) can have different ranges of values, which can affect data analysis.
- Outliers in a dataset can cause scaling issues, as they can have a disproportionate effect on summary statistics such as mean and standard deviation.

To handle scaling issues, we have several techniques such as:

- **Standardization**: It involves scaling each variable to have a mean of zero and a standard deviation of one. This makes the variables comparable in terms of their range of values.
- **Normalization**: It involves scaling each variable to a range between 0 and 1. This is useful when the absolute values of the variables are not as important as their relative values.
- **Logarithmic transformation**: It can be used to scale variables that have a highly skewed distribution. This can make the distribution more symmetric and reduce the influence of outliers.
- **Rescaling**: Rescaling involves transforming variables to a different scale or unit of measurement. This can make the variables comparable and easier to interpret.
- **Using robust statistical methods**: Robust statistical methods are less sensitive to outliers and can provide more accurate results when scaling issues are present.

The following is an example of handling scaling issues using normalization scaling technique which is widely used technique for handling scaling issues:

```
import pandas as pd
import numpy as np
from sklearn.preprocessing import MinMaxScaler
# Load the wind turbine data into a pandas dataframe
df_wind_turbine = pd.read_csv('wind_turbine_with_issues.csv')
# Normalize data using MinMaxScaler
scaler = MinMaxScaler()
timestamps = df_wind_turbine['timestamps']
df_wind_turbine = df_wind_turbine.drop('timestamps', axis = 1)
df_wind_turbine_normalized = pd.DataFrame(scaler.fit_transform(df_wind_turbine), columns=df_wind_turbine.columns)
df_wind_turbine_normalized.insert(0,'timestamps',timestamps)
print(df_wind_turbine_normalized.describe())
df_wind_turbine_normalized.head() # Save the scaled data to a CSV file
df_wind_turbine_normalized.to_csv('wind_turbine_scaled.csv', index=False)
```

The preceding code loads wind turbine data from a CSV file called **`wind_turbine_with_issues.csv`** into a pandas DataFrame called **`df_wind_turbine`**. It then normalizes the data using the **`MinMaxScaler()`** function from scikit-learn.

The timestamps column is extracted from the **`DataFrame`** and saved to a separate variable called timestamps. The **`drop()`** function is then used to remove the timestamps column from **`df_wind_turbine`**.

The **fit_transform()** method of the scaler object is used to normalize the remaining columns of the **df_wind_turbine DataFrame**. The resulting normalized data is saved to a new DataFrame called **df_wind_turbine_normalized**, which has the same columns as the original DataFrame.

The **timestamps** column is then added back into the normalized **DataFrame** using the **insert()** function. The **describe()** function is called to generate summary statistics for the normalized **DataFrame**, and **head()** function is called to display the first five rows of the **DataFrame**.

Finally, the normalized data is saved to a new CSV file called **wind_turbine_scaled.csv** using the **to_csv()** function, with the index parameter set to False to prevent it from being saved to the file.

Handling outliers: Outliers are data points that deviate significantly from the other data points in a dataset. These data points can be unusually high or low in value, or distant from the other data points in some other way. Outliers can occur due to errors in data collection from IoT sensors, measurement, or entry, or they may represent genuine but rare observations. It is important to handle outliers in a dataset because they can have a significant impact on data analysis results, especially if they are not genuine but instead arise from data entry errors or other mistakes. Outliers can have a disproportionate impact on summary statistics such as mean and standard deviation, leading to inaccurate or biased results. Outliers can distort correlation and regression coefficients, leading to inaccurate or misleading relationships between variables. The following are examples of handling outliers:

- **Removing outliers**: Outliers can be removed from the dataset, but this should be done with care to ensure that genuine data points are not removed.
- **Transforming data**: Transforming the data using techniques such as log transformation or trimming can reduce the impact of outliers on summary statistics and machine learning algorithms.
- **Using robust statistical methods**: Robust statistical methods are less sensitive to outliers and can provide more accurate results in the presence of outliers.

The following is an example of a Python program on how to identify and remove outliers:

```
# Box Plot
import seaborn as sns
import pandas as pd
import numpy as np
# Load the wind turbine data into a pandas dataframe
df_wind_turbine = pd.read_csv('wind_turbine_with_issues.csv')
sns.boxplot(df_wind_turbine['rpm'])
```

The preceding program helps us in identifying outliers using a **boxplot** that shows any unusually lower or upper values for the column **rpm**. We could observe that there is some upper value which may cause issues with our data analysis. So, we need to remove them:

```
from scipy import stats
import numpy as np
import pandas as pd
# Load the wind turbine data into a pandas dataframe
df_wind_turbine = pd.read_csv('wind_turbine_with_issues.csv')
z = np.abs(stats.zscore(df_wind_turbine['rpm']))
print(z)
print(np.where(z > 3))
df_wind_turbine = df_wind_turbine[z<3]
z = np.abs(stats.zscore(df_wind_turbine['rpm']))
print(z)
print(np.where(z > 3))
```

This program again loads the wind turbine data into a Pandas **dataframe**. It then calculates the **z-score** for each data point in the **rpm** column and removes any data points with a **z-score** greater than **3** (indicating an outlier). The data with outliers are removed.

Handling duplicate values: Duplicate values in the dataset is one of the major issues we face in data analysis, especially in IoT Data Analytics where due to sensor device malfunction. The duplicate data in the dataset impacts the data analysis significantly with skewness in the data, and inflated sample zine, leading to overfitting. So, it is important to handle duplicate values in the dataset.

The following is a Python code for removing duplicate records from the dataset:

```
import pandas as pd
import numpy as np
# Load the wind turbine data into a pandas dataframe
df_wind_turbine = pd.read_csv('wind_turbine_with_issues.csv')
print(df_wind_turbine.duplicated().sum())
df_wind_turbine = df_wind_turbine.drop_duplicates()
print(df_wind_turbine.duplicated().sum())
```

The preceding program identifies the presence of duplicate records in the dataset and uses **drop_duplicates** function to remove them.

Data aggregation: Aggregating data is necessary for performing time series analysis because it can help to smooth out fluctuations in the data and make it easier to identify trends and patterns over time. IoT data which are time series by nature are typically collected at regular intervals, such as for every second, minute, hourly, daily, weekly, or monthly, and can contain a large amount of noise and variability. Aggregating the data by taking averages or sums over longer time periods can help to reduce the impact of this noise and reveal underlying patterns in the data.

The following is a Python program on how to aggregate data hourly:

```
import pandas as pd
# Read in the turbine data CSV file
df_wind_turbine = pd.read_csv('wind_turbine_with_issues.csv')
# Add a new column to the data indicating the hour of the day
df_wind_turbine['hour'] = pd.to_datetime(df_wind_turbine['timestamps']).dt.hour
# Aggregate the data by hour, taking the mean of each column for each hour
hourly_data = df_wind_turbine.groupby('hour').mean()
# Save the aggregated data to a new CSV file
hourly_data.to_csv('turbine_data_hourly.csv')
```

The preceding program aggregates the data hourly using the mean method to smoothen the data from noise.

Data Visualization using Python

Data visualization is a crucial and effective technique in data analysis that can help identify patterns and communicate insights. It presents data in a manner that is easier to comprehend than other formats, such as tables and rows, and enables decision-makers to understand complex information through simple visual representations. By using charts, graphs, and other visual presentation methods, we can effectively communicate trends, patterns, relationships, and dependencies that may not be immediately obvious from other forms of data representations. Visualization can help in our data analysis tasks by identifying skewness, outliers, anomalies, relationships, and other features of the data that may require further investigation.

Matplotlib is a popular Python library for creating visualizations. This topic covers the basics of Matplotlib, including creating basic plots, customizing plot properties, and saving and exporting plots.

The following is a Python program example of a scattered plot showing how wind speed may increase energy output from the **wind turbine**:

```
import pandas as pd
import numpy as np
import matplotlib.pyplot as plt
# Load the wind turbine data into a pandas DataFrame
df_wind_turbine = pd.read_csv('wind_turbine_with_issues.csv',
parse_dates=['timestamps'])
plt.scatter(df_wind_turbine['wind_speed'], df_wind_turbine['energy_output'])
plt.xlabel('Wind Speed')
plt.ylabel('Energy Output')
```

```
plt.title('Wind Speed vs Energy Output Scatter Plot')
plt.show()
```

The following is another example of the same scattered plot, this time, create the regression plot, which shows the linear relationship between wind speed and energy output:

```
import pandas as pd
import numpy as np
import matplotlib.pyplot as plt
# Load the wind turbine data into a pandas DataFrame
df_wind_turbine = pd.read_csv('wind_turbine_with_issues.csv',
parse_dates=['timestamps'])
sns.regplot(x='wind_speed', y='energy_output', data=df_wind_turbine)
plt.xlabel('Wind Speed')
plt.ylabel('Energy Output')
plt.title('Wind Speed vs Energy Output with Regression Line')
plt.show()
```

Visualization with Seaborn: Seaborn is a Python library to provide a rich visualization experience built on top of Matplotlib.

The following is a Python example of seaborn. This program plots how energy output increases over the increase of wind speed. We use the mean value of the wind speed and range of value to calculate the average energy output:

```
import pandas as pd
import numpy as np
import matplotlib.pyplot as plt
import seaborn as sns
import plotly.express as px
df_wind_turbine = pd.read_csv('wind_turbine_with_issues.csv', parse_dates=['timestamps'])
bins = [0, 5, 10, 15, 20, 25]
labels = [‘0-5’, ‘5-10’, ‘10-15’, ‘15-20’, ‘20-25’]
df_wind_turbine['wind_speed_range'] = pd.cut(df_wind_turbine['wind_speed'], bins=bins, labels=labels,
include_lowest=True)
grouped = df_wind_turbine.groupby('wind_speed_range').mean().reset_index()
plt.bar(grouped['wind_speed_range'], grouped['energy_output'])
```

```
plt.xlabel('Wind Speed Range (m/s)')
plt.ylabel('Mean Energy Output (kW)')
plt.title('Mean Energy Output by Wind Speed Range')
plt.show()
```

Dashboarding with Plotly: Plotly is one of the most useful Python library for creating interactive dashboards. The following is a Python program example that uses Plotly library to create a scatter plot matrix that displays the relationships between the different variables in the wind turbine data, with each variable along both the X and Y axes. The diagonal shows the distribution of each variable, while the off-diagonal cells show the scatter plots of the variable pairs:

```
import pandas as pd
import plotly.express as px
df_wind_turbine = pd.read_csv('wind_turbine_with_issues.csv',
parse_dates=['timestamps'])
fig = px.scatter_matrix(df_wind_turbine, dimensions=['wind_speed', 'rpm', 'temperature', 'pressure',  'energy_output'])
fig.update_layout(title='Wind Turbine Scatter Plot')
fig.show()
```

Conclusion

Python is an excellent language for data analysis and has several advantages over other programming languages. We have discussed the process of installing and configuring Python, Apache Kafka, MQTT, and PostgresSQL, along with important Python packages used for data analysis. We have also covered the basics of Python language with examples, including data analysis and data wrangling techniques. In addition, we have learned to install Python using the pip package manager.

We have also learned how basics of how to simulate Industrial IoT equipment data using Python with an example of a wind turbine.

In the final part of the chapter, we learned data visualization techniques using Matplotlib, Seaborn, and Plotly libraries.

In the next chapter, we will learn about the different data formats of IoT and how to handle them using Python. We will also learn about real-time data steaming, data pipeline, and how to set up a simple data pipeline using data simulation techniques and push the data to MQTT broker. This will mimic the real-time scenario of receiving a wind turbine.

We will also build a data cleansing and transformation engine which will perform data cleaning and transformation tasks for the data pipeline.

Points to Remember

The following are the key takeaways from this lesson:

- Python has several libraries and packages which can be used for performing IoT Data Analytics. Commonly used packages for performing IoT Data Analytics are NumPy, Pandas, paho-mqtt, PyKafka, psycopg2, Matplotlib, Seaborn, Faker, Scikit-learn, TensorFlow, Prophet, SciPy, PuLP, and Pyomo. These packages can be installed using the pip or conda commands, or through the Anaconda interface. It is recommended to create separate virtual environments for each project to avoid version issues and package conflicts.
- There are various data types available in Python to store variables. The main data types in Python are integer, float, string, list, tuple, and boolean. Python dynamically determines the variable type based on the value assigned to it. It is essential to maintain consistency in handling variables to avoid errors in code execution.
- Python provides various operations like mathematical operations, string manipulation, indexing, slicing, and many more for each data type.
- Python is structured with libraries at the top layer, which contains packages, modules, and sub-packages.
- A Python framework provides a structure and building blocks for developing applications. The frameworks have a core code and subsystems, which include pre-written code for common tasks.
- Data simulation of Industrial IoT equipment can be done using Numpy and Pandas packages. In many real-time situations, data simulation is required for developing a data analysis approach.
- NumPy and Pandas are popular Python libraries for performing various data analysis tasks. NumPy offers functions for performing array operations, mathematical operations, and basic statistical analysis such as random, rand, min, max, mean, std, sum, and where. Meanwhile, Pandas provides a wide range of functions for data processing, transformation, cleaning, exploration, and basic statistical analysis, including read_csv, merge, groupby, head, tail, describe, info, fillna, dropna, duplicated, drop_duplicate, mean, median, min, max, std, and corr.
- Matplotlib is a widely used Python library for data visualization, offering various types of plots such as bar, scatter, histogram, heatmap, and box plot. Seaborn built on top of Matplotlib, provides a richer graphical interface with additional visualization types, including regression, relational, and distribution plots. Plotly is a Python library built on top of JavaScript, providing a platform for creating interactive visualizations and dashboards with extensive customization options, making it easy to share high-quality interactive visualizations with others.

CHAPTER 4
Managing Data Pipeline and Cleaning

Introduction

The data generated from IoT sensors will have different formats depending on the IoT devices, gateway, and **Original Equipment Manufacturer (OEM)**.

To effectively leverage this data for meaningful insights and analytics, it is important to understand the different types of data formats encountered in IoT applications and how to handle them. We will learn about data formats like JSON, XML, MessagePack, CSV, Protobuf, Avro, FastAvro, and CBOR data formats in the first section of this chapter. We will also cover Python examples of handling these data formats for simple and complex data types.

In the subsequent section, we will learn about synchronous data streaming, viz-a-vis, realtime data streaming and asynchronous data streaming called data pipeline. Real-time data streaming and data pipeline are two standard methods used in IoT Analytics for processing and analyzing the vast amounts of data generated by IoT devices. Understanding how these methods work and when to use them is crucial for building effective IoT Analytics solutions.

In addition to understanding data formats and processing methods, it is important to understand the overall IoT data flow. This includes dataflow through the network and to the cloud or other storage and processing locations. We will learn about the standard dataflow for any IoT Analytics application in the next section, IoT Dataflow.

Data simulation and digital twin are related concepts that can help organizations improve their IoT Analytics capabilities. Data simulation involves creating a system model or process to simulate how it will behave under different conditions. In contrast, a digital twin creates a digital replica of a physical system to monitor and analyze its performance in real time. There are multiple IoT simulators available in the market which can help simulating various part of the IoT application. We will cover a simple implementation of data simulator using Python, which can help performing IoT Data Analytics. We will be learning about data simulation, IoT Simulators and digital twins in this chapter.

In the final part of the chapter, we will learn about data cleansing and data transformation, which are crucial steps in the **Extract, Transform, Load** (**ETL**) process or data pre-processing, which involve identifying and correcting inaccuracies or errors in the data, and transforming it into a more useful format for downstream analysis.

Structure

In this chapter, we will cover the following topics:

- IoT Data Formats
- Realtime Data Streaming and Data Pipeline
- IoT Dataflow
- Data Simulation and Digital Twin
- IoT Simulator Tools
- IoT Data Simulator Python Implementation
- Data Cleansing Implementation in Python
- Data Transformation Rule Implementation in Python

Objectives

In this chapter, you will learn several essential topics related to IoT Data Analytics. You will learn how to handle and implement different data formats in IoT Data Analytics solutions, including real-time data streaming and data pipeline, critical for processing vast amounts of data in real-time.

You will receive a refresher on IoT Dataflow, which is fundamental to understanding how data is analyzed and processed in IoT systems. Then, you will learn about data simulation, including why it is essential, how to perform it, and the pros and cons of using this technique in IoT Data Analytics.

The chapter covers the Digital Twin, an emerging technology gaining popularity in IoT systems, and the relationship between data simulation and the Digital Twin. You will learn about the Digital Twin provided by Python programs for data simulation implementation. Before learning how to implement a simple Python data simulator, we will cover various IoT Simulator tools available in the market and its functions.

Furthermore, you will learn about various data cleansing techniques using Python, different data transformation rules, and how to implement them using Python.

IoT Data Formats

The **Internet of Things** (**IoT**) sensors generates vast amounts of data in various formats, each with its characteristics and advantages.

Let us investigate the most frequently used formats:

JavaScript Object Notation (**JSON**) is a lightweight data-interchange format that is easy for humans to read and write and for machines to parse and generate. It is widely used in IoT and IIoT applications as it can straightforwardly represent data structures. JSON data is represented using key-value pairs, making extracting specific data pieces easy. The JSON format also supports complex data structures. The following are examples of simple and complex data from IoT sensors:

The following code is the simple JSON data with temperature and humidity values sent from sensors:

```
{"temperature": 23.5,
"humidity": 60.2}
```

The following is the Python example of handling JSON. Before trying the following example, save the preceding JSON data in your current working directory as **`json_data.json`**:

```
import json
# Open the JSON file and read its contents
with open("json_data.json", "r") as file:
    json_data = file.read()
# Parse the JSON data and convert it into a Python dictionary
parsed_data = json.loads(json_data)
# Print the values for the "temperature" and "humidity" keys
print("Temperature: " + str(parsed_data["temperature"]))
print("Humidity: " + str(parsed_data["humidity"]))
```

The following is a more **complex JSON data** of wind turbine. It has header information about an asset and the data from the sensors:

```
{
  "Header": {
    "ID": "Asset123",
    "SNo": "Gateway456",
```

```
        "AType": 5,
        "DType": 1,
        "UID": "Unit789",
        "Ver": "1.0",
        "Dflag": "3;1;1;1;100"
    },
  "data": [
    {
      "rtc": "2022-03-01T10:30:00",
      "temp": 25.4,
      "pressure": 1013.25,
      "wind_speed": 12.3,
      "rpm": 1500,
      "energy_output": 1000
    }
  ]
}
```

The following is a Python program on how to handle the complex XML data. Before executing the following program, save the preceding data in a file named **turbine_data.json** on your current working directory:

```
import json
# Open the JSON file for reading
with open('turbine_data.json', 'r') as f:
    # Load the JSON data into a Python dictionary
    data = json.load(f)
# Access the values in the dictionary using the keys
header = data['Header']
id = header['ID']
sno = header['SNo']
atype = header['AType']
dtype = header['DType']
uid = header['UID']
ver = header['Ver']
```

```
dflag = header['Dflag']
data_values = data['data'][0]
rtc = data_values['rtc']
temp = data_values['temp']
pressure = data_values['pressure']
wind_speed = data_values['wind_speed']
rpm = data_values['rpm']
energy_output = data_values['energy_output']
# Print the values
print('ID:', id)
print('SNo:', sno)
print('AType:', atype)
print('DType:', dtype)
print('UID:', uid)
print('Ver:', ver)
print('Dflag:', dflag)
print('RTC:', rtc)
print('Temp:', temp)
print('Pressure:', pressure)
print('Wind Speed:', wind_speed)
print('RPM:', rpm)
print('Energy Output:', energy_output)
```

XML: Extensible Markup Language (XML) is another popular format used in IoT applications. The markup language uses tags to define elements and attributes to provide additional information. XML is more flexible than JSON as it allows the creation of custom tags, making it more suited for complex data structures. The following are examples of simple and complex data from IoT sensors:

Simple XML data from the sensor with temperature and humidity values:

```
<data>
    <temperature>23.5</temperature>
    <humidity>60.2</humidity>
</data>
```

The Python program parses the XML file and prints the data. Save the preceding data in a file on your current directory before executing the program. The file name should be **xml_data.xml**:

```
import xml.etree.ElementTree as ET
# Parse the XML file and get the root element
tree = ET.parse('xml_data.xml')
root = tree.getroot()
# Retrieve the values for the "temperature" and "humidity" elements
temperature = root.find('temperature').text
humidity = root.find('humidity').text
# Print the values for the "temperature" and "humidity" elements
print("Temperature: " + temperature)
print("Humidity: " + humidity)
```

The following is the complex data in XML format from wind turbine:

```
<root>
  <Header>
    <ID>Asset123</ID>
    <SNo>Gateway456</SNo>
    <AType>5</AType>
    <DType>1</DType>
    <UID>Unit789</UID>
    <Ver>1.0</Ver>
    <Dflag>3;1;1;1;100</Dflag>
  </Header>
  <data>
    <entry>
      <rtc>2022-03-01T10:30:00</rtc>
      <temp>25.4</temp>
      <pressure>1013.25</pressure>
      <wind_speed>12.3</wind_speed>
      <rpm>1500</rpm>
      <energy_output>1000</energy_output>
    </entry>
  </data>
</root>
```

The preceding complex XML data can be parsed using Python. The following is an example of reading the preceding XML data saved in a file called **turbuine_data.xml**:

```
import xml.etree.ElementTree as ET
# Open the XML file for reading
with open('turbine_data.xml', 'r') as f:
    # Parse the XML data
    tree = ET.parse(f)
    root = tree.getroot()
# Access the values in the XML tree using the tag names
header = root.find('Header')
id = header.find('ID').text
sno = header.find('SNo').text
atype = header.find('AType').text
dtype = header.find('DType').text
uid = header.find('UID').text
ver = header.find('Ver').text
dflag = header.find('Dflag').text
data_values = root.find('data').find('entry')
rtc = data_values.find('rtc').text
temp = data_values.find('temp').text
pressure = data_values.find('pressure').text
wind_speed = data_values.find('wind_speed').text
rpm = data_values.find('rpm').text
energy_output = data_values.find('energy_output').text
# Print the values
print('ID:', id)
print('SNo:', sno)
print('AType:', atype)
print('DType:', dtype)
print('UID:', uid)
print('Ver:', ver)
print('Dflag:', dflag)
print('RTC:', rtc)
print('Temp:', temp)
```

```
print('Pressure:', pressure)
print('Wind Speed:', wind_speed)
print('RPM:', rpm)
print('Energy Output:', energy_output)
```

MessagePack is a binary serialization format of JSON and XML. It is a compact format with a variable-length encoding scheme, making it ideal for data transmission in low-bandwidth environments.

The following are examples of simple and complex data:

```
"\x82\xaBtemperature\xCB\x41\x8C\xCC\xCD\xCC\xCD\xCD\xa8humidity\xCB\x40\xCD\x33\x33\x33\x33\x33\x33\x33"
```

This **MessagePack** encoding uses the following format:

- **\x82** indicates that this is a Map with 2 key-value pairs.
- **\xaBtemperature** is the first key, encoded as a String with 11 bytes.
- **\xCB\x41\x8C\xCC\xCD\xCC\xCD\xCD\xCD** is the value associated with the **temperature** key. This is encoded as a 64-bit floating point number (CB code) with the value 23.5.
- **\xa8humidity** is the second key, encoded as a String with 8 bytes.
- **\xCB\x40\xCD\x33\x33\x33\x33\x33\x33\x33** is the value associated with the **humidity** key. This is encoded as a 64-bit floating point number (CB code) with the value 60.2.

MessagePack uses binary encoding, so the preceding is a string of bytes, not a string of characters. If you want to decode this **MessagePack** encoding back into a JSON object, you can use a **MessagePack** library in Python. The following is the Python example of decoding the binaryencoded **MessagePack**. You need to install **msgpack** Python library for handling **MessagePack** data. To install the package, you can use **pip install msgpack** command from your computer's command line.

```
import msgpack
# binary data from the question
binary_data = b'\x82\xabtemperature\xcb@7\x80\x00\x00\x00\x00\x00\xa8humidity\xcb@N\x19\x99\x99\x99\x99\x9a'
# check the Length of the binary data
print(len(binary_data))
# unpack the binary data using msgpack with the raw option set to False
unpacked_data = msgpack.unpackb(binary_data, raw=False)
# print the unpacked data
print(unpacked_data)
#Extract the temperature and humidity values
```

```
temperature = unpacked_data['temperature']
humidity = unpacked_data['humidity']
# Print the values
print('Temperature:', temperature)
print('Humidity:', humidity)
```

The following is a complex data of the wind turbine as shown in the JSON example, packed in **MessagePack** format:


```
"\x82\xa6Header\x87\xa2ID\xa89Asset123\xa3SNo\xaaGateway456\
xa5AType\x05\xa5DType\x01\xa3UID\xa87Unit789\xa3Ver\xa32.0\xa5Dflag\
xaB3;1;1;1;100\xa4data\x91\x86\xa3rtc\xD9\x12\x2B\x81\x1A\xE7\x88\x00\
x00\x00\xa4temp\xCA\x41\x9A\x99\x99\x99\x99\x9A\xa8pressure\xCE\x44\x40\
x07\xD2\x9B\x66\x66\x66\x66\x66\xaAwind_speed\xCD\x40\x2A\x8F\x5C\x28\
xF5\xC3\xF6\xEB\xa3rpm\xCD\x05\xDC\xa3\xC8\xa9energy_output\xCE\x44\x01\
x86\xA0\x00\x00"
```


Try decoding the preceding complex data in Python using the example given for simple data.

Comma Separated Values (CSV) is simple format for storing tabular data, such as sensor readings, in a text file. It is a popular format as it is easy to read and write and can be easily imported into various applications for further analysis. The following are the simple and complex examples of CSV data from IoT sensors:

```
temperature,humidity
23.5,60.2
```

Both **temperature** and **humidity** values are separated by comma with column headers.

The following is the complex data from the wind turbine:

```
Header.ID,Header.SNo,Header.AType,Header.DType,Header.UID,Header.Ver,Header.Dflag,data.rtc,data.temp,data.pressure,data.wind_speed,data.rpm,data.energy_output
Asset123,Gateway456,5,1,Unit789,1.0,3;1;1;1;100,2022-03-01T10:30:00,25.4,1013.25,12.3,1500,1000
```

Since we have seen handling CSV data using Python in various examples of the wind turbine data, we are already familiar with the method to handle any CSV data coming from the IoT sensors. So let us move on to the next format.

Protocol Buffers (Protobuf): It is a language-agnostic binary serialization format used in Google applications. It is becoming increasingly popular due to its efficiency, compactness, and extensibility. **Protobuf** is well-suited for IoT applications requiring high performance, low bandwidth usage, and interoperability between platforms and programming languages. Many IoT platforms and services now support **Protobuf**, and it is becoming a de facto standard in some domains, such as industrial automation and automotive. It is more efficient than JSON and XML and can be used to define complex data structures. **Protobuf** is preferred in IoT applications that require high-performance data processing. To process **Protobuf** data format, we must first define the schema using protoc complier. To download protoc, go to the official protocol buffers GitHub repository: **https://github.com/protocolbuffers/protobuf/releases.** On the release page, select the latest version suitable for your operating system and download the corresponding package. Once you have downloaded the package, you can install protoc by following the instructions provided for your operating system:

- For Windows, download the precompiled binary package from the release page and add the **protoc** binary to your system path.
- For macOS, you can use Homebrew to install **protoc**: **brew install protobuf.**

For example, to install **protoc** on Ubuntu or Debian Linux, you can run the following command: **brew install protobuf**

After installing protoc, you can compile a protobuf schema file using the following command:

```
protoc -I=<directory> --python_out=<output_directory> <schema_file.proto>
```

Replace **<directory>** with where your **protobuf** schema file is located, **<output_directory>** with the directory where you want to generate the Python code, and **<schema_file.proto>** with the name of your **protobuf** schema file.

The following is an example and steps for processing the sample data:

1. Create a new file called **protobuf_data.proto** and copy the schema definition of **SensorData** into it:

```
syntax = "proto3";
package protobuf;
message SensorData {
float temperature = 1;
float humidity = 2;
}
```

2. Compile the schema file to generate the Python code for the **protobuf** message. You can use the **protoc** command line tool to compile the schema file:

```
protoc -I=. --python_out=. protobuf_data.proto
```

This will generate a Python module called **protobuf_data_pb2.py** in the current directory.

You can import the **protobuf_data_pb2** module and use the **SensorData** message to encode and decode binary data.

```
import protobuf_data_pb2
# Create a SensorData message object
sensor_data = protobuf_data_pb2.SensorData()
```

```
# Decode the binary data
binary_data = b'\x0d\x9a\x99\x38\x41\x15\x33\x33\xb3\x40'
sensor_data.ParseFromString(binary_data)
# Print the values of the fields in the message
print("Temperature:", sensor_data.temperature)
print("Humidity:", sensor_data.humidity)
```

The following will be the output:

```
Temperature: 23.5
Humidity: 60.20000076293945
```

The following is the complex data of wind turbine we used for JSON encoded in **Protobuf** format:


```
0A 81 02 0A 09 41 73 73 65 74 31 32 33 12 0B 47 61 74 65 77 61 79 34 35 36 18 0
5 28 05 30 01 3A 07 55 6E 69 74 37 38 39 42 05 31 2E 30 4A 09 33 3B 31 3B 31 3B 3
1 3B 31 30 1A 1B 0A 19 32 30 32 32 2D 30 33 2D 30 31 54 31 30 3A 33 30 3A 30 30
12 9A 99 18 41 15 33 33 B3 40 28 D0 05 31 00 00
```


You can follow the instructions for the simple data to decode the complex data in Python. Make sure you install google package using **pip install google** command.

Avro and FastAvro: Avro is a binary serialization format used for data exchange between systems. It is efficient and supports schema evolution, making it ideal for IoT applications that require backward and forward compatibility. Avro collects sensor data from industrial automation systems, monitors manufacturing processes, and optimizes production. It is used to stream data from connected cars, including telemetry and engine data, collect and analyze data from medical devices, monitor patient health, and optimize healthcare operations.

FastAvro is a Python implementation of the Avro format that provides fast serialization and deserialization of data. It is designed for large datasets and can handle data compression and decompression. The preceding are the serialized simple and complex data:

A simple message in **FastAvro** serialized binary format:


```
\x00\x01\x06temperature\x02=\x00\x06humidity\x02\x9d\x99\x1a@
```


The following is the Python example to deserialize the preceding data sent from the IoT device. Make sure that you install **fastavro** package using **pip install fastavro**, before trying the following example:

```
import fastavro
import io
# Define the schema
schema = {
```

```
    "type": "record",
    "name": "SensorData",
    "fields": [
        {"name": "temperature", "type": "float"},
        {"name": "humidity", "type": "float"}
    ]
}
# Read the binary data
binary_data = b'\x00\x01\x06temperature\x02=\x00\x06humidity\x02\x9d\x99\x1a@'
# Create a BytesIO object from the binary data
bytes_io = io.BytesIO(binary_data)
# Deserialize the binary data using the schema
parsed_data = fastavro.schemaless_reader(bytes_io, schema)
# Print the parsed data
print(parsed_data)
```

Complex data in **FastAvro** serialized binary format:


```
b'\x00\x01\x04Asset123\rGateway456\x05\x01\tUnit789\x061.03;1;1;1;100\x01\x06data\x05\x02\x06rtc\x04temp\n\x1f33333333\xb8@\x15\x85\xeb\x51\xb8\x1a\x8f\xc2\x05\x00\x00'
```


Try out deserializing the preceding complex data in Python using the example given.

Concise Binary Object Representation (CBOR) is a binary serialization format similar to JSON but more compact and efficient. It is designed for low-bandwidth environments and supports data streaming, making it ideal for IoT applications. CBOR is used for encoding and decoding data in industrial automation and control systems to reduce the payload size and improve communication efficiency between devices. It securely and efficiently transmits medical data, such as patient records and vital signs. Smart cities started adopting the CBOR format for transmitting data in smart city applications, such as traffic and waste management. Various other industries use the CBOR formats such as energy management systems, smart grids, renewable energy systems, and automotive for vehicle-to-vehicle communication and telematics.

Simple data in CBOR binary serialized format:


```
A2 78 19 3B 9D 70 FB 40 47 E1 7A 14
```


The following is the Python code to deserialize the received data. Make sure that you install **cbor** package using command **pip install cbor**:

```
import cbor
# JSON data to be serialized
data = {
    "temperature": 23.5,
    "humidity": 60.2
}
# Serialize data in CBOR format
serialized_data = cbor.dumps(data)
# Print serialized data
print("Serialized data: ", serialized_data)
# Deserialize data from CBOR format
deserialized_data = cbor.loads(serialized_data)
# Print deserialized data
print("Deserialized data: ", deserialized_data)
```

Complex data in CBOR binary serialized format:


```
A26848656164 6572A661734E6F184861745970656 35A6F4761746577617934361 85A-
554964553179D901050201056A556E697437383942053 12E30A64444666C6167
3B333B313B313B313030826274633230323 22D30332D30315431303A33303A-
3030C09A991841153333B34028D005310000
```


Try out deserializing the preceding complex data in Python using the example given.

In conclusion, different data formats have advantages and disadvantages, and it is essential to understand how to handle them when working with IoT data. JSON, XML, CSV, MessagePack, Protobuf, Avro, FastAvro, and CBOR are popular formats used in IoT applications. Choosing the format depends on various factors, such as data complexity, bandwidth, and performance requirements. Understanding the differences between these formats can help developers and data scientists choose the most appropriate method to handle and process the data.

Realtime Streaming and Data Pipeline

Real-time data streaming in the context of IoT Data Analytics refers to the continuous and automatic transfer of data from IoT devices to a data processing system in real-time, as the data is generated. This allows for real-time analysis and decision-making based on the data as it is being generated, without any delay or lag. Real-time data streaming is important in IoT Analytics because many applications require immediate analysis and response, such as monitoring equipment performance and detecting anomalies or malfunctions. Additionally, real-time data streaming enables organizations to use data-driven insights to optimize their operations and enhance their products and services in real time.

On the other hand, data pipeline in IoT Analytics refers to multiple interconnected data processing and storage components that collect, process, and analyze large amounts of data generated by IoT sensors and devices. These pipelines have several stages, including data ingestion, storage, processing, and visualization.

Data pipeline in IoT Analytics differs from real-time data streaming regarding data velocity, volume, and complexity. Real-time data streaming is used to process data as it arrives in near real-time, while the IoT Analytics pipeline deals with batch processing of large volumes of data.

Consider the following factors when deciding between real-time data streaming or data pipeline:

- **Data volume:** Data pipelines can store and process large amounts of data in batches, which can be more efficient than processing data in real-time. On the other hand, real-time data streaming is better suited for scenarios where data needs to be processed and analyzed as it is generated, such as monitoring and control applications.
- **Data velocity:** Real-time data streaming may be the best option if the data generated is time-sensitive and requires immediate action. Real-time data streaming can process and analyze data in real-time, allowing immediate responses to events and anomalies. Data pipelines, conversely, can introduce some latency due to batch processing, which may not be suitable for use cases where timely decision-making is critical.
- **Data complexity:** A data pipeline may be the best option if the generated data is complex and requires complex transformations and processing. Data pipelines can use complex data processing and transformation tools, such as machine learning algorithms and modeling, to analyze and transform data before it is stored or sent to downstream applications. On the other hand, real-time data streaming is better suited for simpler data processing and transformation scenarios.

Advantages of Data Pipeline

Advantages of data pipeline are:

- Well suited when a large volume of data processing is required.
- Can process and analyze data at a more granular level.
- Provides more advanced data processing and transformation capabilities.
- Can be more cost-effective compared to real-time data streaming.

Disadvantages of Data Pipeline

Some disadvantages of data pipeline are as follows:

- Can introduce latency due to batch processing.
- May not be suitable for use cases that require immediate action.
- Can be more complex to set up and maintain than real-time data streaming.

Advantages of Real-Time Data Streaming

Some advantages of real-time data streaming are:

- Processes real-time data, allowing immediate responses to events and anomalies.
- Well suited for scenarios that require immediate action or decision-making.
- Easy to set up and maintain, compared to data pipelines.

Disadvantages of Real-Time Data Streaming

Disadvantages of real-time data streaming are as follows:

- May not be suitable for handling large volumes of data.
- Limited data processing and transformation capabilities compared to data pipelines.
- Can be more expensive compared to data pipelines.

IoT Dataflow

IoT Dataflow is a comprehensive process that involves several steps, including data collection, transmission, storage, pre-processing, analysis, visualization, and action-taking based on data obtained from IoT devices. One of the use cases of IoT Dataflow is demonstrated in the example of a wind turbine, where sensors installed on the machine collect data on wind speed, direction, temperature, and vibration, and send it to a gateway device for transmission to the cloud. The collected data is then stored in its raw format and subjected to pre-processing, where useful information is extracted through filtering, aggregation, or feature engineering techniques. The extracted data is then analyzed using statistical, machine learning, or deep learning techniques to derive insights. These insights are visualized through reports or dashboards, and appropriate actions are taken based on the results to enhance the performance of the wind turbine. This example demonstrates how IoT Dataflow can be used to optimize the performance of industrial machines. The following *Figure 4.1* shows the end-to-end flow of any IoT application:

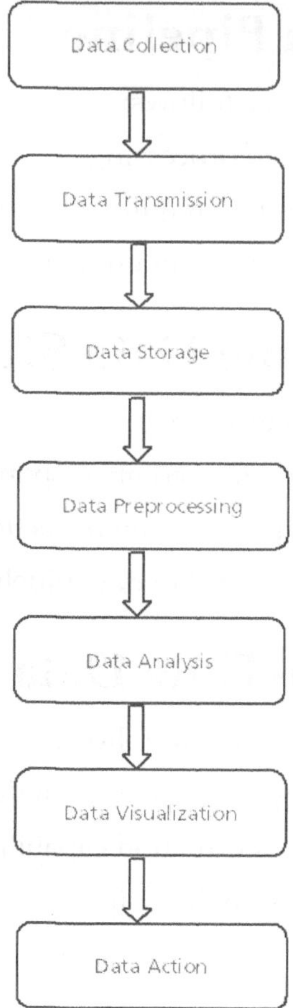

***Figure 4.1:** IoT Dataflow*

As explained in the preceding section, the process of IoT Dataflow involves several steps, from collecting data to taking actions based on insights. Let us take a closer look at each step to understand how IoT Dataflow can enhance the performance of industrial machines, using the example of a wind turbine:

1. **Data collection:** The first step in IoT Dataflow is collecting data from sensors installed on the wind turbine. These sensors can measure wind speed, direction, temperature, and vibration. The data is collected in real-time and sent to a gateway device, which bridges the IoT devices and the cloud.
2. **Data transmission:** The gateway device then transmits the collected data to the cloud using a wireless network like Wi-Fi or cellular network. To ensure security, the data is encrypted before transmission.
3. **Data storage:** After being transmitted, the data is stored in a cloud-based storage system, such as a database or a data lake, in its raw format.

4. **Data pre-processing:** Once the raw data is stored, it goes through pre-processing, which extracts useful information from it. This step can be done in real-time or batch, depending on the application's requirements. Pre-processing may involve filtering, aggregation, or feature engineering. For example, the raw sensor data from the wind turbine may be filtered to remove noise or outliers and aggregated to calculate average wind speed and temperature over a specific period.

5. **Data analysis:** Once the data is pre-processed, it is analyzed to extract insights and make predictions. Statistical analysis, machine learning, or deep learning techniques can be used for data analysis. For instance, machine learning algorithms can predict turbine failure based on sensor data.

6. **Data visualization:** The insights obtained from data analysis are then visualized using dashboards or reports. Visualization helps users understand insights and take appropriate actions. For example, a dashboard can show the real-time wind speed, temperature, and vibration of a wind turbine and highlight any unusual behavior.

7. **Data action:** Insights from data analysis are used to take action to enhance the performance of the wind turbine. Actions can be automated or manual, depending on application requirements. For example, an alert can be sent to the maintenance team to take preventive measures if the machine learning algorithm predicts a possible failure.

IoT Dataflow involves collecting data, transmitting it to the cloud, storing it, pre-processing it to extract useful information, analyzing it to extract insights, visualizing the insights, and taking actions based on the insights. The use case of a wind turbine is just one example of how IoT Dataflow can be used to enhance the performance of industrial machines.

Data Simulation and Digital Twin

Data simulation is a process that involves generating synthetic data to mimic the behavior of real-world IoT devices. This technique is commonly used in IoT Analytics for various purposes, including testing, training machine learning models, and evaluating analytics algorithms. Real-world IoT data is often complex, expensive, and difficult to obtain, making data simulation a practical and cost-effective approach for evaluating IoT Analytics solutions. However, simulation has some disadvantages, such as the inability to fully capture the complexity and variability of real-world data. In this section, we will overview data simulation, industry-standard methods, pitfalls, and examples of its application in IoT Analytics. Additionally, we will go through the relationship between data simulation and digital twins, which are used to monitor, analyze, and control physical assets or systems.

Data Simulation

Data simulation is a technique used in IoT Analytics to mimic the behavior of real-world IoT devices and generate synthetic data that can be used for testing, training machine learning models, and evaluating analytics algorithms. It is required in IoT because real-world IoT data is often complex, expensive, and difficult to obtain. Moreover, it is sometimes required to perform experiments on real-world systems due to safety, cost, or ethical concerns.

Advantages of Data Simulation in IoT Data Analytics

Some advantages of data simulation in IoT Analytics are:

- Provides a controlled environment for testing and validation of IoT Analytics solutions.
- Enables developers and data scientists to evaluate algorithms and models with various simulated scenarios.
- Saves time and cost associated with real-world data collection and experimentation.
- Offers the ability to simulate rare or extreme events that may be difficult to observe in real-world data such as failure of boilers in manufacturing industry is a very rare event, but critical to predict for avoiding major breakdown and accidents.
- Allows for evaluating the impact of changing system parameters on system behaviors.

Disadvantages of Data Simulation in IoT Data Analytics

Some disadvantages of data simulation in IoT Analytics are:

- Simulated data may not fully capture the complexity and variability of real-world data.
- Assumptions, simplifications, or limitations in the models can impact the accuracy and representativeness of the simulation models.
- The generated data may not reflect the true distribution of data in the real world
- There is always a risk of overfitting the models to the simulated data, leading to poor generalization performance in real-world scenarios.

Industry-standard Methods for Data Simulation

Here are the key industry standard methods for data simulation:

- Use accurate mathematical models that describe the behavior of the physical systems.
- Use probabilistic models to capture the uncertainty and variability in the system behavior.
- Calibration and validation of simulation models using real-world data.
- Incorporation of environmental factors that impact system behavior, such as temperature, humidity, and pressure.

Example of Data Simulation

Suppose we want to simulate the behavior of a centrifugal pump in a chemical processing plant. We can model the pump using differential equations that describe the relationship between the pump flow rate, pressure, and impeller speed. We can then use simulation software, such as Matlab/Simulink, to simulate the pump's behavior under different conditions. We can vary the input parameters, such as the fluid viscosity, temperature, and pump speed, to generate different scenarios. The simulated data can be used to train machine learning models to detect anomalies, predict failures, or optimize pump performance.

Mathematical Simulation Models for Data Simulation in IoT

Below are the important mathematical simulation models used in IoT:

- Finite element models
- Computational fluid dynamics models
- System dynamics models
- Agent-based models
- Monte Carlo simulations.

How Data Simulation Helps

Data simulation can save time by providing a way to evaluate IoT Analytics algorithms without the need for expensive and time-consuming real-world experiments. By generating a large amount of synthetic data, data scientists can train machine learning models more efficiently and evaluate the performance of analytics algorithms under various simulated scenarios.

Disadvantages of Data Simulation

Here are some pitfalls of data simulation and how to manage them:

- **Overfitting:** To avoid overfitting, it is important to validate the simulation models against real-world data and use cross-validation techniques to evaluate the generalization performance of the models.
- **Model complexity:** Simulation models can become very complex, making it difficult to interpret the results and identify the most important factors driving system behavior. To manage complexity, it is important to use clear and concise models that capture the essential features of the system behavior.
- **Data quality:** The simulated data's accuracy and representativeness depend on the input data quality and the assumptions made in the simulation models. To ensure data quality, validating the simulation models using real-world data and incorporating sources of uncertainty and variability is important.

  Data simulation in IoT and IIoT can be performed in various scenarios but assessing the need for simulation in each case is important. Some of the scenarios where data simulation can be useful are:

- o **Lack of historical data:** In cases where there is no or limited historical data available, simulation can be used to generate data that can be used for analysis.
- o **System testing:** Simulation can be used to test the system before deployment to ensure it performs as expected.
- o **Scenario testing:** Simulation can test the system's performance in extreme weather conditions or equipment failures.
- o **Predictive maintenance:** Simulation can predict maintenance needs based on equipment usage patterns, enabling proactive maintenance, and reducing downtime.

Digital Twin

Data simulation and digital twins are closely related in that data simulation can create a digital twin of a physical system. A digital twin is a virtual replica of a physical system used for various purposes such as testing, monitoring, and optimization.

In other words, a digital twin is a virtual representation of a physical asset, system, or process that enables the monitoring, analysis, and control of the real-world object through data and analytics. Digital twin technology has gained significant importance in IIoT, which helps optimize operational efficiency, predict maintenance needs, and improve product development processes.

To implement digital twin technology, the physical asset or system must be equipped with sensors and other monitoring devices that collect data on its behavior and performance. The collected data is then used to create a virtual representation of the asset or system, which can be used for monitoring, analysis, and control.

Data simulation can generate the necessary data to create a digital twin that accurately reflects the behavior of the physical system.

Data simulation methods are useful when it is not possible or practical to collect real-world data, or when the physical asset or system is not yet available. However, the digital twin's accuracy depends on the simulation model's accuracy, and it may only be sometimes possible to capture all the complexities and uncertainties of the real-world system.

Data simulation methods create digital twins by simulating the behavior and performance of the physical asset or system. The simulation model can be based on mathematical models or empirical data, and the simulated data can be used to create a digital twin.

There are several open-source products available for implementing digital twin technology. Some of the popular ones are:

- **Eclipse ditto:** It is an open-source project that provides a digital twin framework for IIoT systems.

- **Fiware:** It is an open-source platform that provides tools and components for implementing digital twins.
- **AWS IoT:** It is a cloud-based platform that provides tools and services for building and deploying digital twins.

IoT Simulator Tools

An IoT simulator is a valuable software tool or platform designed to replicate the operation of IoT networks and devices without the need for physical hardware. It serves as a virtual environment for testing, creating, and evaluating IoT applications and systems. By providing a realistic simulation of IoT installations, simulators enable developers and researchers to assess the functionality, dependability, and scalability of their solutions. Here, we will delve into the details of IoT simulators, highlighting their key features, benefits, and some popular options available in the market:

- **Device emulation:** IoT simulators allow developers to emulate a wide range of IoT devices, mimicking their behavior, communication protocols, and data generation. This feature enables comprehensive testing of IoT applications, ensuring compatibility and performance across various device types and configurations.

- **Network simulation:** Simulating different network conditions is crucial for evaluating the performance and reliability of IoT systems. IoT simulators provide the capability to model diverse network scenarios, including varying bandwidth, latency, packet loss, and network congestion. By recreating realistic network environments, developers can gauge the system's behavior and optimize its performance under different conditions. Scalability and Load.

- **Testing:** IoT simulators facilitate testing the scalability of IoT deployments. By simulating many virtual devices, developers can assess the system's ability to handle a high volume of data, requests, and concurrent connections. Load testing capabilities help identify bottlenecks and optimize resource allocation for optimal performance.

- **Cost-effective development:** Utilizing IoT simulators significantly reduces the cost of IoT application development. By eliminating the need for physical devices and infrastructure, developers can iterate and experiment more rapidly, accelerating the development process. Simulators also enable early-stage testing, allowing issues to be identified and resolved before deploying solutions on real hardware.

- **Scenario modeling:** IoT simulators offer the ability to create and simulate various scenarios and use cases. Developers can evaluate how IoT applications perform in different environments, events, and edge cases. This feature helps identify potential vulnerabilities, assess system resilience, and fine-tune algorithms or control strategies.

- **Data analytics and visualization:** IoT simulators often provide tools for data analytics and visualization. They enable developers to generate synthetic data or replay real data sets for analysis, allowing them to gain insights into the system's behavior and performance. Visualization capabilities aid in understanding complex data patterns, identifying anomalies, and making informed decisions based on the analysis. While numerous IoT simulators are available, each with its unique features and capabilities, some popular options include:

- **Cooja**: Cooja is an IoT simulator based on the Contiki operating system. It offers a powerful network simulation environment, enabling developers to evaluate IoT protocols, applications, and system behavior.
- **OMNeT++**: OMNeT++ is a widely used simulation framework that supports network modeling and IoT simulations. It provides an extensive set of tools and libraries for creating detailed and accurate simulations.
- **Contiki-NG**: Contiki-NG is an open-source operating system for IoT devices. It includes a simulator that allows developers to test and evaluate Contiki-based IoT applications and networks.
- **IoTIFY**: IoTIFY offers a cloud based IoT simulation platform that allows developers to create virtual IoT deployments and conduct comprehensive testing. It supports various protocols and offers scalability testing capabilities.
- **ThingWorx**: ThingWorx is a robust IoT platform that includes simulation features for testing IoT applications and systems. It provides a comprehensive environment for modeling, testing, and optimizing IoT deployments.
- **Simics**: Simics is a powerful simulator that enables the virtual modeling and simulation of complete IoT systems, including both hardware and software components. It provides a high-level of accuracy and fidelity, allowing developers to assess system behavior, performance, and security.
- **NetSim**: NetSim is a comprehensive network simulator that includes IoT capabilities. It offers a user-friendly interface and supports the simulation of various IoT protocols, network topologies, and communication scenarios. NetSim allows developers to analyze network performance, evaluate IoT application behavior, and optimize network configurations.

These are just a few examples, and there are many other IoT simulators available in the market, catering to different development and testing requirements. Choosing the most suitable simulator depends on factors such as the specific use case, desired features, scalability needs, and integration capabilities with other.

IoT Data Simulator Python Implementation

You can recollect that we performed data simulation of a wind turbine in *Chapter 3, Setting Up IoT Analytics Environment*. The one we used in *Chapter 3, Setting Up IoT Analytics Environment* is a static data simulator where the data is generated once. The following is an example of continuous data simulation using **mosquitto MQTT** broker:

```
import json
import random
import datetime
import time
import paho.mqtt.client as mqtt
# Function to generate simulated data
def generate_data():
    data = {}
    data['header'] = {}
    data['header']['id'] = '100001'
    data['header']['sno'] = 'G7500001'
    data['header']['atype'] = 5
    data['header']['dtype'] = 1
    data['header']['uid'] = '5200001'
    data['header']['ver'] = 'V 2.0.1'
    data['header']['dflag'] = '3;1;1;1;100'
    data['data'] = []
    current_time = datetime.datetime.now().replace(microsecond=0).isoformat()
    data_point = {}
    data_point['rtc'] = current_time
    data_point['temp'] = round(random.uniform(20, 30), 2)
    data_point['pressure'] = round(random.uniform(1000, 1100), 2)
    data_point['wind_speed'] = round(random.uniform(5, 15), 2)
    data_point['rpm'] = random.randint(1200, 1800)
    data_point['energy_output'] = random.randint(800, 1200)
    data['data'].append(data_point)
    return json.dumps(data)
# MQTT client setup
client = mqtt.Client()
client.connect("localhost", 1883)  # Connect to Mosquitto MQTT broker
# Main program loop to generate data every 1 second
```

```
while True:
    data = generate_data()
    print(data)
    client.publish("wind-turbine-data", data)
    time.sleep(1)
```

This code first imports the Paho **MQTT** client library and sets up a connection to a public **MQTT** broker hosted by **Eclipse.org.** You can change the broker address and port to connect to your **MQTT** broker.

The code then modifies the **generate_data()** function to return the generated data as JSON. After generating the data, the code uses the client to publish the JSON string to the wind turbine-data MQTT topic **.publish()** method.

Finally, the code sleeps for 1 second before generating and publishing the next data set. You can adjust the sleep duration to generate data more or less frequently.

Data Cleansing Implementation in Python

Data cleansing is a critical process in IoT and Analytics that involves identifying and correcting inaccurate, incomplete, or irrelevant data in a dataset. The main goal of data cleansing is to ensure that the data is accurate, reliable, and consistent, which is vital for making well-informed business decisions.

Data cleansing is required for several reasons, including accuracy, consistency, and efficiency. Only accurate or complete data can lead to accurate analyses and insights, while inconsistent data can pose challenges when merging different datasets or conducting analyses over various periods. Clean data is more manageable and requires less time and effort to prepare and analyze.

Data cleansing may require several steps, such as removing duplicate records, correcting spelling errors, eliminating outliers, handling missing values, and standardizing data. Duplicate records can distort analyses and produce misleading insights while spelling errors can affect data accuracy. Outliers, or data points outside the typical range, can skew analyses and should be removed. Missing data can present issues for analyses, and techniques such as imputation or deletion can be used to address it. Standardizing data formats, such as dates, can improve the usability of datasets.

Python is a popular programming language used for data cleansing tasks in IoT Analytics. Python provides many libraries and tools to simplify and automate data cleansing. The following is the Python program that implements data cleansing methods that can perform most of the data cleansing tasks:

```
import paho.mqtt.client as mqtt
import pandas as pd
```

```
import json
import datetime
from data_cleaning_engine import DataCleaningEngine
# initialize the MQTT client
mqtt_client = mqtt.Client()
mqtt_client.connect("localhost", 1883)
# initialize the data cleaning engine
data_cleaner = DataCleaningEngine()
# define the callback function to be executed when a new message is received
def on_message(client, userdata, msg):
    # decode the message payload from bytes to string
    msg_payload = msg.payload.decode('utf-8')
    # parse the message payload as JSON
    msg_data = json.loads(msg_payload)
    # clean the data using the data cleaning engine
    cleaned_data = data_cleaner.clean_data(msg_payload)
    cleaned_data['rtc'] = datetime.datetime.fromtimestamp(cleaned_data['rtc'] / 10**9)
    # do something with the cleaned data
    print(cleaned_data)
        # append the cleaned data to a CSV file
    with open('cleaned_data.csv', 'a') as f:
        f.write(cleaned_data.to_csv(header=f.tell()==0, index=False))
# set the on_message callback function for the MQTT client
mqtt_client.on_message = on_message
# subscribe to the MQTT topic
mqtt_client.subscribe("wind-turbine-data")
# start the MQTT client loop
mqtt_client.loop_forever()
```

This program uses the Paho **MQTT** client library to subscribe to the **wind-turbine-data** topic and listen for incoming messages. Upon receiving a new message, the program decodes the message payload from bytes to string, parses it as JSON, and cleans the data using the data cleaning engine. The cleaned data is then printed and appended to a CSV file called **cleaned_data.csv**. The program uses the **MQTT** client loop to listen for new messages continuously, and the loop runs indefinitely until the program is stopped.

The following is the data cleaning engine implemented in Python:

```
import json
import numpy as np
import pandas as pd
class DataCleaningEngine:
    def __init__(self):
        pass
    def clean_data(self, data):
        # Convert JSON string to dictionary
        data_dict = json.loads(data)
        # Extract data from dictionary
        data_list = data_dict['data']
        # Convert data to pandas dataframe
        df = pd.DataFrame(data_list)
        # Drop duplicate rows
        df = df.drop_duplicates()
        # Drop rows with missing values
        df = df.dropna()
        # Convert string timestamps to datetime format
        df['rtc'] = pd.to_datetime(df['rtc'])
        # # Clean data using additional rules
        # # Remove leading/trailing whitespaces from all columns
        df = df.apply(lambda x: x.str.strip() if x.dtype == "object" else x)
        # # Remove special characters from column names
        df.columns = df.columns.str.replace('[^a-zA-Z0-9_]', '')
        # # Convert all string values to lowercase
        df = df.apply(lambda x: x.str.lower() if x.dtype == "object" else x)
        # # Convert all NaN values to None
        df = df.where(pd.notnull(df), None)
        # # Remove rows with invalid/incorrect data types
        df = df.apply(pd.to_numeric, errors='coerce')
```

```
        df = df.dropna()
        # # # Remove rows with data outside a certain range. They will create noise due to IoT Sensor malfunction
        df = df[(df['temp'] >= 10) & (df['temp'] <= 150)]
        df = df[(df['pressure'] >= 800) & (df['pressure'] <= 1200)]
        df = df[(df['wind_speed'] >= 0) & (df['wind_speed'] <= 200)]
        df = df[(df['rpm'] >= 0) & (df['rpm'] <= 3000)]
        df = df[(df['energy_output'] >= 0) & (df['energy_output'] <= 2000)]
        return df
```

This program defines a class called **DataCleaningEngine** that contains a method called **clean_data**. This method does several things to prepare the data for analysis. First, it takes input data and converts a JSON string into a dictionary. Then, it extracts important information from the dictionary. After that, it cleans the data by removing duplicate rows, removing rows with missing values, changing string timestamps to the **DateTime** format, removing special characters from column names, converting string values to lowercase, and removing rows with incorrect or invalid data types. The method removes rows with data outside a certain range to eliminate noise caused by IoT sensor malfunction. The cleaned data is then returned as a **pandas** data frame. This program provides a comprehensive and automated approach to cleaning and pre-processing data.

Data Transformation Rule Implementation in Python

Data transformation is an essential process in the field of IoT and analytics. It involves modifying or converting data from one structure or format to another to improve the data's quality, usability, and relevance for analytical purposes.

The process of data transformation is needed to convert raw data into a standardized format, integrate data from multiple sources, aggregate data, and reduce the dimensionality of data. For example, data standardization is necessary to ensure that data from different sources is in a consistent format or unit for accurate analysis. The following is the transformation engine built in Python to perform various data transformation tasks:

```
import pandas as pd
import numpy as np
from scipy.signal import savgol_filter
class DataTransformationEngine:
    def __init__(self):
```

```
        pass
    def transform_data(self, df):
        # Check if all required columns are present in the DataFrame
        required_cols = ['rtc', 'temp', 'pressure', 'wind_speed', 'rpm', 'energy_output']
        missing_cols = set(required_cols) - set(df.columns)
        if missing_cols:
            raise KeyError(f"{missing_cols} not in index")
        # Convert rtc column to datetime format
        df['rtc'] = pd.to_datetime(df['rtc'])
        # Group data by hour and calculate mean value for each group
        df = df.set_index('rtc')
        df['wind_speed'] = pd.to_numeric(df['wind_speed'])
        df['temp'] = pd.to_numeric(df['temp'])
        df = df.groupby(pd.Grouper(freq='H')).mean()
        # Normalize the value column
        df['wind_speed'] = (df['wind_speed'] - df['wind_speed'].mean()) / df['wind_speed'].std()
        df['temp'] = (df['temp'] - df['temp'].mean()) / df['temp'].std()
        # Add a column for the weekday
        df['Weekday'] = df.index.weekday
        # Apply a Savitzky-Golay filter to the value column
        df['wind_speed'] = savgol_filter(df['wind_speed'], window_length=3, polyorder=2)
        df['temp'] = savgol_filter(df['temp'], window_length=3, polyorder=2)
        # Add columns for the hour and minute
        df['Hour'] = df.index.hour
        df['Minute'] = df.index.minute
        # Resample the data to 15-minute intervals
        df = df.resample('15T').mean()
        # Remove columns with low variance
        numeric_cols = df.select_dtypes(include=np.number).columns
        variances = df[numeric_cols].var()
```

```
        cols_to_drop = variances[variances < 0.01].index
        df = df.drop(cols_to_drop, axis=1)
        return df
# Load data from the CSV file
df = pd.read_csv('cleaned_data.csv')
# Initialize the data transformation engine
data_transformer = DataTransformationEngine()
try:
    # Transform the data using the data transformation engine
    transformed_data = data_transformer.transform_data(df)
    # Write the transformed data to a CSV file
    transformed_data.to_csv('transformed_data.csv')
    print('Transformation complete. Output saved to transformed_data.csv')
except KeyError as e:
    print(f"Error: {e}")
```

The given program is a Python script that reads data from a CSV file, applies various transformations, and saves the transformed data to a new CSV file. The transformations are performed using a class called **DataTransformationEngine** which has a method **transform_data** that accepts a panda **DataFrame** as input and returns a transformed **DataFrame** as output. The transformations include converting the timestamp column to datetime format, grouping the data by hour and calculating the mean value for each group, normalizing the temperature and wind speed columns, adding columns for the weekday, hour, and minute, resampling the data to 15-minute intervals, applying a *Savitzky-Golay* filter to the temperature and wind speed columns, and dropping columns with low variance. If any required columns are missing from the input **DataFrame**, a **KeyError** is raised. If the transformations are successful, the transformed **DataFrame** is written to a new CSV file, and a success message is printed.

Conclusion

We have learned about various data formats of IoT data and how to handle each format using Python at the beginning of this chapter. Knowing how to handle different data formats from the IoT device is critical to any IoT Analyst.

In the subsequent part of the chapter, we learned about real-time data streaming and data pipelines. The advantage and disadvantages of choosing the right approach to streaming data.

We then discussed the data flow of IoT applications. This section discussed each stage of data flow in any IoT application.

Subsequently, we discussed data simulation, and how it relates to the digital twins. We covered the concept of data simulation, then learnt about IoT simulator tools available in the market and concluded the section with the Python example of simulating wind turbine, equipment, which generates electricity from wind energy. An **MQTT** broker ingests the simulated data.

We discussed the basics of data cleansing and transformation and how to implement various data cleaning and transformation for the pipeline we built to ingest the **MQTT** topic.

In the next chapter, we will learn about the concept and design of a data lake, and why we need a data lake for IoT Analytics implementation. We will learn to set up a data lake using Kafka and PostgreSQL. We will finally implement an end-to-end data pipeline using Python to ingest the data every minute into the data lake. The objective of the next chapter is to build a data lake with continued data streaming into different layers of the data lake for performing analytics in the later chapters.

Points to Remember

Following are the key takeaways from this chapter:

- There are many formats of IoT data received from IoT sensors and devices. The most used formats are JSON, XML, CSV and some other formats which are important to learn are `MessagePack`, `Protobuf`, Avro, FastAvro and, CBOR. Specific Python packages are available for decoding, deserialization, and data processing. Important packages are JSON, `pandas`, `msgpack`, fastavro, and CBOR. The module `xml.etree`, and `ElementTree` is helpful in handling XML data.
- Real time data streaming and data pipeline are the key process in acquiring data from the IoT sensors and devices. Real-time data streaming is a synchronous process that immediately transmits data from the IoT devices to the cloud. The data pipeline is very similar to real time streaming, but the major difference is the delay or batch processing. The data pipeline is used where data from the IoT device is acquired asynchronously.
- IoT Dataflow involves collecting, transmitting, storing, pre-processing, analyzing, visualizing, and acting on data to extract insights and enhance performance. Following are the stages of typical dataflow in IoT:
  - Data collection
  - Data transmission
  - Data storage
  - Data pre-processing
  - Data analysis
  - Data visualization

- Data simulation is a technique used in IoT Analytics to generate synthetic data replicating real-world IoT devices' behavior. This process tests trains machine learning models and evaluates analytics algorithms. It saves time and cost related to data collection and experimentation, allows for the evaluation of system behavior, and can simulate rare or extreme events. Industry-standard methods include accurate mathematical and probabilistic models, calibration, and real-world data validation. Assumptions, simplifications, or limitations may impact the accuracy of the simulation models. Digital Twin technology uses data and analytics to create a virtual replica of a physical system. Data simulation can generate the data required to create a digital twin. The data simulation can be implemented using Python and for digital twin implementation, we have various open-source tools such as Eclipse Ditto, Fiware, and AWS IoT. There are various IoT Simulator tools available in the market such as Cooja, OMNeT++, Contiki-NG, IoTIFY, ThingWorx NetSim and Simics.
- Data cleansing is a crucial process in IoT Data Analytics, necessary for accurate, reliable, and consistent data. Inaccurate or incomplete data can lead to erroneous insights, while inconsistent data can pose challenges when merging datasets or conducting analyses over different periods. Data cleansing involves several steps: removing duplicates, correcting errors, handling outliers and missing data, and standardizing data formats. Clean data is more manageable, requires less time and effort to prepare and analyze, and leads to well-informed business decisions. The data cleansing can be implemented using Python during data ingestion stage of IoT data flow.
- Data transformation is a crucial process in IoT Analytics that involves modifying or converting data from one structure or format to another to improve data quality, usability, and relevance. Data transformation is needed to convert raw data into a standardized format, integrate data from multiple sources, aggregate data, and reduce the dimensionality of data. Data standardization is necessary to ensure that data from different sources are in a consistent format or unit for accurate analysis. We can use Python to perform various data transformations. The transformations can be performed during data ingestion or later stages of dataflow in IoT.

CHAPTER 5
Designing Data Lake and Executing Data Transformation

Introduction

As data from **Internet of Things (IoT)** sensors and devices grows in volume and velocity, it is becoming increasingly important to have a well-defined approach for storing and accessing data for analysis. The concept of a data lake provides a modern solution for managing large amounts of data in a scalable and flexible manner. Unlike traditional data storage systems, a data lake stores data in its native format, making it easier to integrate various data sources. In this chapter, we will introduce the concept of a data lake, its purpose, structure, and benefits.

Chapter 4, Managing Data Pipeline and Cleaning introduced the importance of real-time streaming and data pipelines for batch streaming data from IoT devices. The IoT has transformed how we collect and analyze data, but it also presents new challenges in managing data streams. With an increasing number of connected devices generating vast amounts of data, a new approach is required for storing, processing, and analyzing IoT data. This chapter will introduce IoT data lake streams and demonstrate how to implement data streams into a data lake. We will cover fundamental concepts such as storing data in different zones or segments to facilitate efficient analysis for various purposes.

Structure

In this chapter, we will cover the following topics:

- Data Lake Concept

- Iot Real-time Data Streaming
- Building Data Pipeline to the Raw Zone
- Transformation Zone of the Data Lake
- Building Kpis and Metrics Objectives

Objectives

This chapter's objective is to introduce the concept of data lakes and their implementation for IoT Analytics in a concise manner. It covers creating distinct data zones within an IoT data lake for specific data management and analytics purposes. The practical steps for designing and constructing an IoT data lake are outlined, utilizing the data stream developed in *Chapter 4, Managing Data Pipeline and Cleaning*. This data stream is channeled to Kafka, a real-time data pipeline, and then directed into the data lake.

The chapter explores various data zones that facilitate organized storage, management, and analysis of incoming data. The raw zone is where tables are established to house unprocessed data from IoT devices. In the trusted zone, validated and cleaned data resides, which includes entries checked for completeness, consistency, and accuracy. Moving to the transformation zone, tables contain data augmented with extra details or converted into a more usable format, such as aggregated or combined data.

A separate metrics zone is dedicated to storing **Key Performance Indicators (KPIs)** and metrics, enabling the extraction of meaningful insights from the data lake. This section imparts knowledge on constructing KPIs and metrics, leveraging tools and technologies for data analysis and visualization. This encompasses the design of efficient data pipelines for generating KPIs and metrics, as well as techniques for visualizing and conveying insights to stakeholders.

We will be covering the analytical zone in *Chapter 6, Implementing Descriptive Analytics Using Pandas*.

Data Lake Concept

A data lake is a large repository for storing and analyzing structured and unstructured data. The main objective of a data lake is to provide a centralized location for all data, regardless of its source or type. By learning the data lake concept, you can understand how to build an efficient and scalable data storage infrastructure that can handle large volumes of data. This includes understanding how to design and implement a data lake, ingest process, and analyze data from various sources. In IoT Analytics, the data lake plays a crucial role in acquiring and serving data from IoT devices for different analytics purposes.

The data in a data lake is usually stored in its raw form and is continuously curated, transformed, and served for gaining insights from the data. The data could be served for performing various tasks such as data analysis, reporting, dashboard, and machine learning.

The use of data lakes is crucial for effective IoT Analytics for various reasons:

- **Scalability:** Traditional storage systems are limited in handling the vast amount of data generated by IoT devices. In contrast, data lakes can store and manage this data effectively.
- **Flexibility:** Data lakes can handle various data formats and structures, including unstructured data like images and videos, making, storing, and analyzing data from multiple IoT devices easier.
- **Real-time analytics:** Real-time processing and analysis of IoT data are essential for organizations to make quick decisions, and data lakes enable this.
- **Cost-effective:** Setting up a data lake can be more cost-effective than traditional storage systems, especially when dealing with massive amounts of IoT data.
- **Futureproofing:** Data lakes offer a platform for future data analytics needs, such as artificial intelligence and machine learning applications.

Although both data lakes and traditional data warehouses are used for storing and managing data, there are several key differences between them:

- **Data structure:** Traditional data warehouses store data in a structured format, while data lakes store data in its native format, making it easier to handle unstructured data.
- **Data processing:** Data warehouses are designed for batch processing of structured data, while data lakes are designed for processing large volumes of unstructured data in real-time.
- **Schema:** Data warehouses have a predefined schema, whereas data lakes do not require normalization and can store data without following a specific schema.
- **Data access:** Data warehouses offer limited data access and are primarily used for generating reports. In contrast, data lakes enable self-service data access, allowing data scientists and analysts to explore and discover new insights.

Data lakes offer a flexible, scalable, and real-time platform for handling large volumes of structured and unstructured data, making them an ideal choice for IoT Analytics. However, proper management and governance are crucial to ensuring data quality, security, and compliance. Traditional data warehouses, on the other hand, are better suited for structured data processing and generating reports but lack the flexibility and real-time processing capabilities of data lakes.

Introduction to Data Lake Zones

In Data Lake, the data will be partitioned into various zones to enable easy and efficient access. The standard data lake implementation will have the following data zones:

- **Raw zone:** The raw data zone is the first stage of a data lake, where data is ingested and stored in its raw and unprocessed form.
- **Curated zone:** The curated data zone is the second stage of a data lake, where data is transformed, cleansed, and enriched for analysis.
- **Trusted zone:** The trusted data zone is the third stage of a data lake, where data is enriched with context, meaning, and governance.
- **Analytics zone:** The analytics zone is the fourth stage of a data lake, where data is used for analytics, reporting, and machine learning. We will be covering the analytical zone in the next chapter.

In addition to these industry-standard zones, for IoT Analytics, we might need to add a transformation and metric zone for performing necessary data transformation, KPIs, and metrics specific to the requirements of serving data for IoT Data Analysis, reporting, and dashboards.

Designing Data Lake

Designing a data lake for IoT Analytics involves the following key steps:

1. Defining the business goals that the data lake will support is essential to determine the data types that should ingest, how the data should be processed, and what types of analytics should be performed.
2. Identifying reliable and secure data sources like sensors, machines, equipment, or other devices.
3. The ingestion layer should be designed to handle high-velocity data ingestion. The storage layer should be designed to handle large volumes of data, provide data security and privacy, and enable data partitioning to support scalable and efficient queries.
4. The processing layer should be designed to support various types of data processing. The analytics layer should be designed to support various types of analytics, such as descriptive, predictive, and prescriptive analytics.
5. Finally, implementing governance and security mechanisms, such as access control, data lineage, and data retention policies, ensures the privacy, confidentiality, and integrity of the data stored in the data lake.

Designing a data lake for IoT Analytics requires careful consideration of business goals, data sources, and data processing requirements. By following these steps, organizations can build a scalable, secure, and flexible data lake that supports their IoT Analytics needs.

Architecture of Data Lake

The following *Figure 5.1* is the logical architecture of the data lake with the end-to-end data flow from the IoT devices to different data lake zones:

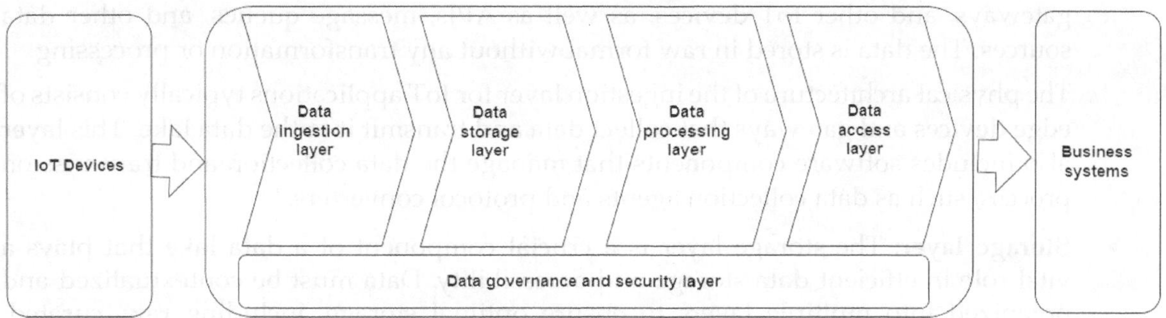

Figure 5.1: Data Lake Logical Architecture

The data lake architecture involves several layers for efficient data management and analysis. These layers include data ingestion, data storage, data processing, data analytics, and data governance and security:

- The **data ingestion layer** collects data from various sources, including IoT devices, sensors, and other data streams. Depending on the IoT environment, the layer must handle different data formats and protocols such as MQTT, HTTP, CoAP, or AMQP.
- The **data storage layer** is responsible for storing the acquired data securely and efficiently to make it available for business use. The data is organized into different zones, such as raw, curated, trusted, transformation, metric, and analytics, each with specific objectives.
- The **data processing layer** transforms raw data into structured data for efficient use for analytics. The processing methodologies and technologies depend on the purpose of the business it needs to serve.
- The **data analytics layer** is where different machine learning algorithms and statistical methods are applied to extract insights from the data. Data visualization tools are used to create interactive dashboards and reports to make it easier to interpret and communicate the insights gained from analyzing the data.
- The **data governance and security layer** ensure that the data's security, integrity, and privacy is stored in the data lake. Access controls, data protection techniques such as encryption, masking, and tokenization, and auditing and monitoring tools are used to comply with various regulations and standards.

Implementation of Data Lake

The physical architecture of a data lake for IoT Analytics consists of several layers that work together to collect, store, manage, and analyze large volumes of IoT data. These layers include:

- **Ingestion layer:** The ingestion layer is the first layer where data is collected from various IoT devices and other sources. This layer includes devices such as sensors, gateways, and other IoT devices, as well as APIs, message queues, and other data sources. The data is stored in raw format without any transformation or processing.

  The physical architecture of the ingestion layer for IoT applications typically consists of edge devices and gateways that collect data and transmit it to the data lake. This layer also includes software components that manage the data collection and transmission process, such as data collection agents and protocol converters.

- **Storage layer:** The storage layer is a crucial component of a data lake that plays a vital role in efficient data storage and accessibility. Data must be contextualized and organized into multiple layers to ensure optimal storage, including raw, curated, transformation, metric, and analytical zones. Each layer stores data according to the specific processing needs of the business.

  The raw zone, part of the storage layer, is responsible for storing raw data and typically uses a distributed file system such as a file-based system. This approach provides cost-effective storage of large volumes of raw data. Alternatively, the raw zone can be designed using NoSQL databases like MongoDB or SQL databases like PostgreSQL.

  For the other zones, such as curated, transformation, metric, and analytical, relational databases are used for efficient storage and easy access via SQL statements. Popular relational database systems such as PostgreSQL, MySQL, MS SQL server, and Oracle are utilized to store data more efficiently. By leveraging these systems, the storage layer can ensure optimized storage and seamless accessibility to data across various processing zones.

- **Processing layer:** The processing layer is where we perform necessary data cleansing, formatting, and transformation of the incoming data from external sources like IoT devices. We can implement the entire processing layer using Python or software components such as Apache Spark, Flink, or Storm. Data processing aims to clean the data and store it in the appropriate zones of the data lake for analytics and machine learning.

- **Analytics layer:** The analytics layer provides insights and visualization of the processed data. This layer includes software components such as Apache Hive, Apache Impala, or Amazon Athena, which enable SQL-based analytics and reporting.

  The physical architecture of the analytics layer typically consists of multiple nodes connected to a high-speed network. Each node usually consists of a processing unit, memory, and storage to handle data access and retrieval.

- **Governance layer:** The governance layer ensures data security, compliance, and quality. This layer includes software components such as Apache Ranger or AWS IAM, which enable access control, auditing, and data lineage tracking.

  The physical architecture of the governance layer typically consists of multiple nodes connected to the speed network. Each node usually consists of a processing unit, memory, and storage to handle data governance and management.

In conclusion, the physical architecture of a data lake for IoT Analytics comprises multiple layers that work together to collect, store, manage, and analyze large volumes of IoT data. These layers and their components provide a comprehensive and scalable solution for managing and extracting value from IoT data.

In many IoT implementations, we need a simpler and more efficient data lake design that can be modular and serve the purpose of any implementation size. Using open-source tools for building a simplified data lake for IoT implementations is becoming popular. This chapter will go through an implementation architecture based on open-source products and tools.

Let us take the wind turbine examples we were going through in *Chapter 4, Managing Data Pipeline and Cleaning,* and build a data lake using **`Mosquitto MQTT`** broker, Apache Kafka, Python, and PostgreSQL, as shown in *Figure 5.2*:

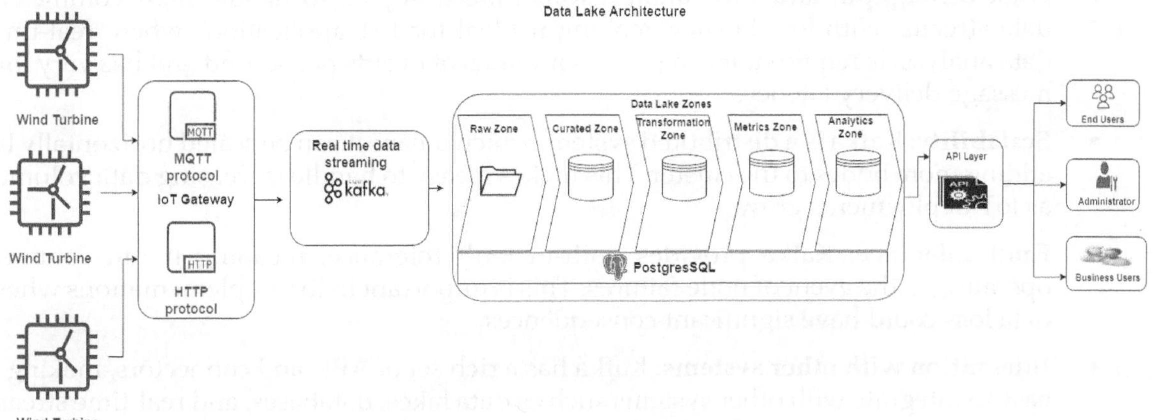

Figure 5.2: Data Lake Architecture

The following is the implementation of each data lake layer:

- **Data ingestion:** The first step is to collect data from the wind turbines using sensors and devices that can communicate using the **`MQTT`** protocol. **`MQTT`** is a lightweight messaging protocol that is used in IoT applications for collecting and transmitting data.
- **Data processing:** After the data is collected using the **`MQTT`** protocol, it needs to be processed and transformed to prepare it for analysis. This is done using Python, which provides many libraries and tools for data manipulation, transformation, and cleaning.
- **Data storage:** Once the data is processed, it must be stored in a data lake in a segregated zone. The number of zones in the data lake depends on its business purpose. We will set up raw, curated, transformation, metrics, and analytics zones for our wind turbine use case. You can notice that the zones defined for our use case differ from those defined in *Figure 5.1*. For the examples in this text, we combined the data lake's curated and trusted zones for simplicity. Both zones represent a similar form of data. Hence, we do not need to keep the data in two different zones. We use the PostgreSQL database for building the data lake. PostgreSQL is an open-source, scalable, and reliable relational database management system that can be used to store processed data.

- **Data analysis:** After storing the data in different zones of the PostgreSQL database and schemas, it can be analyzed using SQL statements or Python programming language.

IoT Real-time Data Streaming

To build a data lake for IoT Analytics, we need to set up real-time data streaming from the IoT devices continuously. The data must be available immediately as and when generated from the sensors. In our example, we will be simulating data for Wind Turbine with various parameters like wind speed, temperature, pressure, rpm, and power output. This will help us analyze wind turbines thoroughly. We need a tool to handle the high volume of data streams in low latency to achieve this. We will use Apache Kafka to stream the data from the IoT devices. The following are the reasons for choosing Apace Kafka for real-time data streaming:

- **High throughput and low latency:** Kafka are designed to handle high volumes of data streams with low latency, making it ideal for IoT applications where real-time data analysis is required. It can process millions of events per second and has very low message delivery latency.
- **Scalability:** Kafka is a distributed system, which means it can be scaled horizontally by adding more nodes to the cluster. This makes it easy to handle increasing data volumes as IoT deployments grow.
- **Fault tolerance:** Kafka provides built-in fault tolerance, meaning it can continue operating in the event of node failures. This is important in IoT implementations where data loss could have significant consequences.
- **Integration with other systems:** Kafka has a rich set of APIs and connectors, making it easy to integrate with other systems such as data lakes, databases, and real-time stream processing frameworks like Apache Flink and Apache Spark.
- **Flexibility:** Kafka is a versatile platform that can be used for a wide range of use cases beyond IoT data streaming, including data integration, messaging, and real-time analytics.

Overall, Apache Kafka provides a reliable, scalable, and flexible platform for real-time data streaming in IoT implementations.

In the first step of any IoT data lake and data streaming implementation, we need to set up a device registration and onboarding process. Also, we need to setup a database layer for storing the raw data. The raw zone is the first layer of the data lake. Let us first go through the device registration and onboarding process and how to implement the same.

Setting up Data Lake

We must create the required database and schema in PostgreSQL before streaming the data into the data lake.

The following are the steps for creating database and schema using PostgreSQL tool called **pgAdmin** that we installed in section *Installation and configuration of PostgreSQL* of *Chapter 3, Setting Up IoT Analytics Environment*:

1. InsectionInstallationandconfigurationofPostgreSQLof*Chapter3,SettingUpIoTAnalytics Environment*, we already created a database server called **IoTAnalytics** as shown in *Figure 5.3*:

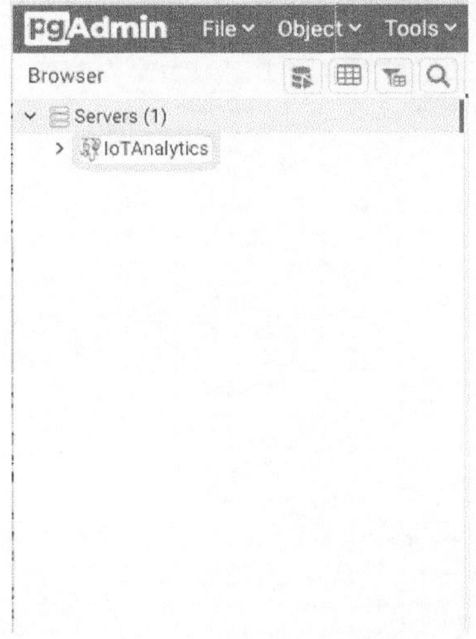

***Figure 5.3:** IoT Analytics Database Server*

2. In the **pgAdmin** screen, expand the node called **Servers** and right-click **IoTAnalytics** to choose **Create | Database....** as shown in the *Figure 5.4*:

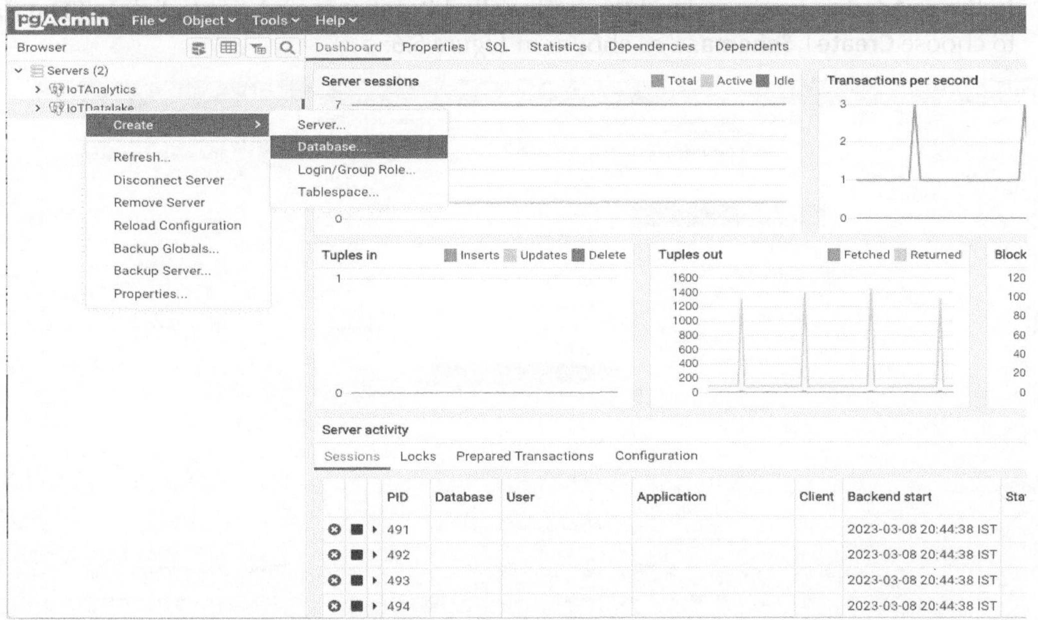

***Figure 5.4:** Creating database*

3. In the **Database** field, provide **IoTDatalake....** as shown in *Figure 5.5* and click **Save** button:

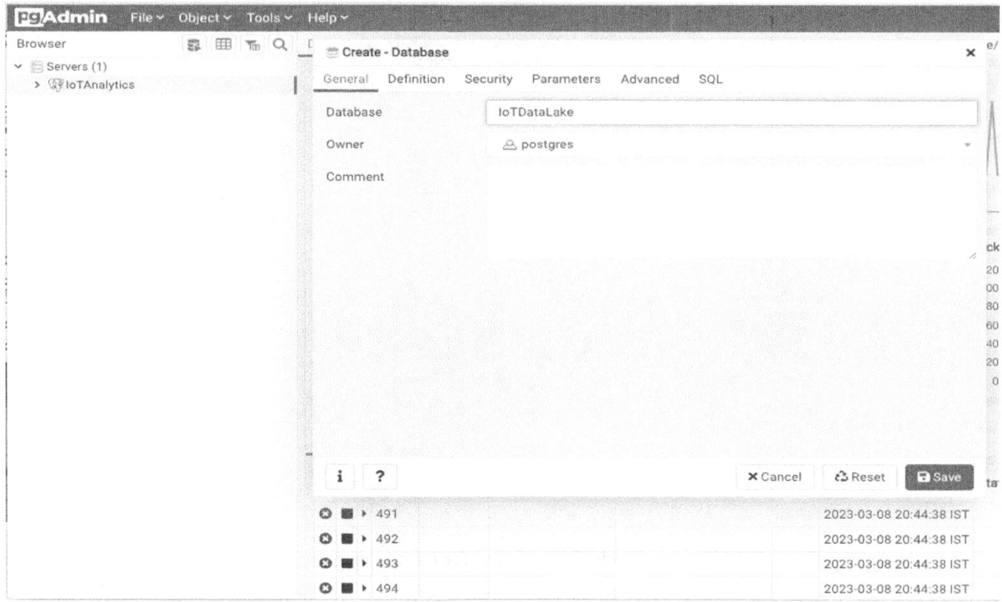

***Figure 5.5**: IoTDatalake database*

4. In the **pgAdmin** screen, expand the node called **Databases** and right-click **IoTDatalake** to choose **Create | Schema....** as shown in *Figure 5.6*:

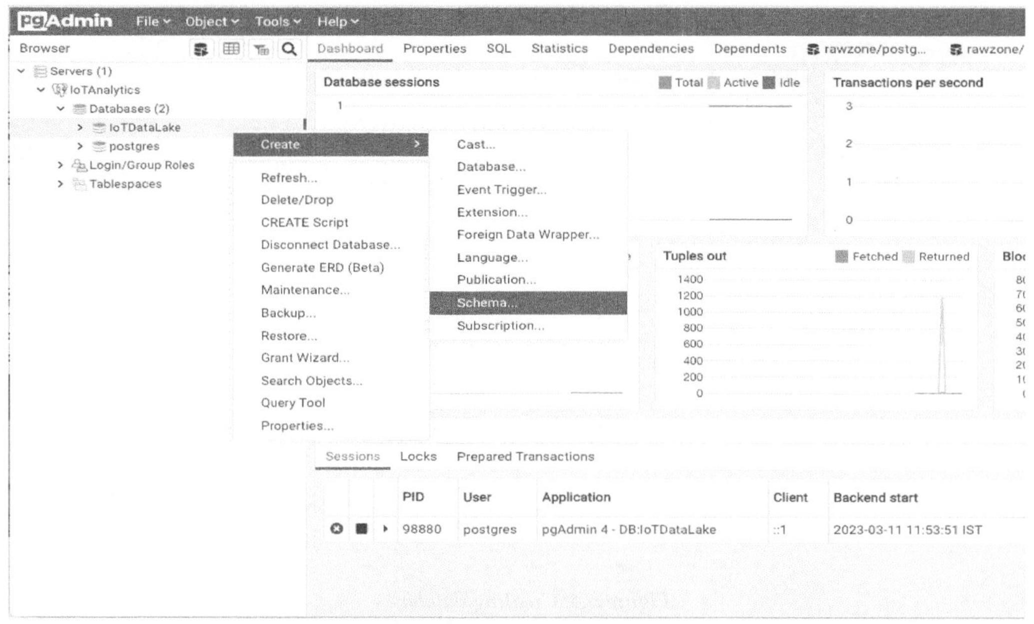

***Figure 5.6**: Creating schema.*

5. Provide **rawzone** in the **Name** field as shown in *Figure 5.7*:

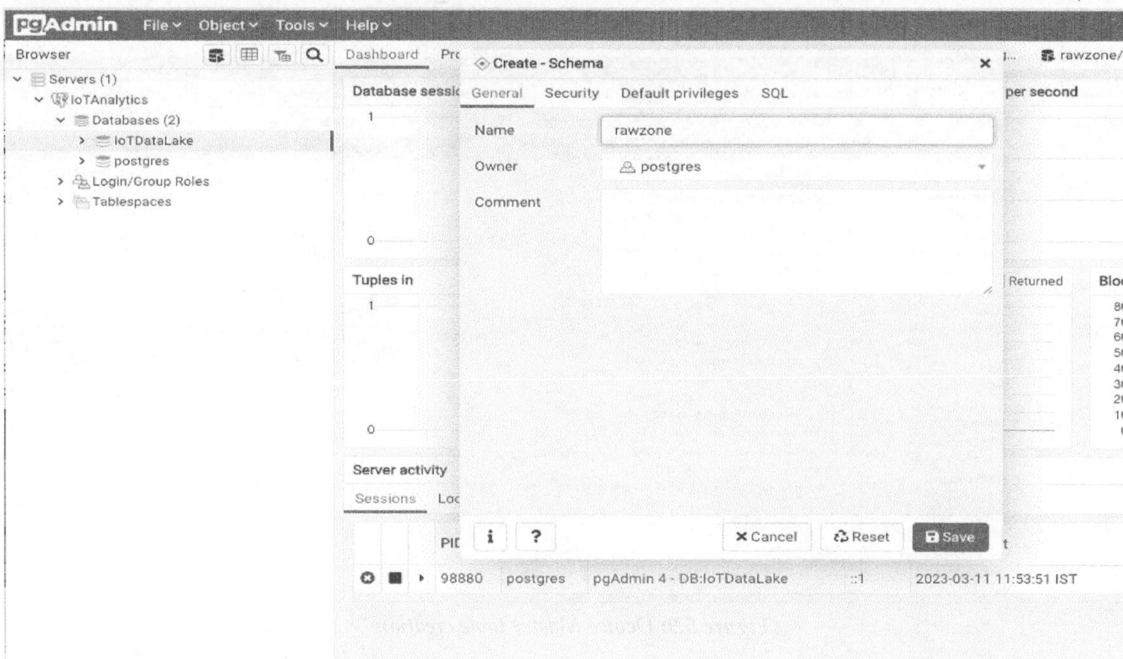

Figure 5.7: rawzone schema.

6. Click on the query tool button and create **ASSET_MASTER** table in the **rawzone** schema as shown *Figure 5.8*:

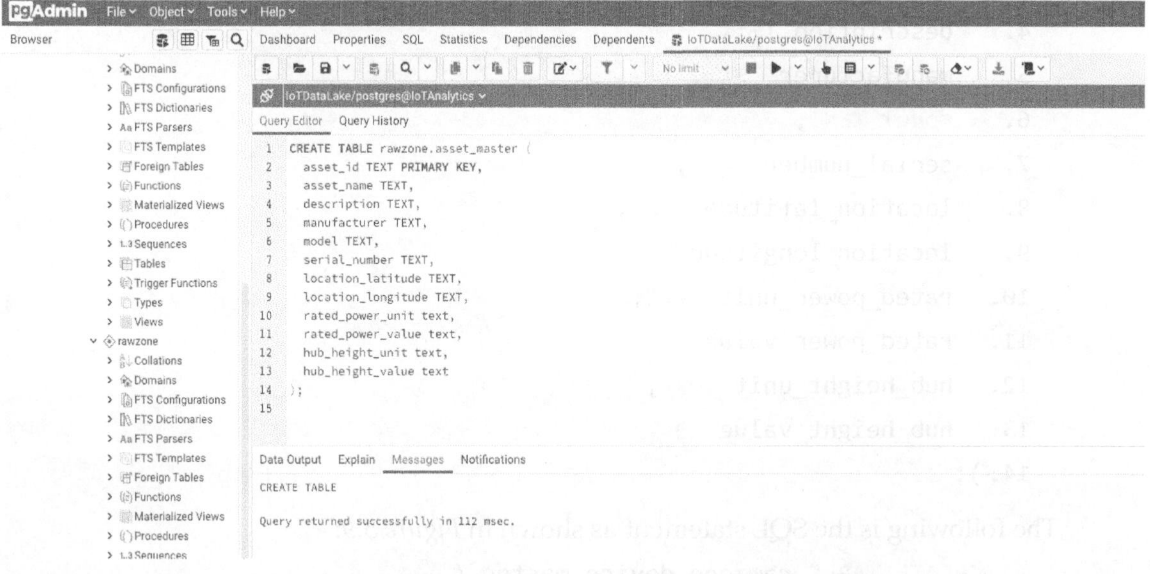

Figure 5.8: Asset Master table creation

7. Click on the **Query** tool button and create **DEVICE_MASTER** table in the **rawzone** schema as shown *Figure 5.9*:

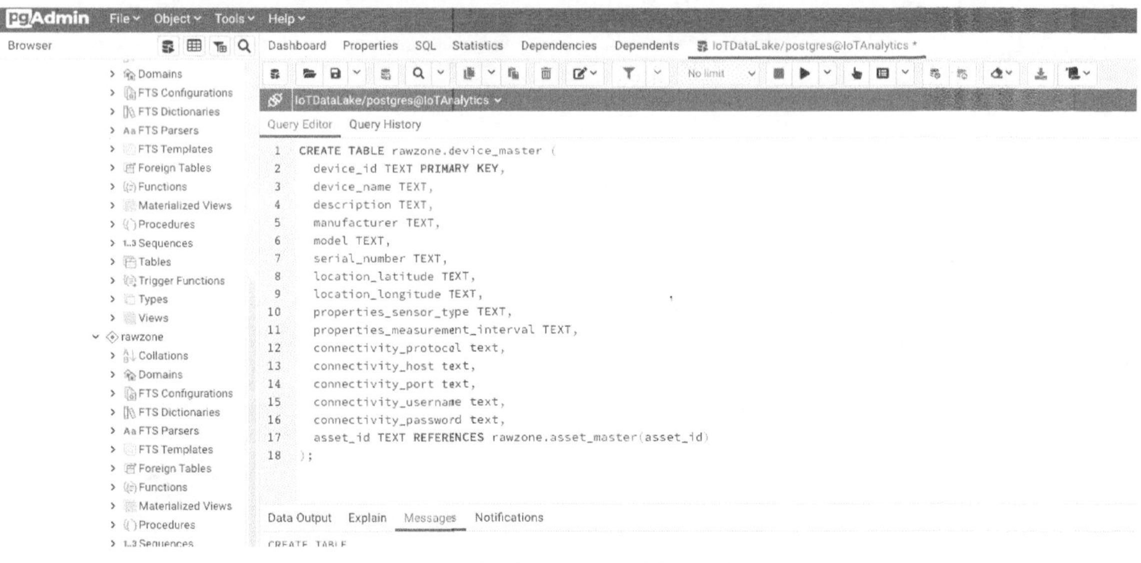

Figure 5.9: Device Master table creation

The following is the SQL statement as shown in *Figure 5.8*:

```
CREATE TABLE rawzone.asset_master (
    asset_id TEXT PRIMARY KEY,
    asset_name TEXT,
    description TEXT,
    manufacturer TEXT,
    model TEXT,
    serial_number TEXT,
    location_latitude TEXT,
    location_longitude TEXT,
    rated_power_unit text,
    rated_power_value text,
    hub_height_unit text,
    hub_height_value text
);
```

The following is the SQL statement as shown in *Figure 5.9*:

```
CREATE TABLE rawzone.device_master (
    device_id TEXT PRIMARY KEY,
```

```
device_name TEXT,
description TEXT,
manufacturer TEXT,
model TEXT,
serial_number TEXT,
location_latitude TEXT,
location_longitude TEXT,
properties_sensor_type TEXT,
properties_measurement_interval TEXT,
connectivity_protocol text,
connectivity_host text,
connectivity_port text,
connectivity_username text,
connectivity_password text,
asset_id TEXT REFERENCES rawzone.asset_master(asset_id)
);
```

8. Create multiple schemas under **IoTDatalake** database using query tool, for **curatezone**, **transformationzone**, **metriczone**, and **analyticszone** using the following commands:

```
CREATE SCHEMA curatedzone;
CREATE SCHEMA transformationzone;
CREATE SCHEMA metriczone;
CREATE SCHEMA analyticszone;
```

The data lake setup is now ready for setting up the real time streaming of IoT data.

Registration and Onboarding of Assets and Devices

Asset and device registration and onboarding is essential on the **Internet of Things (IoT)** ecosystem. It involves the identification, authentication, and authorization of devices and assets before they can be used in an IoT network.

Asset registration is registering and identifying a physical asset or product as an IoT device, which can be done by assigning a unique identifier. This identifier can be a serial number, MAC address, or other unique identifier that enables the device to be recognized and tracked within the IoT network.

Device registration, on the other hand, involves registering the device on the IoT platform, which enables the device to connect to the network and communicate with other devices and the cloud. Registration typically involves authentication and authorization mechanisms, such as certificates, tokens, or passwords.

The purpose of asset and device registration and onboarding is to establish a secure and reliable connection between IoT devices, the cloud, and other components of the IoT infrastructure. This ensures that only authorized devices can access the network, preventing unauthorized access and malicious attacks.

The process of asset and device registration and onboarding typically involves the following steps:

- **Device identification:** Each device is assigned a unique identifier, which enables it to be tracked and recognized within the IoT network.
- **Authentication:** The device is authenticated using certificates, tokens, or passwords, which verify its identity and ensure that it is authorized to access the network.
- **Provisioning:** The device is provisioned with the necessary configuration information, such as network settings and security parameters, which enable it to connect to the network and communicate with other devices and the cloud.
- **Onboarding:** The device is onboarded to the IoT platform, which enables it to be managed, monitored, and controlled remotely.

Overall, asset and device registration and onboarding are a critical process in the IoT ecosystem, which ensures the security and reliability of the network and enables devices to be seamlessly integrated into the IoT infrastructure.

The asset and device registration implementation process may vary depending on an organization's Asset Management and Operation process and the technologies and tools used. A typical implementation happens by getting the asset and device information in a standard format like JSON and maintain the information in database for tracking and analytical purpose.

The following are the implementation steps for asset and device registration using Python. In this implementation, we assume the JSON files with asset and device information is provided by the **Original Equipment Manufacturer (OEM)**:

1. Save the following JSON data in a files into your current working directory as **`wind_turbine_asset.json`**:

```
{
  "asset": {
    "id": "WT001",
    "name": "Wind Turbine 001",
    "description": "A wind turbine that generates electricity from wind energy",
    "manufacturer": "General Electric",
    "model": "GE 2.5-120",
    "serial_number": "12345",
```

```
    "location": {
      "latitude": "40.7128° N",
      "longitude": "74.0060° W"
    },
    "properties": {
      "rated_power": {
        "unit": "kW",
        "value": "2.5"
      },
      "hub_height": {
        "unit": "m",
        "value": "120"
      }
    }
  }
}
```

2. Save the following JSON data in a files into your current working directory as **wind_turbine_devices.json**:

```
{
  "devices": [
    {
      "id": "WT001_S01",
      "name": "Wind Turbine Sensor 01",
      "description": "A sensor for monitoring the wind speed and direction",
      "manufacturer": "General Electric",
      "model": "GE-P7",
      "serial_number": "67890",
      "asset_id":"WT001",
      "location": {
        "latitude": "40.7128° N",
        "longitude": "74.0060° W"
      },
```

```
    "properties": {
      "sensor_type": "Wind Speed and Direction",
      "measurement_interval": "1 minute"
    },
    "connectivity": {
      "protocol": "MQTT",
      "host": "mqtt.example.com",
      "port": "1883",
      "username": "mqtt_user",
      "password": "mqtt_password"
    }
  },
  {
    "id": "WT001_S02",
    "name": "Wind Turbine Sensor 02",
    "description": "A sensor for monitoring the RPM",
    "manufacturer": "General Electric",
    "model": "GE-P7",
    "serial_number": "12345",
    "asset_id":"WT001",
    "location": {
      "latitude": "40.7128° N",
      "longitude": "74.0060° W"
    },
    "properties": {
      "sensor_type": "RPM",
      "measurement_interval": "1 minute"
    },
    "connectivity": {
      "protocol": "MQTT",
      "host": "mqtt.example.com",
      "port": "1883",
      "username": "mqtt_user",
```

```
        "password": "mqtt_password"
      }
    },
    {
      "id": "WT001_S03",
      "name": "Wind Turbine Sensor 03",
      "description": "A sensor for monitoring the temperature",
      "manufacturer": "General Electric",
      "model": "GE-P7",
      "serial_number": "67890",
      "asset_id":"WT001",
      "location": {
        "latitude": "40.7128° N",
        "longitude": "74.0060° W"
      },
      "properties": {
        "sensor_type": "Temperature",
        "measurement_interval": "1 minute"
      },
      "connectivity": {
        "protocol": "MQTT",
        "host": "mqtt.example.com",
        "port": "1883",
        "username": "mqtt_user",
        "password": "mqtt_password"
      }
    },
    {
      "id": "WT001_S04",
      "name": "Wind Turbine Sensor 04",
      "description": "A sensor for monitoring the pressure",
      "manufacturer": "General Electric",
      "model": "GE-P7",
```

```
      "serial_number": "537890",
      "asset_id":"WT001",
      "location": {
        "latitude": "40.7128° N",
        "longitude": "74.0060° W"
      },
      "properties": {
        "sensor_type": "pressure",
        "measurement_interval": "1 minute"
      },
      "connectivity": {
        "protocol": "MQTT",
        "host": "mqtt.example.com",
        "port": "1883",
        "username": "mqtt_user",
        "password": "mqtt_password"
      }
    },
      {
          "id": "WT001_S05",
          "name": "Wind Turbine Sensor 05",
          "description": "A sensor for monitoring the energy output",
          "manufacturer": "General Electric",
          "model": "GE-P7",
          "serial_number": "2150377",
          "asset_id":"WT001",
          "location": {
            "latitude": "40.7128° N",
            "longitude": "74.0060° W"
          },
          "properties": {
            "sensor_type": "energy",
```

```
              "measurement_interval": "1 minute"
            },
            "connectivity": {
              "protocol": "MQTT",
              "host": "mqtt.example.com",
              "port": "1883",
              "username": "mqtt_user",
              "password": "mqtt_password"
            }
          }
        ]
      }
```

3. Save the following JSON data in a files into your current working directory as **gateway_reg.json**:

```
{
  "devices": [
{
  "device_id": "G97210100",
  "device_name": "Smart Gateway",
  "description": "An IoT gateway for collecting and transmitting sensor data",
  "manufacturer": "Teltra Tech",
  "model": "SG-100",
  "serial_number": "SG-100-1234",
  "location": {
        "latitude": "40.7128° N",
        "longitude": "74.0060° W"
    },
  "properties": {
        "measurement_interval": "1 minute"
    },
  "connectivity": {
        "protocol": "MQTT",
```

```
            "host": "mqtt.example.com",
            "port": "1883",
            "username": "mqtt_user",
            "password": "mqtt_password"
        },
    "asset_id": "WT001"
}
]
}
```

4. Execute the following Python program, which will insert the data into **asset_master** table in the postgresSQL. You can save the Python program as **asset_registration.py** on your current working directory to execute the same:

```
import json
import psycopg2
# Connect to the PostgreSQL database
conn = psycopg2.connect(
    host="localhost",
    database="IoTDataLake",
    user="postgres",
    password=""
)
# Open the JSON file and load the data
with open("wind_turbine_asset.json") as f:
    data = json.load(f)
# Extract the asset data from the JSON
asset_data = data["asset"]
# Insert the asset data into the asset_master table
cur = conn.cursor()
cur.execute(
    """
    INSERT INTO rawzone.asset_master (
        asset_id,
        asset_name,
```

```
            description,
            manufacturer,
            model,
            serial_number,
            location_latitude,
            location_longitude,
            rated_power_unit,
            rated_power_value,
            hub_height_unit,
            hub_height_value
        ) VALUES (%s, %s, %s, %s, %s, %s, %s, %s, %s, %s, %s, %s)
        """,
        (
            asset_data["id"],
            asset_data["name"],
            asset_data["description"],
            asset_data["manufacturer"],
            asset_data["model"],
            asset_data["serial_number"],
            asset_data["location"]["latitude"],
            asset_data["location"]["longitude"],
            asset_data["properties"]["rated_power"]["unit"],
            asset_data["properties"]["rated_power"]["value"],
            asset_data["properties"]["hub_height"]["unit"],
            asset_data["properties"]["hub_height"]["value"]
        )
)
conn.commit()
# Close the database connection
conn.close()
```

5. Execute the following Python program, to insert the data into **device_master** table in the postgresSQL. You can save the Python program as **device_registration.py** on your current working directory to execute the same:

```
import json
import psycopg2
```

```
# Connect to the PostgreSQL database
conn = psycopg2.connect(database="IoTDataLake", user="postgres", password="", host="localhost", port="5432")
# Open the JSON file and load the data
with open("wind_turbine_devices.json", "r") as f:
    data = json.load(f)
# Loop through the devices and insert them into the database
for device in data["devices"]:
    cur = conn.cursor()
    cur.execute(
        """
        INSERT INTO rawzone.device_master (device_id, device_name, description, manufacturer, model, serial_number, asset_id, location_latitude, location_longitude, properties_sensor_type, properties_measurement_interval, connectivity_protocol, connectivity_host, connectivity_port, connectivity_username, connectivity_password)
        VALUES (%s, %s, %s, %s, %s, %s, %s, %s, %s, %s, %s, %s, %s, %s, %s, %s);
        """,
        (
            device["id"],
            device["name"],
            device["description"],
            device["manufacturer"],
            device["model"],
            device["serial_number"],
            device["asset_id"],
            device["location"]["latitude"],
            device["location"]["longitude"],
            device["properties"]["sensor_type"],
            device["properties"]["measurement_interval"],
            device["connectivity"]["protocol"],
            device["connectivity"]["host"],
            device["connectivity"]["port"],
            device["connectivity"]["username"],
```

```
                device["connectivity"]["password"]
            )
        )
        conn.commit()
# Close the database connection
conn.close()
```

6. Execute the following Python program which will insert the data into **device_master** table in the postgresSQL. You can save the Python program as **gateway_reg.py** on your current working directory to execute the same:

```
import json
import psycopg2
# Connect to the PostgreSQL database
conn = psycopg2.connect(database="IoTDataLake", user="postgres", password="", host="localhost", port="5432")
# Open the JSON file and load the data
with open("gateway_reg.json", "r") as f:
    data = json.load(f)
# Loop through the devices and insert them into the database
for device in data["devices"]:
    cur = conn.cursor()
    cur.execute(
        """
        INSERT INTO rawzone.device_master (device_id, device_name, description, manufacturer, model, serial_number, asset_id, location_latitude, location_longitude, properties_measurement_interval, connectivity_protocol, connectivity_host, connectivity_port, connectivity_username, connectivity_password)
        VALUES (%s, %s, %s, %s, %s, %s, %s, %s, %s, %s, %s, %s, %s, %s, %s);
        """,
        (
            device["device_id"],
            device["device_name"],
            device["description"],
            device["manufacturer"],
```

```
                device["model"],
                device["serial_number"],
                device["asset_id"],
                device["location"]["latitude"],
                device["location"]["longitude"],
                device["properties"]["measurement_interval"],
                device["connectivity"]["protocol"],
                device["connectivity"]["host"],
                device["connectivity"]["port"],
                device["connectivity"]["username"],
                device["connectivity"]["password"]

        )
    )
    conn.commit()
# Close the database connection
conn.close()
```

7. Go to the query tool of **pgAdmin** and execute the following SQL SELECT statement, to check that the asset and device registration is successful:

```
select * from rawzone.asset_master
select * from rawzone.device_master
```

Building Data Pipeline to the Raw Zone

In *IoT data simulator Python implementation* section of *Chapter 4, Managing Data Pipeline and Cleaning,* we have performed a data simulation of IoT sensors for wind turbine equipment and published the simulated data in MQTT topic. The following is the same simulation program with minor modification on the header data to capture the **asset_id**:

```
import json
import random
import datetime
import time
import paho.mqtt.client as mqtt
# Function to generate simulated data
def generate_data():
```

```
    data = {}
    data['header'] = {}
    data['header']['asset_id'] = 'WT001',
    data['header']['serial_number'] = '12345'
    data['data'] = []
    current_time = datetime.datetime.now().replace(microsecond=0).
isoformat()
    data_point = {}
    data_point['rtc'] = current_time
    data_point['temp'] = round(random.uniform(20, 30), 2)
    data_point['pressure'] = round(random.uniform(1000, 1100), 2)
    data_point['wind_speed'] = round(random.uniform(5, 15), 2)
    data_point['rpm'] = random.randint(1200, 1800)
    data_point['energy_output'] = random.randint(800, 1200)
    data['data'].append(data_point)
    return json.dumps(data)
# MQTT client setup
client = mqtt.Client()
client.connect("localhost", 1883)  # Connect to Mosquitto MQTT broker
# Main program Loop to generate data every 1 second
while True:
    data = generate_data()
    print(data)
    client.publish("wind-turbine-data", data)
    time.sleep(1)
```

We will now send the preceding generated IoT data from MQTT topic to Kafka. The reason we need Kafka is explained in the beginning of IoT real-time data streaming section.

Before streaming the data to Kafka, ensure the Kafka zookeeper and server are up and running. To start the zookeeper, go to the Kafka installation folder using command line window and execute following command and do not close the command window:

```
bin/zookeeper-server-start.sh config/zookeeper.properties
```

To start the Kafka server, execute the following command from the Kafka installation directory using a new command line window and do not close existing command window:

```
bin/kafka-server-start.sh config/server.properties
```

Now, we are ready to setup a data stream from MQTT broker to Kafka topic. The following is the Python code for streaming the data from MQTT to Kafka topic:

```
from kafka import KafkaProducer
import paho.mqtt.client as mqtt
import json
# Define constants
MQTT_BROKER_HOST = "localhost"
MQTT_BROKER_PORT = 1883
MQTT_TOPIC = "wind-turbine-data"
KAFKA_BROKER_HOST = "localhost"
KAFKA_BROKER_PORT = 9092
KAFKA_TOPIC = "wind-turbine-data"
# Create a Kafka producer configuration
producer_config = {
    "bootstrap_servers": f"{KAFKA_BROKER_HOST}:{KAFKA_BROKER_PORT}",
    "value_serializer": lambda x: json.dumps(x).encode('utf-8')
}
# Create a Kafka producer instance
producer = KafkaProducer(**producer_config)
# Define the MQTT client callbacks
def on_connect(client, userdata, flags, rc):
    print(f"Connected to MQTT broker with result code {rc}")
    # Subscribe to the MQTT topic
    client.subscribe(MQTT_TOPIC)
def on_message(client, userdata, msg):
    # Parse the JSON message
    json_data = json.loads(msg.payload.decode())
    # Print the received message
    print(f"Received message: {json_data}")
    # Send the message to Kafka topic
    producer.send(KAFKA_TOPIC, json_data)
def on_disconnect(client, userdata, rc):
    if rc != 0:
```

```
    print(f"Disconnected from MQTT broker with result code {rc}")
# Create a MQTT client instance
client = mqtt.Client()
# Set the MQTT client callbacks
client.on_connect = on_connect
client.on_message = on_message
client.on_disconnect = on_disconnect
# Connect to the MQTT broker
client.connect(MQTT_BROKER_HOST, MQTT_BROKER_PORT)
# Start the MQTT loop
client.loop_forever()
```

The preceding program publishes the data from MQTT wind-turbine-data to Kafka topic with the same name. We are finally ready to setup a data stream which can insert data into rawzone of the data lake we built earlier in the subsection *setting up data lake* of section *IoT real time data streaming*.

The following is the Python program which automatically creates SQL table to insert the data from the Kafka topic:

```
from kafka import KafkaConsumer
import psycopg2
import json
# Set up Kafka consumer
consumer = KafkaConsumer('wind-turbine-data', bootstrap_servers=['localhost:9092'])
# Set up Postgres connection
conn = psycopg2.connect(
    host="localhost",
    database="IoTDataLake",
    user="postgres",
    password=""
)
cur = conn.cursor()
# Create table if not exists
cur.execute('''
    CREATE TABLE IF NOT EXISTS rawzone.r_wind_turbine_data (
```

```
        id SERIAL PRIMARY KEY,
        rtc TIMESTAMP,
        wind_speed FLOAT,
        rpm FLOAT,
        temp FLOAT,
        pressure FLOAT,
        energy_output FLOAT,
        asset_id VARCHAR(20),
        serial_number VARCHAR(20)
    )
''')
conn.commit()
# Read data from Kafka topic and insert into Postgres
for message in consumer:
    data = json.loads(message.value.decode('utf-8'))
    header = data['header']
    asset_id = header['asset_id'][0]
    serial_number = header['serial_number']
    data = data['data'][0]
    rtc = data['rtc']
    wind_speed = data['wind_speed']
    rpm = data['rpm']
    temp = data['temp']
    pressure = data['pressure']
    energy_output = data['energy_output']
    cur.execute(f"INSERT INTO rawzone.r_wind_turbine_data (rtc, wind_speed, rpm, temp, pressure, energy_output, asset_id, serial_number) VALUES ('{rtc}', {wind_speed}, {rpm}, {temp}, {pressure}, {energy_output}, '{asset_id}', '{serial_number}')")
    conn.commit()
    print(f"Inserted data: {data}")
# Close Postgres connection
cur.close()
conn.close()
```

The preceding program read data from the Kafka topic. The code extracts the relevant data from the JSON payload for each message read from Kafka, including the asset ID, serial number, timestamp, wind speed, RPM, temperature, pressure, and energy output. The code then inserts this data into the PostgreSQL database using an SQL query, and the database connection is committed. If the table for storing the raw table is unavailable, the program automatically creates the table **r_wind_turbine_data** in the **rawzone** schema to ingest the data from Kafka.

Curated Zone of the Data Lake

The curated zone of the data lake plays a critical role in performing necessary clean-up and transformation of raw data stored in the raw zone of the data lake. The purpose of the curated zone is to ensure that this data is cleaned, transformed, high quality, and ready for analysis. This will help the data analyst and data scientist to make necessary analysis quickly without doing many data engineering tasks.

Let us use the data cleaning engine we built in *Chapter 4, Managing Data Pipeline and Cleaning* to consume data from the raw zone of the data lake and apply data cleansing methods to clean and insert the data into the curated zone of the data lake.

Building Data Cleaning Engine

The data cleaning tasks can be grouped as a module in Python. Various data cleaning tasks can be applied to the raw data received from the IoT devices:

```
import json
import numpy as np
import pandas as pd

class DataCleaningEngine:
    def __init__(self):
        pass

    def clean_data(self, df):
        # Drop duplicate rows
        df = df.drop_duplicates()
        # Drop rows with missing values
        df = df.dropna()
        # # Convert string timestamps to datetime format
        df['rtc'] = pd.to_datetime(df['rtc'])
```

```
        # # # Clean data using additional rules
        # # # Remove leading/trailing whitespaces from all columns
        df = df.apply(lambda x: x.str.strip() if x.dtype == "object" else x)
        # # # Remove special characters from column names
        df.columns = df.columns.str.replace('[^a-zA-Z0-9_]', '')
        # # # Convert all string values to lowercase
        df = df.apply(lambda x: x.str.lower() if x.dtype == "object" else x)
        # # # drop rows which are empty
        df = df.dropna()
        # # # # Remove rows with data outside a certain range. They will create noise due to IoT Sensor malfunction
        df = df[(df['temp'] >= 10) & (df['temp'] <= 150)]
        df = df[(df['pressure'] >= 800) & (df['pressure'] <= 1200)]
        df = df[(df['wind_speed'] >= 0) & (df['wind_speed'] <= 200)]
        df = df[(df['rpm'] >= 0) & (df['rpm'] <= 3000)]
        df = df[(df['energy_output'] >= 0) & (df['energy_output'] <= 2000)]
        return df
```

This preceding Python program defines a class called **DataCleaningEngine**, which has a method called **clean_data**. This method uses pandas **dataframe df** as an argument and applies various data cleaning operations. Save the file as **data_cleaning_engine.py** on your current working directory to apply the required data cleaning methods explained below:

- The first operation drops any duplicate rows in the dataframe using the **drop_duplicates** method. The second operation drops any rows containing missing values using the **dropna** method.
- The second operation converts the **rtc** column in the dataframe from a string timestamp to a datetime format using the **pd.to_datetime** method.
- The third operation applies additional cleaning rules to the dataframe. It removes leading and trailing whitespaces from all columns using the apply method and a lambda function. It removes any special characters from column names using the **str.replace** method. It converts all string values in the **dataframe** to lowercase using another lambda function.
- The fourth operation again drops any rows containing empty values using the **dropna** method.

- Finally, the last operation removes any rows containing data outside certain ranges. This is done to remove noise due to IoT sensor malfunction. The range for each column is specified using conditional statements.

The cleaned **dataframe** is then returned from the **clean_data** method. This program can be useful in cleaning and pre-processing raw data before further analysis or modelling. Let us now use this data cleaning engine for creating a data pipeline to the curated zone of the data lake.

Data Pipeline to Curated Zone

We can now setup a data pipeline to the curated zone of the data lake which takes the raw data and perform the data cleaning tasks defined in the data cleaning engine. The resulted data is inserted into a table **c_wind_turbine_data** on the **curatedzone** schema.

The following is the Python program for performing continuous cleanup of data from the raw table and insert the curated data into the curated zone:

```
import psycopg2
import pandas as pd
from data_cleaning_engine import DataCleaningEngine
from apscheduler.schedulers.background import BackgroundScheduler
from datetime import datetime, timedelta
from data_cleaning_engine import DataCleaningEngine
def clean_data():
    # Connect to the database
    conn = psycopg2.connect(
        host="localhost",
        database="IoTDataLake",
        user="postgres",
        password=""
    )
    # Initialize last run timestamp
    last_run_timestamp = '2023-03-11 11:39:35.922405'  # Replace with code to read the timestamp
    # Read the data inserted after the last run from the raw data table
    cur = conn.cursor()
    # Create the last run timetamp table if it doesn't exist
    cur.execute('''
        CREATE TABLE IF NOT EXISTS curatedzone.last_run_timestamp (
```

```
            rtc timestamp without time zone,
            job_id SERIAL PRIMARY KEY
            )
    ‹››)
    #select the latest record with the recent timestamp
    cur.execute("SELECT rtc FROM curatedzone.last_run_
timestamp ORDER BY job_id DESC LIMIT 1")
    result_timestamp = cur.fetchone()
    if result_timestamp is not None:
        last_run_timestamp = result_timestamp[0]
    print("last_run_timestamp ", last_run_timestamp)
    cur.execute("SELECT * FROM rawzone.r_wind_turbine_
data WHERE rtc > %s", (last_run_timestamp,))
    data = pd.DataFrame(cur.fetchall(), columns=['id','rtc', 'wind_speed',
'rpm', 'temp', 'pressure', 'energy_output', 'asset_id', 'serial_number'])
    print("data " , data)
    # Clean the data using the DataCleaningEngine
    clean_engine = DataCleaningEngine()
    cleaned_data = clean_engine.clean_data(data)
    print(cleaned_data)
    # Create the c_wind_turbine_data table if it doesn't exist
    cur.execute('''
        CREATE TABLE IF NOT EXISTS curatedzone.c_wind_turbine_data (
            id integer PRIMARY KEY,
            rtc TIMESTAMP,
            wind_speed FLOAT,
            rpm FLOAT,
            temp FLOAT,
            pressure FLOAT,
            energy_output FLOAT,
            asset_id VARCHAR(20),
            serial_number VARCHAR(20)
        )
    ‹››)
```

```
    # Insert the cleaned data into the c_wind_turbine_data table
    for i, row in cleaned_data.iterrows():
        last_timestamp = row['rtc']
        cur.execute("""INSERT INTO curatedzone.c_wind_turbine_
data (id, rtc, wind_speed, rpm, temp, pressure, energy_output, asset_
id, serial_number) VALUES (%s ,%s, %s, %s, %s, %s, %s, %s, %s)
            """, (row['id'], row['rtc'], row['wind_
speed'], row['rpm'], row['temp'],row['pressure'],row['energy_out-
put'],row['asset_id'],row['serial_number']))
        conn.commit()
    # Update the timestamp of the last run to the current time
    cur.execute("INSERT INTO curatedzone.last_run_timestamp (rtc) VALUES
(%s) ON CONFLICT (job_id) DO UPDATE SET rtc = EXCLUDED.rtc", (datetime.now(),))
    conn.commit()
# Create a scheduler that runs the clean_data function every 1 minute
scheduler = BackgroundScheduler()
scheduler.add_job(clean_data, 'interval', minutes=1)
# Start the scheduler
scheduler.start()
# Keep the program running
while True:
    pass
```

The preceding Python program is designed to clean and curate data from a wind turbine sensor system. It uses the PostgreSQL database to store raw and cleaned data. The program connects to the database and reads the last run timestamp from the **curatedzone.last_run_timestamp** table. Then, it selects all the data from the **rawzone.r_wind_turbine_data** table that was inserted after the last run timestamp. The selected data is then cleaned using a data cleaning engine- **DataCleaningEngine**. The cleaned data is inserted into the **curatedzone.c_wind_turbine_data** table. Finally, the last run timestamp is updated in the **curatedzone.last_run_timestamp** table to the current time.

The program also uses the **apscheduler** module to schedule the **clean_data** function to run every 1 minute in the background. The program keeps running in a loop to ensure the scheduler continues running.

Transformation Zone of the Data Lake

The transformation zone of the data lake plays a crucial role in preparing the raw data collected from IoT devices for analytics. We will apply various transformation methods to standardize, smooth and convert data for quicker visualization and data analysis by business analyst and data scientist.

The objective of the transformation zone is to ensure that the data is stored for immediate access for necessary analytics such as predictive and prescriptive analytics to drive business insights and optimize operations.

We will build a data transformation engine like the one we built on section Data Transformation rule Implementation in Python of *Chapter 4, Managing Data Pipeline and Cleaning*. But this time, the data transformation engine will take curated data as a input and continuously transform the data to ingest the transformed data in the transformation zone of the data lake. Let us now investigate the transformation engine.

Building Data Transformation Engine

The following is the transformation engine code in Python, where we apply series of data transformation rules to the input data from the curated zone and insert the transformed data into the transformation zone of the data lake in **t_wind_turbine_data** table:

```
import pandas as pd
import numpy as np
from scipy.signal import savgol_filter
class DataTransformationEngine:
    def __init__(self):
        pass
    def transform_data(self, df):
        # Check if all required columns are present in the DataFrame
        required_cols = ['rtc', 'temp', 'pressure', 'wind_speed', 'rpm', 'energy_output']
        missing_cols = set(required_cols) - set(df.columns)
        if missing_cols:
            raise KeyError(f"{missing_cols} not in index")
        # # # Normalize the value column
        df['wind_speed'] = (df['wind_speed'] - df['wind_speed'].mean()) / df['wind_speed'].std()
        df['temp'] = (df['temp'] - df['temp'].mean()) / df['temp'].std()
        # # Remove columns with low variance
        numeric_cols = df.select_dtypes(include=np.number).columns
        variances = df[numeric_cols].var()
        cols_to_drop = variances[variances < 0.01].index
```

```
        df = df.drop(cols_to_drop, axis=1)
        # Create a new column 'energy_output_per_rpm' which represents energy output per rpm
        df['energy_output_per_rpm'] = df['energy_output'] / df['rpm']
        # Apply a rolling mean to the 'energy_output_per_rpm' column
        df['energy_output_per_rpm'] = df['energy_output_per_rpm'].rolling(window=3).mean()
        # Create a new column 'pressure_temp_ratio' which represents the ratio of pressure to temperature
        df['pressure_temp_ratio'] = df['pressure'] / df['temp']
        # Apply a rolling median to the 'pressure_temp_ratio' column
        df['pressure_temp_ratio'] = df['pressure_temp_ratio'].rolling(window=3).median()
        #Unit conversion for pressure: Convert the pressure values from Pascals (Pa) to kilopascals (kPa) and add a new column pressure_kPa to the DataFrame.
        df['pressure_kPa'] = df['pressure'] / 1000
        #Unit conversion for energy_output: Convert the energy output values from joules (J) to kilowatt-hours (kWh) and add a new column energy_output_kWh to the DataFrame.
        df['energy_output_kWh'] = df['energy_output'] / 3600000
        #Format conversion for pressure: Convert the pressure values to a string with two decimal places and add a new column pressure_str to the DataFrame.
        df['pressure_str'] = df['pressure'].apply(lambda x: '{:.2f}'.format(x))
        return df
```

This Python program is a data transformation engine that takes a dataset in the form of a **DataFrame** as input and applies several transformations to it. The purpose of these transformations is to pre-process the data to be ready for analysis or modeling.

The program first checks if all the required columns are in the **DataFrame**. The program raises an error if any of the required columns are missing.

The program then normalizes two columns, **wind_speed** and **temp**, by subtracting their means and dividing by their standard deviations. It then drops columns with low variance.

Next, the program creates two new columns: **energy_output_per_rpm**, calculated by dividing the **energy_output** column by the rpm column, and **pressure_temp_ratio**, calculated by dividing the pressure column by the temp column.

The program then applies rolling means to the **energy_output_per_rpm** column and rolling medians to the **pressure_temp_ratio** column. It converts the pressure values from Pascals to kilopascals and adds a new column **pressure_kPa** to the DataFrame. Similarly, it converts the energy output values from joules to kilowatt-hours and adds a new column **energy_output_kWh** to the **DataFrame**.

Finally, the program converts the pressure values to strings with two decimal places and adds a new column **pressure_str** to the **DataFrame**. The program then returns the transformed **DataFrame** as output.

Data Pipeline to Transformation Zone

After building the data transformation engine we can use the same for building a data pipeline to stream the data into transformation zone of the data lake for the **t_wind_turbine_data** table. The following is the python program which show the data pipeline implementation for the data lake:

```
import psycopg2
import pandas as pd
from DataTransformationEngine import DataTransformationEngine
from apscheduler.schedulers.background import BackgroundScheduler
from datetime import datetime, timedelta

def transform_data():
    # Connect to the database
    conn = psycopg2.connect(
        host="localhost",
        database="IoTDataLake",
        user="postgres",
        password=""
    )
        # Assign the timestamp
    last_run_timestamp = '2023-03-11 11:39:35.922405'  # Replace with code to read the timestamp
    # Read the data inserted after the last run from the curated data table
    cur = conn.cursor()
    # Create the last_run_timestamp table if it doesn't exist
    cur.execute('''
```

```
        CREATE TABLE IF NOT EXISTS transformationzone.last_run_timestamp (
            rtc timestamp without time zone,
            job_id SERIAL PRIMARY KEY
            )
    ‹››)
    cur.execute("SELECT rtc FROM transformationzone.last_run_timestamp ORDER BY job_id DESC LIMIT 1")
    result_timestamp = cur.fetchone()
    if result_timestamp is not None:
        last_run_timestamp = result_timestamp[0]
    print("last_run_timestamp ", last_run_timestamp)
    cur = conn.cursor()
    cur.execute("SELECT * FROM curatedzone.c_wind_turbine_data WHERE rtc > %s", (last_run_timestamp,))
    data = pd.DataFrame(cur.fetchall(), columns=['id','rtc', 'wind_speed', 'rpm', 'temp', 'pressure', 'energy_output', 'asset_id', 'serial_number'])
    data_transformer = DataTransformationEngine()
    transformed_data = data_transformer.transform_data(data)
    print(transformed_data.columns)
    # Create the t_wind_turbine_data table if it doesn't exist
    cur.execute('''
        CREATE TABLE IF NOT EXISTS transformationzone.t_wind_turbine_data (
            id integer PRIMARY KEY,
            rtc TIMESTAMP,
            wind_speed FLOAT,
            rpm FLOAT,
            temp FLOAT,
            pressure FLOAT,
            energy_output FLOAT,
            asset_id VARCHAR(20),
            serial_number VARCHAR(20),
            energy_output_per_rpm FLOAT,
```

```
            pressure_temp_ratio FLOAT,
            pressure_kPa FLOAT,
            energy_output_kWh FLOAT,
            pressure_str varchar(80)
        )
    ‹››)
    # Insert the transformed data into the t_wind_turbine_data table in the transformation zone of the data lake
    for i, row in transformed_data.iterrows():
        cur.execute("""INSERT INTO transformationzone.t_wind_turbine_data (id, rtc, wind_speed, rpm, temp, pressure, energy_output, asset_id, serial_number,
            energy_output_per_rpm, pressure_temp_ratio, pressure_kPa, energy_output_kWh, pressure_str) VALUES (%s ,%s, %s, %s, %s, %s, %s , %s, %s, %s, %s, %s, %s, %s)
            """, (row['id'], row['rtc'], row['wind_speed'], row['rpm'], row['temp'],row['pressure'],row['energy_output'],row['asset_id'],row['serial_number'],
                row['energy_output_per_rpm'], row['pressure_temp_ratio'], row['pressure_kPa'], row['energy_output_kWh'], row['pressure_str'] ))
        conn.commit()
    # Update the timestamp of the last run to the current time
    cur.execute("INSERT INTO transformationzone.last_run_timestamp (rtc) VALUES (%s) ON CONFLICT (job_id) DO UPDATE SET rtc = EXCLUDED.rtc", (datetime.now(),))
    conn.commit()
# Create a scheduler that runs the transform_data function every 1 minute
scheduler = BackgroundScheduler()
scheduler.add_job(transform_data, 'interval', minutes=1)
# Start the scheduler
scheduler.start()
# Keep the program running
while True:
    pass
```

This preceding program is designed to transform and insert data from a curated data table into a new table in a transformation zone of a data lake. The program first connects to a database using **psycopg2** library, then sets a timestamp for the last run of the transformation process. The data inserted after the last run is then read from the curated data table, and this data is transformed using a **DataTransformationEngine** object, which contains a **transform_data** method. The transformed data is then inserted into a new table, **t_wind_turbine_data**, in the transformation zone of the data lake.

The program uses a **BackgroundScheduler** object to schedule the **transform_data** method to run every minute, and a while true loop is used to keep the program running indefinitely. The program also checks whether certain tables already exist in the database and creates them if they do not. Finally, the program updates the timestamp of the last run to the current time after every transformation process.

Building KPIs and Metrics

In IoT Analytics, the metric zone is a crucial component of a data lake. Its purpose is to store and analyze KPIs and metrics that are essential for monitoring and optimizing the performance of IoT devices and systems. The metric zone plays a critical role in real-time monitoring and identifying opportunities for improvement.

The metric zone centralizes the storage and analysis of KPIs and metrics, enabling stakeholders to make data-driven decisions that can help optimize operations and reduce costs. This zone typically contains KPIs, metrics, and thresholds. KPIs are used to measure the performance of IoT systems and processes, while metrics are specific measures used to calculate KPIs. Thresholds are established to determine acceptable levels for each KPI and trigger alerts or actions when performance falls outside these levels.

Building KPIs and metrics for IoT data requires several steps, including defining business objectives, identifying relevant data sources, determining calculation methods, and setting thresholds. Monitoring and refining KPIs and metrics are crucial to ensure they align with business objectives.

In summary, the metric zone is a vital component of a data lake in the context of IoT Analytics. It enables organizations to gain valuable insights into the performance of their IoT initiatives and optimize their operations accordingly. By building KPIs and metrics in this zone, stakeholders can make data-driven decisions that help reduce costs and improve customer experiences.

To implement the data pipeline for the metric zone of the data lake, we will first follow the design of building metric engine similar to data cleaning and transformation engine. The purpose of the metric engine is to take the curated data as an input and calculate metrics.

After building the metric engine, we will implement a data pipeline to which uses the metric engine and calculate metrics to store the results in the metric zone of the data lake.

Building Metric Engine

The following is a Python program that calculates various metrics related to wind turbine operations. It takes in data about the performance of a wind turbine (stored in the curated zone of the data lake) and calculates metrics such as the turbine's capacity factor, mean time between failures, and mean time to repair. It also calculates various statistics related to the turbine's performance such as the maximum and minimum wind speed, average RPM, and average temperature. The program returns a new **DataFrame** containing all the calculated metrics and statistics.

```
import pandas as pd
class MetricEngine:
    def __init__(self, rated_capacity=2000):
        self.rated_capacity = rated_capacity # kW
    def calculate_metrics(self, df):
        # Calculate the metrics
        if len(df) > 1:
            total_runtime = (df["rtc"].iloc[-1] - df["rtc"].iloc[0]).total_seconds() / 3600 # hours
        else:
            total_runtime = 0
        downtime = 0 # hours
        num_failures = 0
        for index, row in df.iterrows():
            if pd.isna(row["energy_output"]):
                downtime += 10 / 60 # Assuming 10 mins to repair
                num_failures += 1
            elif row["energy_output"] == 0:
                downtime += 10 # Assuming 10 hours to repair
                num_failures += 1
        if num_failures > 0:
            mtbf = total_runtime / num_failures
            mttr = downtime / num_failures
        else:
            mtbf = 0
            mttr = 0
        capacity_factor = (df["energy_output"].
```

```
sum() / (24 * 1000 * 4.32 * self.rated_capacity)) * 100
        if len(df['rtc']) > 0:
            hours_in_period = (max(df['rtc']) - min(df['rtc'])).total_seconds() / 3600
        else:
            hours_in_period = 0
        max_wind_speed = df['wind_speed'].max()
        min_wind_speed = df['wind_speed'].min()
        avg_wind_speed = df['wind_speed'].mean()
        max_rpm = df['rpm'].max()
        min_rpm = df['rpm'].min()
        avg_rpm = df['rpm'].mean()
        max_temperature = df['temp'].max()
        min_temperature = df['temp'].min()
        avg_temperature = df['temp'].mean()
        max_pressure = df[‘pressure’].max()
        min_pressure = df[‘pressure’].min()
        avg_pressure = df['pressure'].mean()
        max_energy_output = df['energy_output'].max()
        actual_energy_output = df['energy_output'].sum()
        if len(df) > 0:
            df_new = pd.DataFrame({
                'capacity_factor': [capacity_factor],
                'mtbf': [mtbf],
                'mttr': [mttr],
                'downtime': [downtime],
                'max_wind_speed': [max_wind_speed],
                'min_wind_speed': [min_wind_speed],
                'avg_wind_speed': [avg_wind_speed],
                'max_rpm': [max_rpm],
                'min_rpm': [min_rpm],
                'avg_rpm': [avg_rpm],
                'max_temperature': [max_temperature],
```

```
                'min_temperature': [min_temperature],
                'avg_temperature': [avg_temperature],
                'max_pressure': [max_pressure],
                'min_pressure': [min_pressure],
                'avg_pressure': [avg_pressure],
                'max_energy_output': [max_energy_output],
                'actual_energy_output': [actual_energy_output],
                'hours_in_period': [hours_in_period]
            })
        else:
            df_new = pd.DataFrame()
        return df_new
```

The preceding Python program defines a module called **MetricEngine** that calculates various metrics from a Pandas **DataFrame**. Save the python file on your working directory as **MetricEngine.py**.

The **calculate_metrics** method takes a Pandas **DataFrame** as input and calculates various metrics based on the data in the **DataFrame**.

Metrics include total runtime, downtime, number of failures, mean time between failures, mean time to repair, capacity factor, hours in period, and various other variables.

The calculated metrics are returned in a new **DataFrame**.

Data Pipline to Metric Zone

Let us create a python program that uses the metric engine to process the wind turbine's curated data and insert the resulting metric data into the metric zone of the data lake. The metrics can be used immediately for building dashboards and reports.

The following is the Python program:

```
import psycopg2
import pandas as pd
from MetricEngine import MetricEngine
from apscheduler.schedulers.background import BackgroundScheduler
from datetime import datetime, timedelta
def calculate_metrics_data():
    # Connect to the database
    conn = psycopg2.connect(
```

```
        host="localhost",
        database="IoTDataLake",
        user="postgres",
        password=""
    )
        # Read the timestamp of the last run from a separate table or file
    last_run_timestamp = '2023-03-11 11:39:35.922405'  # Replace with code to read the timestamp
    cur = conn.cursor()
    # Create the last run timetamp table if it doesn't exist
    cur.execute('''
        CREATE TABLE IF NOT EXISTS metriczone.last_run_timestamp (

            rtc timestamp without time zone,
            job_id SERIAL PRIMARY KEY
            )
    ‹››)
    #select the latest record with the recent timestamp
    cur.execute("SELECT rtc FROM metriczone.last_run_timestamp ORDER BY job_id DESC LIMIT 1")
    result_timestamp = cur.fetchone()
    if result_timestamp is not None:
        last_run_timestamp = result_timestamp[0]
    print("last_run_timestamp ", last_run_timestamp)
    cur = conn.cursor()
    cur.execute("SELECT * FROM curatedzone.c_wind_turbine_data WHERE rtc > %s", (last_run_timestamp,))
    data = pd.DataFrame(cur.fetchall(), columns=['id','rtc', 'wind_speed', 'rpm', 'temp', 'pressure', 'energy_output', 'asset_id', 'serial_number'])
    # Calculate the metrics using the MetricEngine
    data_for_metrics = MetricEngine()
    metric_data = data_for_metrics.calculate_metrics(data)
    # Create the m_wind_turbine_metrics table if it doesn't exist
    cur.execute('''
```

```
        CREATE TABLE IF NOT EXISTS metriczone.m_wind_turbine_metrics (
            id serial PRIMARY KEY,
            capacity_factor FLOAT,
            max_wind_speed FLOAT,
            min_wind_speed FLOAT,
            avg_wind_speed FLOAT,
            max_rpm FLOAT,
            min_rpm FLOAT,
            avg_rpm FLOAT,
            max_temperature FLOAT,
            min_temperature FLOAT,
            max_pressure FLOAT,
            min_pressure FLOAT,
            avg_pressure FLOAT,
            actual_energy_output FLOAT,
            max_energy_output FLOAT,
            mtbf FLOAT,
            mttr FLOAT,
            downtime FLOAT,
            hours_in_period FLOAT
        )
    ‹››)
    # Insert the calculated metric data into the m_wind_turbine_metrics table
    for i, row in metric_data.iterrows():
        cur.execute("""INSERT INTO metriczone.m_wind_turbine_metrics (capacity_factor, mtbf, mttr, downtime, max_wind_speed, min_wind_speed, avg_wind_speed,
            max_rpm, min_rpm, avg_rpm, max_temperature, min_temperature, max_pressure, min_pressure, avg_pressure, max_energy_output, actual_energy_output,
            hours_in_period ) VALUES (%s, %s, %s, %s, %s, %s,  %s, %s,%s, %s, %s, %s, %s, %s, %s, %s,%s, %s)
            """, (row['capacity_factor'], row['mtbf'], row['mttr'],row['downtime'],row['max_wind_speed'],row['min_wind_speed'],row['avg_wind_speed'],row['max_rpm'],
                row['min_rpm'],row['avg_rpm'],row['max_temperature'],row['min_temperature'],row['max_pressure'],row['min_
```

```
pressure'],row['avg_pressure'],
            row['max_energy_output'],row['actual_energy_output'], row['hours_in_period']))
        conn.commit()
    # Update the timestamp of the last run to the current time
    cur.execute("INSERT INTO metriczone.last_run_timestamp (rtc) VALUES (%s) ON CONFLICT (job_id) DO UPDATE SET rtc = EXCLUDED.rtc", (datetime.now(),))
    conn.commit()
calculate_metrics_data()
```

This preceding Python program is to calculate metrics for wind turbine data and insert the calculated metric data into a PostgreSQL database. The program first connects to the database and reads the timestamp of the last run from a separate table or file. If no such timestamp exists, it defaults to a hardcoded value. The program selects all records with a timestamp greater than the last run timestamp from the **`curatedzone.c_wind_turbine_data`** table and creates a **`Pandas DataFrame`** with the selected data. Using the **`MetricEngine`**, the program calculates the required metrics and stores the results in a new Pandas **`DataFrame`**.

The program then creates the **`m_wind_turbine_metrics`** table if it does not already exist and inserts the calculated metric data into the table row by row. Finally, the program updates the timestamp of the last run to the current time. To schedule the program to run at regular intervals, the program can be integrated with the **`apscheduler`** library. Overall, the program provides a robust and automated solution for calculating metrics for wind turbine data and storing the results in a PostgreSQL database.

Conclusion

This chapter highlights the significance of data lakes in IoT Analytics and guides designing and building one. It outlines the data zones required for data lake creation and discusses the benefits, including scalability, flexibility, real-time analytics, cost-effectiveness, and futureproofing. However, proper management and governance are crucial to ensure data quality, security, and compliance.

Real-time data streaming from IoT devices is essential, and Apache Kafka can be used for this purpose. Asset and device registration and onboarding are critical for establishing a secure and reliable connection between IoT devices and the cloud.

Python and MQTT can be used to build data pipelines to the raw zone, while the curated zone provides clean, transformed, and high-quality data for analysis. The transformation and metric zones prepare raw data for analytics and centralize the storage and analysis of KPIs and metrics, respectively.

The next chapter will cover descriptive analysis and building the analytical zone of the data lake. It will cover various statistical methods, including time series analysis using Python with seasonal, stationary, non-stationary, trend analysis, and pattern recognition. Additionally, essential testing methods such as Granger Causality Test, Augmented Dickey-Fuller test, Kwiatkowski-Phillips-Schmidt-Shin test, and Philips Perron test will be discussed.

Points to Remember

Following are the key takeaways from this chapter:

- A data lake is a centralized repository for both structured and unstructured data.
- Data lakes offer scalability, flexibility, real-time analytics, cost-effectiveness, and futureproofing for IoT Analytics.
- Proper management and governance are crucial for data quality, security, and compliance.
- Data lakes have different zones for efficient data management. The data lake is divided into several zones: raw, curated, trusted, transformation, and analytical.
- The first step in building the data lake is setting up the required database and schema using the PostgreSQL tool **`pgAdmin`**.
- Asset and device registration and onboarding are essential processes in the IoT ecosystem. JSON is a standard format for the OEMs to send the asset and device information for registration.
- We performed a data simulation of IoT sensors for wind turbine equipment and published the simulated data in an MQTT topic.
- Kafka is used for real-time data streaming and helps to ensure data durability and availability. It is a powerful tool for handling high volumes of data streams with low latency, making it ideal for IoT applications.
- The raw zone is where the data is initially stored in its original, unprocessed format. It serves as a landing zone for all data types, whether structured or unstructured, where data is first ingested into the data lake.
- The curated zone of the data lake is critical in performing the necessary clean-up and transformation of raw data. The data cleaning engine built in Python can perform various data cleaning operations on raw data and store the clean data in the curated zone. The curated data is immediately available for Data Analysis and Data Science tasks without performing any data engineering operations.
- The transformation engine in Python applies several transformations to pre-process the data so it is ready for analysis or modelling. The transformed data is stored in the transformation zone for building dashboards, reports, and analysis.
- The metric zone centralizes the storage and analysis of KPIs and metrics that are essential for monitoring and optimizing the performance of IoT devices and systems. Python's metric engine helps calculate various metrics and KPIs and store the results in the metric zone of the data lake for building dashboards and reports. Monitoring and refining KPIs and metrics are crucial to ensure they align with business objectives.

CHAPTER 6

Implementing Descriptive Analytics Using Pandas

Introduction

This chapter will discuss various techniques and tools for performing descriptive data analysis on **Internet of Things (IoT)** data using Python's Pandas package. Descriptive Analysis is the preliminary step toward understanding and analysing the data set. We will cover the basics of central tendency and various statistical measures such as mean, median mode, harmonic mean, variance, P-variance, and standard deviation, which can help us understand the data distribution. We will demonstrate how to build an analytical zone of the data lake for storing the results of descriptive analysis.

We will then move on to time series analysis, which analyses time series data to extract meaningful insights. We will cover seasonal analysis, trend analysis, autocorrelation, and partial autocorrelation, which are crucial for understanding patterns in time series data. We will also discuss various testing methods of time series data, including the **Granger causality** test, **Augmented Dickey-Fuller** test (**ADF** test for stationary), **Kwiatkowski-Phillips-Schmidt-Shin (KPSS)** test (trend stationary), and **Philips Perron (PP)** test.

This chapter aims to understand descriptive analysis comprehensively and time series analysis using Python's Pandas package for IoT data. We will cover various techniques and tools to help us extract insights and make informed decisions from the vast amounts of data generated by IoT devices.

Structure

In this chapter, we will covers the following topics:

- Descriptive Data Analysis
- Time Series Analysis
- Testing Methods for Time Series Data

Objectives

This chapter will discuss on implementing descriptive analytics using Pandas for IoT Analytics in Python. You will learn the basic approach to descriptive data analysis, and how to use the Pandas package for data analysis in Python. In Python, we will learn how to calculate central tendency measures such as mean, median, mode, harmonic mean, variance, P-variance, and standard deviation.

Moving further, we will dive into time series analysis, where we will explore seasonal analysis and how to identify patterns in the data. You will learn how to perform stationary and non-stationary analysis, de-seasonalize the data, and perform trend analysis. We will also cover detrending, autocorrelation and partial autocorrelation, data lag identification, and data smoothing.

In addition to the preceding topics, this chapter will introduce you to the basics of forecasting analysis, various testing methods for time series data, noise analysis, and statistical tests like Granger causality test, Augmented Dickey Fuller test, Kwiatkowski-Phillips-Schmidt-Shin test, and Philips Perron test. Upon completing this chapter, you will have a strong foundation in both descriptive data analysis and time series analysis. You can apply these skills to analyse IoT data using Python.

Descriptive Data Analysis

Descriptive data analysis is a crucial process in understanding key data characteristics through statistical and visual tools, allowing for identification of patterns, trends, and relationships. In IoT Analytics, descriptive data analysis plays a significant role in comprehending data gathered from IoT devices and sensors. With enormous volumes of data generated, this analysis is essential for extracting valuable insights to improve system performance and business processes.

To illustrate, consider wind turbine sensor data as an example. These turbines are equipped with sensors that collect data on wind speed, direction, temperature, and pressure. Analysing this data makes it possible to understand the turbine's performance and optimize its efficiency.

Methods of descriptive data analysis in the context of IoT Analytics:

- **Statistical analysis:** Descriptive statistics such as mean, median, mode, variance, standard deviation can be used to summarize the data collected from wind turbine sensors.

For example, the mean wind speed recorded by the sensor can give us an idea of the typical wind speed at a particular location, which can help us optimize the blade pitch angle for optimal energy output.

- **Visualization:** Graphs and charts such as histograms, scatter plots, and box plots can be used to visualize the data and identify patterns or outliers.

  For example, a scatter plot of wind and rotor speed can help us identify the relationship between these variables and optimize the rotor speed for optimal energy output.

  For example, clustering the data based on wind direction can help us identify the areas where the wind speed is consistently high, allowing us to optimize the location of wind turbines.

Approaches of descriptive data analysis in the context of IoT Analytics:

- **Univariate analysis:** This approach involves analysing a single variable simultaneously to understand its distribution, central tendency, and variability.

  For example, analysing the distribution of wind speeds recorded by the sensor can help us understand the typical wind conditions at a particular location.

- **Bivariate analysis:** This approach involves analysing two variables simultaneously to understand the relationship between them.

  For example, analysing the relationship between wind speed and temperature can help us understand how wind speed changes due to temperature impact the wind turbine's energy output.

- **Multivariate analysis:** This approach involves analysing multiple variables simultaneously to understand their interrelationships and identify patterns in the data.

  For example, analysing the relationship between wind speed, wind direction, and pressure can help us optimize the performance of the wind turbine.

  In conclusion, descriptive data analysis is an important tool in IoT Analytics, allowing us to make sense of the vast amounts of data generated by IoT devices such as Wind Turbine sensors. By analysing this data using statistical and visual tools, we can identify patterns and trends that can be used to optimize system performance and improve business processes.

Download Wind Turbine Dataset

So far, we were using data simulation technique to perform our exercises and implementation using Python. Let us use a real-world dataset for data analysis and machine learning tasks. The **National Renewable Energy Laboratory** (**NREL**) is a national laboratory of the U.S. Department of Energy. It is operated by Alliance for Sustainable Energy LLC under the office of Energy Efficiency and Renewable Energy. NREL's National Wind Technology centre and wind energy program consist of researchers, scientists, and analysts working on open-source datasets and multifidelity predictive modelling and simulation capabilities to benefit the wind energy industry.

One such dataset available for demonstration is the central Asia wind data. This dataset contains wind-speed, temperature, and direction values at varying heights (80m, 100m, and 120m above the surface) and air pressure (at the surface, 100m, and 200m above the surface) for the year 2015. The data was produced using WRF v3.7 with a 15-minute time resolution and a spatial resolution of 3 km2 over Kazakhstan and 9 km2 over the surrounding region. The U and V components derived wind speed using 41 pressure levels.

The following are the steps to download the dataset:

1. Go to the web site **https://developer.nrel.gov/signup/** and provide the required information in the following screen as shown in *Figure 6.1*:

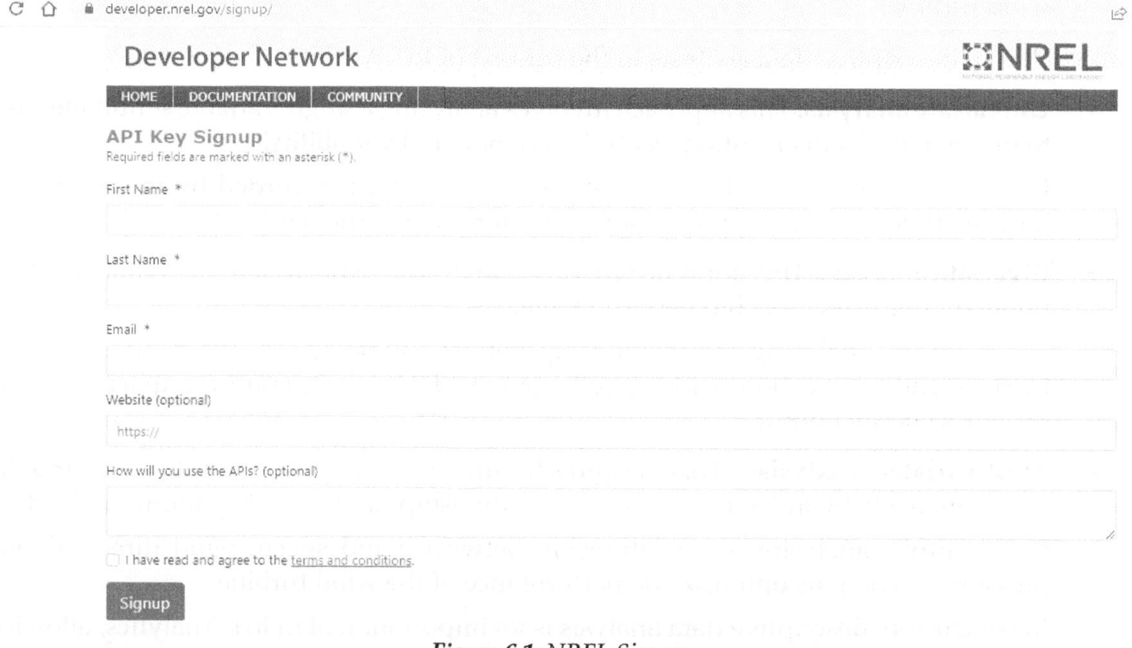

***Figure 6.1**: NREL Signup*

2. Verify that you received the **API Key** on your email ID in *Figure 6.1*.

3. Execute the following Python code from your python IDE or command line:

```
import requests
url = "https://developer.nrel.gov/api/wind-toolkit/v2/wind/central-asia-wind-download.json"
params = {
    "wkt": "POINT(55.81054 46.01222)",
    "api_key": "Your_Api_key",
            "attributes":   "temperature_100m,temperature_120m,temperature_80m,winddirection_100m,winddirection_120m,winddirec-
```

```
    tion_80m,windspeed_100m,windspeed_120m,windspeed_80m,pressure_200m,-
    pressure_100m,pressure_0m",
7.      "names": "2015",
8.      "full_name": "First_Name Second_Name",
9.      "email": "your_email_id@abc.com",
10.     "affiliation": "BPB",
11.     "mailing_list": "false",
12.     "reason": "learning",
13.     "leap_day": "true",
14.     "utc": "false",
15.     "interval": "15",
16.     "csv_format": "csv"
17. }
18. response = requests.get(url, params=params)
19. if response.status_code == 200:
20.     with open("central-asia-wind-data.json", "wb") as f:
21.         f.write(response.content)
22.     print("Data downloaded successfully!")
23. else:
24.     print("Failed to download data. Error code:", response.status_code)
```

Make sure you modify the preceding Python code with the API Key information (line#8) received on your email, along with your full name and email ID (line#11 and 12 respectively).

4. After the execution of the above Python code, you receive a download link on your email ID from NREL.
5. On clicking on the link will automatically initiate the download of a **.zip** file with the dataset.
6. Extract the **.zip** file on your working directory to start working on the dataset.
7. Calculate the power output from the wind turbine as the original dataset we downloaded above will not provide power output calculation. After the power output calculation, we will insert the data in the curated zone of the data lake for the further analysis. Here is the detailed Python program to accomplish the tasks:

```
import pandas as pd
import numpy as np
```

```
import psycopg2
# Read the CSV file which is downloaded and renamed
df = pd.read_csv('wind_data_new.csv', skiprows=6)
# Convert the time columns to a datetime object and add a new column called rtc
df['rtc'] = pd.to_datetime(df[['Year', 'Month', 'Day', 'Hour', 'Minute']])
cols = list(df.columns)
cols.remove('rtc')
cols = ['rtc'] + cols
df = df[cols]
# Define the constants
rho = 1.225 # Air density at sea level (kg/m^3)
d = 150 # Diameter of the rotor (m)
r = d/2 # Radius of the rotor (m)
A = np.pi*r**2 # Swept area of the rotor (m^2)
Cp = 0.38 # Power coefficient of the turbine
# Calculate wind speed at hub height 80m
df['Wind Speed at 80m (m/s)'] = df['Wind Speed at 80m (m/s)']*np.log(80/0.1)/np.log(120/0.1)
# Calculate wind speed at hub height 100m
df['Wind Speed at 100m (m/s)'] = df['Wind Speed at 100m (m/s)']*np.log(80/0.1)/np.log(120/0.1)
# Calculate wind speed at hub height 120m
df['Wind Speed at 120m (m/s)'] = df['Wind Speed at 120m (m/s)']*np.log(80/0.1)/np.log(120/0.1)
# Calculate the power output for 80m, 100m and 120m
df['Power Output at 80m (kW)'] = 0.5*rho*A*Cp*(df['Wind Speed at 80m (m/s)']*1000/3600)**3
df['Power Output at 100m (kW)'] = 0.5*rho*A*Cp*(df['Wind Speed at 100m (m/s)']*1000/3600)**3
df['Power Output at 120m (kW)'] = 0.5*rho*A*Cp*(df['Wind Speed at 120m (m/s)']*1000/3600)**3

# Set up database connection
```

```
conn = psycopg2.connect(database="IoTDataLake", user="postgres", password="", host="localhost", port="5432")
cur = conn.cursor()
# Create wind turbine data table if it doesn't exist
cur.execute("""
    CREATE TABLE IF NOT EXISTS curatedzone.c_external_wind_turbine_data (
        id SERIAL PRIMARY KEY,
        rtc TIMESTAMP NOT NULL,
        year INTEGER NOT NULL,
        month INTEGER NOT NULL,
        day INTEGER NOT NULL,
        hour INTEGER NOT NULL,
        minute INTEGER NOT NULL,
        temperature_100 FLOAT,
        temperature_120 FLOAT,
        temperature_80 FLOAT,
        wind_direction_100 FLOAT,
        wind_direction_120 FLOAT,
        wind_direction_80 FLOAT,
        wind_speed_100 FLOAT,
        wind_speed_120 FLOAT,
        wind_speed_80 FLOAT,
        pressure_200 FLOAT,
        pressure_100 FLOAT,
        pressure_0 FLOAT,
        power_output_80 FLOAT,
        power_output_100 FLOAT,
        power_output_120 FLOAT
    )
""")
# Insert the transformed data into the c_external_wind_turbine_data table in the curated zone of the data lake
for i, row in df.iterrows():
```

```
cur.execute("""INSERT INTO curatedzone.c_external_wind_turbine_data (rtc, year, month, day, hour, minute, temperature_100, temperature_120,
temperature_80, wind_direction_100, wind_direction_120, wind_direction_80, wind_speed_100, wind_speed_120, wind_speed_80, pressure_200, pressure_100, pressure_0,
 power_output_80, power_output_100, power_output_120) VALUES (%s, %s, %s, %s, %s, %s, %s, %s, %s, %s, %s, %s, %s, %s ,%s, %s, %s, %s , %s, %s, %s)
     """, (row['rtc'], row['Year'], row['Month'], row['Day'], row['Hour'],row['Minute'], row['Temperature at 100m (C)'],row['Temperature at 120m (C)'],
     row['Temperature at 80m (C)'], row['Wind Direction at 100m (Degrees)'], row['Wind Direction at 120m (Degrees)'], row['Wind Direction at 80m (Degrees)'],
     row['Wind Speed at 100m (m/s)'], row['Wind Speed at 120m (m/s)'], row['Wind Speed at 80m (m/s)'], row['Pressure at 200m (atm)'], row['Pressure at 100m (atm)'],
     row['Pressure at 0m (atm)'], row['Power Output at 80m (kW)'], row['Power Output at 100m (kW)'], row['Power Output at 120m (kW)'] ))
 conn.commit()
cur.close()
conn.close()
```

Descriptive Analysis using Python

The first step in descriptive analysis on the dataset is to understand the data distribution in the dataset. The Pandas package has a very simple method to achieve this. Let us write a Python program which query the wind turbine data from the curated zone and create a Pandas dataframe. Then we will use the describe method of Pandas to understand the distribution of the data such as total count, mean, median, standard deviation, minimum, maximum, 25%, 50% and 75% of the distribution. We will be using Jupyter Notebook for executing the following codes in the rest of this chapter:

```
import pandas as pd
from scipy.stats import chi2_contingency
import psycopg2
# Define database connection parameters
host = 'localhost'
```

```
dbname = 'IoTDataLake'
user = 'postgres'
password = ""
# Define function to execute SQL query and return result as DataFrame
def execute_query(query):
    # Connect to database
    conn = psycopg2.connect(
        host=host,
        database=dbname,
        user=user,
        password=""
    )
    # Execute query and fetch result
    cur = conn.cursor()
    cur.execute(query)
    result = cur.fetchall()
    # Get column names from cursor description
    col_names = [desc[0] for desc in cur.description]
    # Convert result to pandas DataFrame
    df = pd.DataFrame(result, columns=col_names)
    # Close cursor and database connection
    cur.close()
    conn.close()
    # Return DataFrame
    return df
# Load the wind turbine dataset from the curated zone of the data lake
df = execute_query('SELECT * FROM curatedzone.c_external_wind_turbine_data')
# assume df is your original DataFrame
stats = df.describe()
# reset the index of the stats DataFrame
stats.reset_index(inplace=True)
# create a list of descriptions
```

```
descriptions = ['count', 'mean',  'std', 'min', '25%', '50%', '75%', 'max']
# create a new DataFrame with descriptions as a column
stats_t = pd.DataFrame({'description': descriptions})
# merge the stats and stats_t DataFrames
stats_t = pd.concat([stats_t, stats], axis=1)
stats_t = stats_t.drop('index', axis=1)
# Change the data type of the "description" column to text
stats_t[‘description’] = stats_t[‘description’].astype(str)
table_name = "analyticszone.a_stats_wind_turbine"
#Connect to database
conn = psycopg2.connect(
        host=host,
        database=dbname,
        user=user,
        password=""
    )
# Create cursor object
cur = conn.cursor()
# Create table query
create_query = f"""
    CREATE TABLE IF NOT EXISTS {table_name} (
        metric_description TEXT,
        id DOUBLE PRECISION,
        temperature_100 DOUBLE PRECISION,
        temperature_120 DOUBLE PRECISION,
        temperature_80 DOUBLE PRECISION,
        wind_direction_100 DOUBLE PRECISION,
        wind_direction_120 DOUBLE PRECISION,
        wind_direction_80 DOUBLE PRECISION,
        wind_speed_100 DOUBLE PRECISION,
        wind_speed_120 DOUBLE PRECISION,
        wind_speed_80 DOUBLE PRECISION,
        pressure_200 DOUBLE PRECISION,
```

```
        pressure_100 DOUBLE PRECISION,
        pressure_0 DOUBLE PRECISION,
        power_output_80 DOUBLE PRECISION,
        power_output_100 DOUBLE PRECISION,
        power_output_120 DOUBLE PRECISION
    );
"""
# Execute create table query
cur.execute(create_query)
# Commit the changes
conn.commit()
# Insert the transformed data into the a_basic_stats_wind_turbine table in the analytics zone of the data lake
for i, row in stats_t.iterrows():
    cur.execute("""INSERT INTO analyticszone.a_stats_wind_turbine (metric_description, id, temperature_100, temperature_120, temperature_80, wind_direction_100,
    wind_direction_120, wind_direction_80, wind_speed_100, wind_speed_120, wind_speed_80, pressure_200, pressure_100,
    pressure_0, power_output_80, power_output_100, power_output_120) VALUES (%s, %s, %s, %s, %s, %s, %s,%s, %s, %s, %s, %s, %s, %s, %s, %s, %s)
    """, (row['description'], row['id'], row['temperature_100'], row['temperature_120'], row['temperature_80'],row['wind_direction_100'],row['wind_direction_120'],
    row['wind_direction_80'],row['wind_speed_100'], row['wind_speed_120'], row['wind_speed_80'], row['pressure_200'],
    row['pressure_100'], row['pressure_0'], row['power_output_80'], row['power_output_100'], row['power_output_120']  ))
    conn.commit()
cur.close()
conn.close()
# display the new DataFrame
print(stats_t)
```

The program loads the wind turbine dataset from the curated zone of the data lake using the **execute_query** function. Then, it uses the **describe()** function to get descriptive statistics of the **DataFrame**. The index of the stats **DataFrame** is reset, and a new **DataFrame** called **stats_t** is created with the description column. The stats and **stats_t DataFrames** are merged, and the index column is dropped.

Afterward, the data type of the description column in the **stats_t DataFrame** is changed to text. The program then creates a new table in the analytics zone of the data lake using a create table query. It then inserts the transformed data into the new table using a for loop and executes the insert query for each row in the **stats_t DataFrame**. Finally, the program displays the new **DataFrame**.

In *Chapter 5, Designing Data Lake and Executing Data Transformation,* we built data cleaning and data transformation engine. Similarly, we will build a data analytical engine to perform basic descriptive analysis and store the results for quick access in the analytical zone of the data lake. Save the following Python program with the file **DataAnalyticsEngine.py** on your current working directory:

```
import json
import numpy as np
import pandas as pd
class DataAnalyticsEngine:
    def __init__(self):
        pass
    def analyze_data(self, df):
        # Check if all required columns are present in the DataFrame
        required_cols = ['id', 'rtc','temperature_100', 'temperature_120', 'temperature_80', 'wind_direction_100', 'wind_direction_120',
        'wind_direction_80', 'wind_speed_100', 'wind_speed_120', 'wind_speed_80', 'pressure_200', 'pressure_100', 'pressure_0', 'power_output_80',
        'power_output_100', 'power_output_120']
        missing_cols = set(required_cols) - set(df.columns)
        if missing_cols:
            raise KeyError(f"{missing_cols} not in index")
        #Wind Speed to Power Output ratio calculation
        df['wind_speed_to_power_output_ratio_120'] = df['wind_speed_120'] / df['power_output_120']
        df['wind_speed_to_power_output_ratio_100'] = df['wind_speed_100'] / df['power_output_100']
        df['wind_speed_to_power_output_ratio_80'] = df['wind_speed_80'] / df['power_output_80']
```

```
        # Wind direction to Wind speed Ratio
        df['wind_direction_wind_speed_ratio_120'] = df['wind_direction_120'] / df['wind_speed_120']
        df['wind_direction_wind_speed_ratio_100'] = df['wind_direction_100'] / df['wind_speed_100']
        df['wind_direction_wind_speed_ratio_80'] = df['wind_direction_80'] / df['wind_speed_80']
        # Wind Speed to Pressure Ratio
        df['wind_speed_to_pressure_ratio_120'] = df['wind_speed_120'] / df['pressure_200']
        df['wind_speed_to_pressure_ratio_100'] = df['wind_speed_100'] / df['pressure_100']
        df['wind_speed_to_pressure_ratio_80'] = df['wind_speed_80'] / df['pressure_0']
        # Temperature to Power Output ratio
        df['temp_to_power_output_ratio_120'] = df['temperature_120'] / df['power_output_120']
        df['temp_to_power_output_ratio_100'] = df['temperature_100'] / df['power_output_100']
        df['temp_to_power_output_ratio_80'] = df['temperature_80'] / df['power_output_80']
        # Temperature to Wind Speed ratio
        df['temp_wind_speed_ratio_120'] = df['temperature_120'] / df['wind_speed_120']
        df['temp_wind_speed_ratio_100'] = df['temperature_100'] / df['wind_speed_100']
        df['temp_wind_speed_ratio_80'] = df['temperature_80'] / df['wind_speed_80']
        # Correlation between Wind Speed and Power Output
        df['wind_speed_to_power_output_corr_120'] = df['wind_speed_120'].corr(df['power_output_120'])
        df['wind_speed_to_power_output_corr_100'] = df['wind_speed_100'].corr(df['power_output_100'])
        df['wind_speed_to_power_output_corr_80'] = df['wind_speed_80'].corr(df['power_output_80'])
        # Correlation between Wind Direction and Wind Speed
        df['wind_direction_wind_speed_corr_120'] = df['wind_
```

```
direction_120'].corr(df['wind_speed_120'])
        df['wind_direction_wind_speed_corr_100'] = df['wind_direction_100'].corr(df['wind_speed_100'])
        df['wind_direction_wind_speed_corr_80'] = df['wind_direction_80'].corr(df['wind_speed_80'])
        # Correlation between Temperature and Wind Speed
        df['temp_wind_speed_corr_120'] = df['temperature_120'].corr(df['wind_speed_120'])
        df['temp_wind_speed_corr_100'] = df['temperature_100'].corr(df['wind_speed_100'])
        df['temp_wind_speed_corr_80'] = df['temperature_80'].corr(df['wind_speed_80'])
        # Correlation between Temperature and Power Output
        df['temp_power_output_corr_120'] = df['temperature_120'].corr(df['power_output_120'])
        df['temp_power_output_corr_100'] = df['temperature_100'].corr(df['power_output_100'])
        df['temp_power_output_corr_80'] = df['temperature_80'].corr(df['power_output_80'])
        # Correlation between Pressure and Wind Speed
        df['pressure_wind_speed_corr_120'] = df['pressure_200'].corr(df['wind_speed_120'])
        df['pressure_wind_speed_corr_100'] = df['pressure_100'].corr(df['wind_speed_100'])
        df['pressure_wind_speed_corr_80'] = df['pressure_0'].corr(df['wind_speed_80'])
        # Correlation between Pressure and Power Output
        df['pressure_power_output_corr_120'] = df['pressure_200'].corr(df['power_output_120'])
        df['pressure_power_output_corr_100'] = df['pressure_100'].corr(df['power_output_100'])
        df['pressure_power_output_corr_80'] = df['pressure_0'].corr(df['power_output_80'])
        return df
```

This is a Python program that defines a class named **DataAnalyticsEngine** that has a method named **analyze_data**. The method aims to analyse a given **DataFrame df** by computing various ratios and correlations between the columns of the **DataFrame**. We use this as a module to re-use this data analytical engine for any **dataframes**.

The **analyze_data** method first checks whether all the required columns are in the **DataFrame**. If any required column is missing, it raises a **KeyError** with the name of the missing column.

After verifying that all required columns are present, the method proceeds to compute various ratios and correlations between the columns of the **DataFrame**. The ratios are computed by dividing one column by another, and the correlations using the **corr** method of the **DataFrame**.

The computed ratios and correlations are added as new columns to the **DataFrame**, with names that include the names of the original columns and a description of the ratio or correlation being computed. For example, the ratio of wind speed to power output at 120m is computed as wind_speed_120 / power_output_120 and added as a new column named wind_speed_to_power_output_ratio_120.

Finally, the method returns the modified **DataFrame** with the added columns.

Let us now write a Python program to query the wind turbine dataset from the curated zone of the data lake and invoke the Python module **DataAnalyticsEngine** to perform basic descriptive analysis and insert the results into the analytical zone of the data lake:

```
import psycopg2
import pandas as pd
from DataAnalyticsEngine import DataAnalyticsEngine
from apscheduler.schedulers.background import BackgroundScheduler
from datetime import datetime, timedelta
def analyze_data():
    # Connect to the database
    conn = psycopg2.connect(
        host="localhost",
        database="IoTDataLake",
        user="postgres",
        password=""
    )
        # Assign the timestamp
    last_run_timestamp = '2000-01-11 11:39:35.922405'  # Replace with code to read the timestamp
    # Read the data inserted after the last run from the curated data table
    cur = conn.cursor()
    # Create the last_run_timestamp table if it doesn't exist
    cur.execute('''
        CREATE TABLE IF NOT EXISTS analyticszone.last_run_timestamp_wt (
```

```
            rtc timestamp without time zone,
            job_id SERIAL PRIMARY KEY
            )
    ‹››)
    cur.execute("SELECT rtc FROM analyticszone.last_run_timestamp_wt ORDER BY job_id DESC LIMIT 1")
    result_timestamp = cur.fetchone()
    if result_timestamp is not None:
        last_run_timestamp = result_timestamp[0]
    print("last_run_timestamp ", last_run_timestamp)
    cur = conn.cursor()
    cur.execute("SELECT * FROM curatedzone.c_external_wind_turbine_data WHERE rtc > %s", (last_run_timestamp,))
    data = pd.DataFrame(cur.fetchall(), columns=['id','rtc','year', 'month', 'day', 'hour', 'minute', 'temperature_100', 'temperature_120',  'temperature_80', 'wind_direction_100', 'wind_direction_120',
     'wind_direction_80', 'wind_speed_100','wind_speed_120','wind_speed_80',' pressure_200','pressure_100','pressure_0','power_output_80','power_output_100',
     'power_output_120'])
    data_analyzer =  DataAnalyticsEngine() #call the data analytical engine
    anlyzed_data = data_analyzer.analyze_data(data)
    print(anlyzed_data.head(5))
    # Create the a_external_wind_turbine_data table if it doesn't exist
    cur.execute('''
        CREATE TABLE IF NOT EXISTS analyticszone.a_external_wind_turbine_data (
            wind_speed_to_power_output_ratio_100 FLOAT,
            wind_speed_to_power_output_ratio_120 FLOAT,
            wind_speed_to_power_output_ratio_80 FLOAT,
            wind_direction_wind_speed_ratio_100 FLOAT,
            wind_direction_wind_speed_ratio_120 FLOAT,
            wind_direction_wind_speed_ratio_80 FLOAT,
```

```
            wind_speed_to_pressure_ratio_100 FLOAT,
            wind_speed_to_pressure_ratio_120 FLOAT,
            wind_speed_to_pressure_ratio_80 FLOAT,
            temp_to_power_output_ratio_100 FLOAT,
            temp_to_power_output_ratio_120 FLOAT,
            temp_to_power_output_ratio_80 FLOAT,
            temp_wind_speed_ratio_100 FLOAT,
            temp_wind_speed_ratio_120 FLOAT,
            temp_wind_speed_ratio_80 FLOAT,
            wind_speed_to_power_output_corr_100 FLOAT,
            wind_speed_to_power_output_corr_120 FLOAT,
            wind_speed_to_power_output_corr_80 FLOAT,
            wind_direction_wind_speed_corr_100 FLOAT,
            wind_direction_wind_speed_corr_120 FLOAT,
            wind_direction_wind_speed_corr_80 FLOAT,
            temp_wind_speed_corr_100 FLOAT,
            temp_wind_speed_corr_120 FLOAT,
            temp_wind_speed_corr_80 FLOAT,
            temp_power_output_corr_100 FLOAT,
            temp_power_output_corr_120 FLOAT,
            temp_power_output_corr_80 FLOAT,
            pressure_wind_speed_corr_100 FLOAT,
            pressure_wind_speed_corr_120 FLOAT,
            pressure_wind_speed_corr_80 FLOAT,
            pressure_power_output_corr_100 FLOAT,
            pressure_power_output_corr_120 FLOAT,
            pressure_power_output_corr_80 FLOAT
        )
    ‹››)
    # Insert the analyzed data into the a_external_wind_turbine_data table in the analytical zone of the data lake
    for i, row in anlyzed_data.iterrows():
        cur.execute("""INSERT INTO analyticszone.a_external_wind_turbine_data (wind_speed_to_power_output_ratio_100,
```

```
            wind_speed_to_power_output_ratio_120 ,
            wind_speed_to_power_output_ratio_80 ,
            wind_direction_wind_speed_ratio_100 ,
            wind_direction_wind_speed_ratio_120 ,
            wind_direction_wind_speed_ratio_80 ,
            wind_speed_to_pressure_ratio_100 ,
            wind_speed_to_pressure_ratio_120 ,
            wind_speed_to_pressure_ratio_80 ,
            temp_to_power_output_ratio_100 ,
            temp_to_power_output_ratio_120 ,
            temp_to_power_output_ratio_80 ,
            temp_wind_speed_ratio_100 ,
            temp_wind_speed_ratio_120 ,
            temp_wind_speed_ratio_80 ,
            wind_speed_to_power_output_corr_100 ,
            wind_speed_to_power_output_corr_120 ,
            wind_speed_to_power_output_corr_80 ,
            wind_direction_wind_speed_corr_100 ,
            wind_direction_wind_speed_corr_120 ,
            wind_direction_wind_speed_corr_80 ,
            temp_wind_speed_corr_100 ,
                  temp_wind_speed_corr_120 ,
                  temp_wind_speed_corr_80 ,
                  temp_power_output_corr_100 ,
                  temp_power_output_corr_120 ,
                  temp_power_output_corr_80 ,
                  pressure_wind_speed_corr_100 ,
                  pressure_wind_speed_corr_120 ,
                  pressure_wind_speed_corr_80 ,
                  pressure_power_output_corr_100 ,
                  pressure_power_output_corr_120 ,
                  pressure_power_output_corr_80 ) VALUES (%s ,%s, %s, %
s, %s, %s, %s, %s, %s, %s, %s, %s, %s, %s, %s, %s, %s, %s, %s,%s ,%s
, %s, %s, %s, %s,
```

```
                    %s, %s, %s, %s,%s ,%s, %s)
                    """, (row['wind_speed_to_power_output_ratio_100'], row['wind_speed_to_power_output_ratio_120'], row['wind_speed_to_power_output_ratio_80'], row['wind_direction_wind_speed_ratio_100'],
                     row['wind_direction_wind_speed_ratio_120'], row['wind_direction_wind_speed_ratio_80'],row['wind_speed_to_pressure_ratio_100'],
                     row['wind_speed_to_pressure_ratio_120'],row['wind_speed_to_pressure_ratio_80'], row['temp_to_power_output_ratio_100'],
                     row['temp_to_power_output_ratio_120'], row['temp_to_power_output_ratio_80'], row['temp_wind_speed_ratio_100'], row['temp_wind_speed_ratio_120'],
                        row['temp_wind_speed_ratio_80'], row['wind_speed_to_power_output_corr_100'], row['wind_speed_to_power_output_corr_120'],
                        row['wind_speed_to_power_output_corr_80'], row['wind_direction_wind_speed_corr_100'],row['wind_direction_wind_speed_corr_120'],
                        row['wind_direction_wind_speed_corr_80'], row['temp_wind_speed_corr_100'], row['temp_wind_speed_corr_120'],
                        row['temp_wind_speed_corr_80'], row['temp_power_output_corr_100'], row['temp_power_output_corr_120'],
                        row['temp_power_output_corr_80'],row['pressure_wind_speed_corr_100'], row['pressure_wind_speed_corr_120'],row['pressure_wind_speed_corr_80'],
                        row['pressure_power_output_corr_100'],row['pressure_power_output_corr_120'], row['pressure_power_output_corr_80']  ))
            conn.commit()
        # Update the timestamp of the last run to the current time
        cur.execute("INSERT INTO analyticszone.last_run_timestamp_wt (rtc) VALUES (%s) ON CONFLICT (job_id) DO UPDATE SET rtc = EXCLUDED.rtc", (datetime.now(),))
        conn.commit()
    analyze_data()
```

The preceding Python program performs data analysis on the external wind turbine dataset. The program reads data from the curated data table of an IoT data lake, analyses the data using an instance of the **DataAnalyticsEngine**, and stores the analysis results in the data lake's analytical zone.

The program uses the psycopg2 module to connect to a PostgreSQL database and the pandas module to handle data frames. It also uses the **BackgroundScheduler** class from the **apscheduler.schedulers.background** module to schedule the **analyze_data()** function to run periodically in the background. Use the scheduler if required. For our example we did not schedule the analytical pipeline.

The **analyze_data()** function first connects to the database using the **psycopg2.connect()** method and assigns a timestamp to **last_run_timestamp**. It then creates a table named **last_run_timestamp_wt** if it does not exist and retrieves the most recent timestamp from the table using a SQL query.

Next, the function reads the data inserted after the last run from the curated data table named **c_external_wind_turbine_data** using the **pd.DataFrame()** method converts the query result to a Pandas data frame. The **DataAnalyticsEngine** instance then analyses the data using the **analyze_data()** method, and the results are stored in **analyzed_data**.

The function creates a table called a**_external_wind_turbine_data** if it doesn't already exist. Then, it adds the analysed data to the table using a **for loop** that goes through each row of the data and adds it to the table using the "**cur.execute()**" method.

Finally, the function prints the first five rows of the **analyzed_data** data frame using the **head()** method.

We can see from the preceding data that all 80m, 100m, and 120m parameters have similar data. So here onwards, we will be using 100m as our example instead of performing analysis on every other parameters.

Let us perform additional analysis using various statistical methods to gain insights on the dataset:

- Perform analysis to understand percentage of **NULL** values in the dataset using Python:

```
import psycopg2
import pandas as pd
import matplotlib.pyplot as plt
import seaborn as sns
#Print the plot within the page
%matplotlib inline
# set seaborn theme
sns.set(style="white")

conn = psycopg2.connect(
        host="localhost",
        database="IoTDataLake",
```

```
        user="postgres",
        password=""
    )
cur = conn.cursor()
cur.execute("SELECT * FROM curatedzone.c_external_wind_turbine_data")
data_external = pd.DataFrame(cur.fetchall(), columns=['id','rtc','year', 'month', 'day', 'hour', 'minute', 'temperature_100', 'temperature_120', 'temperature_80', 'wind_direction_100', 'wind_direction_120',
      'wind_direction_80', 'wind_speed_100','wind_speed_120','wind_speed_80','pressure_200','pressure_100','pressure_0','power_output_80','power_output_100',
      'power_output_120'])
# Inspecting the percentages of Null values again
print(round(100*(data_external.isnull().sum()/len(data_external.index)), 2))
```

The preceding program prints the percentage of **NULL** values on each dataset column. Here is the output of the preceding Python program:

```
id                  0.0
rtc                 0.0
year                0.0
month               0.0
day                 0.0
hour                0.0
minute              0.0
temperature_100     0.0
temperature_120     0.0
temperature_80      0.0
wind_direction_100  0.0
wind_direction_120  0.0
wind_direction_80   0.0
wind_speed_100      0.0
wind_speed_120      0.0
wind_speed_80       0.0
pressure_200        0.0
pressure_100        0.0
pressure_0          0.0
```

```
power_output_80         0.0
power_output_100        0.0
power_output_120        0.0
dtype: float64
```

- Understand the distribution of wind speed of the wind turbine dataset. Ensure you have the dataframe **data_external** created from the wind turbine data using above point#1. Let us use only the **wind_speed_100** instead of other two **wind_speed_80** and **wind_speed_120**.

```
plt.figure(figsize=(18,6))
plt.title('Distribution of wind_speed_100')
sns.distplot(data_external.wind_speed_100)
plt.show()
```

The preceding Python program shows the distribution of wind speed as shown in *Figure 6.2*:

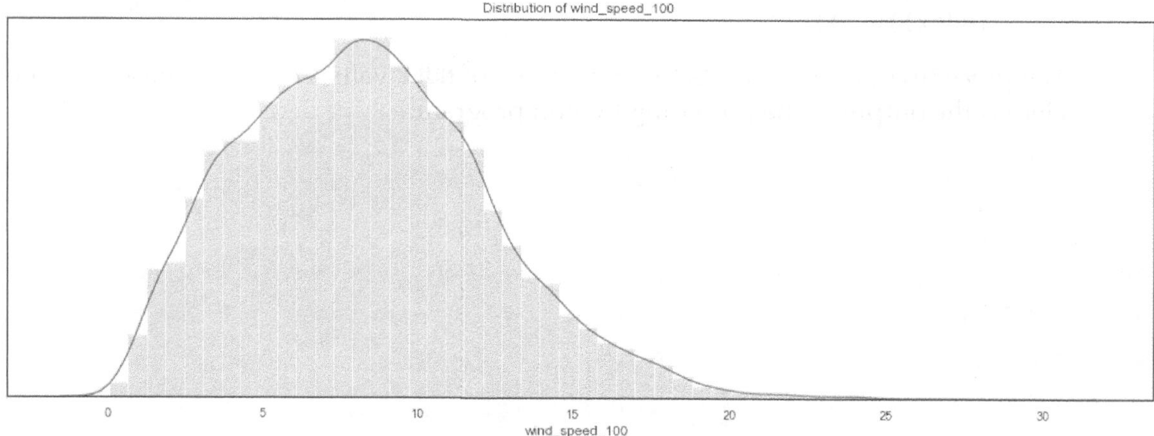

***Figure 6.2:** Distribution of wind speed*

You can perform the same distribution check using other columns of the dataset. The distribution plot shows how data is distributed over range of values. This is usually the first step in the univariate analysis. Analysing each column individually to ensure quality data helps us with further analysis.

- Next important step in the univariate analysis is understanding outliers and data distribution in different quartiles using box plot. The following is the example of plotting a box plot of a variable using Python:

```
#Using the Box plot will help us understand the outliers
plt.figure(figsize=(18,6))
```

```
3. plt.title('Distribution of wind_speed_100 ')
4. sns.boxplot(y=data_external.wind_speed_100)
```

The preceding Python program show the box plot as shown in *Figure 6.3*. You can repeat the similar analysis on other variables:

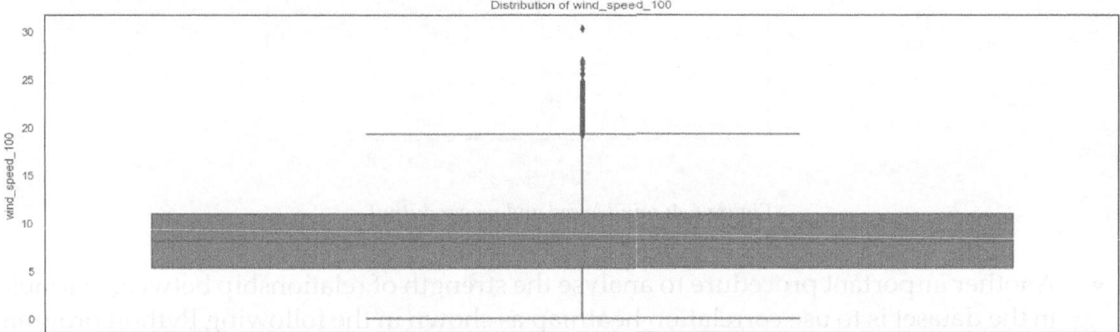

***Figure 6.3:** Boxplot of wind speed*

The preceding figure shows minimum and maximum values of the wind speed by the whiskers of the box plot. The median value is shown as a horizontal line inside the box. The first quartile is the value below which 25% of the data falls, while the third is below which 75% falls. These values will be represented by the bottom and top of the box, respectively. Outliers are represented by dots or other symbols outside the whiskers of the box plot.

The box plot describes key features of the distribution, such as the data's range, center, and spread. You can also observe any outliers in the dataset and their potential impact on the overall distribution.

- Once we understood each variable's distributions and outliers as part of univariate analysis, we can perform multivariate analysis. Here is the Python program to visualize relationship between wind speed and power output using scattered plot:

```
1. # Visual inspection of linearity using scat-
   ter plot for wind speed and power output
2. sns.scatterplot(data=data_external, x='wind_speed_100', y='power_
   output_100')
3. plt.show()
```

The preceding Python program shows scattered plot (see *Figure 6.4*) which explains the relationship between wind speed and power output. They have a linear relationship, as the power output will rise with increased wind speed:

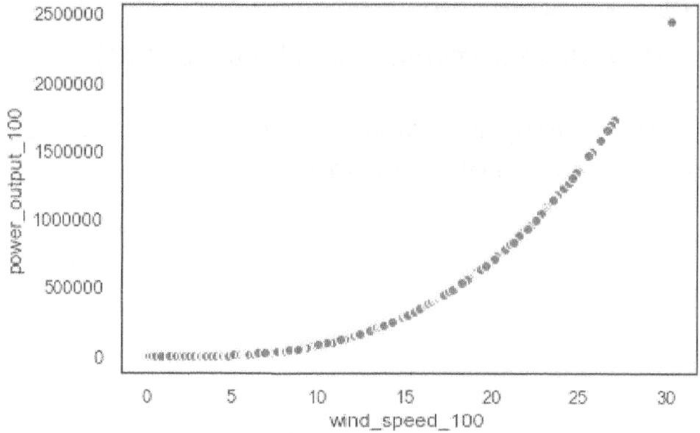

***Figure 6.4:** wind speed and power output*

- Another important procedure to analyse the strength of relationship between variables in the dataset is to use correlation heatmap as shown in the following Python program:

```
1. data_filtered = data_external.loc[:, ['month','day','hour','minute','temperature_100', 'wind_direction_100', 'wind_speed_100', 'pressure_100','power_output_100']]
2. plt.figure(figsize = (16,10))
3. sns.heatmap(data_filtered.corr(),annot = True)
```

The preceding Python program shows heatmap (see *Figure 6.5*) which explains the relationship between all the variables selected in line#1 of the Python program.

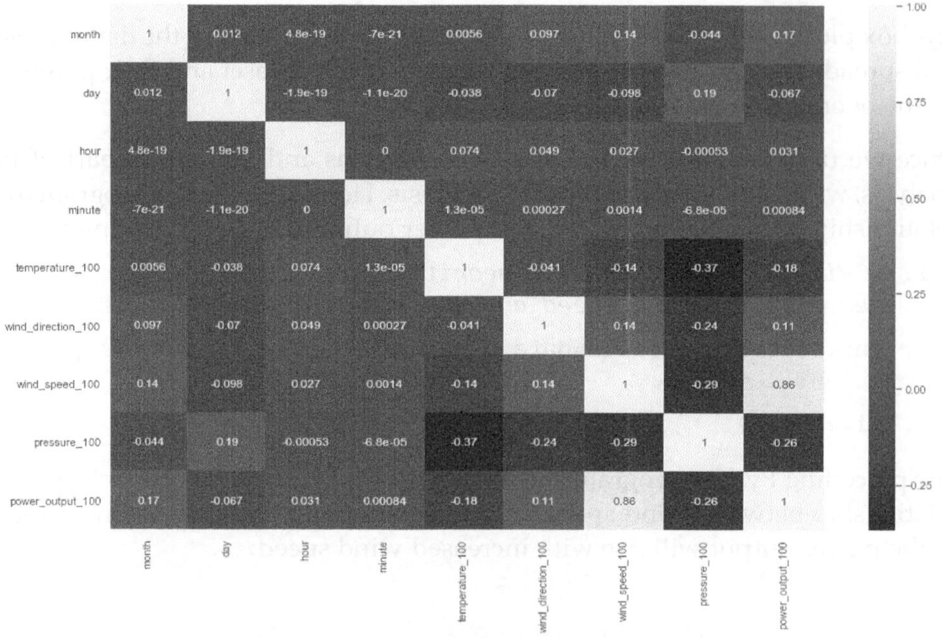

***Figure 6.5:** Correlation between variables*

The heatmap presented in *Figure 6.5* indicates a strong correlation between wind speed and power output. This correlation is also supported by our common sense and experience, which suggests that an increase in wind speed will result in a corresponding increase in power output. Additionally, we can observe an inverse relationship between temperature and wind speed, meaning that an increase in temperature will harm the wind speed. As a result, an increase in temperature will also lead to a decrease in power output.

Calculating correlation coefficients is essential in understanding the relationship between variables and their significance. One of the most commonly used calculations is the Pearson correlation coefficient, which measures the strength and direction of a linear relationship between two variables. It ranges from -1 to +1, with a value of -1 representing perfect negative correlation, +1 representing perfect positive correlation, and 0 indicating no correlation.

The variables are positively correlated when the Pearson correlation coefficient value is positive. This suggests that the other variable also increases as one variable increases. In contrast, a negative coefficient value indicates negative correlation, meaning the other variable tends to decrease as one variable increases.

The p-value is another critical aspect of correlation coefficient analysis. The p-value indicates the probability of observing the correlation coefficient or a more extreme value if the variables are not correlated in the population. When the p-value is less than the predetermined level of significance, typically 0.05, the correlation is statistically significant. This suggests that the observed correlation is unlikely due to chance.

Let us now check the correlation coefficient between **power_output_100** and **wind_speed_100** using Pearson method:

```
# Linearity testing using Pearson correlation coefficient for power output and wind speed
from scipy.stats import pearsonr, spearmanr
corr, p = pearsonr(data_external['power_output_100'], data_external['wind_speed_100'])
print('Pearson correlation coefficient between power output and wind speed:', corr)
print('p-value:', p)
```

The following is the output of the preceding Python program:

```
Pearson correlation coefficient between power output and wind speed: 0.8648957697795068
p-value: 0.0
```

The preceding output shows the strength and significance of the relationship between power output and wind speed.

In conclusion, the descriptive analysis we performed on the wind turbine dataset gives us more insights about the dataset. How each variable impacts the power output of the wind turbine.

Time Series Analysis

Time series analysis is a widely used statistical technique in IoT Analytics to analyse data that changes over time. This method is useful in identifying patterns and trends in the data, providing valuable insights into future events and predictions.

The wind turbine dataset includes variables such as wind speed, wind direction, pressure, temperature, and power output, which are measured over time to assess the turbine's performance. Using time series analysis techniques on this data, patterns and insights can be extracted, and future behaviour can be predicted.

Trend analysis, seasonal analysis, autocorrelation, and forecasting are the primary techniques used in time series analysis. Trend analysis identifies the overall trend of the data over time, while seasonal analysis identifies recurring patterns. Forecasting leverages past data to make predictions about future outcomes.

Overall, time series analysis is essential for optimizing the performance of IoT devices such as wind turbines. It reduces downtime, ensures efficient and reliable operation, and enhances overall performance.

Time Series Analysis using Python

Let us now implement various time series analyses to gain insights from the wind turbine data we downloaded:

- **Trend and seasonality:** Analysing the trend and seasonality of a time series data can help us identify various patterns and changes in a system. This understanding is critical to optimize the performance of a system and increase the output it generates. In the case of wind turbines, it has been observed that the power output is primarily dependent on wind speed, with wind direction also playing a significant role in achieving higher wind speeds. Additionally, seasonal conditions can affect power output, such as a higher output during the spring season when wind speeds are stronger. Therefore, it is crucial to analyse the trend and seasonality of the power output to optimize the performance of wind turbines. The following is the Python example of the trend and seasonality using wind turbine dataset:

```
import psycopg2
import pandas as pd
import matplotlib.pyplot as plt
import seaborn as sns
#Print the plot within the page
%matplotlib inline
# set seaborn theme
sns.set(style="white")
```

```
conn = psycopg2.connect(
        host="localhost",
        database="IoTDataLake",
        user="postgres",
        password=""
    )
cur = conn.cursor()
cur.execute("SELECT * FROM curatedzone.c_external_wind_turbine_data")
data_external = pd.DataFrame(cur.fetchall(), columns=['id','rtc','year', 'month', 'day', 'hour', 'minute', 'temperature_100', 'temperature_120', 'temperature_80', 'wind_direction_100', 'wind_direction_120',
      'wind_direction_80', 'wind_speed_100','wind_speed_120','wind_speed_80','pressure_200','pressure_100','pressure_0','power_output_80','power_output_100',
      'power_output_120'])
def plot_df(new_data, x, y, title="", xlabel='Time', ylabel='Power Output', dpi=100):
    # Resample the data to a 15-minute interval
    resampled_data = new_data.set_index('rtc').resample('15T').sum().reset_index()
    # Create a datetime index for the resampled data
    resampled_data['datetime'] = pd.to_datetime(resampled_data['rtc'])
    # Plot the resampled data
    plt.figure(figsize=(15,4), dpi=dpi)
    plt.plot(resampled_data['datetime'], resampled_data[y], color='blue')
    plt.gca().set(title=title, xlabel=xlabel, ylabel=ylabel)
    plt.show()
plot_df(data_external, x=data_external['rtc'], y='power_output_100', title='Trend and Seasonality of power output (15-minute interval)')
```

The following *Figure 6.6* is the output of the preceding Python program which shows the trend and pattern of the power output over time:

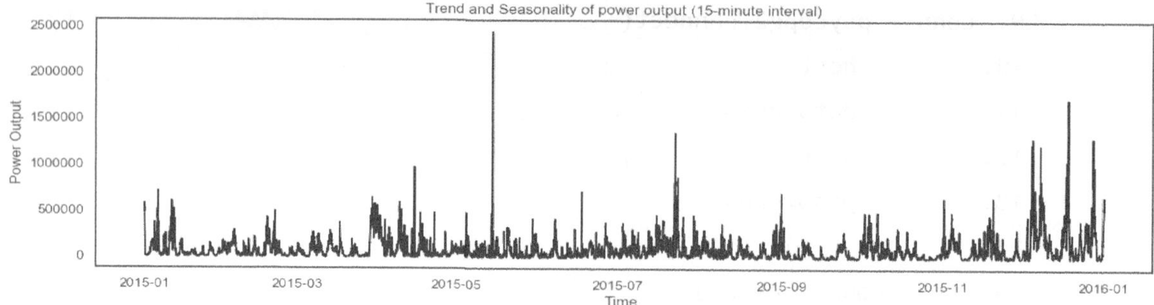

Figure 6.6: Trend and Seasonality of power output

- Let us now find the trend and seasonality of wind speed using Python:

```
def plot_df(wind_speed_df, x, y, title="", xlabel='rtc', ylabel='Wind Speed', dpi=100):
    plt.figure(figsize=(15,4), dpi=dpi)
    decomposition = sm.tsa.seasonal_decompose(y, model='additive', freq=30) # perform seasonal decomposition. If you are using different version of the statsmodels, you may need to use period parameter instead of "freq"
    trend = decomposition.trend # extract trend component
    seasonal = decomposition.seasonal # extract seasonal component
    plt.plot(x, y, color='yellow', label='Original Data') # plot original data in gray
    plt.plot(x, trend, color='blue', label='Trend') # plot trend component in blue
    plt.plot(x, seasonal, color='red', label='Seasonality') # plot seasonal component in red
    plt.gca().set(title=title, xlabel=xlabel, ylabel=ylabel)
    plt.legend()
    plt.show()
plot_df(data_external, x=data_external['rtc'], y=data_external['wind_speed_100'], title='Trend and Seasonality of wind speed')
```

The following *Figure 6.7* is the output of the preceding Python program which shows the trend and pattern of the wind speed:

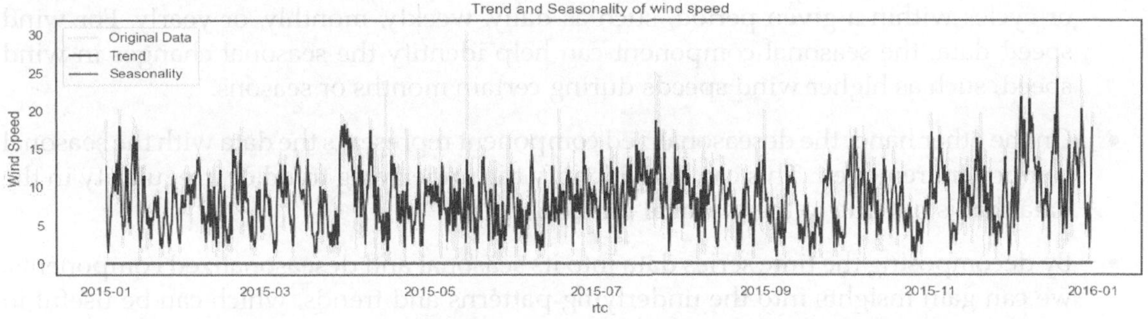

Figure 6.7: Trend and Seasonality of wind speed

- Let us now use a method to decomposes the time series into its parts - the trend, seasonal, and residual components:

```
1. import statsmodels.api as sm
2. decomposition = sm.tsa.seasonal_decompose(data_external['power_
   output_100'], model='additive',freq=7) #If you are using different
   version of the statsmodels, you may need to use period parameter
   instead of "freq"
3. fig = decomposition.plot()
4. plt.show()
```

The following *Figure 6.8* is the output the preceding program which shows the trend, seasonal and residual components:

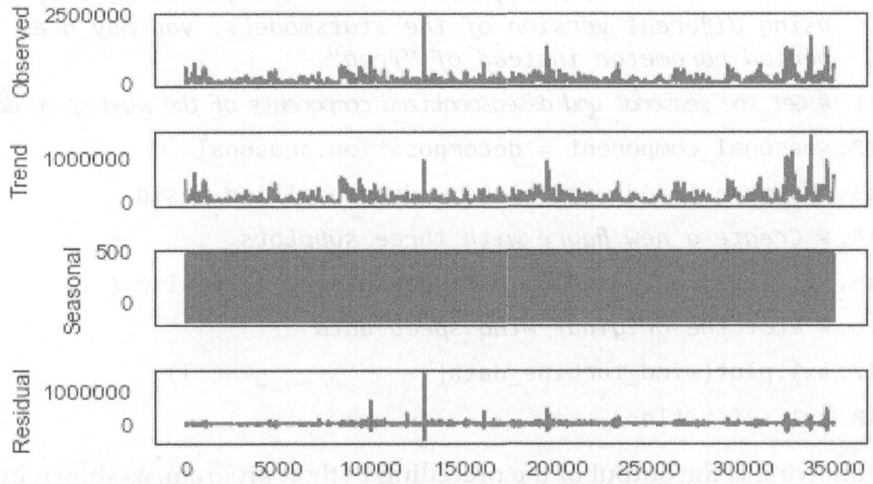

Figure 6.8: Trend and Seasonality of power output with residual

- Let us perform the trend and seasonal analysis on the wind speed variable as they impact the power output. The seasonal component can help identify recurring patterns or cycles within a given period, such as daily, weekly, monthly, or yearly. For wind speed data, the seasonal component can help identify the seasonal changes in wind speed, such as higher wind speeds during certain months or seasons.

- On the other hand, the deseasonalized component represents the data with the seasonal component removed. This can help identify the underlying trend or irregularity in the data that is not due to the seasonal pattern.
- By decomposing the time series data into its seasonal and deseasonalized components, we can gain insights into the underlying patterns and trends, which can be useful in making forecasts, identifying anomalies or outliers, and improving the accuracy of predictive models. The following is the Python program for the same:

```
import pandas as pd
import numpy as np
import statsmodels.api as sm
import matplotlib.pyplot as plt
# Load the wind turbine data with weekly frequency
wind_turbine_data = data_external[['rtc', 'wind_speed_100']]
# Set the timestamp column as the index of the DataFrame
wind_turbine_data.set_index("rtc", inplace=True)
# Perform seasonal decomposition on the wind speed data
decomposition = sm.tsa.seasonal_decompose(wind_turbine_data["wind_speed_100"], model="additive", freq=7) # If you are using different version of the statsmodels, you may need to use period parameter instead of "freq"
# Get the seasonal and deseasonalized components of the wind speed data
seasonal_component = decomposition.seasonal
deseasonalized_wind_speed = decomposition.resid
# Create a new figure with three subplots
fig, (ax1, ax2, ax3) = plt.subplots(3, 1, figsize=(12, 8))
# Plot the original wind speed data
ax1.plot(wind_turbine_data["wind_speed_100"])
ax1.set(title="Original Wind Speed Data")
```

The following is the output of the preceding Python program, as shown in *Figure 6.9*:

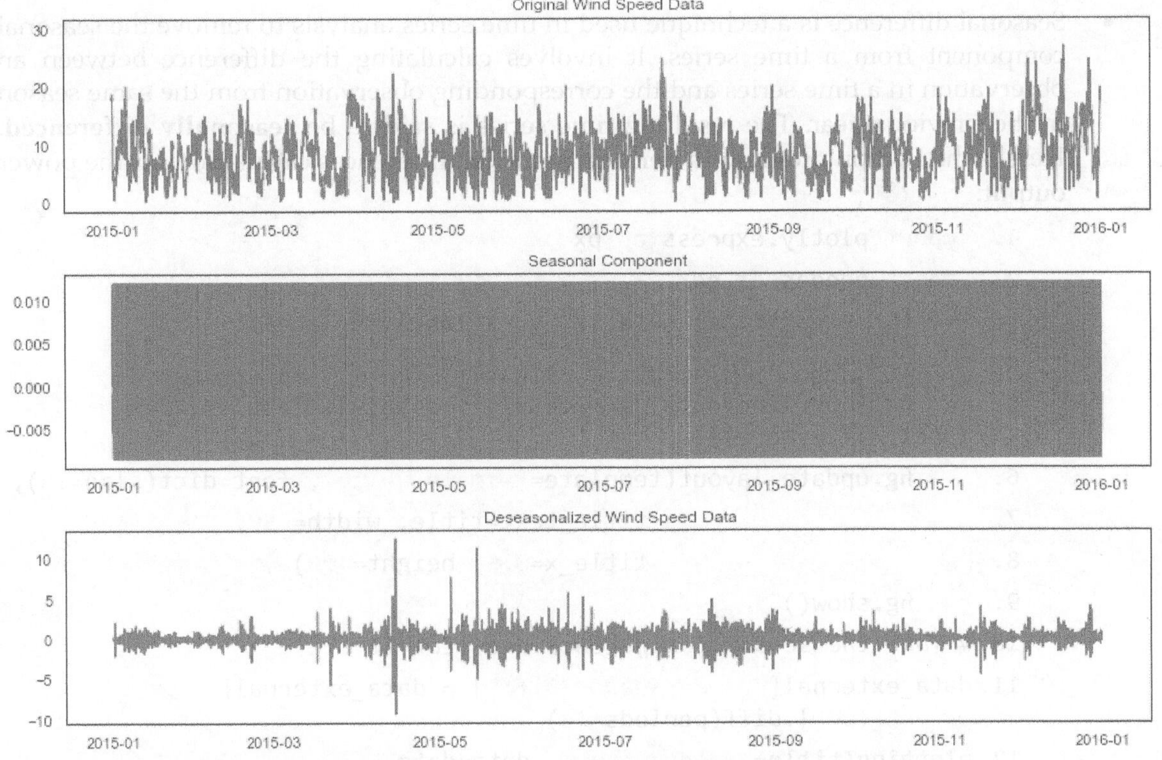

Figure 6.9: Seasonal and De-seasonalized component of wind speed

This Python program performs seasonal decomposition on wind speed data using the **statsmodels** library, and plots the original wind speed data along with its seasonal and deseasonalized components.

First, the program loads the wind turbine data with weekly frequency from an external source and sets the timestamp column as the index of the DataFrame. Then, it performs seasonal decomposition on the wind speed data using the additive model and a frequency of 7, which assumes a weekly seasonal component.

Next, the program retrieves the seasonal and deseasonalized components of the wind speed data from the decomposition object. The seasonal component represents the seasonal pattern in the data, while the deseasonalized component represents the data with the seasonal component removed.

The program then creates a new figure with three subplots using the matplotlib library. In the first subplot, it plots the original wind speed data. The second subplot plots the seasonal component of the wind speed data. In the third subplot, it plots the deseasonalized wind speed data.

Finally, the program sets titles for each subplot and displays the figure using the **plt.show()** method. This allows us to visualize the seasonal pattern in the data and the effect of removing it on the wind speed time series.

- Seasonal difference is a technique used in time series analysis to remove the seasonal component from a time series. It involves calculating the difference between an observation in a time series and the corresponding observation from the same season in the previous year. The resulting time series is said to be **seasonally differenced**. Here is the Python program to perform seasonal differences calculation for the power output:

```
import plotly.express as px
import pandas as pd
def plotting(title, data, x, y, x_label, y_label):
    """General function to plot the Power data."""
    fig = px.line(data, x=data[x], y=data[y], labels={x: x_label, y: y_label})
    fig.update_layout(template="simple_white", font=dict(size=18),
                      title_text=title, width=650,
                      title_x=0.5, height=400)
    fig.show()
# Take the seasonal difference and plot it
data_external["power_Season_Diff"] = data_external["power_output_100"].diff(periods=12)
plotting(title='Power Ouput', data=data_external, x='rtc', y='power_Season_Diff',
         x_label='Date', y_label='Power Output<br>Seasonal Difference')
```

The following *Figure 6.10* is the output of the preceding Python program which shows the power output:

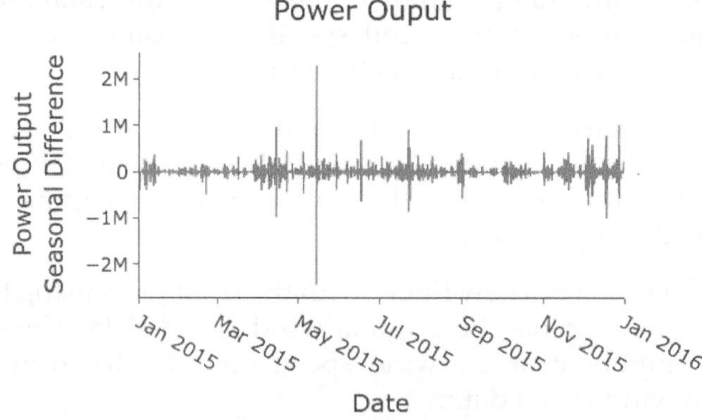

***Figure 6.10**: Seasonal difference of power output*

- The following is the Python program which performs time series forecasting of wind turbine power output using an ARIMA model. The significance of the program is to provide insights into future power generation, which can be useful for planning and decision-making:

```
import pandas as pd
import numpy as np
import statsmodels.api as sm
import matplotlib.pyplot as plt
# Load the wind turbine data into a Pandas DataFrame
wind_turbine_data = data_external[['rtc','power_output_100']]
# Set the timestamp column as the index of the DataFrame
wind_turbine_data.set_index("rtc", inplace=True)
# Fit an ARIMA model to the data
model = sm.tsa.ARIMA(wind_turbine_data["power_output_100"], order=(1, 1, 1))
fitted_model = model.fit()
# Generate forecasts for the next month
forecasts = fitted_model.forecast(steps=720)
# Convert the forecasted dates to the same format as the original dates
last_date = wind_turbine_data.index[-1]
forecasted_dates = pd.date_range(last_date, periods=720+1, freq="H")[1:]
# Extract the forecasted values from the forecasts array
forecasted_values = forecasts[0]
# Create a new figure with two subplots
fig, (ax1, ax2) = plt.subplots(2, 1, figsize=(12, 8))
# Plot the actual wind speed data and the forecasts
ax1.plot(wind_turbine_data["power_output_100"], label="Actual Power Output")
ax1.plot(forecasted_dates, forecasted_values, label="Forecasted Power Output", color="red")
ax1.set(title="Actual and Forecasted Power Output Data", ylabel="Power Output")
ax1.legend()
# Plot the residuals of the model
ax2.plot(fitted_model.resid)
```

```
ax2.set(title="Residuals of the ARIMA Model", ylabel="Residuals")
# Adjust the Layout of the subplots
plt.tight_layout()
# Display the plot
plt.show()
```

The program first loads the wind turbine data from an external source and sets the timestamp column as the index of the DataFrame. Then, an ARIMA model is fitted to the data using the statsmodels library. The order of the model is specified as (1, 1, 1), indicating that the model uses a first-order differencing for both the **Autoregressive** (**AR**) and **Moving Average** (**MA**) components.

The program generates forecasts for the next month by calling the **`forecast()`** function of the fitted model. The forecasted dates are then converted to the same format as the original dates, and the forecasted values are extracted from the forecasts array.

A new figure with two subplots is created using the **`subplots()`** function of the matplotlib library. The first subplot plots the actual wind turbine power output data along with the forecasted power output data. The second subplot plots the residuals of the ARIMA model.

Due to space limitation, the plots are not displayed here. We encourage readers to execute the above Python code and see the results themselves.

Testing Methods for Time Series Data

Different methods can be employed to understand the data better when testing time series data. Stationary and non-stationary and noise analysis are commonly used methods in IoT Analytics.

Stationary analysis involves examining the data to determine whether it is stable over time. It is deemed stationary if the data displays no significant changes in its statistical properties over time. Non-stationary analysis, however, entails data that exhibits a changing mean or variance over time. Understanding whether the data is stationary or non-stationary can help identify trends and patterns and predict future behaviour.

Noise analysis is another method used to test time series data. This analysis enables us to identify any random or unpredictable elements in the data that may affect the system's overall performance. By removing noise from the data, we can better understand the system's behaviour and make more accurate predictions.

For instance, in the context of IoT Analytics for wind turbines, stationary analysis can help determine if the turbine's performance is consistent over time or if there are significant fluctuations in its behaviour. Non-stationary analysis can help identify changing trends in wind speed or power output. In contrast, noise analysis can help filter out unpredictable factors affecting the turbine's performance.

Statistical tests are frequently used in this context to identify patterns and relationships between variables, to provide an objective, rigorous method for testing hypotheses and quantifying the strength and significance of relationships.

Statistical tests for time series data analysis are based on several key principles. Firstly, they assume that the data is random and that the observations are independent. Secondly, the tests presuppose that the data distribution is known or can be estimated. Lastly, they assume that the data is stationary, meaning that the statistical properties of the data remain consistent over time.

Various statistical tests are used in time series data analysis, including parametric and non-parametric tests. Parametric tests assume that the data follows a normal distribution, and the variances are equal. In contrast, non-parametric tests do not require any specific distribution assumption or equal variances.

Statistical tests for time series data analysis can be classified into univariate and multivariate. Univariate tests focus on a single variable, while multivariate tests examine the relationships between multiple variables. Some common statistical tests used in time series analysis include **autocorrelation, Augmented Dickey-Fuller (ADF), Granger causality**, and **Phillips-Perron (PP)** tests.

In summary, testing methods such as stationary and non-stationary and noise analysis are essential for analysing time series data. They are particularly useful in the context of IoT Analytics for wind turbines.

Statistical tests are crucial to time series data analysis in IoT Analytics. The choice of the appropriate test depends on the research question, the type of data being analysed, and the assumptions that can be made about the data.

Implementing Time Series Tests

After gaining a solid understanding of time series analysis and the various tests available, it is time to implement them in Python.

Implementing time series tests using Python involves using a variety of libraries and tools to perform statistical analysis on the data. In this section, we will use Python to explore how to implement stationary and non-stationary tests, noise analysis, and statistical tests like autocorrelation, ADF, Granger causality, and PP.

We will also discuss how to visualize and interpret the results of these tests to gain insights into the underlying trends and patterns in the time series data:

- **Stationary and non-stationary test:** In Python we can use **statsmodels** package to perform stationary and non-stationary test. Here is the Python program for the same:

```
import pandas as pd
import numpy as np
import matplotlib.pyplot as plt
```

```
from statsmodels.tsa.stattools import adfuller
from statsmodels.tsa.seasonal import seasonal_decompose
wind_turbine_data = data_external[['power_output_100']]
# perform stationary analysis
def stationary_analysis(wind_turbine_data ):
    # calculate rolling mean and standard deviation
    rolmean = wind_turbine_data .rolling(window=12).mean()
    rolstd = wind_turbine_data.rolling(window=12).std()
    # plot rolling statistics
    plt.plot(wind_turbine_data , color='blue', label='Original')
    plt.plot(rolmean, color='red', label='Rolling Mean')
    plt.plot(rolstd, color='black', label='Rolling Std')
    plt.legend(loc='best')
    plt.title('Rolling Mean & Standard Deviation')
    plt.show()
    # perform Augmented Dickey-Fuller test
    print('Results of Augmented Dickey-Fuller Test:')
    adf_test = adfuller(wind_turbine_data['power_output_100'], autolag='AIC')
    adf_output = pd.Series(adf_test[0:4], index=['Test Statistic','p-value','#Lags Used','Number of Observations Used'])
    for key,value in adf_test[4].items():
        adf_output['Critical Value (%s)'%key] = value
    print(adf_output)
# perform non-stationary analysis
def non_stationary_analysis(wind_turbine_data):
    decomposition = seasonal_decompose(wind_turbine_data, model='additive', freq=12) # If you are using different version of the statsmodels, you may need to use period parameter instead of "freq"
    # plot the decomposition
    fig, (ax1,ax2,ax3,ax4) = plt.subplots(4,1, figsize=(15,8))
    wind_turbine_data.plot(ax=ax1)
    ax1.set(title='Original Data')
    decomposition.trend.plot(ax=ax2)
    ax2.set(title='Trend Component')
    decomposition.seasonal.plot(ax=ax3)
```

```
    ax3.set(title='Seasonal Component')
    decomposition.resid.plot(ax=ax4)
    ax4.set(title='Residual Component')
    plt.tight_layout()
    plt.show()
# call the functions
stationary_analysis(wind_turbine_data)
non_stationary_analysis(wind_turbine_data)
```

The program defines two functions, **stationary_analysis** and **non_stationary_analysis**, to perform stationary and non-stationary analysis, on the **wind_turbine_data**.

The **stationary_analysis** function calculates the rolling mean and standard deviation for the given window size of 12 using the **rolling()** pandas method. It then plots the original data, rolling mean, and rolling standard deviation on a single graph using **matplotlib.pyplot**. Finally, it performs the **Augmented Dickey-Fuller** (**ADF**) test using the **adfuller()** method from **statsmodels.tsa.stattools** and prints the test results on the console.

The **non_stationary_analysis** function decomposes the time series into trend, seasonal, and residual components using the **seasonal_decompose()** method from **statsmodels.tsa.seasonal**. It then plots the original data, trend, seasonal, and residual components on separate subplots using **matplotlib.pyplot**.

Finally, the program calls the two functions, **stationary_analysis** and **non_stationary_analysis**, with the **wind_turbine_data** as the input to perform the stationary and non-stationary analysis on the **power_output_100** column of the **data_external** dataframe. The results are displayed using various plots and console outputs.

The following is the stationary test result of the preceding Python program (see *Figure 6.11*):

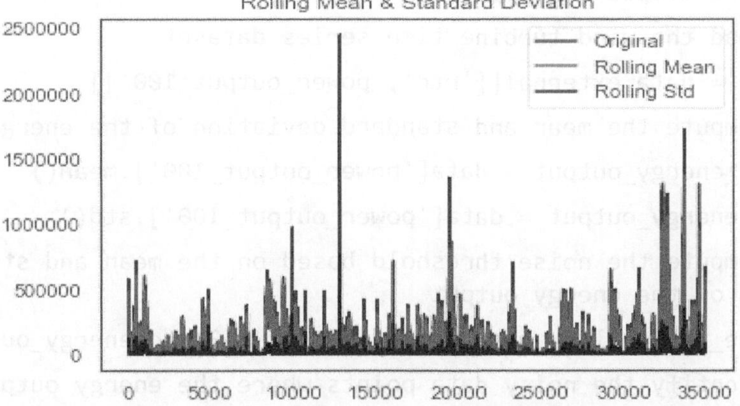

***Figure 6.11:** Rolling mean and Standard deviation*

The following is the non-stationary test result of the preceding Python program (see *Figure 6.12*):

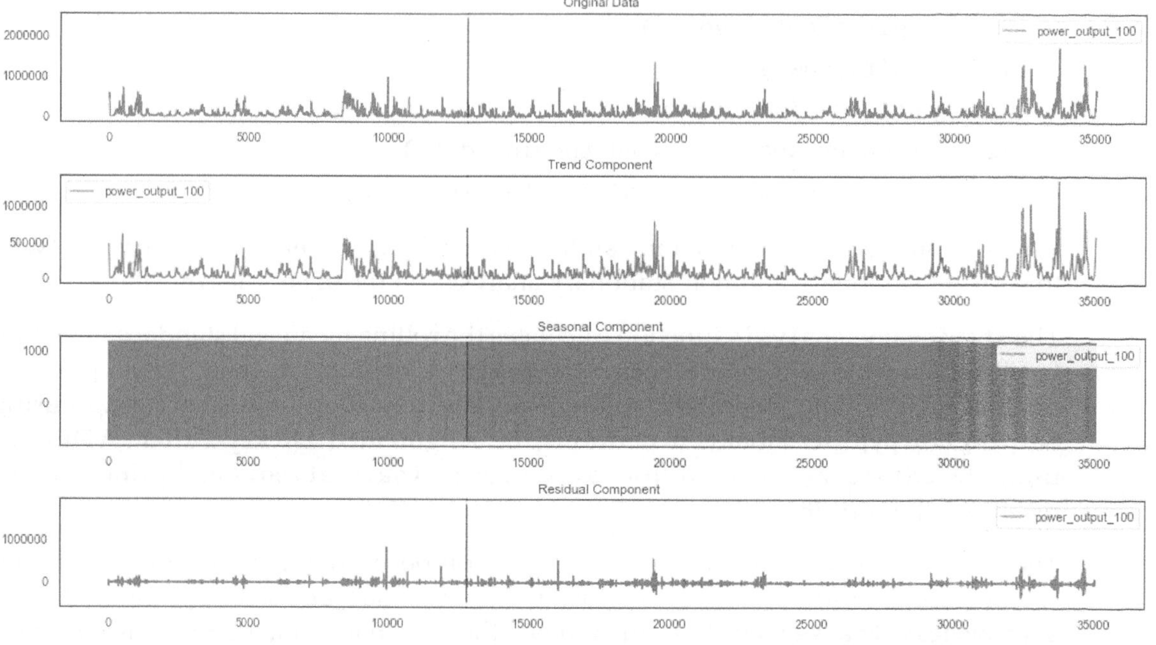

***Figure 6.12:** Original, Trend, seasonal and residual components*

- **Noise analysis:** The Python program analyses noise on a wind turbine time series dataset. The purpose of noise analysis is to identify and filter out the data points that are not meaningful or are erroneous:

```
import pandas as pd
import numpy as np
import matplotlib.pyplot as plt
# Load the wind turbine time series dataset
data = data_external[['rtc','power_output_100']]
# Compute the mean and standard deviation of the energy output
mean_energy_output = data['power_output_100'].mean()
std_energy_output = data['power_output_100'].std()
# Compute the noise threshold based on the mean and standard deviation of the energy output
noise_threshold = mean_energy_output + 3*std_energy_output
# Identify the noisy data points where the energy output exceeds the noise threshold
```

```
noisy_data = data[data['power_output_100'] > noise_threshold]
# Plot the noisy data points
plt.figure()
plt.plot(data['rtc'], data['power_output_100'], 'b-
', label='Energy Output')
plt.plot(noisy_data['rtc'], noisy_data['power_
output_100'], 'ro', label='Noisy Data')
plt.fill_between(data['rtc'], noise_threshold, data['power_out-
put_100'], alpha=0.2, color='grey', label='Noise Threshold')
plt.title('Wind Turbine Time Series with Noisy Data Points')
plt.xlabel('timestamp')
plt.ylabel('power_output_100')
plt.legend()
plt.show()
```

The preceding program reads in a time series dataset for wind turbine data and selects two specific columns: **rtc** which represents timestamps, and **power_output_100** which is the energy output. Next, it calculates the mean and standard deviation of the energy output column. It computes a noise threshold set at three times the standard deviation preceding the mean energy output using these values. Any data points that surpass this threshold are classified as noisy data. The program then generates a plot of the wind turbine time series, marking the noisy data points with red dots and the noise threshold with a gray shaded region. This visualization enables easy identification of the noisy data points and the noise threshold.

The following *Figure 6.13* is the output of the preceding program:

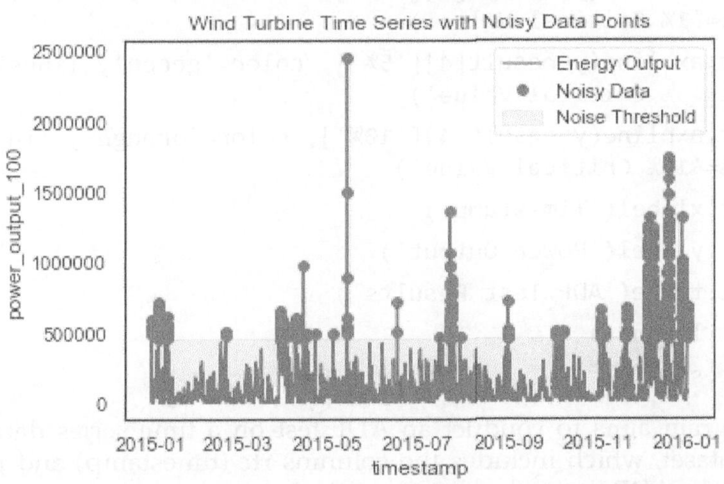

***Figure 6.13:** Noise analysis of power output*

- The **Augmented Dickey-Fuller** (**ADF**) test is a statistical method used to determine whether a time series is stationary or non-stationary. A stationary time series has a constant mean and variance over time, while a non-stationary time series has a changing mean and variance over time. The ADF test calculates a test statistic and p-value based on the null hypothesis that the time series is non-stationary. If the p-value is below a specified significance level (0.05), the null hypothesis is rejected, and the time series is considered stationary:

```
import pandas as pd
import matplotlib.pyplot as plt
from statsmodels.tsa.stattools import adfuller
# Load the time series data
data = data_external[['rtc', 'power_output_100']]
# Perform ADF test
result = adfuller(data['power_output_100'])
# Print the test results
print('ADF Statistic: %f' % result[0])
print('p-value: %f' % result[1])
print('Critical Values:')
for key, value in result[4].items():
    print('\t%s: %.3f' % (key, value))
# Plot the time series data with critical values
plt.plot(data.index, data['power_output_100'], color='blue', label='Power Output')
plt.axhline(y=result[4]['1%'], color='red', linestyle='-', label='1% Critical Value')
plt.axhline(y=result[4]['5%'], color='green', linestyle='-', label='5% Critical Value')
plt.axhline(y=result[4]['10%'], color='orange', linestyle='-', label='10% Critical Value')
plt.xlabel('Timestamp')
plt.ylabel('Power Output')
plt.title('ADF Test Results')
plt.legend()
plt.show()
```

This Python program aims to conduct an ADF test on a time series dataset. The program first loads the dataset, which includes the columns **rtc** (timestamp) and **`power_output_100`** (energy output). The ADF test is then performed on the **`power_output_100`** column using the **`statsmodels.tsa.stattools`** library.

The ADF test returns several statistics, including the test statistic, p-value, and critical values. The critical values serve as thresholds for the test statistic, where values below the critical values indicate stationarity. The program prints the ADF test results and plots the time series data with the critical values, allowing for visual identification of stationary regions. The following *Figure 6.14* is output of the preceding program:

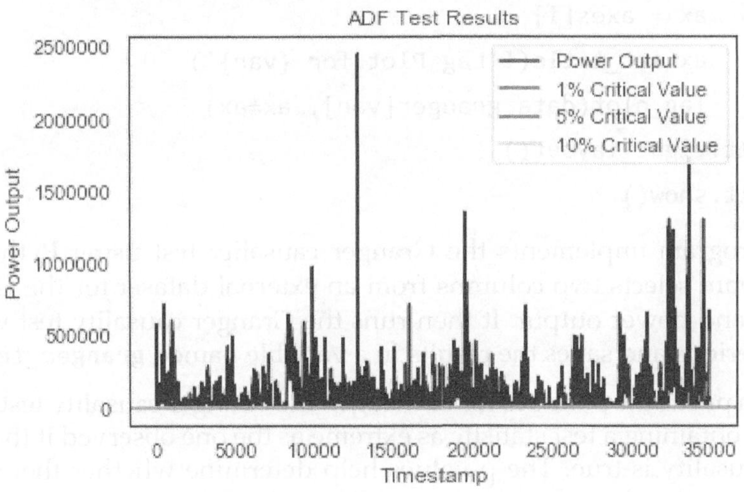

***Figure 6.14:** ADF test result*

- **Granger causality tests**: It is a statistical technique used to determine whether one time series can be used to predict another time series. It is named after Nobel laureate *Clive Granger*, who developed this method in the 1960s. The Granger causality test examines the causal relationship between two time series by comparing the accuracy of the forecast of one time series with and without the lagged values of the other time series:

```
import pandas as pd
from statsmodels.tsa.stattools import grangercausalitytests
import matplotlib.pyplot as plt
# Select two columns for the Granger Causality Test
data_granger = data_external[['wind_speed_100', 'power_
output_100']]
# Run the Granger Causality Test with a maximum lag of 5 time periods
maxlag = 5
granger_test_results = grangercausalitytests(data_
granger, maxlag=maxlag, verbose=False)
# Print the p-values for each lag
for lag in range(1, maxlag+1):
    print(f'Lag {lag}: p-value = {granger_test_results[lag][0]
```

```
    ["ssr_ftest"][1]:.3f}')
# Plot the lag plot for the Granger Causality Test
fig, axes = plt.subplots(nrows=2, ncols=1, figsize=(8, 6))
for i, var in enumerate(['wind_speed_100', 'power_output_100']):
    ax = axes[i]
    ax.set_title(f'Lag Plot for {var}')
    lag_plot(data_granger[var], ax=ax)
plt.tight_layout()
plt.show()
```

The preceding program implements the Granger causality test using Python's statsmodels library. The program selects two columns from an external dataset for the Granger causality test: wind speed and power output. It then runs the Granger causality test with a maximum lag of five time periods and saves the results in a variable named **granger_test_results**.

The program then prints the p-values for each lag in the Granger causality test, which indicates the probability of obtaining a test statistic as extreme as the one observed if the null hypothesis of no Granger causality is true. The p-values help determine whether there is a statistically significant causal relationship between the two time series.

Finally, the program plots the lag plot for the Granger causality test using the matplotlib library. The lag plot shows the correlation between a variable and its lagged values and helps identify whether the time series is stationary or exhibits any patterns or trends.

Overall, this program helps to identify the causal relationship between wind speed and power output, which can be used to make better decisions in various fields such as energy management and climate research. Here is the output of the above Python program, as shown in *Figure 6.15*:

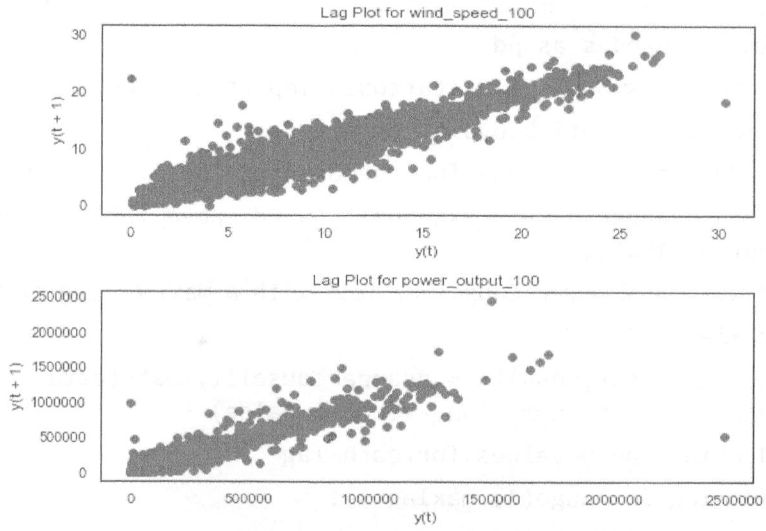

***Figure 6.15:** Lag plots of wind speed and power output*

- The **Kwiatkowski-Phillips-Schmidt-Shin (KPSS)** test, is used to determine whether a time series is stationary or non-stationary. A stationary time series maintains its statistical properties, such as the mean, variance, and autocorrelation, consistently over time. On the other hand, a non-stationary time series demonstrates trends, seasonality, and variable statistical properties over time. The following is a Python code for performing the KPSS test:

```
import pandas as pd
import matplotlib.pyplot as plt
from statsmodels.tsa.stattools import kpss
# Load the time series data
data = data_external[['rtc', 'power_output_100']]
# Perform KPSS test
result = kpss(data['power_output_100'], regression='c')
# Print the test results
print('KPSS Statistic: %f' % result[0])
print('p-value: %f' % result[1])
print('Critical Values:')
for key, value in result[3].items():
    print('\t%s: %.3f' % (key, value))
# Plot the time series data with critical values
plt.plot(data['rtc'], data['power_output_100'])
plt.axhline(y=result[3]['1%'], color='y', linestyle='-')
plt.axhline(y=result[3]['5%'], color='g', linestyle='-')
plt.axhline(y=result[3]['10%'], color='r', linestyle='-')
plt.xlabel('Timestamp')
plt.ylabel('Power Output')
plt.title('KPSS Test Results')
plt.show()
```

The program first loads the time series data, which includes a timestamp column **rtc** and **power_output_100**. It then performs the KPSS test on the **power_output_100** column with a constant trend. The test results include the KPSS statistic, p-value, and critical values.

Finally, the program plots the time series data with the critical values marked as horizontal lines on the plot. The critical values are based on the significance level chosen, such as 1%, 5%, and 10%. The following *Figure 6.16* is the output of the preceding Python program:

```
KPSS Statistic: 2.600551
```

```
p-value: 0.010000
Critical Values:
	10%: 0.347
	5%: 0.463
	2.5%: 0.574
	1%: 0.739
```

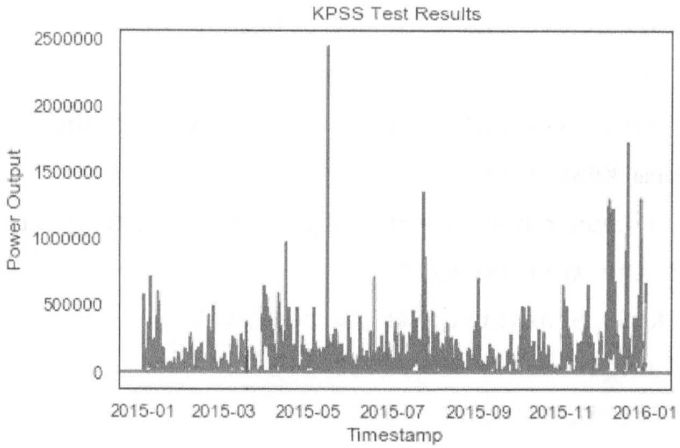

***Figure 6.16:** KPSS test results*

- The **Phillips-Perron (PP)** test is a statistical test used to test for stationarity in time series data. The PP test is similar to the more well-known Dickey-Fuller test, but it is more robust to certain forms of non-stationarity and can also account for serial correlation. The following is the Python code for implementing PP test:

```
import pandas as pd
import statsmodels.tsa.stattools as ts
import matplotlib.pyplot as plt
# Load the time series data
data = data_external[['rtc', 'power_output_100']]
# Extract the power output column
power_output = data['power_output_100']
# Run the Phillips-Perron test
pp_test = ts.adfuller(power_output, regression='ct')
# Print the test results
print('Phillips-Perron Test Results:')
print('ADF Statistic:', pp_test[0])
print('p-value:', pp_test[1])
```

```
print('Critical Values:')
for key, value in pp_test[4].items():
    print('\t%s: %.3f' % (key, value))
# Plot the time series data with critical values
plt.plot(data['rtc'], power_output, label='Power Output')
plt.axhline(y=pp_test[4]['1%'], color='y', linestyle='--', label='1% Critical Value')
plt.axhline(y=pp_test[4]['5%'], color='g', linestyle='--', label='5% Critical Value')
plt.axhline(y=pp_test[4]['10%'], color='r', linestyle='--', label='10% Critical Value')
plt.legend()
plt.title('Phillips-Perron Test Results')
plt.xlabel('Timestamp')
plt.ylabel('Power Output')
plt.show()
```

The preceding Python program implements the **Phillips-Perron** (**PP**) test for a wind turbine power output data time series.

The program first loads the necessary libraries: **`pandas`**, **`statsmodels.tsa.stattools`**, and **`matplotlib.pyplot`**.

Then, it loads the time series data from an external source into a Pandas **`DataFrame`** and selects the **real-time clock** (**`rtc`**) and **`power_output_100`** columns.

Next, the program extracts the **`power_output_100`** column from the **`DataFrame`** and stores it in the **`power_output`** variable.

The PP test is then run using the **`adfuller()`** function from the **`statsmodels.tsa.stattools`** library, with the **`power_output`** variable passed in as an argument. The **`regression='ct'`** parameter specifies that the regression model should include a constant and a linear trend.

The program then prints out the results of the PP test, including the ADF statistic, p-value, and critical values. The critical values are printed using a for loop that iterates over the items in the dictionary returned by the **`adfuller()`** function.

Finally, the program plots the time series data and the critical values using the **`plot()`** function from the **`matplotlib.pyplot`** library. The critical values are plotted as horizontal lines using the **`axhline()`** function, with their respective levels and colors specified. The legend, title, and axis labels are also set using various **`plt`** functions.

The following is the output of the preceding Python program (see *Figure 6.17*):

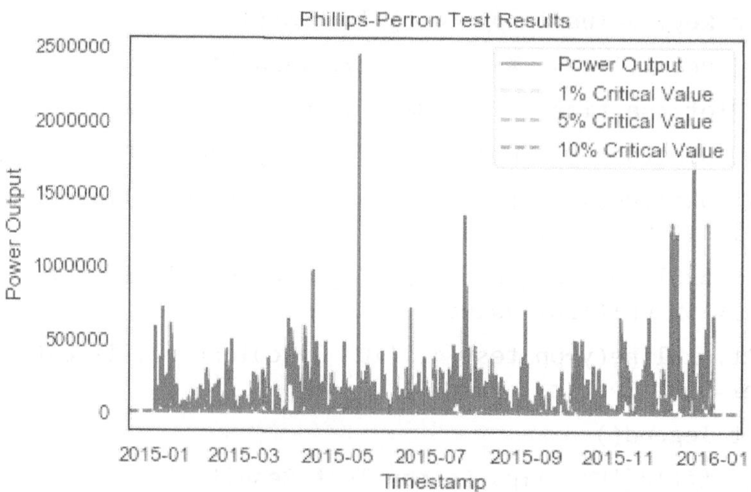

Figure 6.17: *PP test results*

Conclusion

In this chapter, we explored statistical techniques and analysis methods for time series data, using the wind turbine dataset from NREL as an illustration. The dataset records wind speed, direction, pressure, temperature, and power output.

We summarized the data using descriptive statistics such as mean, median, mode, variance, and standard deviation, and visualized it using graphs and charts like histograms, scatter plots, and box plots. We also covered Univariate, Bivariate, and Multivariate analysis to study single, two, and multiple variables, respectively, to understand their distribution, central tendency, and variability, and to identify patterns and interrelationships.

Furthermore, we discussed time series analysis, which involves various statistical tests such as trend analysis, seasonal analysis, autocorrelation, forecasting, stationary and non-stationary analysis, noise analysis, and various autocorrelation and causality tests like the **Augmented Dickey-Fuller** (**ADF**) test, Granger causality tests, and **Phillips-Perron** (**PP**) tests.

Using the wind turbine dataset, we applied these techniques to optimize turbine performance and gain valuable insights into other time series datasets.

In next chapter, we will focus on forecasting techniques for time series data using **Autoregressive** (**AR**) models. The AR model is a popular approach for predicting future values based on past observations.

We will explore the **Auto Regressive Integrated Moving Average** (**ARIMA**) and **Moving Average** (**MA**) techniques for estimating future values of a time series. Additionally, we will dive into several Python libraries such as **Tsfresh** and **AutoTS**, which provide scalable hypothesis tests and automatic time series forecasting for high accuracy.

We will also apply these techniques to industrial equipment. We will use these models to predict future availability and productivity of equipment, as well as perform predictive maintenance and identify potential equipment failures.

We will build metric tables to store the predictions in SQL tables to facilitate easy access and usage of the prediction results. These tables will be used for planning and scheduling.

Points to Remember

Following are the key takeaways from this chapter:

- Summarizing time series datasets using descriptive statistics, including mean, median, mode, variance, and standard deviation. Graphs and charts such as histograms, scatter plots, and box plots can be used to visualize the data and identify patterns or outliers.

- Univariate analysis is used to examine a single variable at a time, and it aids in understanding the distribution, central tendency, and variability of the wind turbine sensor's wind speed measurements. On the other hand, Bivariate analysis examines the relationship between two variables, such as wind speed and temperature, to comprehend how changes in wind speed due to temperature impact energy output.

- Multivariate analysis analyzes multiple variables simultaneously to identify patterns and understand their interrelationships. The relationship between wind speed, wind direction, and pressure, for example, can be studied to optimize the performance of the wind turbine.

- Time series analysis, which is frequently employed in IoT Analytics to analyze data that changes over time, is a statistical method that assists in identifying patterns and trends. It can forecast future events and make predictions based on historical data. The wind turbine dataset obtained from NREL contains variables such as wind speed, wind direction, pressure, temperature, and power output. By applying time series analysis techniques to this data, valuable insights into the turbine's performance can be obtained, and patterns can be identified.

- Various techniques, including trend analysis, seasonal analysis, autocorrelation, and forecasting, are utilized in time series analysis. Trend analysis identifies the overall direction of the data over time, whereas seasonal analysis identifies recurring patterns within the data.

- Autocorrelation and forecasting leverage past data to make predictions about future outcomes. Additionally, stationary and non-stationary analyses, noise analyses, autocorrelation tests, the **Augmented Dickey-Fuller** (**ADF**) tests, **Granger causality** tests, and **Phillips-Perron** (**PP**) tests are used to perform statistical tests on time series datasets.

Join our book's Discord space

Join the book's Discord Workspace for Latest updates, Offers, Tech happenings around the world, New Release and Sessions with the Authors:

https://discord.bpbonline.com

CHAPTER 7

Time Series Forecasting and Predictions

Introduction

In this chapter, we will focus on time series analysis and forecasting. We will cover key topics such as autocorrelation, partial autocorrelation, data lag identification, data smoothening, and various forecasting models such as autoregressive models, **Auto Regressive Integrated Moving Average** (**ARIMA**), and **Moving Average** (**MA**) models.

We will also explore Python libraries such as Tsfresh and AutoTS, designed specifically for high accuracy in the Time Series feature extraction and forecasting. We will use these libraries to demonstrate how to build powerful predictive models for various industries, such as wind turbines and automobiles.

Finally, we will discuss how to store **Analytical Base Table** (**ABT**) in the analytical zone of the data lake using SQL tables.

Structure

In this chapter, we will cover the following topics:

- Data Smoothing
- Data Lag Identification
- Autocorrelation and Partial Autocorrection
- Forecasting using an ar Model.

- Moving Average
- Arima
- Time Series Feature Extraction
- Automatic Time Series
- Storing Wind Turbine Predictions in the Analytical Zone
- Analytical Base Table

Objectives

By the end of this chapter, you will be able to understand the basics of time series analysis and forecasting. You can apply techniques such as data smoothening, data lag identification, autocorrelation, and partial autocorrelation, to analyze time series data.

The chapter will cover various forecasting models such as **Autoregressive (AR)**, MA, and ARIMA models. You will learn how to build models using Python libraries such as Tsfresh and AutoTS. These libraries are designed for high accuracy in time series feature extraction and forecasting.

You can also apply the techniques learned in this chapter to build predictions for industrial equipment such as wind turbines. Predictive maintenance and equipment failures will be covered in the *Chapter 8, Monitoring and Preventive Maintenance.*

Finally, you will learn how to store the ABT in the analytical zone of the data lake using Python and SQL.

The chapter will provide you with the essential skills and knowledge to analyze and forecast the **Industrial Internet of Things (IIoT)** data using Python, resulting in a comprehensive understanding of time series analysis and forecasting.

Data Smoothing

Data smoothing is a method that involves averaging out the fluctuations in time series data to eliminate noise or irregularities. Its primary objective in IoT Analytics is to enhance the accuracy of predictive models and detect patterns and trends in the data.

Data smoothing is advantageous when working with inconsistent or noisy data, such as sensor readings from IoT devices. Eliminating noise and irregularities makes recognizing underlying trends and patterns in the data easier, resulting in more precise predictions and decisions.

For instance, in the wind turbine dataset, data smoothing can remove power output fluctuations triggered by changes in environmental variables such as wind speed and temperature. This helps to identify power output trends, such as energy efficiency changes and maintenance requirements, for more accurate predictions of future performance. Moving averages, exponential smoothing, or Gaussian smoothing are some techniques available. The selection of a particular method depends on the data's characteristics and the specific application's requirements.

The requirements for applying data smoothing techniques depend on the dataset and the problems we will solve. It is imperative to perform basic checks to ensure that data smoothing techniques will help improve the accuracy of the prediction before implementing such techniques. Let us go through a Python example on the same.

Data Smoothing using Python

The following Python program showcases the application of data smoothing on time series data within IoT Analytics. The program connects with the **IoTDataLake** database and retrieves wind turbine data from the **c_external_wind_turbine_data** table in the **curatedzone** schema. It calculates the moving average of the power output using a window size of 24 and displays the original data and the moving average on a graph. The program also displays the smoothed data obtained by subtracting the moving average from the original data. Finally, a comparison graph of the original data, moving average, and smoothed data is displayed.

```
import pandas as pd
import matplotlib.pyplot as plt
import psycopg2
#Connect to datalake
conn = psycopg2.connect(
        host="localhost",
        database="IoTDataLake",
        user="postgres",
        password=""
    )
cur = conn.cursor()
#Query curated zone of the data lake for the wind turbine table and create a dataframe
cur.execute("SELECT * FROM curatedzone.c_external_wind_turbine_data")
wind_turbine_data= pd.DataFrame(cur.fetchall(), columns=['id','rtc','year', 'month', 'day', 'hour', 'minute', 'temperature_100', 'temperature_120', 'temperature_80', 'wind_direction_100', 'wind_direction_120',
      'wind_direction_80', 'wind_speed_100','wind_speed_120','wind_speed_80','pressure_200','pressure_100','pressure_0','power_output_80','power_output_100',
```

```
        'power_output_120'])
# Calculate moving average of power output
window_size = 24 # choose window size
rolling_avg = wind_turbine_data['power_output_100'].rolling(window_size).mean()
# Plot original data and moving average
plt.plot(wind_turbine_data['rtc'], wind_turbine_data['power_output_100'], label='Original Data')
plt.plot(wind_turbine_data['rtc'], rolling_avg, label='Moving Average')
# Set plot labels and legend
plt.xlabel('Time')
plt.ylabel('Power Output')
plt.title('Original Data vs. Moving Average')
plt.legend()
# Show the plot
plt.show()
# Plot smoothed data against original data
plt.plot(wind_turbine_data['rtc'], wind_turbine_data['power_output_100'], label='Original Data')
plt.plot(wind_turbine_data['rtc'], rolling_avg, label='Moving Average')
plt.plot(wind_turbine_data['rtc'], wind_turbine_data['power_output_100'] - rolling_avg, label='Smoothed Data')
print("Here is the comparison of original data and smoothed data")
# Set plot labels and legend
plt.xlabel('Time')
plt.ylabel('Power Output')
plt.title('Original , Moving Average and Smoothed Data')
plt.legend()
# Show the plot
plt.show()
```

Here is the output from the preceding program which shows the original data and moving average which has smoothened the data without having significant noise. We can observe that the data in yellow is much more consistent than the data in blue (see *Figure 7.1*):

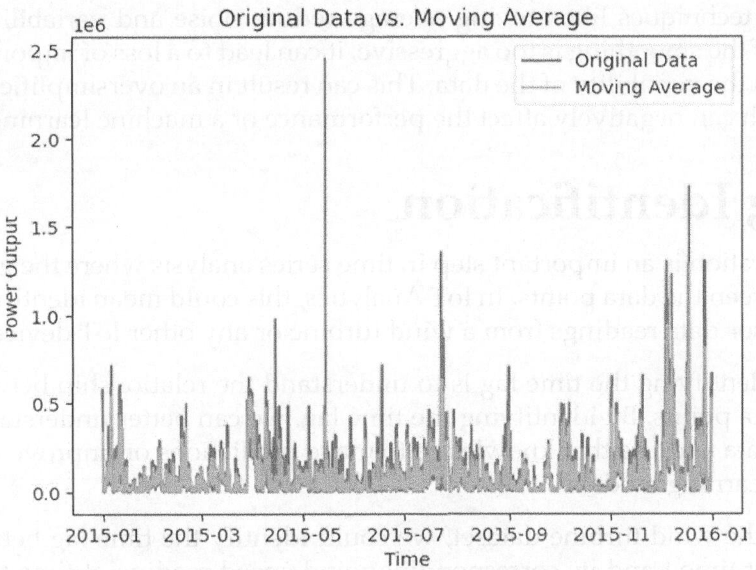

***Figure 7.1:** Data Smoothing using Moving Average method*

Let us see the result of further smoothening to check the data distribution against original and moving average data. Here is the output on the comparison (see *Figure 7.2*):

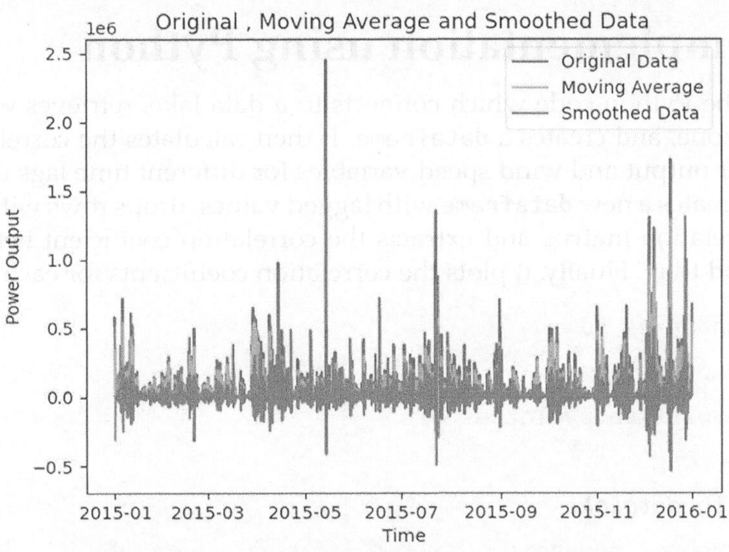

***Figure 7.2:** Moving Average after smoothening*

We can see that the green-coloured data is more consistent than the moving average. But we need to be mindful that this kind of smoothening may impact the prediction, and sometimes lead to underfitting.

Data smoothing techniques like moving average reduce noise and variability in time series data. However, if the smoothing is too aggressive, it can lead to a loss of important information and a decrease in the variability of the data. This can result in an oversimplified representation of the data, which can negatively affect the performance of a machine learning model.

Data Lag Identification

Data lag identification is an important step in time series analysis where the goal is to identify the time lag between the data points. In IoT Analytics, this could mean identifying the time lag between the sensor data readings from a wind turbine or any other IoT device.

The reason for identifying the time lag is to understand the relationship between the current and previous data points. By identifying the time lag, we can better understand the temporal patterns in the data and use that knowledge to make predictions or improve the performance of our machine learning models.

For instance, in the wind turbine dataset, we could identify the time lag between the power output reading at time t and its corresponding wind speed reading at time t - k. This would allow us to determine how much wind speed is required to generate a certain power output level.

Overall, data lag identification is a crucial step in time series analysis as it helps us uncover the temporal patterns in the data and enables us to build better predictive models.

Data Lag Implementation using Python

The following is the Python code which connects to a data lake, retrieves wind turbine data from the curated zone, and creates a **dataframe**. It then calculates the correlation coefficients between the power output and wind speed variables for different time lags up to a maximum lag value of 10. It creates a new **dataframe** with lagged values, drops rows with missing values, calculates the correlation matrix, and extracts the correlation coefficient between the power output at time t and t-lag. Finally, it plots the correlation coefficients for each lag value:

```
import pandas as pd
import numpy as np
import matplotlib.pyplot as plt
import psycopg2
#Connect to datalake
conn = psycopg2.connect(
        host="localhost",
        database="IoTDataLake",
        user="postgres",
        password=""
```

```
    )
cur = conn.cursor()
#Query curated zone of the data Lake for the wind turbine table and create a dataframe
cur.execute("SELECT * FROM curatedzone.c_external_wind_turbine_data")
wind_turbine_data= pd.DataFrame(cur.fetchall(), columns=['id','rtc','year',  'month', 'day', 'hour', 'minute', 'temperature_100', 'temperature_120', 'temperature_80', 'wind_direction_100', 'wind_direction_120',
        'wind_direction_80', 'wind_speed_100','wind_speed_120','wind_speed_80','pressure_200','pressure_100','pressure_0','power_output_80','power_output_100',
        'power_output_120'])
# Define the maximum lag value to consider
max_lag = 10
# Create a list to store the correlation coefficients for each lag value
corrs = []
# Calculate the correlation coefficients for each lag value up to max_lag
for lag in range(1, max_lag+1):
    # Create a new dataframe with lagged values
    cols_to_lag = ['power_output_100', 'wind_speed_100']
    for i in range(1, lag+1):
        for col in cols_to_lag:
            wind_turbine_data[col + '(t-' + str(i) + ')'] = wind_turbine_data[col].shift(i)
    # Drop rows with NaN values
    df_lagged = wind_turbine_data.dropna()
    # Calculate the correlation matrix
    corr_matrix = df_lagged.corr()
    # Extract the correlation coefficient between the power output at time t and time t-lag
    corr = corr_matrix.loc['power_output_100', 'power_output_100(t-' + str(lag) + ')']
    # Append the correlation coefficient to the list of correlations
    corrs.append(corr)
```

```
# Plot the correlation coefficients for each lag value
plt.plot(range(1, max_lag+1), corrs)
plt.xlabel('Lag')
plt.ylabel('Correlation Coefficient')
plt.show()
```

Here is the output of the preceding program (see *Figure 7.3*):

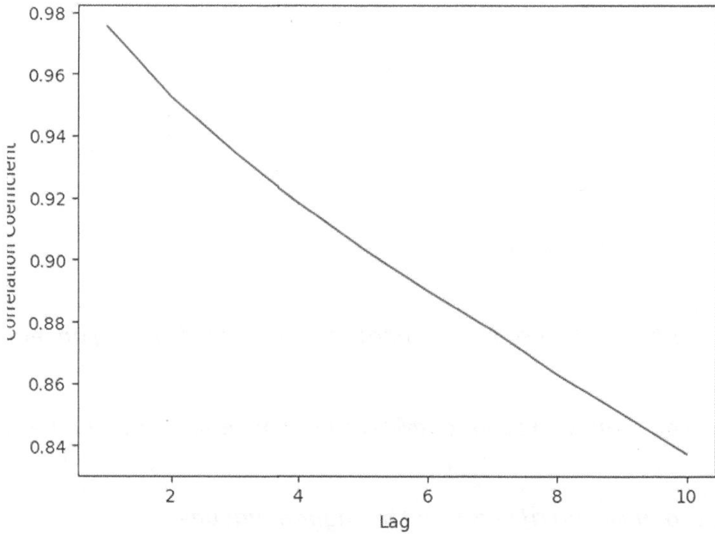

Figure 7.3: *Data Lag diagram*

The significance of the lag plot lies in the fact that it helps identify the correlation between a variable and its lagged values. In this case, the lag plot shows that the correlation coefficient between the wind turbine power output and its lagged values decreases as the lag increases. A high correlation coefficient at low lags (For example: lags 1-4) indicates that the current value of the variable is highly dependent on its recent past values. On the other hand, a low correlation coefficient at high lags (for example, lag 10) indicates that the current value of the variable is less dependent on its distant past values. By identifying the correlation coefficients at different lags, we can understand the temporal dependence structure of the variable and use it to make predictions or take other data-driven decisions.

Autocorrelation and Partial Autocorrection

Autocorrelation: In time series analysis, it refers to the correlation between the values of a time series and its lagged values. In simpler terms, it measures how closely a given observation relates to its past values. Autocorrelation is useful for identifying patterns in a time series, such as periodic or seasonal behavior, and for understanding the degree of predictability of future values based on past values.

On the other hand, Partial Autocorrelation measures the correlation between two observations in a time series while controlling for the correlations with the intervening values. It helps to determine the direct relationship between two observations and is useful for identifying the order of an autoregressive model.

In Industrial IoT Data Analytics, autocorrelation and partial autocorrelation are fundamental techniques for time series analysis and forecasting industrial equipment such as wind turbine and automobiles. With sensors and other monitoring devices, industrial IoT devices generate vast amounts of time series data that can provide insights into potential equipment failures. For example, autocorrelation can detect recurring patterns in sensor readings from wind turbine equipment, such as spikes in temperature or air pressure. We can forecast future values based on past data by detecting these patterns. On the other hand, partial autocorrelation can be used to identify the lag time between events in the equipment's operations. This information can help predict when maintenance is required to prevent equipment failure, such as replacing a worn-out part. Overall, autocorrelation and partial autocorrelation are essential for time series analysis and forecasting in Industrial IoT Data Analytics, allowing for predictive maintenance and reducing downtime.

Overall, autocorrelation and partial autocorrelation are fundamental techniques in time series analysis and forecasting for Industrial IoT Data Analytics, helping to improve the reliability and efficiency of industrial equipment and processes.

Implementing Autocorrelation Technique using Python

The following is the Python code which connects to a PostgreSQL database named **IoTDataLake** using the **psycopg2** library. The code then executes a SQL query to retrieve data from the **curatedzone.c_external_wind_turbine_data** table and creates a Pandas **DataFrame** named **wind_turbine_data**.

The code then computes the autocorrelation of the **power_output_100** variable using the Pandas **autocorr()** function and stores the result in the **autocorr** variable. It then plots the autocorrelation of **power_output_100** using the Pandas **autocorrelation_plot()** function and displays the plot using Matplotlib. The plot shows the lagged correlation between the **power_output_100** variable and its past values. The plot's title shows the Lag-1 autocorrelation of **power_output_100**, the correlation between the variable and its immediate past value.

```
import pandas as pd
import matplotlib.pyplot as plt
import psycopg2
#Print the plot within the page
%matplotlib inline
#Connect to datalake
conn = psycopg2.connect(
```

```
        host="localhost",
        database="IoTDataLake",
        user="postgres",
        password=""
    )
cur = conn.cursor()
#Query curated zone of the data lake for the wind turbine table and create a dataframe
cur.execute("SELECT * FROM curatedzone.c_external_wind_turbine_data")
wind_turbine_data= pd.DataFrame(cur.fetchall(), columns=['id', 'rtc','year', 'month', 'day', 'hour', 'minute', 'temperature_100', 'temperature_120', 'temperature_80', 'wind_direction_100', 'wind_direction_120',
      'wind_direction_80', 'wind_speed_100','wind_speed_120','wind_speed_80','pressure_200','pressure_100','pressure_0','power_output_80','power_output_100',
      'power_output_120'])
# Compute autocorrelation
autocorr = wind_turbine_data['power_output_100'].autocorr()
# Plot autocorrelation
fig, ax = plt.subplots(figsize=(12, 6))
pd.plotting.autocorrelation_plot(wind_turbine_data['power_output_100'], ax=ax)
ax.set_title(f"Autocorrelation of 'power_output_100' (Lag-1 autocorrelation: {autocorr:.2f})")
plt.show()
```

Here is the output of the preceding Python program (see *Figure 7.4*):

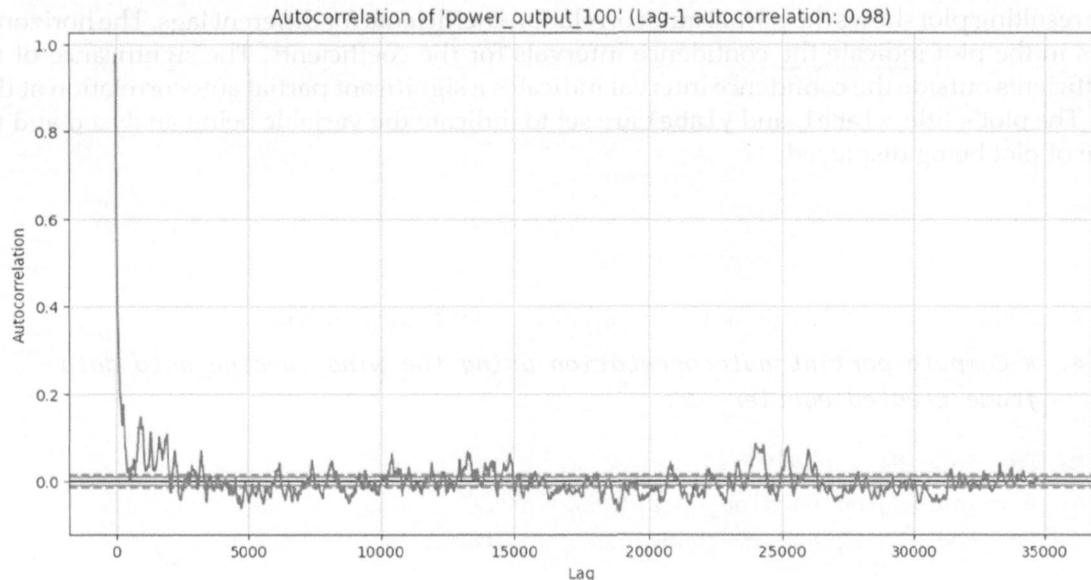

Figure 7.4: Autocorrelation

A Lag-1 autocorrelation value of 0.98 indicates a strong positive relationship between the current power output and its value at the previous time step, highlighting the temporal nature of time series data. However, an autocorrelation plot shows the correlation between the power output and its lagged values at various lags, not just at Lag-1. Most of the values on the plot are close to 0.0, indicating that the power output does not have a significant correlation with its past values at those lags. While the high Lag-1 autocorrelation value and the autocorrelation plot at various lags demonstrate the temporal dependency of power output, both need to be considered to fully comprehend the relationship between the variables.

Python Implementation of the Partial-autocorrelation

The following Python code aims to compute and plot the partial autocorrelation of the **`power_output_100`** variable in the **`wind_turbine_data dataframe`**. The partial autocorrelation is a statistical measure that describes the linear dependence between an observation in a time series and its lagged values while considering the indirect effects of the intermediate lags. In simpler terms, it is the correlation between the variable and its lagged values, but after removing the effects of the intervening lags.

The **`plot_pacf`** function from the **`statsmodels.graphics.tsaplots`** library generates the partial autocorrelation plot. The **`lags`** parameter specifies the number of lags to include in the plot, and the **`method`** parameter specifies the method used to estimate the partial autocorrelation coefficients.

The resulting plot shows the partial autocorrelation coefficients for different lags. The horizontal lines in the plot indicate the confidence intervals for the coefficients. The significance of the coefficients outside the confidence interval indicates a significant partial autocorrelation at that lag. The plot's title, **xlabel**, and **ylabel** are set to indicate the variable being analysed and the type of plot being displayed:

```
import pandas as pd
import matplotlib.pyplot as plt
from statsmodels.graphics.tsaplots import plot_pacf
# Compute partial autocorrelation using the wind_turbine_data dataframe created earlier
fig, ax = plt.subplots()
plot_pacf(wind_turbine_data['power_output_100'], lags=20, method='ols', ax=ax)
# Plot partial autocorrelation
ax.set_title("Partial Autocorrelation of 'power_output_100'")
ax.set_xlabel("Lag")
ax.set_ylabel("Partial Autocorrelation")
plt.show()
```

Here is the output of the preceding code (see *Figure 7.5*):

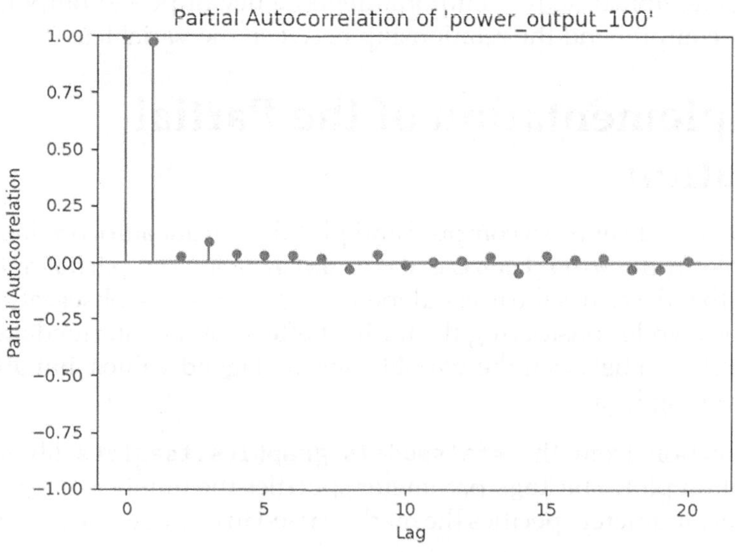

Figure 7.5: *Partial Autocorrelation*

A partial autocorrelation plot shows the correlation between a time series and its lagged values after controlling for the effect of intervening lags. The partial autocorrelation plot's significance and interpretation can help identify the appropriate order of autoregression (p) in a time series model.

In our case, a partial autocorrelation value of 1 for lags 0 to 3 suggests a strong correlation between the power output and its lagged values at those lags, even after controlling for the effect of intervening lags. This means that the current value of the power output is highly dependent on its past values up to lag 3.

The fact that most of the partial autocorrelation values after lag 3 and up to lag 20 are near zero suggests that there is no significant correlation between the power output and its lagged values at those lags, after controlling for the effect of intervening lags. This means that the current value of the power output is not significantly dependent on its past values at those lags.

Therefore, it might be appropriate to choose an autoregressive model with an order of p=3 to capture the significant partial autocorrelation values up to lag 3 and exclude the insignificant partial autocorrelation values at higher lags. However, the final choice of the order of p should also be based on other criteria such as model fit, residual diagnostics, and the purpose of the analysis.

Forecasting using AR Model

Autoregressive (**AR**) models are commonly used in IoT Data Analytics to forecast future values of time series data such as wind turbine power output. In an AR model, the future values of the variable of interest are predicted based on its past values. This means that an AR model assumes that a time series' future values depend on its past values, and not on the values of other variables.

For example, we can use an AR model to forecast the future power output of a wind turbine based on its past power output values. The model uses a set of past observations of the power output and the associated time index to predict the power output at future time points. The forecast accuracy depends on the AR model's order, which refers to the number of past observations used to predict future values.

One advantage of using AR models for forecasting is that they are simple to implement and can provide accurate results for many types of time series data, including wind turbine power output. Another advantage is that AR models can be extended to include other variables and additional explanatory factors, such as weather data or maintenance schedules, to improve the accuracy of the forecasts.

However, one disadvantage of AR models is that they assume a linear relationship between past and future values, which may not always hold for complex time series data. Additionally, the accuracy of the forecasts can be affected by changes in the underlying patterns of the data, such as sudden shifts or trends, which may require model retraining or adjustments.

AR models are useful in IoT Data Analytics for forecasting future values of time series data such as wind turbine power output. Their simplicity and ability to incorporate additional explanatory factors make them popular for many applications. Still, care must be taken to ensure the model's assumptions hold for the analysed data.

Implementing Autoregressive Model using Python

The following Python program connects to a PostgreSQL database, queries a table containing wind turbine data from the curated zone of the data lake, and creates a Pandas **DataFrame** from the results. It then applies a rolling window average with a window size of 24, to smooth the power output data, and splits the data into training and test sets. The program defines the number of lags for an **Autoregressive (AR)** model and fits the model to the smoothed training data using the **AutoReg** function from **statsmodels.tsa.ar_model** module. The program then generates predictions on the test set and calculates the **Root Mean Squared Error (RMSE)** using the **mean_squared_error** function from the **sklearn.metrics** module. Finally, the program plots the actual and smoothed power output data and the predicted values using matplotlib. The actual power output data is in blue, the smoothed power output data is in green, and the predicted values are in red. The plot shows the difference between the actual and predicted values and how the smoothed data is more consistent than the raw data.

```
import pandas as pd
import numpy as np
import matplotlib.pyplot as plt
from statsmodels.tsa.ar_model import AutoReg
from sklearn.metrics import mean_squared_error
import psycopg2
#Connect to datalake
conn = psycopg2.connect(
        host="localhost",
        database="IoTDataLake",
        user="postgres",
        password=""
    )
cur = conn.cursor()
#Query curated zone of the data lake for the wind turbine table and create a dataframe
cur.execute("SELECT * FROM curatedzone.c_external_wind_turbine_data")
wind_turbine_data= pd.DataFrame(cur.fetchall(), columns=['id','rtc',
```

```
'year', 'month', 'day', 'hour', 'minute', 'temperature_100', 'temperature_120', 'temperature_80', 'wind_direction_100', 'wind_direction_120',
    'wind_direction_80', 'wind_speed_100','wind_speed_120','wind_speed_80',' pressure_200','pressure_100','pressure_0','power_output_80','power_output_100',
    'power_output_120'])
# Smooth the power output using a rolling window average with a window size of 24
wind_turbine_data['power_output_100_smoothed'] = wind_turbine_data['power_output_100'].rolling(window=24).mean()
# Split the data into training and test sets
train_size = int(len(wind_turbine_data) * 0.8)
train, test = wind_turbine_data.iloc[:train_size], wind_turbine_data.iloc[train_size:]
# Define the number of lags for the AR model
lags = 10
# Fit the AR model to the smoothed training data
ar_model = AutoReg(train['power_output_100_smoothed'].dropna(), lags=lags)
ar_fit = ar_model.fit()
# Generate predictions on the test set
predictions = ar_fit.predict(start=len(train), end=len(train)+len(test)-1, dynamic=False)
# Calculate the root mean squared error (RMSE)
mse = mean_squared_error(test['power_output_100'], predictions)
rmse = np.sqrt(mse)
print('Test RMSE: %.3f' % rmse)
# Plot the actual and smoothed power output along with the predicted values
plt.plot(test.index, test['power_output_100'], label='Actual', color='blue')
plt.plot(wind_turbine_data.index, wind_turbine_data['power_output_100_smoothed'], label='Smoothed', color='green')
plt.plot(test.index, predictions, label='Predicted', color='red')
```

```
plt.xlabel('Time')
plt.ylabel('Power Output')
plt.legend()
plt.show()
```

The following is the preceding program's output, which shows the AR model's result using the smoothened data. Blue colored shows the actual data, green colored lines shows the smoothened data and the red line shows the predicted values (see *Figure 7.6*).

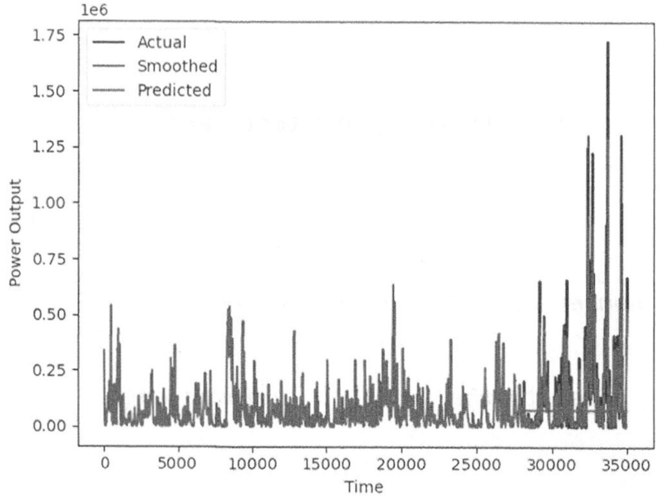

Figure 7.6: *Actual, smoothed vs Prediction using Autoregressive method*

The following is prediction of power output without using any data smoothening techniques.

This Python program performs time series forecasting using an AR model. The program splits the existing wind turbine data into training and test sets. The training set is used to fit the AR model, and the test set is used to evaluate the model's performance.

The AR model is defined by specifying the number of lags (the number of previous time steps) to include in the model. The model is fitted to the training set using the **`AutoReg`** function from the **`statsmodels.tsa.ar_model`** module.

Once the model is trained, it generates predictions on the test set using the predict function. The RMSE is then calculated to evaluate the performance of the model.

Finally, the predicted and actual values are plotted on a graph using the **`matplotlib.pyplot`** module. The X-axis represents time, while the Y-axis represents the wind turbine's power output. The predicted values are plotted in a different color from the actual values to distinguish them from each other.

```
import pandas as pd
import numpy as np
import matplotlib.pyplot as plt
from statsmodels.tsa.ar_model import AutoReg
from sklearn.metrics import mean_squared_error
# Split the data into training and test sets
train_size = int(len(wind_turbine_data) * 0.8)
train, test = wind_turbine_data.iloc[:train_size], wind_turbine_data.iloc[train_size:]
# Define the number of lags for the AR model
lags = 10
# Fit the AR model to the training data
ar_model = AutoReg(train['power_output_100'], lags=lags)
ar_fit = ar_model.fit()
# Generate predictions on the test set
predictions = ar_fit.predict(start=len(train), end=len(train)+len(test)-1, dynamic=False)
# Calculate the root mean squared error (RMSE)
mse = mean_squared_error(test['power_output_100'], predictions)
rmse = np.sqrt(mse)
print('Test RMSE: %.3f' % rmse)
# Plot the predicted and actual values
plt.plot(test.index, test['power_output_100'], label='Actual')
plt.plot(test.index, predictions, label='Predicted')
plt.xlabel('Time')
plt.ylabel('Power Output')
plt.legend()
plt.show()
```

Here is the output of the preceding program which shows the prediction of AR model (see *Figure 7.7*):

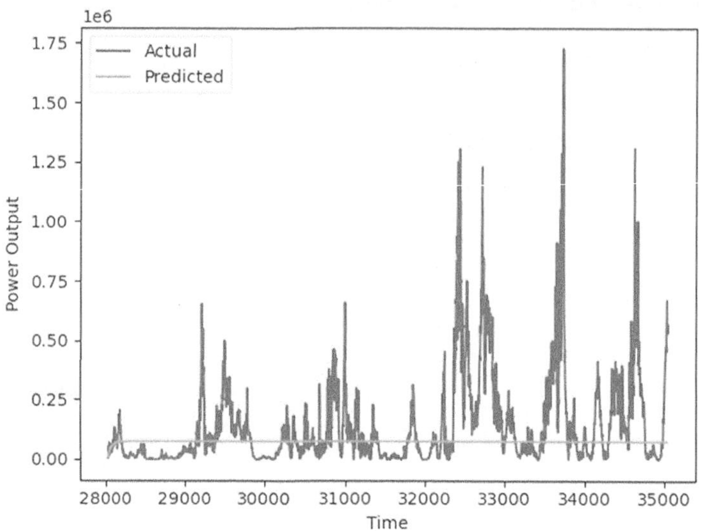

Figure 7.7: *Actual versus Prediction using Autoregressive method*

The blue lines are the data distribution, and the yellow line shows the prediction.

Moving Average

Moving Average (MA) is a time series analysis technique used to smooth out random fluctuations in data and make underlying trends more visible. It involves calculating the average of a fixed number of consecutive data points and then shifting the calculation window by one point to create a moving average series. MA is significant because it helps forecast future values and identify trends in noisy data. It can be used to identify the seasonality of time series data, and it is particularly useful in IoT Data Analytics for detecting anomalies in sensor data from IoT devices. For example, in the case of wind turbine data, MA can be applied to smooth out the random fluctuations in power output to perform better forecasting.

Implementing MA using Python

The below code establishes a connection to a database called **`IoTDataLake`** and retrieves data from the **`curatedzone.c_external_wind_turbine_data`** table. Then, it computes the moving average of the **`power_output_100`** variable using a window size of 24 hours. The original data and the moving average are plotted on a graph using Matplotlib. The graph's x-axis represents time, and the y-axis shows the wind turbine's power output. Calculating the moving average reduces noise and highlights long-term trends or patterns in the data, making it useful for time series analysis. This technique is not specific to the wind turbine example and can be applied to any time series data.

```
import pandas as pd
import matplotlib.pyplot as plt
```

```
import psycopg2
#Connect to datalake
conn = psycopg2.connect(
        host="localhost",
        database="IoTDataLake",
        user="postgres",
        password=""
    )
cur = conn.cursor()
#Query curated zone of the data lake for the wind turbine table and create a dataframe
cur.execute("SELECT * FROM curatedzone.c_external_wind_turbine_data")
wind_turbine_data= pd.DataFrame(cur.fetchall(), columns=['id','rtc','year', 'month', 'day', 'hour', 'minute', 'temperature_100', 'temperature_120', 'temperature_80', 'wind_direction_100', 'wind_direction_120',
    'wind_direction_80', 'wind_speed_100','wind_speed_120','wind_speed_80',' pressure_200','pressure_100','pressure_0','power_output_80','power_output_100',
    'power_output_120'])
# Calculate moving average of power output
window_size = 24 # choose window size
rolling_avg = wind_turbine_data['power_output_100'].rolling(window_size).mean()
# Plot original data and moving average
plt.plot(wind_turbine_data['rtc'], wind_turbine_data['power_output_100'], label='Original Data')
plt.plot(wind_turbine_data['rtc'], rolling_avg, label='Moving Average')
# Set plot labels and legend
plt.xlabel('Time')
plt.ylabel('Power Output')
plt.title('Original Data vs. Moving Average')
plt.legend()
# Show the plot
plt.show()
```

Here is the output of the preceding code (see *Figure 7.8*):

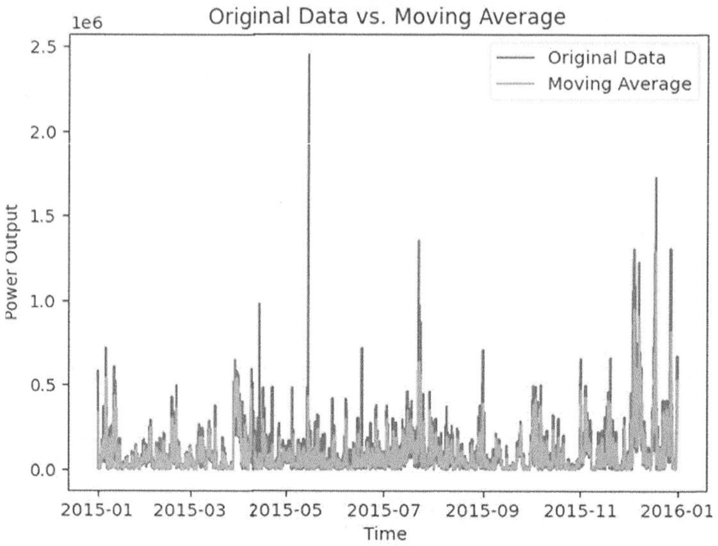

***Figure 7.8:** Original Vs Moving Average data*

The preceding graph shows the moving average in yellow-colored lines and comparing the same with the original values in blue lines. This demonstrate how we can reduce the noise and fluctuations in data, and the method will be very useful for forecasting future values.

ARIMA

ARIMA is a time series analysis technique used in IoT Data Analytics to forecast future values based on past observations. ARIMA models are commonly used to analyse and predict complex time series data such as wind turbine power output. The technique uses the past values of the time series to forecast future values. The advantage of ARIMA is that it can be used to model complex time series data with trends, seasonality, and irregularities. However, the disadvantage is that it requires significant data for accurate predictions. For example, an ARIMA model can be used to predict the power output of a wind turbine based on historical data. The model can be used to optimize the turbine's operation to maximize energy production.

Implementing ARIMA Model using Python

The following is the Python code which connects to a PostgreSQL database named **`IoTDataLake`** and reads data from the **`curatedzone.c_external_wind_turbine_data`** table. The code then pre-processes the data by keeping only relevant columns, converting the date-time column to a datetime object, setting the date-time column as the index, and splitting the data into training and testing sets.

The code fits an ARIMA model to the training data, using wind speed as an exogenous variable. ARIMA models are commonly used for time series forecasting, and they can consider the temporal dependencies between consecutive observations, seasonal patterns, and trends.

After fitting the model, the code uses it to predict the power output for the test data using wind speed as an input. The actual and predicted power output are then plotted on a graph, and the **Mean Squared Error** (MSE) is calculated to measure the model's performance.

ARIMA models are widely used in IoT Data Analytics for forecasting, anomaly detection, and root cause analysis. However, ARIMA models assume that the time series is stationary, and they may not perform well when the data has trends, seasonality, or other non-stationary patterns. In this example, wind speed is used as an exogenous variable to improve the model's performance, but selecting the appropriate exogenous variables can be challenging:

```
import pandas as pd
import matplotlib.pyplot as plt
from statsmodels.tsa.arima.model import ARIMA
import psycopg2
#Connect to datalake
conn = psycopg2.connect(
        host="localhost",
        database="IoTDataLake",
        user="postgres",
        password=""
    )
cur = conn.cursor()
#Query curated zone of the data lake for the wind turbine table and create a dataframe
cur.execute("SELECT * FROM curatedzone.c_external_wind_turbine_data")
wind_turbine_data= pd.DataFrame(cur.fetchall(), columns=['id','rtc','year', ' month', 'day', 'hour', 'minute', 'temperature_100', 'temperature_120', 'temperature_80', 'wind_direction_100', 'wind_direction_120',
     'wind_direction_80', 'wind_speed_100','wind_speed_120','wind_speed_80',' pressure_200','pressure_100','pressure_0','power_output_80','power_output_100',
     'power_output_120'])
# Keep only the relevant columns
data = wind_turbine_data[["rtc", "wind_speed_100", "power_output_100"]]
# Convert the 'rtc' column to a datetime object
data["rtc"] = pd.to_datetime(data["rtc"])
```

```
# Set the 'rtc' column as the index
data = data.set_index("rtc")
# Split the data into training and testing sets
train_size = int(len(data) * 0.8)
train_data = data.iloc[:train_size]
test_data = data.iloc[train_size:]
# Fit the ARIMA model
model = ARIMA(train_data["power_output_100"], exog=train_data["wind_
speed_100"], order=(1, 1, 1))
model_fit = model.fit()
# Predict the power output for the test data
predictions = model_fit.predict(start=test_data.index[0], end=test_data.
index[-1], exog=test_data["wind_speed_100"])
# Plot the actual and predicted power output
plt.plot(test_data.index, test_data["power_output_100"], label="Actual")
plt.plot(predictions.index, predictions, label="Predicted")
plt.legend()
plt.show()
# Evaluate the model's performance
mse = ((predictions - test_data["power_output_100"]) ** 2).mean()
print("ARIMA Test MSE:", mse)
```

Here is output of the preceding Python program (see *Figure 7.9*):

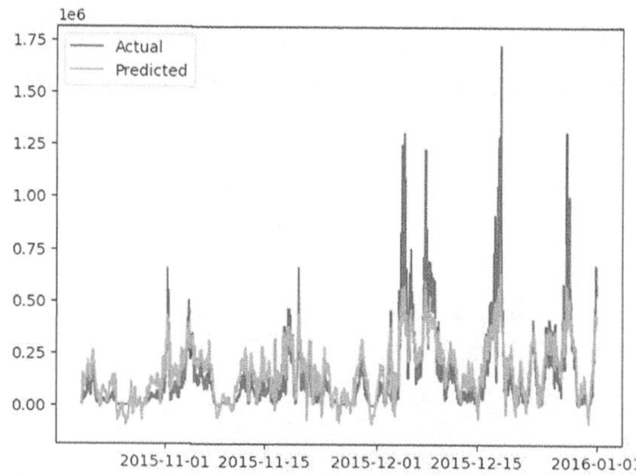

***Figure 7.9:** Actual vs predicted using ARIMA model*

The preceding graph clearly shows the advantage of using ARIMA model for prediction. The yellow lines are the predicted value compared to the actual values in blue lines.

Time Series Feature Extraction

Time Series Feature Extraction (**TSFresh**) is a tool for extracting relevant features from time series data. It identifies and quantifies patterns in time series data, which can be used for machine learning and statistical modeling. TSFresh is particularly useful when working with large datasets, as it can automate the feature extraction process and reduce the risk of human error.

TSFresh is typically used with machine learning and statistical techniques to analyze time series data. It is particularly useful in IoT Analytics, as many IoT devices generate large amounts of time series data. For example, in the case of wind turbine data, TSFresh can be used to extract features such as wind speed, rotor speed, and power output, which can be used to predict future power output and identify potential maintenance issues.

One advantage of TSFresh is that it automates the feature extraction process, reducing the time and effort required to identify relevant features. Additionally, TSFresh can extract a wide range of statistical, spectral, and time series features, allowing for a comprehensive data analysis.

However, one disadvantage of TSFresh is that it may extract irrelevant or redundant features, leading to overfitting or reduced model performance. It is important to carefully evaluate the extracted features and select only the most relevant ones for the analysis.

Overall, TSFresh is a valuable tool for time series analysis and can be particularly useful in IoT Data Analytics, where large amounts of time series data are generated. By automating the feature extraction process, TSFresh can reduce the risk of human error and enable a more comprehensive data analysis.

Implementing TSFresh using Python

The following Python program retrieves wind turbine data from a curated zone in a data lake by connecting to it first. The timestamp column is converted to datetime, and relevant columns are selected, with the index set to the timestamp column. Tsfresh is then used to extract features from the time series data, using the exhaustive setting for feature calculation. To handle missing values, the extracted features are imputed.

The data is then split into training and testing sets, and a random forest regressor is trained using the training set. The performance of the model is evaluated on the testing set using the R^2 score, and predictions are made on the testing set using the trained model. Finally, a plot of the actual vs predicted values is generated to visualize the model's performance.

```
import pandas as pd
from tsfresh import extract_features, select_features
from tsfresh.utilities.dataframe_functions import impute
from sklearn.ensemble import RandomForestRegressor
from sklearn.model_selection import train_test_split
```

```
import matplotlib.pyplot as plt
import psycopg2
#Connect to datalake
conn = psycopg2.connect(
        host="localhost",
        database="IoTDataLake",
        user="postgres",
        password=""
    )
cur = conn.cursor()
#Query curated zone of the data lake for the wind turbine table and create a dataframe
cur.execute("SELECT * FROM curatedzone.c_external_wind_turbine_data")
wind_turbine_data= pd.DataFrame(cur.fetchall(), columns=['id','rtc','year', 'month', 'day', 'hour', 'minute', 'temperature_100', 'temperature_120', 'temperature_80', 'wind_direction_100', 'wind_direction_120',
      'wind_direction_80', 'wind_speed_100','wind_speed_120','wind_speed_80',' pressure_200','pressure_100','pressure_0','power_output_80','power_output_100',
      'power_output_120'])
# Convert the timestamp column to datetime
wind_turbine_data['rtc'] = pd.to_datetime(wind_turbine_data['rtc'])
# Select the relevant columns
wind_turbine_df = wind_turbine_data[['id', 'rtc', 'wind_speed_100', 'power_output_100']].head(10000)
# Set the index to the timestamp column
wind_turbine_df.set_index('rtc', inplace=True)
# Extract features using the "exhaustive" settings for feature calculation
extracted_features = extract_features(wind_turbine_df, column_id='id')
# Impute missing values
imputed_features = impute(extracted_features)
# Split the data into training and testing sets
```

```
X_train, X_test, y_train, y_test = train_test_split(imputed_features,
    wind_turbine_df['power_output_100'], test_size=0.2, random_state=42)
# Train a random forest regressor
rf = RandomForestRegressor()
rf.fit(X_train, y_train)
# Evaluate the model on the testing set
score = rf.score(X_test, y_test)
print('R^2 score:', score)
# Predict on the testing set
y_pred = rf.predict(X_test)
# Plot actual vs predicted values
plt.figure(figsize=(10, 5))
plt.plot(y_test, y_pred, 'o', label='Actual vs Predicted')
plt.plot([y_test.min(), y_test.max()], [y_test.min(), y_test.max()], ‘k--’, label=’Ideal’)
plt.xlabel('Actual')
plt.ylabel('Predicted')
plt.title('Actual vs Predicted Power Output')
plt.legend()
plt.show()
```

Here is the output of the preceding Python program (see *Figure 7.10*):

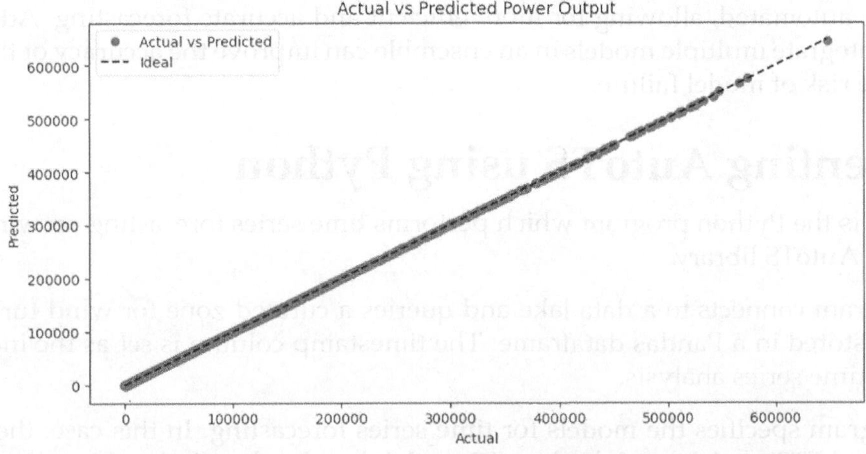

***Figure 7.10:** Actual vs predicted using tsfresh and RandomForestRegressor*

The preceding graph clearly shows the performance of the model we build to predict the wind turbine's power output. It also shows a high R^2 score of 0.9999979057417828 indicates that the model has a very high accuracy in predicting the power output of wind turbines based on the extracted features from the time series data. However, it is important to note that the R^2 score should not be the only metric used to evaluate the performance of a model, and other metrics such as MAE and RMSE should also be considered.

Automatic Time Series

Automatic Time Series (AutoTS) is a Python package that automates the process of forecasting time series data. Time series forecasting is common in many industries, including finance, sales, and manufacturing. It involves predicting future values of a variable based on its historical values.

AutoTS is used to simplify the time series forecasting process by automating the selection and tuning of forecasting models. It allows users to input time series data and receive accurate and reliable forecasts without requiring extensive domain knowledge or expertise in time series analysis.

The advantages of AutoTS include the ability to save time and reduce human error by automating the selection and tuning of forecasting models. It also allows for more systematic and thorough parameter space exploration. Additionally, AutoTS supports integrating multiple models in an ensemble, which can improve the accuracy and robustness of the forecasts.

However, the disadvantage of AutoTS is that it may not always result in the best possible forecast, as the accuracy of the forecast depends on the quality of the input data and the appropriateness of the selected models.

In IoT Data Analytics, AutoTS can forecast time series data from IoT devices, such as wind turbine data. Wind turbine data can be used to predict the power output of the wind turbines, which can be useful for energy production and management. By using AutoTS, the forecasting process can be automated, allowing for more efficient and accurate forecasting. Additionally, the ability to integrate multiple models in an ensemble can improve the accuracy of the forecast and reduce the risk of model failure.

Implementing AutoTS using Python

The following is the Python program which performs time series forecasting on wind turbine data using the AutoTS library.

First, the program connects to a data lake and queries a curated zone for wind turbine data, which is then stored in a Pandas dataframe. The timestamp column is set as the index of the dataframe for time series analysis.

Next, the program specifies the models for time series forecasting. In this case, the program uses ARIMA and ETS models, and the AutoTS model then fits the wind turbine data using the specified models.

Once the model is fit, the program uses it to make predictions. These predictions are stored in a Pandas dataframe.

Finally, the program creates a plot to visualize the actual and predicted values of the power output for the last 24 hours. This plot helps to assess the performance of the model:

```
from autots import AutoTS
import pandas as pd
import matplotlib.pyplot as plt
import psycopg2
# Connect to datalake
conn = psycopg2.connect(
        host="localhost",
        database="IoTDataLake",
        user="postgres",
        password=""
    )
cur = conn.cursor()
# Query curated zone of the data lake for the wind turbine table and create a dataframe
cur.execute("SELECT * FROM curatedzone.c_external_wind_turbine_data")
wind_turbine_data = pd.DataFrame(cur.fetchall(), columns=['id', 'rtc', 'year', 'month', 'day', 'hour', 'minute', 'temperature_100', 'temperature_120', 'temperature_80', 'wind_direction_100', 'wind_direction_120','wind_direction_80', 'wind_speed_100','wind_speed_120','wind_speed_80','pressure_200','pressure_100','pressure_0', 'power_output_80','power_output_100','power_output_120'])
# Set the index to the timestamp column
wind_turbine_data.set_index('rtc', inplace=True)
# Specify the models to use
models = ['ARIMA', 'ETS']
# Fit AutoTS model with specified models
model = AutoTS(forecast_length=24, frequency='H', ensemble='weighted', max_generations=5, num_validations=2, model_list=models)
model.fit(wind_turbine_data['power_output_100'])
# Fit AutoTS model with Prophet
```

```
#model = AutoTS(forecast_length=24, frequency='H', ensemble='weighted', max_generations=5, num_validations=2)
#model.fit(df['power_output_100'])
# Make predictions
predictions = model.predict()
# Create a new figure with a bigger size
fig = plt.figure(figsize=(10, 6))
# Plot actual vs predicted
plt.plot(wind_turbine_data.index[-24:], wind_turbine_data['power_output_100'][-24:], label='Actual')
plt.plot(predictions.forecast.index[-24:], predictions.forecast[-24:], label='Predicted')
plt.legend()
```

`plt.show()`Here is the output of the above Python program (see *Figure 7.11*):

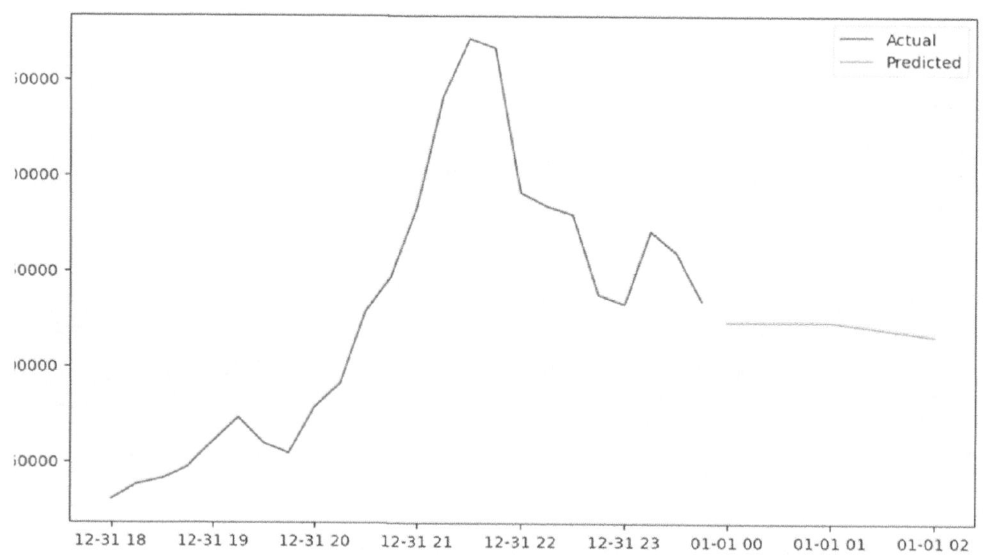

***Figure 7.11:** Actual vs Predicted using AutoTS*

The actual data shows in blue line and the orange line shows the predicted values.

Storing Wind Turbine Predictions

Storing the machine learning predicted values along with the actual values in a table is crucial because it allows for easy and quick access to the predictions and comparison with the actual values. This is particularly useful when the model needs to be frequently updated or retrained with new data. By storing the predicted values in a table, users can quickly see how the model performs and if any adjustments need to be made to improve its accuracy. This historical data can also be useful for trend analysis and forecasting, allowing businesses to make data-driven decisions and adjust their strategies accordingly. Overall, storing predicted values in a table can help streamline the machine learning process and improve the accuracy and effectiveness of predictive models.

Here is an improved version of the same Python program that uses the **tsfresh** library to extract features and predict the power output using the **RandomForestRegressor** algorithm. This time, we will also show you how to store the predicted and actual values in the **analyticszone** of the data lake. This data can be extracted later for analysis:

```
import pandas as pd
from tsfresh import extract_features, select_features
from tsfresh.utilities.dataframe_functions import impute
from sklearn.ensemble import RandomForestRegressor
from sklearn.model_selection import train_test_split
import matplotlib.pyplot as plt
import psycopg2
# Connect to datalake
conn = psycopg2.connect(
        host=”localhost”,
        database=”IoTDataLake”,
        user=”postgres”,
        password=””
    )
cur = conn.cursor()
# Query curated zone of the data lake for the wind turbine table and create a dataframe
cur.execute(“SELECT * FROM curatedzone.c_external_wind_turbine_data”)
wind_turbine_data = pd.DataFrame(cur.fetchall(), columns=[‘id’, ‘rtc’, ‘year’,
‘month’, ‘day’, ‘hour’, ‘minute’,  ‘temperature_100’, ‘temperature_120’,
‘temperature_80’,  ‘wind_direction_100’, ‘wind_direction_120’,
‘wind_direction_80’, ‘wind_speed_100’,’wind_speed_120’,
‘wind_speed_80’,’pressure_200’,’pressure_100’,’pressure_0’,
‘power_output_80’,’power_output_100’,’power_output_120’])
# Convert the timestamp column to datetime
wind_turbine_data[‘rtc’] = pd.to_datetime(wind_turbine_data[‘rtc’])
```

```
# Select the relevant columns
wind_turbine_df = wind_turbine_data[['id', 'rtc', 'wind_speed_100', 'power_output_100']].head(10000)
# Set the index to the timestamp column
wind_turbine_df.set_index('rtc', inplace=True)
# Extract features using the "exhaustive" settings for feature calculation
extracted_features = extract_features(wind_turbine_df, column_id='id')
# Impute missing values
imputed_features = impute(extracted_features)
# Split the data into training and testing sets
X_train, X_test, y_train, y_test = train_test_split(imputed_features, wind_turbine_df['power_output_100'], test_size=0.2, random_state=42)
# Train a random forest regressor
rf = RandomForestRegressor()
rf.fit(X_train, y_train)
# Evaluate the model on the testing set
score = rf.score(X_test, y_test)
print('R^2 score:', score)
# Predict on the testing set
y_pred = rf.predict(X_test)
# Insert actual and predicted values into a new table
cur.execute('CREATE TABLE IF NOT EXISTS analyticszone.a_predicted_power_output (rtc TIMESTAMP, actual NUMERIC, predicted NUMERIC)')
for I in range(len(y_test)):
    cur.execute""INSERT INTO analyticszone.a_predicted_power_output (rtc, actual, predicted) VALUES (%s, %s, %s"",
                (str(y_test.index[i]), y_test.iloc[i], y_pred[i]))
# Commit the changes and close the connection
conn.commit()
cur.close()
conn.close()
```

After storing the data in the **analyticszone** of the data lake, we can perform further analysis using the same data. Here is an example of plotting the actual vs predicted values using the stored data:

```
import psycopg2
import pandas as pd
import matplotlib.pyplot as plt
# Connect to the PostgreSQL database
conn = psycopg2.connect(
    host”"localhos”",
    database”"IoTDataLak”",
    user”"postgre”",
    password”””"
)
# Query the analyticszone.a_predicted_power_output table and create a DataFrame
cur = conn.cursor()
cur.execute“"SELECT rtc, actual, predicted FROM analyticszone.a_predicted_power_outpu”")
results = cur.fetchall()
# Unpack the results into separate lists
timestamps = [r[0] for r in results]
actual_values = [r[1] for r in results]
predicted_values = [r[2] for r in results]
# Create a time series line plot
fig, ax1 = plt.subplots(figsize=(10,5))
# Add scatter plot of actual vs predicted values
ax1 = ax1.twinx()
ax1.scatter(actual_values, predicted_values, color’'re'’, label’'Actual vs Predicte’')
ax1.plot([min(actual_values), max(actual_values)], [min(actual_values), max(actual_values)],‘'--'’, label’'Idea'’)
ax1.set_ylabel‘'Predicte'’)
ax1.legend()
plt.show()
```

Here is the output of the above Python program (see *Figure 7.12*):

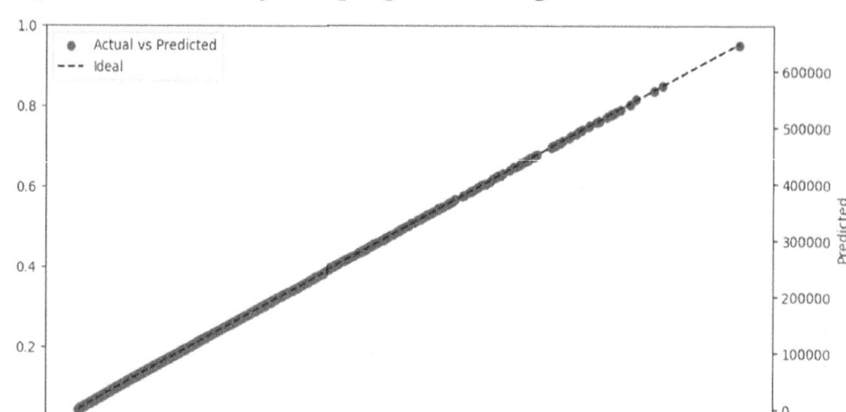

***Figure 7.12:** Actual vs Predicted using Analytics zone data*

The above graph can be generated from the **`analyticszone`** of the data lake.

Analytical Base Table

Analytical Base Table (**ABT**) is a concept used in Data Analytics and Data Science. ABT is a table containing all the relevant data required for analysis, modeling, and data mining. ABT is created after data pre-processing and data cleaning.

ABT facilitates the modeling process by providing a table with all the relevant information. It is used in cases where there is a need to analyze data from multiple sources, with different structures and levels of granularity.

Creating ABT involves merging and aggregating data from various sources to form a table with relevant features. The ABT can be further used for exploratory data analysis, feature engineering, and machine learning.

The advantage of using ABT is that it provides a comprehensive overview of the data, simplifying the modeling process. It saves time and effort by providing all the relevant features in one place. It enables the creation of reproducible workflows and facilitates collaboration between different team members.

However, one disadvantage of using ABT is that it can be computationally expensive to create and maintain, especially when dealing with large datasets. Also, it requires careful selection and engineering of features, which can be challenging.

In IoT Data Analytics, ABT can be useful in handling large amounts of data collected from different sources such as wind turbine operations. It can help create a comprehensive table with relevant features required for predictive maintenance, identify potential failures, and improve overall operational efficiency. ABT can simplify modeling, enabling data-driven decision-making in the Industrial IoT applications.

Implementation of ABT using Python

The code below creates an ABT for wind turbine data stored in a database. First, the code connects to the database using the psycopg2 library and retrieves the wind turbine data from the curated zone of the data lake. The data is then filtered to include only the relevant columns and converted to a Pandas DataFrame.

Next, several new columns are created to extract useful information from the date-time index of the data. These columns include the hour of the day, the day of the week, the month of the year, the season of the year, and the wind speed and power output ranges.

After the data has been cleaned and transformed, the code creates a new table in the database called **wind_turbine_abt** using a SQL statement. The ABT has columns for wind speed, power output, wind direction, temperature, pressure, hour, day of the week, month, season, wind speed range, and power output range.

Finally, the cleaned and transformed data is inserted into the **wind_turbine_abt** table using a SQL insert statement. This new table can be used as a starting point for building machine learning models and performing further analysis on the wind turbine data.

```
import pandas as pd
import numpy as np
import psycopg2
#Connect to dataLake
conn = psycopg2.connect(
        host="localhost",
        database="IoTDataLake",
        user="postgres",
        password=""
    )
cur = conn.cursor()
#Query curated zone of the data lake for the wind turbine table and create a dataframe
cur.execute("SELECT * FROM curatedzone.c_external_wind_turbine_data")
wind_turbine_data= pd.DataFrame(cur.fetchall(), columns=['id','rtc','year', 'month', 'day', 'hour', 'minute', 'temperature_100', 'temperature_120', 'temperature_80', 'wind_direction_100', 'wind_direction_120',
     'wind_direction_80', 'wind_speed_100','wind_speed_120','wind_speed_80','pressure_200','pressure_100','pressure_0','power_output_80','power_output_100',
```

```
        'power_output_120'])
# Keep only the relevant columns
wind_turbine_data = wind_turbine_data[["rtc", "wind_speed_100", "power_output_100",'wind_direction_100','temperature_100','pressure_100']]
# Convert the 'rtc' column to a datetime object
wind_turbine_data["rtc"] = pd.to_datetime(wind_turbine_data["rtc"])
# Set the 'rtc' column as the index
wind_turbine_data = wind_turbine_data.set_index("rtc")
# Create a new column for the hour of the day
wind_turbine_data["hour"] = wind_turbine_data.index.hour
# Create a new column for the day of the week
wind_turbine_data["day_of_week"] = wind_turbine_data.index.dayofweek
# Create a new column for the month of the year
wind_turbine_data["month"] = wind_turbine_data.index.month
# Create a new column for the season of the year
seasons = [(0, "winter"), (3, "spring"), (6, "summer"), (9, "fall")]
wind_turbine_data["season"] = pd.cut((wind_turbine_data.index.month % 12 + 3) // 3, bins=[s[0] for s in seasons] + [12], labels=[s[1] for s in seasons], right=False)
# Create a new column for the wind speed range
bins = [-np.inf, 3, 6, 9, 12, np.inf]
labels = ["<3", "3-6", "6-9", "9-12", ">12"]
wind_turbine_data["wind_speed_range"] = pd.cut(wind_turbine_data["wind_speed_100"], bins=bins, labels=labels)
# Create a new column for the power output range
bins = [-np.inf, 500, 1000, 1500, 2000, np.inf]
labels = ["<500", "500-1000", "1000-1500", "1500-2000", ">2000"]
wind_turbine_data["power_output_range"] = pd.cut(wind_turbine_data["power_output_100"], bins=bins, labels=labels)
# Define create table statement
create_table = """
CREATE TABLE analyticszone.wind_turbine_abt (
    wind_speed_100 FLOAT,
    power_output_100 FLOAT,
    wind_direction_100 FLOAT,
```

```
    temperature_100 FLOAT,
    pressure_100 FLOAT,
    hour INTEGER,
    day_of_week INTEGER,
    month INTEGER,
    season TEXT,
    wind_speed_range TEXT,
    power_output_range TEXT
);
"""
# drop and create table
cur.execute(f"DROP TABLE IF EXISTS analyticszone.wind_turbine_abt")
cur.execute(create_table)
conn.commit()
cur.close()
# Insert the data into the table
insert_cursor = conn.cursor()
abt_records = []
for index, row in wind_turbine_data.iterrows():
    value = (row['wind_speed_100'], row['power_output_100'], row['wind_direction_100'], row['temperature_100'],
             row['pressure_100'], row['hour'], row['day_of_week'], row['month'], row['season'],
             row['wind_speed_range'], row['power_output_range'])
    abt_records.append(value)
query = "INSERT INTO analyticszone.wind_turbine_abt VALUES (%s, %s, %s, %s, %s, %s, %s, %s, %s, %s, %s)"
insert_cursor.executemany(query,  abt_records)
conn.commit()
insert_cursor.close()
conn.close()
```

After inserting the records in the analytics zone of the data lake, we can use the table for building machine learning tasks quickly. Here is the example of the same:

```
import psycopg2
import pandas as pd
```

```
import numpy as np
from sklearn.model_selection import train_test_split
from sklearn.ensemble import RandomForestRegressor
from sklearn.metrics import r2_score
import matplotlib.pyplot as plt
# Connect to the database
db_connection = psycopg2.connect(
    host="localhost",
    database="IoTDataLake",
    user="postgres",
    password=""
)
# Read the data into a Pandas dataframe
data_df = pd.read_sql_query("SELECT wind_speed_100, power_output_100, wind_direction_100, temperature_100, pressure_100, hour, day_of_week, month, season, wind_speed_range, power_output_range FROM analyticszone.wind_turbine_abt;", db_connection)
# One-hot encode categorical columns
data_df = pd.get_dummies(data_df, columns=['season', 'wind_speed_range', 'power_output_range'])
# Split the dataset into training and test sets
X_train, X_test, y_train, y_test = train_test_split(data_df.drop(['power_output_100'], axis=1), data_df['power_output_100'], test_size=0.2, random_state=42)
# Train a Random Forest Regressor model on the training set
rf_model = RandomForestRegressor(n_estimators=100, random_state=42)
rf_model.fit(X_train, y_train)
# Predict power output for the training and test sets
y_train_pred = rf_model.predict(X_train)
y_test_pred = rf_model.predict(X_test)
# Plot the predicted values for the training and test sets
fig, ax = plt.subplots()
ax.scatter(y_train_pred, y_train, alpha=0.5, label='Training Set')
ax.scatter(y_test_pred, y_test, alpha=0.5, label='Test Set')
ax.set_xlabel('Predicted Power Output')
```

```
ax.set_ylabel('Actual Power Output')
ax.legend()
plt.show()
# Test the model on the test set and print the results
train_r2 = r2_score(y_train, y_train_pred)
test_r2 = r2_score(y_test, y_test_pred)
print(f"R^2 Score on Training: {train_r2:.4f}")
print(f"R^2 Score on Test: {test_r2:.4f}")
# Close the database connection
db_connection.close()
```

Above Python program queries the analytical base table from the analytical zone of the data lake. Here is the output of the above program (see *Figure 7.13*):

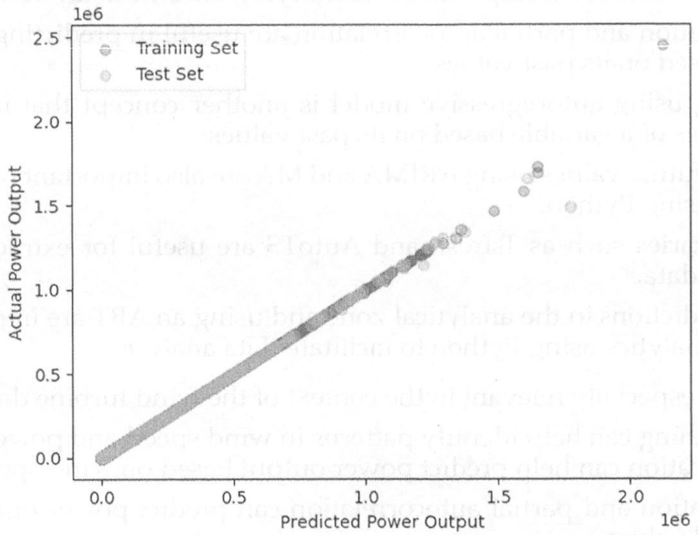

***Figure 7.13:** Train vs Test prediction using ABT data*

Conclusion

IoT Data Analytics empowers comprehensive examination and accurate prediction using data from IoT devices. In this chapter, we explored various techniques for analysing time series data using Python, with the help of Wind Turbine dataset. We covered data smoothing, data lag identification, autocorrelation, and partial autocorrelation. We also looked at different models for forecasting and predicting future values, such as AR model, ARIMA, and MA. Furthermore, we discussed Python libraries such as Tsfresh and AutoTS for time series feature extraction and high-accuracy forecasting.

Finally, we demonstrated how to store the wind turbine predictions in the analytical zone using the ABT.

In the next chapter, we will explore time series monitoring and predictive maintenance. This will include condition monitoring, condition-based maintenance, corrective maintenance, preventive maintenance, and predictive maintenance. These topics are critical for ensuring the longevity of IoT devices and optimizing their performance, and we will cover them in detail using Python examples.

Points to Remember

IoT Data Analytics using Python involves several important concepts that help extract insights from IoT data. Here is the summary of our learnings from this chapter:

- Data smoothing is a concept that involves removing noise from data to highlight trends and patterns.
- Data lag identification is important in identifying the time delay between two variables.
- Autocorrelation and partial autocorrelation are useful in predicting future values of a variable based on its past values.
- Forecasting using autoregressive model is another concept that involves predicting future values of a variable based on its past values.
- Predicting future values using ARIMA and MA are also important concepts in IoT Data Analytics using Python.
- Python libraries such as Tsfresh and AutoTS are useful for extracting insights from time series data.
- Storing predictions in the analytical zone and using an ABT are important concepts in IoT Data Analytics using Python to facilitate data analysis.

These concepts are especially relevant in the context of the wind turbine dataset:

- Data smoothing can help identify patterns in wind speed and power output, and data lag identification can help predict power output based on wind speed.
- Autocorrelation and partial autocorrelation can predict power output based on past wind speed values.
- Forecasting using an AR model can also help predict power output based on past wind speed values.
- ARIMA and MA models can predict future power output values based on past wind speed values.
- Python libraries such as Tsfresh and AutoTS can help with high accuracy in feature extraction and automatic time series forecasting.
- Storing predictions in the analytical zone can help compare the performance of different models, and an ABT can be created by combining data from various sources for analysis.

These techniques and tools can provide valuable insights and help make informed decisions in IoT applications.

Chapter 8
Monitoring and Preventive Maintenance

Introduction

Industrial automation heavily relies on machines and equipment to drive productivity and efficiency. However, these components are prone to wear and tear, resulting in unexpected downtime, increased maintenance costs, and reduced output. Therefore, monitoring machines' conditions is critical to detect early signs of failure and prevent breakdowns. This is where condition monitoring comes in, utilizing various techniques to monitor equipment's health and detect deviations or anomalies from normal operating conditions.

The primary goal of condition monitoring is to improve machines' and equipment's reliability. This can be achieved through various maintenance strategies, including Corrective, Preventive, **Condition-Based Maintenance** (**CBM**), and Predictive Maintenance. CBM involves monitoring the health of machines and performing maintenance only when necessary. Corrective maintenance is carried out after a breakdown, while Preventive Maintenance is performed regularly to avoid unexpected failures. Predictive Maintenance uses data analytics to predict equipment failures before they occur.

This chapter focuses on time-series monitoring and preventive maintenance in **Industrial IoT** (**IIoT**) analytics. Specifically, we will explore how different equipment parameters, such as pressure, and power input or output, can predict equipment failure using machine learning algorithms in Python. We will discuss using time-series data analysis techniques to extract insights, visualize data, and predict equipment failure. Additionally, we will examine the use of text mining techniques to analyze product manuals and build association rules against incoming tag values for improved predictive maintenance. Lastly, we will cover creating maintenance tickets based on predictions to complete the end-to-end benefit of time-series monitoring and preventive maintenance in IoT Data Analytics. By the end of this chapter, readers will have a comprehensive understanding of how to implement time-series monitoring and preventive maintenance techniques for IIoT Data Analytics using Python.

Structure

In this chapter, we will cover the following topics:

- Condition Monitoring
- Condition-based Maintenance
- Corrective Maintenance
- Preventive Maintenance
- Predictive Maintenance
- Text Mining the Product Manual
- Automating the Creation of Maintenance Ticket

Objectives

This chapter aims to comprehensively understand time-series monitoring and Preventive Maintenance techniques for Industrial IoT Analytics. Through this chapter, readers will learn about the importance of condition monitoring, which involves using various techniques to continuously monitor the health of machines and equipment to detect deviations or anomalies from normal operating conditions.

The chapter will cover different maintenance strategies, including corrective, preventive, condition-based, and predictive maintenance. Specifically, we will explore how various equipment parameters, such as pressure and power input or output, can be used to predict equipment failure using machine learning algorithms in Python.

Furthermore, the chapter will use time-series data analysis techniques to extract insights, visualize data, and predict equipment failure. Additionally, readers will learn about using text mining techniques to analyze product manuals and build association rules against incoming tag values for improved predictive maintenance. Finally, the chapter will discuss creating maintenance tickets based on predictions to complete the end-to-end benefit of time-series monitoring and Preventive Maintenance in IoT Data Analytics.

Condition Monitoring

Condition Monitoring is a critical aspect of Industrial IoT that involves continuously monitoring the health of machines and equipment to detect any anomalies or deviations from normal operating conditions. For instance, in the case of a wind turbine dataset, condition monitoring would involve monitoring various parameters such as vibration, temperature, wind speed, and power output to detect any early signs of failure.

The importance of condition monitoring lies in its ability to improve the reliability of machines and equipment, prevent breakdowns, reduce maintenance costs, and increase productivity. By monitoring the health of machines in real time, operators can detect potential failures and address them before they cause any significant damage.

Condition monitoring is essential in the manufacturing, energy, and transportation industries. Various industry standards have been developed to guide the implementation of condition monitoring using IoT sensors and machine learning. In addition, Python libraries such as Pandas and Scikit-learn have been developed to implement condition-monitoring algorithms.

Overall, condition monitoring in Industrial IoT is becoming increasingly important in ensuring the efficiency and reliability of machines and equipment. Its benefits range from reduced maintenance costs to increased productivity, making it a critical aspect of any IIoT system.

Implementing Condition Monitoring using Python

The below Python program implements a simple condition monitoring system for wind turbine data. The program checks if certain parameters of the wind turbine data are above or below a certain threshold or if they have been continuously above a threshold for a given duration.

The program defines three functions:

- **`above_threshold(df, column, threshold)`**: Checks if the given column in the DataFrame df is above the given threshold.
- **`below_threshold(df, column, threshold)`**: Checks if the given column in the DataFrame df is below the given threshold.
- **`continuous_threshold(df, column, threshold, duration)`**: Checks if the given column in the DataFrame df has been continuously above the given threshold for the given duration.

The program then provides an example usage of these functions with a sample wind turbine dataset.

The first example checks if the wind speed is above 25 m/s and generates an alert if it is. The second example checks if the power output is below 1000 kW and generates an alert if it is. The third example checks if wind speed has been continuously above 20 m/s for 5 minutes and generates an alert if it is.

```
import pandas as pd
import numpy as np
def above_threshold(df, column, threshold):
    '''
    Function to check if the given column is above the threshold
    '''
```

```
    if df[column].max() > threshold:
        alert_msg = f"{column} is above the threshold of {threshold}"
        return alert_msg
    else:
        return None
def below_threshold(df, column, threshold):
    '''
    Function to check if the given column is below the threshold
    '''
    if df[column].min() < threshold:
        alert_msg = f"{column} is below the threshold of {threshold}"
        return alert_msg
    else:
        return None
def continuous_threshold(df, column, threshold, duration):
    '''
    Function to check if the given column is above the threshold continuously for the given duration
    '''
    continuous_count = 0
    for value in df[column]:
        if value > threshold:
            continuous_count += 1
        else:
            continuous_count = 0
        if continuous_count >= duration:
            alert_msg = f"{column} is continuously above the threshold of
                        {threshold} for {duration} minutes"
            return alert_msg
    return None
# Example usage
wind_turbine_data = pd.DataFrame({'temperature_100': [30, 25, 30],
                                  'pressure_100': [2000, 1100, 1200],
                                  'wind_speed_100': [30, 15, 20],
                                  'power_output_100': [1500, 2000, 2500]})
```

```
# Alert for wind speed above 25 m/s
alert1 = above_threshold(wind_turbine_data, 'wind_speed_100', 25)
if alert1:
    print(alert1)
# Alert for power output below 1000 kW
alert2 = below_threshold(wind_turbine_data, 'power_output_100', 1000)
if alert2:
    print(alert2)
# Alert for wind speed continuously above 20 m/s for 5 minutes
alert3 = continuous_threshold(wind_turbine_data, 'wind_speed_100', 20, 5)
if alert3:
    print(alert3)
```

Here is the output from the above program which shows the **`wind_speed_100`** is above the threshold of 25 for the given data:

```
wind_speed_100 is above the threshold of 25
```

Condition Based Maintenance

CBM is an important concept in the **Industrial Internet of Things** (**IIoT**) that helps to minimize maintenance costs while maximizing equipment performance. CBM involves monitoring equipment data in real-time to detect any anomalies or changes in equipment behavior, which can then be used to predict when maintenance is required. CBM helps to prevent unscheduled downtime and minimize maintenance costs by enabling predictive maintenance.

IoT Data Analytics plays a crucial role in the implementation of CBM. By collecting data from sensors and other IoT devices, IoT Data Analytics can help to identify patterns and trends in equipment behavior. By analyzing this data, predictive maintenance algorithms can be developed to detect when maintenance is required.

Let us go through an example of how CBM can be implemented using IoT Data Analytics is wind turbine data. By collecting data from sensors on a wind turbine, IoT Data Analytics can be utilized to monitor equipment performance and detect any anomalies or changes in behavior. By analyzing this data, predictive maintenance algorithms can be developed to detect when maintenance is required. This helps to prevent unscheduled downtime and minimize maintenance costs by enabling predictive maintenance. Overall, CBM is an important concept in IIoT that can help organizations optimize equipment performance and reduce maintenance costs.

CBM Implementation using Python

Here is the Python program demonstrating how to implement a condition-based monitoring approach for wind turbines using machine learning. The CBM approach is based on monitoring critical parameters of wind turbines and detecting when they exceed a certain threshold, which may indicate potential faults. The program uses data from a data lake and applies a machine learning model to predict whether each data point is above or below a set threshold. The program uses the Python libraries pandas, **`numpy`**, **`sklearn`**, and **`psycopg2`** to query, preprocess, and model the data. The program output is a list of alerts for each input data point, indicating whether it is above or below the threshold. This program provides a practical example of how machine learning can be used for CBM in industrial applications:

```
import pandas as pd
import numpy as np
from sklearn.preprocessing import StandardScaler
from sklearn.ensemble import RandomForestClassifier
import psycopg2
# Connect to datalake
conn = psycopg2.connect(
        host="localhost",
        database="IoTDataLake",
        user="postgres",
        password=""
    )
cur = conn.cursor()
# Query curated zone of the data lake for the wind turbine table and create a dataframe
cur.execute("SELECT * FROM curatedzone.c_external_wind_turbine_data")
wind_turbine_data = pd.DataFrame(cur.fetchall(), columns=['id', 'rtc', 'year', 'month', 'day', 'hour', 'minute',
 'temperature_100', 'temperature_120', 'temperature_80', 'wind_direction_100', 'wind_direction_120', 'wind_direction_80', 'wind_speed_100','wind_speed_120', 'wind_speed_80','pressure_200','pressure_100','pressure_0', 'power_output_80','power_output_100','power_output_120'])
# Define the threshold values for each parameter
thresholds = {'temperature_100': 25, 'pressure_100': 1100, 'wind_speed_100': 15, 'power_output_100': 2000}
```

```
# Create a new column 'Above_Threshold' in the training dataset based on the threshold values
train_data = wind_turbine_data.sample(frac=0.8, random_state=42)
train_data['Above_Threshold'] = np.where((train_data['temperature_100'] > thresholds['temperature_100']) |
                                         (train_data['pressure_100'] > thresholds['pressure_100']) |
                                         (train_data['wind_speed_100'] > thresholds['wind_speed_100']) |
                                         (train_data['power_output_100'] >
                                         thresholds['power_output_100']),
                                         1, 0)
# Select the columns to use for modeling
features = ['temperature_100', 'pressure_100', 'wind_speed_100', 'power_output_100']
# Split the data into training and testing sets
test_data = wind_turbine_data.drop(train_data.index)
# Standardize the data
scaler = StandardScaler()
scaler.fit(train_data[features])
train_data_scaled = scaler.transform(train_data[features])
test_data_scaled = scaler.transform(test_data[features])
# Build the model
model = RandomForestClassifier(n_estimators=100, random_state=42)
model.fit(train_data_scaled, train_data['Above_Threshold'])
# Predict using the model
def predict_threshold(df, columns, model, scaler, thresholds):
    # Standardize the input data
    input_data_scaled = scaler.transform(df[columns])
    # Make predictions using the model
    predictions = model.predict(input_data_scaled)
    # Check if each prediction is above or below threshold
```

```
    alerts = []
    for i in range(len(predictions)):
        if predictions[i] == 1:
            alerts.append(f"Row {i}: Above threshold")
        else:
            alerts.append(f"Row {i}: Below threshold")
    return alerts
# Example usage
input_data = pd.DataFrame({'temperature_100': [20, 25, 30],
                           'pressure_100': [1000, 1100, 1200],
                           'wind_speed_100': [10, 15, 20],
                           'power_output_100': [1500, 2000, 2500]})
alerts = predict_threshold(input_data, features, model, scaler, thresholds)
for alert in alerts:
    print(alert)
```

Here is the output of the above program with the input data, the model predicts the threshold based on past data:

```
Row 0: Below threshold
Row 1: Above threshold
Row 2: Above threshold
```

We can use the same model prediction for the incoming data in a real-time data streaming scenario. Here is an example where we will simulate wind turbine data to demonstrate how to use condition-based monitoring for real-time data streaming.

Before applying condition-based monitoring, let us publish simulated data in Kafka topic. We covered about installation and configuration of Kafka in *Chapter 5, Designing Data Lake and Executing Data Transformation.* Make sure that Kafka Zookeeper and server services are up and running. Here is the Python program which simulates data and pushes the data into Kafka topic:

```
import json
import pandas as pd
from kafka import KafkaConsumer
# Kafka consumer setup
consumer = KafkaConsumer('wind-turbine-data', bootstrap_servers=['local-
```

```
host:9092'], value_deserializer=lambda m: json.loads(m.decode('utf-8')))
# Create an empty Pandas DataFrame
columns = ['rtc', 'temperature_100', 'pressure_100', 'wind_speed_100', 'power_output_100']
df = pd.DataFrame(columns=columns)
# Consume data from Kafka topic
for message in consumer:
    data = message.value
    df = df.append(pd.json_normalize(data['data']), ignore_index=True)
    # Print the latest row of data
    print(df.tail(1))
```

The following Python program demonstrates how to apply CBM for the above real-time data stream:

```
import pandas as pd
import numpy as np
from sklearn.preprocessing import StandardScaler
from sklearn.ensemble import RandomForestClassifier
import psycopg2
import json
from kafka import KafkaConsumer
# Connect to datalake
conn = psycopg2.connect(
        host="localhost",
        database="IoTDataLake",
        user="postgres",
        password=""
    )
cur = conn.cursor()
# Query curated zone of the data lake for the wind turbine table and create a dataframe
cur.execute("SELECT * FROM curatedzone.c_external_wind_turbine_data")
wind_turbine_data = pd.DataFrame(cur.fetchall(), columns=['id', 'rtc', 'year', 'month', 'day', 'hour', 'minute',
'temperature_100', 'temperature_120', 'temperature_80', 'wind_direction_100', 'wind_direction_120',
'wind_direction_80', 'wind_speed_100','wind_speed_120', 'wind_speed_80','pressure_200','pressure_100','pressure_0', 'power_output_80','power_output_100','power_output_120'])
```

```
# Define the threshold values for each parameter
thresholds = {'temperature_100': 25, 'pressure_100': 1100, 'wind_speed_100': 15, 'power_output_100': 2000}
# Create a new column 'Above_Threshold' in the training dataset based on the threshold values
train_data = wind_turbine_data.sample(frac=0.8, random_state=42)
train_data['Above_Threshold'] = np.where((train_data['temperature_100'] > thresholds['temperature_100']) |
                                         (train_data['pressure_100'] > thresholds['pressure_100']) |
                                         (train_data['wind_speed_100'] > thresholds['wind_speed_100']) |
                                         (train_data['power_output_100'] > thresholds['power_output_100']),
                                         1, 0)
# Select the columns to use for modeling
features = ['temperature_100', 'pressure_100', 'wind_speed_100', 'power_output_100']
# Split the data into training and testing sets
test_data = wind_turbine_data.drop(train_data.index)
# Standardize the data
scaler = StandardScaler()
scaler.fit(train_data[features])
train_data_scaled = scaler.transform(train_data[features])
test_data_scaled = scaler.transform(test_data[features])
# Build the model
model = RandomForestClassifier(n_estimators=100, random_state=42)
model.fit(train_data_scaled, train_data['Above_Threshold'])
# Predict using the model
def predict_threshold(df, columns, model, scaler, thresholds):
    # Standardize the input data
    input_data_scaled = scaler.transform(df[columns])
    # Make predictions using the model
    predictions = model.predict(input_data_scaled)
    # Check if each prediction is above or below threshold
    alerts = []
    for i in range(len(predictions)):
```

```
        if predictions[i] == 1:
            alerts.append(f"Row {i}: Above threshold")
        else:
            alerts.append(f"Row {i}: Below threshold")
    return alerts
# Kafka consumer setup
consumer = KafkaConsumer('wind-turbine-data', bootstrap_servers=['localhost:9092'], value_deserializer=lambda m: json.loads(m.decode('utf-8')))
# Create an empty Pandas DataFrame
columns = ['rtc', 'temperature_100', 'pressure_100', 'wind_speed_100', 'power_output_100']
df = pd.DataFrame(columns=columns)
# Consume data from Kafka topic
for message in consumer:
    data = message.value
    df = df.append(pd.json_normalize(data['data']), ignore_index=True)
    # Print the latest row of data
    print(df.tail(1))
#Invoke Predict function to pass the dataframe, features, model, scaler and thresholds. This will predict and return the threshold alert.
alerts = predict_threshold(df, features, model, scaler, thresholds)
for alert in alerts:
    print(alert)
```

The above Python program demonstrates how to use condition-based monitoring to monitor the health of wind turbines. The program uses machine learning to predict whether certain parameters of the wind turbines, such as temperature, pressure, wind speed, and power output, are above or below a predefined threshold. An alert is generated if these parameters exceed their respective threshold value.

The program begins by connecting to a database that stores wind turbine data. It then retrieves the wind turbine data and creates a Pandas **DataFrame**. The threshold values for each parameter are defined and a new column **Above_Threshold** is created based on the threshold values.

Next, the program selects the features to use for modeling and splits the data into training and testing sets. The data is then standardized using the **StandardScaler** function from scikit-learn.

A random forest classifier is used to build the model, and the **predict_threshold** function is invoked to make predictions using the model. The **predict_threshold** function standardizes the input data and makes predictions using the model. The function then checks whether each prediction is above or below the threshold and generates alerts accordingly.

The program creates a Kafka consumer to consume data from a Kafka topic. It then creates an empty Pandas **DataFrame** and adds new rows of data to the **DataFrame** as they are consumed from the Kafka topic. Finally, the **predict_threshold** function is invoked on the **DataFrame** to generate alerts based on the threshold values defined earlier, and these alerts are then printed out. This program can monitor wind turbines in real-time and generate alerts when certain parameters exceed their threshold values.

Corrective Maintenance

Corrective Maintenance is a strategy that involves fixing an asset or equipment after it has failed or malfunctioned. It aims to restore the asset's original functionality to prevent further damage or failure. Corrective maintenance is essential in industries using IIoT, where assets are constantly monitored and analyzed for performance and condition. In the context of wind turbine data, corrective maintenance would involve identifying and fixing any issues or faults that arise in the turbine's components, such as the blades, generator, or gearbox.

Corrective maintenance can be applied when predictive or preventive maintenance strategies have not effectively prevented failures or malfunctions. It can also be used as a backup plan for situations where it is not feasible to implement predictive or preventive maintenance strategies. In IIoT, corrective maintenance can be used as a last resort to ensure the continuity of operations and prevent equipment downtime.

Python can be used for corrective maintenance implementation in IoT Data Analytics. For example, using wind turbine data, a Python program can analyze the data, identify potential issues or faults, and create alerts when certain thresholds are exceeded. A Python program can also monitor and track the corrective maintenance activities, including work orders, parts replacement, and labor hours. This information can be used to evaluate the corrective maintenance strategy's effectiveness and identify improvement areas.

Corrective maintenance is a vital maintenance strategy for industries using IIoT and IoT Data Analytics, where equipment and assets are constantly monitored and analyzed. It can be applied when other maintenance strategies are ineffective or not feasible. Python can implement and monitor corrective maintenance activities, including data analysis, alert creation, and tracking of maintenance activities.

Implementing Maintenance Process

Automating the creation of maintenance tickets is a critical requirement for any Industrial IoT implementation, regardless of whether it involves corrective, preventive, or predictive maintenance. We will implement a simple maintenance process in this section to achieve this. However, in real-time scenarios, it is common to integrate with tools such as ServiceNow for creating maintenance tickets.

Here are the instructions to create **maintenancezone** of the datalake and the table to store the maintenance ticket. We will demonstrate how to use this table later in this chapter.

1. Create a new database schema **maintenancezone** in the **IoTDataLake** database. Please refer *Setting up Data Lake* section of *Chapter 5, Designing Data Lake and Executing Data Transformation* for how to create a database schema.
2. Create a table using the following SQL statement:

```
CREATE TABLE maintenancezone.maintanence_rec (
            maint_id SERIAL PRIMARY KEY,
            maint_actual_start TIMESTAMP,
            maint_actual_end TIMESTAMP,
            maint_schedule_start TIMESTAMP,
            maint_schedule_end TIMESTAMP,
            reason VARCHAR(180),
            vendor VARCHAR(80),
            description VARCHAR(250),
            Assignee VARCHAR(80),
            status VARCHAR(40),
            equipment_location VARCHAR(80),
            priority VARCHAR(12)
        );
```

Implementing Corrective Maintenance Methods

Here is the Python program which uses data stored in a PostgreSQL database to perform corrective maintenance on wind turbine equipment. It connects to the **IoTDataLake** database and queries the **c_external_wind_turbine_data** table to create a Pandas DataFrame.

The program sets a power output threshold and identifies periods where the power output is below that threshold. It calculates the duration of each low-power period. It identifies any periods where corrective maintenance should be performed based on whether the low-power period is longer than three hours.

Suppose there are any corrective maintenance periods identified. In that case, the program creates a new entry in a **maintenance_rec** table in the database with relevant information about the maintenance period such as its start and end times, reason, vendor, description, assignee, status, equipment location, and priority.

Finally, the program outputs the corrective maintenance periods and closes the connection to the database:

```
import psycopg2
import pandas as pd
```

```
# Connect to PostgreSQL database
try:
    conn = psycopg2.connect(
        host="localhost",
        database="IoTDataLake",
        user="postgres",
        password=""
    )
except:
    print("Unable to connect to database")

# Query the wind turbine data from the curated zone of the data lake
try:
    cur = conn.cursor()
    cur.execute("SELECT * FROM curatedzone.c_external_wind_turbine_data")
    wind_turbine_data = pd.DataFrame(cur.fetchall(), columns=['id', 'rtc', 'year', 'month', 'day', 'hour', 'minute',
                                        'temperature_100', 'temperature_120', 'temperature_80',
                                        'wind_direction_100', 'wind_direction_120',
                                        'wind_direction_80', 'wind_speed_100','wind_speed_120',
                                        'wind_speed_80','pressure_200','pressure_100','pressure_0',
                                        'power_output_80','power_output_100','power_output_120'])
    cur.close()
except:
    print("Unable to fetch wind turbine data")
# Define the threshold for power output
threshold = 20
# Identify the time periods when the power output is below the threshold
```

```
low_power_periods = wind_turbine_data[wind_turbine_data['power_output_100'] < threshold]
# Calculate the duration of each low-power period
low_power_periods['Duration'] = low_power_periods['rtc'] - low_power_periods['rtc'].shift()
# Identify the time periods when corrective maintenance should be performed
corrective_maintenance_periods = low_power_periods[low_power_periods['Duration'] > pd.Timedelta('3 hour')]
# Insert a new record in the maintenance table for each corrective maintenance period
if len(corrective_maintenance_periods) > 0:
    maint_actual_start = corrective_maintenance_periods.iloc[0]['rtc']
    maint_actual_end = corrective_maintenance_periods.iloc[-1]['rtc'] + pd.Timedelta('1 hour')
    maint_schedule_start = maint_actual_start
    maint_schedule_end = maint_actual_end + pd.Timedelta('7 days')
    reason = 'Low power output'
    vendor = 'ABC Wind Turbine Services'
    description = 'Corrective maintenance for low power output'
    assignee = 'John Doe'
    status = 'Open'
    equipment_location = 'Wind turbine A'
    priority = 'High'

    try:
        cur = conn.cursor()
        cur.execute("INSERT INTO maintenancezone.maintanenence_rec (maint_actual_start, maint_actual_end, maint_schedule_start, maint_schedule_end, reason, vendor, description, assignee, status, equipment_location, priority) VALUES (%s, %s, %s, %s, %s, %s, %s, %s, %s, %s, %s)", (maint_actual_start, maint_actual_end, maint_schedule_start, maint_schedule_end, reason, vendor, description, assignee, status, equipment_location, priority))
        conn.commit()
        cur.close()
```

```
    except:
        print("Unable to insert maintenance record")
# Output the corrective maintenance periods
print(corrective_maintenance_periods[['rtc', 'power_output_100', 'Duration']])
# Close the database connection
conn.close()
```

Preventive Maintenance

Preventive Maintenance (PM) is a proactive maintenance approach essential in Industry IoT. Its importance lies in identifying and addressing potential equipment failures before they occur, which can significantly reduce equipment downtime and maintenance costs.

PM is implemented by performing routine maintenance tasks on equipment at predetermined intervals, such as cleaning, lubrication, and inspection. The frequency of these tasks is based on the equipment manufacturer's recommendations, environmental conditions, and other factors that can affect equipment performance.

Preventive maintenance is the planned maintenance of equipment to prevent failures before they occur. This differs from other maintenance approaches, such as condition-based monitoring and corrective maintenance, which are performed after a failure. PM can help extend the equipment's life, improve its performance, and reduce downtime. It can also help to prevent costly repairs and replacements. CM and CBM involve monitoring equipment performance and identifying problems as they occur, while corrective maintenance involves addressing equipment failures after they have already occurred.

For example, PM can be implemented in wind turbines by regularly monitoring power output, wind speed, and other parameters to identify any changes that could indicate potential issues. Based on this data, performing routine maintenance tasks on wind turbines makes it possible to prevent unexpected downtime and reduce maintenance costs.

IoT Data Analytics plays a crucial role in PM by collecting, processing, and analyzing data from various sensors and equipment to identify trends and patterns that could indicate potential issues. By using Predictive Analytics, it is possible to identify potential failures before they occur, enabling maintenance teams to take proactive measures to address them.

Implementing Preventive Maintenance using Python

In the below Python program, we implement a preventive maintenance system for wind turbines using data from the IoT data lake. This system identifies time periods when the power output of the wind turbines is below a certain threshold and initiates maintenance activities during those periods to prevent downtime and equipment failure.

To begin with, we connect to a PostgreSQL database using the **psycopg2** library and fetch data from the curated zone of the IoT data lake. We then define a threshold for power output and calculate the moving average of the power output over 24 hours.

Next, we identify the time periods when the power output is below the threshold and the rolling average using the pandas library and calculate the duration of each low-power period. We then identify the time periods when maintenance should be performed, based on a threshold of one day, and compute the start and end times of the maintenance period.

Once the maintenance period is identified, we create a single maintenance record using pandas and insert it into the maintenance table in the database using SQL. The maintenance record contains the maintenance schedule start and end times, the reason for maintenance, vendor details, equipment location, and priority.

The following Python program is a great example of implementing preventive maintenance using data-driven insights. By identifying low-power periods and scheduling maintenance activities during those periods, we can reduce equipment downtime and prevent costly repairs:

```
import psycopg2
import pandas as pd
# Connect to the PostgreSQL database
try:
    conn = psycopg2.connect(
        host="localhost",
        database="IoTDataLake",
        user="postgres",
        password=""
    )
except Exception as e:
    print("Unable to connect to the database")
    print(e)

# Query the wind turbine data from the curated zone of the data lake
try:
    cur = conn.cursor()
    cur.execute("SELECT * FROM curatedzone.c_external_wind_turbine_data")
    wind_turbine_data = pd.DataFrame(cur.fetchall(), columns=['id',
'rtc', 'year', 'month', 'day', 'hour', 'minute',
```

```
        'temperature_100', 'temperature_120', 'temperature_80',
        'wind_direction_100', 'wind_direction_120',
        'wind_direction_80', 'wind_speed_100','wind_speed_120',
        'wind_speed_80','pressure_200','pressure_100','pressure_0',
        'power_output_80','power_output_100','power_output_120'])
    cur.close()
except Exception as e:
    print("Unable to fetch wind turbine data")
    print(e)

# Define the threshold for power output
threshold = 2000

# Calculate the moving average of the power output
rolling_avg = wind_turbine_data['power_output_100'].rolling(window=24).mean()

# Identify the time periods when the power output is below the threshold and the rolling average
low_power_periods = wind_turbine_data.loc[(wind_turbine_data['power_output_100'] < threshold) & (wind_turbine_data['power_output_100'] < rolling_avg)]

# Calculate the duration of each low-power period
low_power_periods['Duration'] = (low_power_periods['rtc'] - low_power_periods['rtc'].shift())

# Identify the time periods when maintenance should be performed
maintenance_periods = low_power_periods.loc[low_power_periods['Duration'] > pd.Timedelta('1 day')]
```

```

# Compute the start and end times of the maintenance period
maint_start = maintenance_periods['rtc'].min()
maint_end = maintenance_periods['rtc'].min() + pd.Timedelta('6 hours')

# Create a single maintenance record
maintenance_record = pd.DataFrame({
    'maint_actual_start': [maint_start],
    'maint_actual_end': [maint_end],
    'maint_schedule_start': [maint_start + pd.Timedelta('1 day')],
    'maint_schedule_end': [maint_end + pd.Timedelta('1 day')],
    'reason': ['Preventive Maintenance'],
    'vendor': ['ABC Company'],
    'description': ['Inspect and clean the turbine blades'],
    'assignee': ['John Doe'],
    'status': ['Scheduled'],
    'equipment_location': ['Turbine 1'],
    'priority': ['High']
})

# Insert the maintenance record into the maintenance table
try:
    cur = conn.cursor()
    cur.execute("INSERT INTO maintenancezone.maintanenence_rec (maint_
    schedule_start, maint_schedule_end, reason, vendor, description, assign-
    ee, status, equipment_location, priority) VALUES (%s, %s, %s, %s, %s,
    %s, %s, %s, %s)",
        (maintenance_record['maint_schedule_start'][0], maintenance_re-
    cord['maint_schedule_end'][0], maintenance_record['reason'][0], main-
    tenance_record['vendor'][0], maintenance_record['description'][0],
    maintenance_record['assignee'][0], maintenance_record['status'][0],
    maintenance_record['equipment_location'][0], maintenance_record['priori-
    ty'][0]))
    # Commit
    conn.commit()
```

```
    print("Maintenance record inserted successfully")
except:
    print("Unable to insert maintenance record")
finally:
    # Close the cursor and connection
    cur.close()
    conn.close()
```

Predictive Maintenance

Predictive Maintenance is an innovative technique that deploys machine learning algorithms and data analysis to identify possible equipment failures before they occur. This advanced approach helps organizations detect and resolve issues before they cause significant damages, minimize downtime, and reduce maintenance costs. In contrast, preventive maintenance is a schedule-based method that involves conducting regular inspections, maintenance, and replacement of components to avoid equipment failures.

The primary contrast between predictive and preventive maintenance is the timing and method used for maintenance. Preventive maintenance involves conducting routine maintenance on equipment at fixed intervals, irrespective of its condition. On the other hand, predictive maintenance uses real-time data and machine learning algorithms to analyze equipment performance and identify potential issues before they cause significant damage. This approach enables organizations to optimize maintenance schedules, reduce downtime, and lower maintenance costs.

For instance, wind turbines can use predictive maintenance to monitor performance data and detect when components are likely to fail. By predicting possible failures, maintenance teams can proactively address issues before they cause significant damage and avoid unplanned downtime. On the other hand, preventive maintenance would involve performing routine maintenance on the turbines at predetermined intervals, regardless of their condition.

While preventive maintenance is still useful, it can be expensive and time-consuming. On the other hand, predictive maintenance allows organizations to optimize maintenance schedules, minimize downtime, and prevent unexpected equipment failures.

Implementing Predictive Maintenance using Python

Predictive Maintenance is an important aspect of machine health management that can help minimize downtime and reduce repair costs. In this context, the **Mean Absolute Error (MAE)** is a commonly used metric for evaluating the performance of predictive maintenance models. The MAE calculates the difference between machine performance metrics' actual and predicted values, such as power output or vibration levels.

In the following Python program, MAE is used to determine whether a wind turbine requires maintenance. After splitting the wind turbine data into training and testing sets, a linear regression model is trained on the training data using the wind speed, temperature, and pressure as input features and the power output as the target feature. The model is then used to predict the power output on the testing data, and the MAE is calculated between the predicted and actual power output.

The calculated MAE is then compared to a pre-defined threshold, which serves as a decision boundary to determine whether the wind turbine requires maintenance. If the MAE exceeds the threshold, the model's predictions significantly differ from the actual values, suggesting that the wind turbine may require maintenance. Conversely, if the MAE is below the threshold, the model's predictions are accurate, suggesting that the wind turbine does not require maintenance:

```
import pandas as pd
import numpy as np
from sklearn.model_selection import train_test_split
from sklearn.linear_model import LinearRegression
import psycopg2
from sklearn.metrics import mean_absolute_error
import matplotlib.pyplot as plt

# Connect to the PostgreSQL database
try:
    conn = psycopg2.connect(
        host="localhost",
        database="IoTDataLake",
        user="postgres",
        password=""
    )
except:
    print("Unable to connect to the database")

# Query the wind turbine data from the curated zone of the data lake
try:
    cur = conn.cursor()
    cur.execute("SELECT * FROM curatedzone.c_external_wind_turbine_data")
    wind_turbine_data = pd.DataFrame(cur.fetchall(), columns=['id', 'rtc', 'year', 'month', 'day', 'hour', 'minute',
```

```
                                        'temperature_100', 'temperature_120', 'temperature_80',
                                        'wind_direction_100', 'wind_direction_120',
                                        'wind_direction_80', 'wind_speed_100','wind_speed_120',
                                        'wind_speed_80','pressure_200','pressure_100','pressure_0',
                                        'power_output_80','power_output_100','power_output_120'])
    cur.close()
except:
    print("Unable to fetch wind turbine data")

# Split the data into training and testing sets
train, test = train_test_split(wind_turbine_data, test_size=0.2)

# Train a linear regression model on the training data
model = LinearRegression()
model.fit(train[['wind_speed_100', 'temperature_100', 'pressure_100']], train['power_output_100'])
# Predict the power output on the testing data
test['predicted_power_output'] = model.predict(test[['wind_speed_100', 'temperature_100', 'pressure_100']])
#finding MAE (Mean Absolute Error)
mae = mean_absolute_error(test['power_output_100'], test['predicted_power_output'])
# Set a threshold for the MAE to determine whether the wind turbine requires maintenance or not
threshold = 20
# Check if the MAE exceeds the threshold
if mae > threshold:
    print("The wind turbine requires maintenance.")
else:
    print("The wind turbine does not require maintenance.")

# Visualize the predicted vs actual power output on a scatter plot
colors = ['red' if p_actual > p_predicted else 'blue' for p_actual, p_predicted in zip(test['power_output_100'], test['predicted_pow-
```

```
er_output'])]
plt.scatter(test['power_output_100'], test['predicted_power_out-
put'], color=colors)
plt.xlabel('Actual Power Output')
plt.ylabel('Predicted Power Output')
```

Here is the output of the above code with its result (see *Figure 8.1*):

```
The wind turbine requires maintenance
```

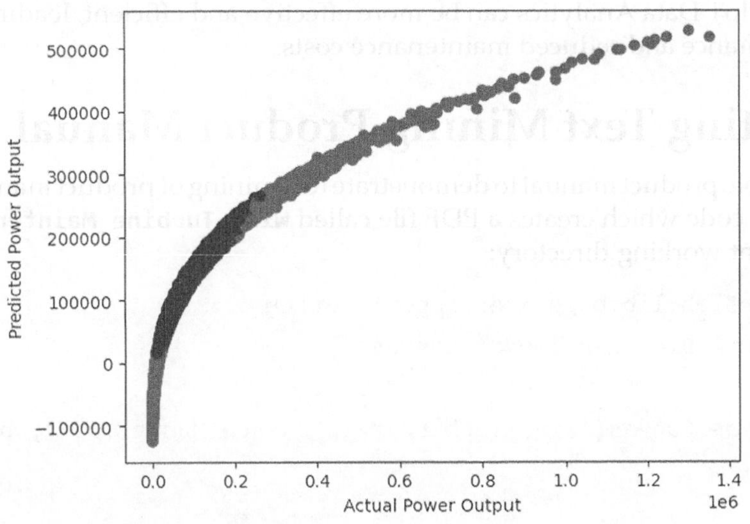

***Figure 8.1:** Actual vs Predicted Power Output*

The graph above shows the accuracy of the linear regression model we built earlier. The MAE is greater than the given threshold of 20, indicating that the wind turbine needs maintenance. We can automate the creation of a maintenance ticket using the Python program for preventive maintenance above. You can try modifying the program to automate the creation of a maintenance record.

Text Mining the Product Manual

Text Mining involves extracting meaningful information from unstructured textual data. Text mining of product manuals can help determine equipment thresholds for various maintenance types. For instance, threshold values can be determined for corrective maintenance, preventive maintenance, and predictive maintenance based on the information present in product manuals.

Automating text mining for Industrial IoT and IoT Data Analytics can be a significant advancement. This can enable faster and more accurate determination of equipment thresholds, reducing the need for manual effort and expertise. By leveraging the vast amounts of unstructured textual data available in product manuals, text mining can provide valuable insights into maintenance requirements for different types of equipment.

For instance, text mining can extract information on equipment usage patterns, environmental factors, and other parameters that may impact equipment performance. This can then be used to determine optimal maintenance thresholds, leading to improved equipment reliability and reduced downtime.

Overall, text mining of product manuals can provide valuable information for determining equipment thresholds and optimizing maintenance schedules. By automating this process, Industrial IoT and IoT Data Analytics can be more effective and efficient, leading to improved equipment performance and reduced maintenance costs.

Implementing Text Mining Product Manual

Let us create a sample product manual to demonstrate text mining of product manuals ourselves. Here is the Python code which creates a PDF file called **`Wind_Turbine_Maintenance_Manual.pdf`** on your current working directory:

```
from reportlab.lib.pagesizes import letter
from reportlab.pdfgen import canvas
# Create a new PDF document with 1 page
pdf = canvas.Canvas('Wind_Turbine_Maintenance_Manual.pdf', pagesize=letter)
# Add content to the page
pdf.setFont("Helvetica-Bold", 20)
pdf.drawCentredString(300, 700, "Wind Turbine Maintenance Manual")
pdf.setFont("Helvetica", 12)
pdf.drawString(50, 650, "Introduction:")
pdf.drawString(50, 620, "This manual provides guidelines for maintaining the wind turbine to ensure optimal performance and prevent breakdowns. It covers all aspects of the turbine's operation, from routine inspections to major repairs.")
pdf.drawString(50, 580, "Thresholds for Preventive Maintenance:")
pdf.drawString(50, 550, "- Temperature: The temperature of the turbine should not exceed 20°C. If it exceeds this threshold, maintenance is required to prevent overheating.")
pdf.drawString(50, 520, "- Wind Speed: The turbine should be shut down if wind speeds exceed 25 meters per second. If the turbine operates in high wind conditions, it may cause damage to the blades and other components.")
pdf.drawString(50, 490, "- Power Output: If the power output drops by more than 20%, it may indicate a problem with the turbine. Maintenance should be performed to identify and resolve any issues.")
```

```
pdf.drawString(50, 450, "These are general guidelines and may vary based on the specific model of the turbine. Please refer to the manufacturer's manual for detailed maintenance instructions.")
# Save the PDF document
pdf.save()
```

After creating the PDF file above, let us proceed to extract threshold information from the PDF file:

```
import psycopg2
import pandas as pd
import numpy as np
import PyPDF2
import re
import nltk
from nltk.tokenize import word_tokenize, sent_tokenize
from nltk.corpus import stopwords
from sklearn.feature_extraction.text import TfidfVectorizer
# Read the Wind Turbine Maintenance Manual PDF file
with open('wind_turbine_maintenance_manual.pdf', 'rb') as pdf_file:
    pdf_reader = PyPDF2.PdfReader(pdf_file)
    # Extract text from the first page of the PDF
    first_page = pdf_reader.pages[0]
    manual_text = first_page.extract_text()
print(manual_text)
# Remove stop words from the text
stop_words = set(stopwords.words('english'))
filtered_tokens = [word for word in word_tokenize(manual_text) if word.lower() not in stop_words]
# Define keywords for identifying relevant information in the manual
relevant_keywords = ['power output', 'wind speed', 'temperature']
# Identify sentences containing relevant information using the keywords
relevant_sentences = []
for sentence in nltk.sent_tokenize(manual_text):
    for keyword in relevant_keywords:
        if keyword in sentence.lower():
            relevant_sentences.append(sentence)
```

```
            break
# Extract the relevant information from the relevant sentences using regular expressions
power_output_regex = r'power output.*?(\d+)\s*%'
wind_speed_regex = r'wind speed.*?(\d+)\s*meters per second'
temperature_regex = r'temperature.*?(\d+)\s*°c'
power_output_threshold, wind_speed_threshold, temperature_threshold = None, None, None
for sentence in relevant_sentences:
    match = re.search(power_output_regex, sentence, re.IGNORECASE)
    if match:
        power_output_threshold = int(match.group(1))
    match = re.search(wind_speed_regex, sentence, re.IGNORECASE)
    if match:
        wind_speed_threshold = int(match.group(1))
    match = re.search(temperature_regex, sentence, re.IGNORECASE)
    if match:
        temperature_threshold = int(match.group(1))
# Print the extracted thresholds
if power_output_threshold is not None:
    print("Threshold for power output:", power_output_threshold)
if wind_speed_threshold is not None:
    print("Threshold for wind speed:", wind_speed_threshold)
if temperature_threshold is not None:
    print("Threshold for temperature:", temperature_threshold)
# Connect to the PostgreSQL database
try:
    conn = psycopg2.connect(
        host="localhost",
        database="IoTDataLake",
        user="postgres",
        password=""
    )
except:
    print("Unable to connect to the database")
```

```
# Create a table if it does not already exist
with conn.cursor() as cursor:
    cursor.execute("""
        CREATE TABLE IF NOT EXISTS maintenancezone.maint_thresholds (
            tag VARCHAR(80),
            threshold INTEGER
        )
    """)
    # Insert the tag and threshold values into the table
    cursor.execute("""
        INSERT INTO maintenancezone.maint_thresholds (tag, threshold)
        VALUES (%s, %s), (%s, %s), (%s, %s)
    """, ("power output", power_output_threshold, "wind speed", wind_speed_threshold, "temperature", temperature_threshold))
# Commit the changes and close the connection
conn.commit()
conn.close()
```

The Python program is designed to extract threshold information from a product manual using **Natural Language Processing** (**NLP**) and regular expressions. It first reads a PDF file containing the manual using the PyPDF2 library and extracts text from the first page of the PDF. It then removes the stop words from the text using the NLTK library.

Next, the program identifies relevant information in the manual by defining keywords such as **`power output`**, **`wind speed`**, and **`temperature`**. It extracts sentences containing these keywords and saves them in a list.

The program then uses regular expressions to extract the relevant information from the identified sentences. It defines regular expressions for extracting power output, wind speed, and temperature thresholds. It then loops over the relevant sentences, searches for the regular expressions, and extracts the threshold values. If found, the threshold values are saved in variables.

Finally, the program connects to a PostgreSQL database, creates a table if it does not exist, and inserts the extracted threshold values into the table. The program does not insert any values into the database if no threshold values were extracted.

Automating the Creation of Maintenance Ticket

As part of the above section on text mining product manual, we have extracted the threshold information from the wind turbine product manual and stored it in the maintenance zone of the data lake. Using the same information let us automate creating a maintenance ticket based on the predictive maintenance result and the threshold value of the temperature for the wind turbine. Here is the Python code for the same:

```
import psycopg2
import pandas as pd
import datetime
# Connect to the PostgreSQL database
try:
    conn = psycopg2.connect(
        host="localhost",
        database="IoTDataLake",
        user="postgres",
        password=""
    )
except:
    print("Unable to connect to the database")
# Query the wind turbine data from the curated zone of the data lake
try:
    cur = conn.cursor()
    cur.execute("SELECT * FROM curatedzone.c_external_wind_turbine_data")
    wind_turbine_data = pd.DataFrame(cur.fetchall(), columns=['id', 'rtc', 'year', 'month', 'day', 'hour', 'minute',
                                                              'temperature_100', 'temperature_120', 'temperature_80',
                                                              'wind_direction_100', 'wind_direction_120',
                                                              'wind_direction_80', 'wind_speed_100','wind_speed_120',
                                                              'wind_speed_80','pressure_200','pressure_100','pressure_0',
                                                              'power_output_80','power_output_100','power_output_120'])
    cur.close()
except:
    print("Unable to fetch wind turbine data")
#Query the maint_threshold table for temperature threshold extracted from product manual
```

```
# Query the wind turbine data from the curated zone of the data lake
try:
    conn = psycopg2.connect(
    host="localhost",
    database="IoTDataLake",
    user="postgres",
    password=""
    )
    cur = conn.cursor()
    cur.execute("SELECT * FROM maintenancezone.maint_thresholds")
    maint_threshold_data = pd.DataFrame(cur.fetchall(), columns=['tag', 'threshold'])
    cur.close()
except:
    print("Unable to fetch maint threshold data")
# Define the threshold for temperature
threshold = 'temperature'
temperature_threshold = maint_threshold_data[maint_threshold_data['tag'] == threshold]['threshold'].iloc[0]
print(f"The temperature threshold is {temperature_threshold}")
# Identify the time periods when the temperature is above the threshold
high_temperature_periods = wind_turbine_data.loc[wind_turbine_data['temperature_100'] > temperature_threshold]
# Calculate the duration of each high-temperature period
high_temperature_periods['Duration'] = (high_temperature_periods['rtc'] - high_temperature_periods['rtc'].shift())
# Identify the time periods when maintenance should be performed
maintenance_periods = high_temperature_periods.loc[high_temperature_periods['Duration'] > pd.Timedelta('1 hour')]
# Create a maintenance record
if not maintenance_periods.empty:
    maint_actual_start = None
    maint_actual_end = None
    maint_schedule_start = datetime.datetime.now() + datetime.timedelta(hours=2)
    maint_schedule_end = maint_schedule_start + datetime.timedel-
```

```
ta(hours=2)
    reason = "Preventive Maintenance based on high temperature"
    vendor = "Wind Turbine Solutions"
    description = "Perform preventive maintenance to reduce wear and tear due to high temperature"
    assignee = "John Doe"
    status = "Open"
    equipment_location = "Wind Turbine #1"
    priority = "High"
  # Insert the maintenance record into the Postgres database
    cur = conn.cursor()
    cur.execute("INSERT INTO maintenancezone.maintanence_rec (maint_actual_start, maint_schedule_start, maint_schedule_end, reason, vendor, description, assignee, status, equipment_location, priority) VALUES (%s, %s, %s, %s, %s, %s, %s, %s, %s, %s)", (maint_actual_start, maint_schedule_start, maint_schedule_end, reason, vendor, description, assignee, status, equipment_location, priority))
    conn.commit()
    print("Maintenance record inserted successfully")
    conn.close()
else:
    print("No maintenance required")
```

The above Python program connects to a PostgreSQL database and queries wind turbine data from the curated zone of the data lake. It also queries the **`maint_threshold`** table for temperature thresholds extracted from the product manual. Based on the threshold and the wind turbine data, it identifies the time periods when maintenance should be performed and creates a record if necessary. The maintenance record includes the scheduled start and end times, reason, vendor, description, assignee, status, equipment location, and priority. The program inserts the maintenance record into the PostgreSQL database if maintenance is required. Otherwise, it prints **`No maintenance required`**.

Conclusion

This chapter explored the importance of continuously monitoring machines' conditions to detect early signs of failure and prevent breakdowns. We discussed various maintenance strategies, including corrective, preventive, condition-based, and predictive maintenance. We focused on time-series monitoring and preventive maintenance in Industrial IoT Data Analytics, where machine learning algorithms in Python can predict equipment failure by analyzing different equipment parameters. We also covered using time-series data analysis techniques to extract insights, visualize data, and predict equipment failure and text mining techniques to analyze product manuals for improved predictive maintenance. Lastly, we discussed creating maintenance tickets based on predictions to complete the end-to-end benefit of time-series monitoring and preventive maintenance in IoT Data Analytics. By implementing these techniques, organizations can improve the reliability of their machines and equipment, reduce maintenance costs, and avoid unexpected downtime.

In the next chapter, *Model Deployment on Edge Devices using FAST API* will cover several topics related to deploying machine learning models on edge devices. The chapter will begin by discussing installing and configuring FastAPI, a Python library for building APIs. It will then move on to the model building, requests, responses, and endpoint creation using FastAPI. The chapter will also cover the process of exposing the model using FastAPI and the concepts of continuous and adaptive learning. The chapter's primary focus will be providing readers with a comprehensive understanding of deploying machine learning models on edge devices using FastAPI. By the end of the chapter, readers will have the necessary knowledge to deploy their machine-learning models on edge devices using FastAPI, a powerful and flexible Python library. The chapter will conclude by summarizing the key takeaways from the discussion and highlighting the importance of continuous and adaptive learning in model deployment.

Points to Remember

Following are the key takeaways from this chapter:

- Monitoring machines' condition is critical to detect early signs of failure and prevent breakdowns.
- The primary goal of condition monitoring is to improve machines and equipment's reliability.
- Maintenance strategies include corrective, preventive, **Condition-Based Maintenance (CBM)**, and predictive maintenance.
- The first is corrective maintenance, which involves repairing equipment after a breakdown. This reactive approach to maintenance is typically more expensive than other strategies.
- The second is preventive maintenance, which involves regular maintenance to avoid unexpected failures. This proactive approach can increase equipment lifespan.
- The third strategy is condition-based maintenance, which involves monitoring machine health and performing maintenance only when necessary. This approach is more cost-effective than corrective maintenance since it reduces the likelihood of unexpected breakdowns.
- The fourth strategy is predictive maintenance, which uses data analytics and machine learning algorithms to anticipate equipment failures before they occur. It's the most advanced and cost-effective maintenance strategy.

- Python can be used to implement time-series monitoring and preventive maintenance techniques for **Industrial IoT (IIoT)** analytics.
- Machine learning algorithms in Python can predict equipment failure using various equipment parameters such as pressure, and power input/output.
- Time-series data analysis techniques can extract insights, visualize data, and predict equipment failure.
- Text mining techniques can analyze product manuals and build association rules against incoming tag values for improved predictive maintenance.
- Creating maintenance tickets based on predictions can complete the end-to-end benefit of time-series monitoring and preventive maintenance in IoT Data Analytics.

Join our book's Discord space

Join the book's Discord Workspace for Latest updates, Offers, Tech happenings around the world, New Release and Sessions with the Authors:

https://discord.bpbonline.com

Chapter 9
Model Deployment on Edge Devices

Introduction

This chapter will explore Edge Analytics and Model Deployment using Python and FastAPI. We will start by introducing the concept of Edge Computing, which involves processing data closer to its source on devices located at the Edge of the network to reduce latency and improve response times. We will also explore some of the IoT system simulators available for simulating various IoT scenarios.

Next, we will explore the challenges of deploying machine learning models on edge devices, such as limited resources like memory and processing power. We will then demonstrate how to overcome these challenges using the Python library FastAPI, which provides a simple and fast way to build web APIs for machine learning models.

We will guide readers through the installation and configuration of FastAPI, showing them how to build a machine-learning model using Python and expose it using FastAPI. We will cover essential concepts such as request, response, and endpoint and show readers how to make real-time predictions on data from edge devices.

Additionally, we will discuss the concepts of continuous and adaptive learning, which can enhance the model's accuracy over time. Continuous learning involves updating the model using new data as it becomes available, while adaptive learning involves adjusting the model in response to changes in the data or environment.

By the end of this chapter, readers will have a comprehensive understanding of Edge Analytics and Model Deployment using Python and FastAPI. They will be equipped to develop and deploy machine learning models on edge devices, providing real-time insights that can help optimize maintenance schedules, improve machine performance, and reduce costs.

Structure

In this chapter, we will cover the following topics:

- Introduction to Edge Computing and Analytics
- Simulators for IoT Systems
- Installation and Configuration of Edge Devices
- Installation and Configuration of FastAPI
- Model Building and Reuse
- Expose Models Using FastAPI
- Deploying Machine Learning Model
- Concept of Continuous Learning
- Concept of Adaptive Learning

Objectives

This chapter aims to learn about Edge Analytics and Model Deployment using Python and provide the readers with the tools and knowledge needed to perform these tasks successfully. By the end of this chapter, readers will have a thorough understanding of edge computing and its benefits, including reduced latency and increased privacy, as well as the ability to deploy machine learning models on edge devices.

The chapter introduces FastAPI, a Python web framework that simplifies API creation and covers its installation and configuration. Readers will learn to build models, make requests and responses, and create endpoints using FastAPI. Additionally, the chapter covers exposing models using FastAPI, making them accessible to other users.

Another important topic discussed in this chapter is continuous learning, where readers will learn how to enhance models by incorporating new data over time. This will allow readers to develop models that can adapt to changes in their environment, resulting in better accuracy and efficiency.

Finally, the chapter explores the concept of adaptive learning, where models can modify their behavior based on changing circumstances. Readers will gain an in-depth understanding of this topic and learn how it can be applied to edge computing scenarios.

Overall, this chapter introduces the concept of Edge Computing and Analytics, and IoT system simulators.

This chapter also equips readers with the skills and knowledge to perform Edge Analytics and Model Deployment using Python. Readers will learn how to deploy machine learning models on edge devices, improve accuracy using continuous and adaptive learning, and make models accessible using FastAPI. This chapter is essential for anyone interested in IoT Data Analytics and machine learning in Edge computing scenarios.

Introduction to Edge Computing and Analytics

Edge Computing and Analytics are innovative technologies that enable data processing and analysis closer to where the data is generated. This allows for real-time insights and more efficient data management, which is particularly useful in IoT Data Analytics and IIoT applications.

By using Edge Computing and Analytics, businesses can improve operational efficiency, reduce latency, and improve privacy. For instance, Edge Analytics can monitor wind turbines' performance in real-time, detect possible faults or anomalies, and trigger maintenance procedures before any breakdown.

Edge Computing and Analytics offer several advantages, such as faster decision-making, reduced data transfer requirements, and more efficient use of cloud resources. However, there are also some downsides, including increased complexity, security risks, and the need for specialized hardware and software.

Despite these challenges, Edge Computing and Analytics are being increasingly adopted by businesses in various sectors, such as manufacturing, healthcare, and transportation. They can help to optimize production processes, reduce downtime, and improve overall operational efficiency.

In summary, Edge Computing and Analytics are game changers in IoT Data Analytics and IIoT. By enabling real-time insights and more efficient data management, they give businesses a competitive edge in their operations. While there are some challenges, the benefits of adopting Edge Computing and Analytics make it a technology worth considering.

Simulators for IoT Systems

In our exploration of IoT systems, we cannot overlook the vital role that simulation plays in their development and evaluation. As researchers and developers, simulation empowers us to create detailed models and analyze the intricate behavior of IoT networks. We can delve into the performance of communication protocols and examine how various factors influence the system's overall behavior.

To aid us in this journey, there exists a diverse range of popular simulators designed explicitly for simulating IoT systems. Each simulator comes equipped with unique features and capabilities, offering us a wealth of opportunities to enhance our understanding of IoT technologies. Let us take a closer look at these simulators and see how they can empower us to create innovative and robust IoT solutions:

- **IFogSim2**: `IFogSim2` is an extended version of `IFogSim`, a popular simulator for fog computing research. IFogSim2 is designed to support large-scale and complex fog computing scenarios with a focus on multi-objective optimization. It allows researchers and developers to model and simulate fog computing architectures and applications. The simulator considers various factors such as network latency, node heterogeneity, application distribution, and service placement policies. IFogSim2 aims to provide insights into the performance, resource utilization, and energy efficiency of fog computing systems. It is written in Java and built on the `CloudSim` framework.

- **iFogSim**: `iFogSim` is the predecessor of IFogSim2, and it is widely used for modeling and simulating fog computing scenarios. It supports the evaluation of applications running on the cloud, fog, and IoT devices in a hierarchical architecture. iFogSim enables the study of resource management strategies, task scheduling algorithms, and data distribution mechanisms in fog computing environments. It is built on the `CloudSim` framework, allowing users to leverage its features and extend it for specific research needs.
- **COSSIM**: COSSIM (COntext-aware and Scalable SIMulator for smart city applications) is a simulator designed specifically for smart city applications. It focuses on modeling large-scale and complex smart city scenarios where multiple IoT devices interact with cloud and fog computing nodes. COSSIM supports the simulation of various smart city applications, such as traffic management, environmental monitoring, and healthcare. It provides researchers and city planners with insights into the performance and scalability of different smart city architectures and services.
- **ns-3**: `ns-3` is another popular discrete-event network simulator that supports the simulation of various communication networks, including IoT and fog computing. It offers a wide range of pre-built models and modules for simulating different network protocols and technologies. ns-3 is written in C++ and provides a high degree of flexibility and customization for researchers working on IoT and fog computing projects.
- **NetSim**: `NetSim` is a popular network simulator designed specifically for IoT and **wireless sensor network** (**WSN**) applications. It offers a comprehensive platform for modeling, simulating, and analyzing IoT systems, protocols, and applications. `NetSim` provides a wide range of features, including realistic channel modeling, support for various IoT communication protocols, energy modeling, and visualization tools. It enables researchers and developers to evaluate the performance, reliability, and scalability of IoT networks and applications.
- **MiXiM**: **Mixed Simulator** (**MiXiM**) is a simulation framework specifically designed for wireless and mobile networks, including IoT and WSNs. It is an extension of the OMNeT++ simulator and provides additional models and modules for simulating IoT and wireless communication protocols. MiXiM offers a rich set of features, including realistic radio and channel models, energy models, mobility models, and protocol implementations. It enables researchers to simulate and analyze the behavior and performance of IoT networks under different conditions and configurations.

Each simulator mentioned above has its strengths and focuses on different aspects of fog computing and IoT. You need to choose the most suitable simulator based on the specific requirements and the complexity of the scenarios you want to model and simulate.

Installation and Configuration of Edge Devices

We use Raspberry Pi to demonstrate Edge Computing and Analytics using Python. It is a popular choice for edge computing due to its small size, low power consumption, and affordable cost. Raspberry Pi can run various software applications and operating systems, including Linux and Windows, making it a versatile Edge Computing and Analytics platform.

Raspberry Pi has many use cases in edge computing, such as monitoring and controlling IoT devices, running data analysis and machine learning algorithms, and performing image and video processing. Raspberry Pi can also be used in edge analytics to pre-process data, reduce latency, and improve data security and privacy.

In the current chapter, *Model Deployment on Edge Devices*, we will focus on deploying the earlier-built models on Raspberry Pi. The same can be applied to other widely used edge devices such as BeagleBone Black, Intel NUC, and NVIDIA Jetson Nano. All these edge devices support Python and machine learning deployment.

Here are the steps to set up Raspberry Pi:

1. **Get the necessary hardware:** You will need a Raspberry Pi board, a power supply, a microSD card with Raspbian OS, and a case (optional but recommended).
2. **Install Raspbian:** Download the latest Raspbian image from the official Raspberry Pi website and flash it onto the microSD card using a tool like Etcher.
3. **Boot up the Pi:** Insert the microSD card, connect the power supply, and connect a monitor, keyboard, and mouse to the Pi.
4. **Configure the Pi:** Once Raspbian boots up, follow the setup wizard to configure the basic settings such as language, password, and Wi-Fi.
5. **Install necessary packages:** Use the terminal to install necessary packages for edge computing and analytics, such as Python, NumPy, Pandas, Scikit-learn, Requests, and FastAPI.

Let us now focus on how we can deploy the models we built on the edge devices in *Chapter 8, Monitoring and Predictive Maintenance*.

Note: We assume that you have a Python environment setup on Raspberry Pi. If not, do not worry. You can just use your usual Python environment to try out these examples, as they will not differ from the Edge devices environment. You can apply the same to any Edge devices if they support a Python environment. If the requirement is to use limited-capacity single-board microcontrollers, then we can use MicroPython. The topics on MicroPython are covered next chapter, Chapter 10 - Understanding Edge Computing with MicroPython.

Installation and Configuration of FastAPI

FastAPI is a modern, fast (high-performance) web framework for building APIs with Python 3.6+ based on standard Python-type hints. In this section, we will go through the installation and configuration process of FastAPI:

Installation of FASTAPI:

- First, open the terminal on your system.
- To install FastAPI, run the following command:
  ```
  pip install fastapi
  pip install "uvicorn[standard]"
  ```

Configuration process:

- First, import the FastAPI class from the fastapi module:
  ```
  from fastapi import FastAPI
  ```
- Next, create an instance of the FastAPI class:
  ```
  app = FastAPI()
  ```
- You can define the endpoints (also known as routes) of your application using the `@ app.route` decorator:
  ```
  @app.get("/")
  def read_root():
    return {"Hello": "World"}
  ```
- Once you have defined the endpoints, you can start the application by running the following command:
  ```
  @app.get("/items/{item_id}")
  def read_item(item_id: int, q: Union[str, None] = None):
    return {"item_id": item_id, "q": q}
  ```

After the successful execution of the above command, it starts the application on the local host at port 8000.

Now, you can test your FastAPI application by navigating to http://localhost:8000 in your web browser or using tools like Postman to test the API endpoints.

These are the basic steps to install and configure FastAPI. You can further customize your FastAPI application by using additional libraries and modules.

You can also try accessing **http://localhost:8000** in your web browser of, Raspberry Pi. Ensure you are in the same network and configured for the incoming requests.

Model Building and Reuse

When building machine learning models, the first step is to train a model using a dataset, which can be used to predict new data. Popular machine learning libraries in Python, such as sci-kit-learn, TensorFlow, and PyTorch, are commonly used.

Once a model is built and trained, it can be saved as a file in a format that can be used for making predictions, also known as model serialization or pickling. Multiple file formats are available for serialized models, including pickle, `joblib`, HDF5, and ONNX.

After serialization, the model can be downloaded and used to predict new data, known as model deployment. Typically, this involves setting up a service that can accept input data and return model predictions. Web frameworks such as Flask, Django, or FastAPI can be used to build such a service.

In addition to building and deploying machine learning models, pre-trained models can also be reused. This is particularly useful when the model is complex, large, or requires a large amount of training data, making it impractical or expensive to train from scratch. Pre-trained models can be found in various sources, such as open-source model repositories, cloud-based machine learning services, or proprietary software vendors. These models can be easily downloaded and used to predict new data.

In summary, building, downloading, and reusing machine learning models using Python involves data preparation, model training, serialization, deployment, and reuse, all depending on the specific use case and requirements.

Implementing Model Building and Reuse

Here is the Python program demonstrating how to download a machine learning model as a file locally for later reuse.

First, it imports the necessary libraries such as **`pandas`**, **`numpy`**, **`StandardScaler`**, **`RandomForestClassifier`**, pickle, and psycopg2 for connecting to the **`datalake`**. Then, it connects to the **`datalake`** and queries the curated zone for the wind turbine data table and creates a Panda DataFrame from the data.

Next, the program defines the threshold values for each parameter and creates a new column, **`'Above_Threshold'`**, in the training dataset based on the threshold values. It selects the columns to use for modeling and splits the data into training and testing sets. The data is then standardized using **`StandardScaler`**.

The program builds the machine learning model using **`RandomForestClassifier`** and fits the model to the training data. Finally, it saves the model as a pickle file with the name **`'alert_model.pkl'`** and the scaler and threshold values using the **`'pickle.dump()'`** function. The file is saved locally for later use.

To use this model for prediction on a new data row example, one could simply load the **`'alert_model.pkl'`** file using the **`'pickle.load()'`** function and pass the new data through the scaler and then use the loaded model's **`'predict()'`** function to get the prediction result for that single row:

```
import pandas as pd
import numpy as np
from sklearn.preprocessing import StandardScaler
```

```
from sklearn.ensemble import RandomForestClassifier
import pickle
import psycopg2
# Connect to datalake
conn = psycopg2.connect(
        host="localhost",
        database="IoTDataLake",
        user="postgres",
        password=""
    )
cur = conn.cursor()
# Query curated zone of the data lake for the wind turbine table and create a dataframe
cur.execute("SELECT * FROM curatedzone.c_external_wind_turbine_data")
wind_turbine_data = pd.DataFrame(cur.fetchall(), columns=['id', 'rtc', 'year', 'month', 'day', 'hour', 'minute',
 'temperature_100', 'temperature_120', 'temperature_80', 'wind_direction_100', 'wind_direction_120', 'wind_direction_80', 'wind_speed_100','wind_speed_120', 'wind_speed_80','pressure_200','pressure_100','pressure_0', 'power_output_80','power_output_100','power_output_120'])
# Define the threshold values for each parameter
thresholds = {'temperature_100': 25, 'pressure_100': 1100, 'wind_speed_100': 15, 'power_output_100': 2000}
# Create a new column 'Above_Threshold' in the training dataset based on the threshold values
wind_turbine_data['Above_Threshold'] = np.where((wind_turbine_data['temperature_100'] > thresholds['temperature_100']) |
                                                (wind_turbine_data['pressure_100'] > thresholds['pressure_100']) |
                                                (wind_turbine_data['wind_speed_100'] > thresholds['wind_speed_100']) |
                                                (wind_turbine_data['power_output_100'] > thresholds['power_output_100']),
                                                1, 0)
# Select the columns to use for modeling
features = ['temperature_100', 'pressure_100', 'wind_speed_100', 'pow-
```

```
    er_output_100']
# Split the data into training and testing sets
train_data = wind_turbine_data.sample(frac=0.8, random_state=42)
test_data = wind_turbine_data.drop(train_data.index)
# Standardize the data
scaler = StandardScaler()
scaler.fit(train_data[features])
train_data_scaled = scaler.transform(train_data[features])
test_data_scaled = scaler.transform(test_data[features])
# Build the model
model = RandomForestClassifier(n_estimators=100, random_state=42)
model.fit(train_data_scaled, train_data['Above_Threshold'])
# Save the model as a pickle file
with open('alert_model.pkl', 'wb') as f:
    pickle.dump((model, scaler, thresholds), f)
```

The below Python program demonstrates how to load a previously built machine learning model to perform predictions.

The first step is to load the saved model from the file **"alert_model.pkl"** using the **"pickle.load()"** method. The saved model is stored as a tuple containing the model, the scaler used for standardization, and the thresholds used for creating the **"Above_Threshold"** column during training.

The next step is to define a function called **"predict_threshold()"** that takes in a DataFrame and a list of column names. The input data is first standardized inside the function using the scaler object loaded earlier. Then, the **"predict()"** method is used to predict whether each row of the input data is above or below the threshold. If the prediction is higher than the threshold, the row is added to the alerts list with the message "**Above threshold**". Otherwise, the message is "**Below threshold**".

Lastly, the function is called with an example input data to obtain the alerts. The alerts are then printed out one by one using a for loop:

```
# Load the model from the file
with open('alert_model.pkl', 'rb') as f:
    model, scaler, thresholds = pickle.load(f)
# Define a function to predict alerts based on the input data
def predict_threshold(df, columns):
```

```
    # Standardize the input data
    input_data_scaled = scaler.transform(df[columns])
    # Make predictions using the model
    predictions = model.predict(input_data_scaled)
    # Check if each prediction is above or below threshold
    alerts = []
    for i in range(len(predictions)):
        if predictions[i] == 1:
            alerts.append(f"Row {i}: Above threshold")
        else:
            alerts.append(f"Row {i}: Below threshold")
    return alerts
# Example usage
input_data = pd.DataFrame({'temperature_100': [20],
                           'pressure_100': [1000],
                           'wind_speed_100': [10],
                           'power_output_100': [1500]})
alerts = predict_threshold(input_data, features)
for alert in alerts:
    print(alert)
```

Expose Models using FastAPI

FastAPI is a modern, fast, and web framework for building Python APIs. It offers many benefits for deploying machine learning models as APIs, including fast development, automatic documentation generation, and easy integration with other Python libraries.

To expose a machine learning model using FastAPI, you must first create a Python function that takes in some input data, performs some processing, and returns the prediction result. This function can be based on any machine learning library or algorithm of your choice.

Next, you can use FastAPI to create a web endpoint that will receive user input data and call your prediction function to generate predictions. FastAPI will automatically handle serialization and deserialization of data, input validation, and error handling.

Once your FastAPI endpoint is set up, you can deploy your machine learning model as a live API service that other developers or applications can access over the internet. FastAPI also provides an interactive documentation UI that allows users to explore and test your API easily.

Implementing Model Exposure using FastAPI

The following Python program explains how to invoke machine learning models via an API call. First, it loads a machine learning model, a scaler, and thresholds from a file. It then defines a function, **predict_threshold**, that takes in a panda **DataFrame** and a list of column names, standardizes the input data, makes predictions using the model, and checks whether each prediction is above or below a specified threshold.

The program uses the **FastAPI** framework to define a web API. It defines a request body schema, **InputData**, with four float fields representing temperature, pressure, wind speed, and power output. It also defines a response schema, **OutputData**, which contains a list of alerts.

The program defines a POST endpoint, **/predict**, that takes in an **InputData** object, converts it to a panda **DataFrame**, and makes predictions using the **predict_threshold** function. It then returns an **OutputData** object containing the list of alerts.

```
import pickle
from fastapi import FastAPI
from pydantic import BaseModel
import pandas as pd
from typing import List
# Load the model from the file
with open('alert_model.pkl', 'rb') as f:
    model, scaler, thresholds = pickle.load(f)
# Define a function to predict alerts based on the input data
def predict_threshold(df, columns):
    # Standardize the input data
    input_data_scaled = scaler.transform(df[columns])
    # Make predictions using the model
    predictions = model.predict(input_data_scaled)
    # Check if each prediction is above or below threshold
    alerts = []
    for i in range(len(predictions)):
        if predictions[i] == 1:
            alerts.append(f"Row {i}: Above threshold")
        else:
            alerts.append(f"Row {i}: Below threshold")
    return alerts
```

```python
# Define the FastAPI app
app = FastAPI()
# Define a request body schema
class InputData(BaseModel):
    temperature_100: float
    pressure_100: float
    wind_speed_100: float
    power_output_100: float
# Define a response schema
class OutputData(BaseModel):
    alerts: List[str]
# Define a POST endpoint for making predictions
@app.post("/predict", response_model=OutputData)
async def predict(input_data: InputData):
    # Convert input data to a pandas DataFrame
    input_df = pd.DataFrame(input_data.dict(), index=[0])
    # Define the list of feature column names
    features = ['temperature_100', 'pressure_100', 'wind_speed_100', 'power_output_100']
    # Make predictions using the machine learning model
    alerts = predict_threshold(input_df, features)
    # Create the response object
    output_data = OutputData(alerts=alerts)
    return output_data
```

Save the program to a file called **api.py** and run the API server with the command **uvicorn api1:app --reload --host <IP address> --port 8000** from the command line window. This command will keep the API running for responding to incoming requests. Make sure that you change the IP address to your computer's IP address on the above command line.

FastAPI Documents

When you run a FASTAPI application and navigate to the /docs endpoint (for example, **http://192.168.1.8:8000/docs**), you will be presented with an interactive web interface that allows you to explore the API and test its endpoints.

This web interface is generated automatically based on the metadata defined in your application's code, such as function signatures, parameter types, and response models. The documentation includes information about API use, such as the available endpoints, required parameters, expected responses, and response codes.

Using the **http://192.168.1.8:8000/docs** endpoint can be very helpful for developers who want to understand how to interact with an API or for testing and debugging purposes. It can also help ensure that your API is well-documented and easy to use for other developers who may want to integrate with it in the future. The following is the sample screen showing machine learning API (see *Figure 9.1*):

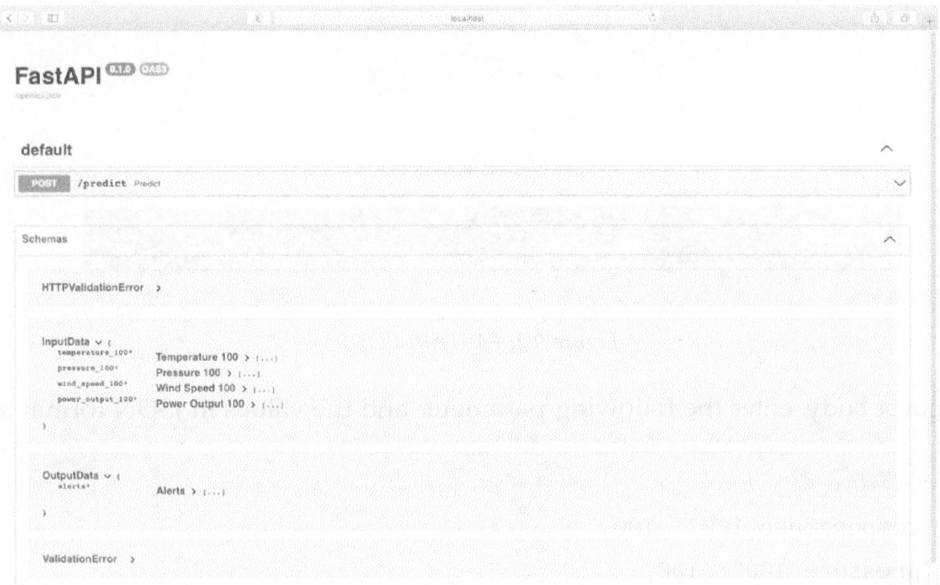

***Figure 9.1:** FASTAPI documents*

We can perform testing our API using the above-shown web interface. To access the Try it Out, please follow the instructions in the following figure. The red lines indicate the steps you need to take.

First, click on the **Post** button, and then you will see the **Try it Out** button. Click on the **Try it Out** button to execute the API from the Swagger web interface (see *Figure 9.2*):

Figure 9.2: FASTAPI POST

On the request body, enter the following parameter and the values in JSON format as shown below:

```
{
   "temperature_100": 100,
   "pressure_100": 100,
   "wind_speed_100": 1000,
   "power_output_100": 1000
}
```

After entering the parameters, click on the **Execute** button. This will invoke the API from the swagger user interface and show the output on the same screen as shown below (see *Figure 9.3*):

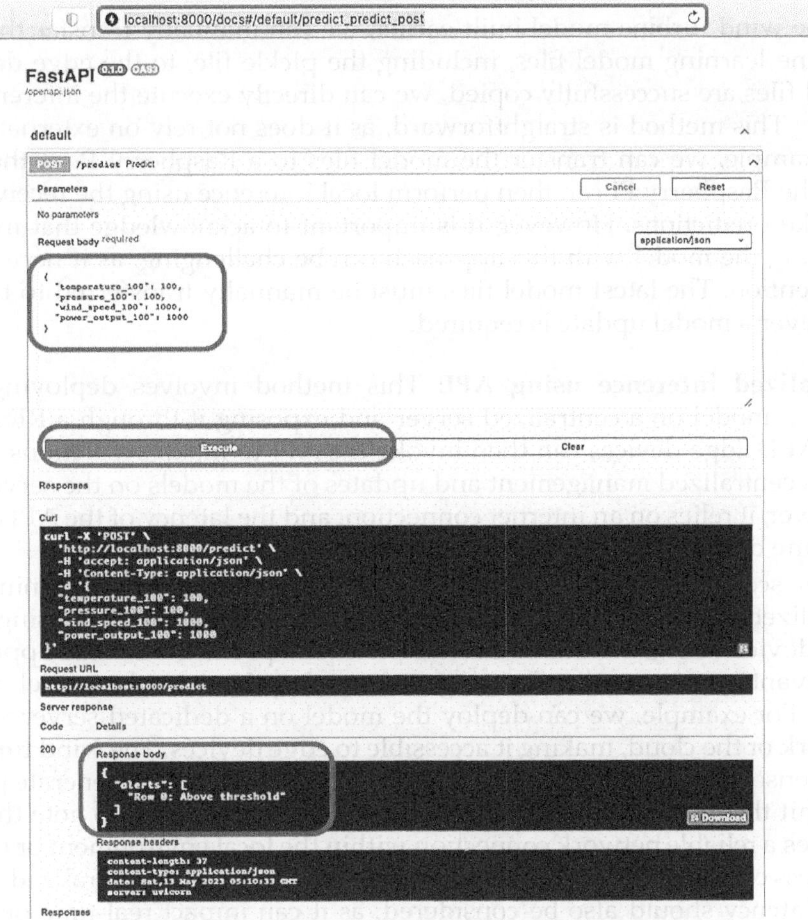

Figure 9.3: FASTAPI request, Execute, and output

The Swagger UI is the best user interface to test and validate APIs built using FASTAPI. The upcoming section, *Implementing Centralized Inference using API,* will show you how to invoke the FAST API from Python code.

Deploying Machine Learning Model

Deploying machine learning models is a critical step in the machine learning workflow, and there are various industry-standard methods for deploying pre-built models. These methods offer different approaches to deploying and managing models in diverse environments effectively. Let us explore these methods and their advantages:

- **Manual copying of model files:** This method manually copies machine learning model files, such as the pickle file, onto the edge device. Once the model files are copied, the inference code can be executed locally on the device. This method is straightforward and does not require external dependencies. However, maintaining and updating the models can be challenging since manual intervention is required.

For the wind turbine model built earlier, we can manually transfer the wind turbine machine learning model files, including the pickle file, to the edge device. Once the model files are successfully copied, we can directly execute the inference code on the device. This method is straightforward, as it does not rely on external dependencies. For example, we can transfer the model files to a Raspberry Pi at the wind turbine site. The Raspberry Pi can then perform local inference using the received sensor data to make predictions. However, it is important to acknowledge that maintaining and updating the model with this approach can be challenging, as it necessitates manual intervention. The latest model files must be manually transferred to the edge device whenever a model update is required.

- **Centralized inference using API:** This method involves deploying the machine learning model on a centralized server and exposing it through a REST API, such as FASTAPI. Edge devices can then invoke the API to make predictions. This approach allows centralized management and updates of the models on the server or the cloud. However, it relies on an internet connection, and the latency of the API calls may affect real-time decision-making on edge devices.

  In this scenario, we can deploy the wind turbine machine learning model on a centralized server or the cloud and expose it through a REST API using FASTAPI. The edge devices can then utilize this API to make predictions. This approach provides the advantage of centralized management and updates for the model on the server or cloud. For example, we can deploy the model on a dedicated server within the local network or the cloud, making it accessible to edge devices. The wind turbines can send their sensor data to this server, which will utilize the model to generate predictions and transmit the results to the turbines for action. It is important to note that this method requires a reliable network connection within the local environment or on the cloud for seamless communication between the edge devices and the centralized server. The API calls' latency should also be considered, as it can impact real-time decision-making, particularly in time-sensitive scenarios.

- **Machine Learning Operations (MLOps):** MLOps is an implementation practice integrating machine learning into software development and operations processes. The objective of MLOPs is to automate the end-to-end process of building, testing, and deploying machine learning models. It is a scalable and automated model deployment and management framework, ensuring consistency and reproducibility. The key advantage of MLOps is streamlining the deployment process, making it faster and more efficient. It also facilitates model monitoring and management. However, implementing MLOps requires significant time, resources, and expertise as it effectively manages complex tools and technologies.

  In MLOps, we can leverage robust tools like Apache Airflow or Kubeflow to construct a streamlined pipeline that automates the entire model development, testing, and deployment process. We can trigger this pipeline by harnessing real-time data from edge devices, ensuring prompt updates and the model stays current.

- **Containerization and orchestration:** Containerization involves packaging models and their dependencies into containers, ensuring consistent execution across different computing environments. Orchestration platforms like Docker and Kubernetes help manage and scale these containers. The main advantage of containerization is providing a portable and isolated environment for running machine learning models. It simplifies deployment and management, allowing models to be deployed across various environments. However, containerization and orchestration can be complex and require expertise to set up and manage effectively. Additionally, they may require substantial storage and processing resources.

We can encapsulate the wind turbine model and its requisite dependencies within a container through containerization. Subsequently, this container can be effortlessly deployed onto the edge devices, guaranteeing consistent and efficient execution. We can employ orchestration platforms like Kubernetes to handle and scale these containers effectively, seamlessly managing the model across various edge environments.

- **Cloud-based deployment:** Cloud-based deployment involves hosting machine learning models on cloud platforms like AWS, Azure, or Google Cloud. Cloud platforms provide scalable infrastructure and a wide range of services to deploy and manage models effectively. The benefits of cloud-based deployment include scalability, cost-effectiveness, and access to advanced tools and services for automation and orchestration. However, cloud-based deployment may require infrastructure and expertise investment, and security considerations and compliance should be addressed.

  For example, we can deploy the wind turbine model on renowned cloud platforms such as AWS or Azure. We can create tailor-made serverless endpoints that specifically cater to the model's needs by harnessing the power of services like AWS Lambda or Azure Functions. This simplifies the process of invoking the model from the edge devices.

  Considering the distinctive advantages and considerations associated with each deployment method is imperative. The ultimate choice hinges upon factors like the specific use case, available resources, technical expertise, scalability requirements, and the desired level of automation. A meticulous evaluation of these factors is essential to determine the most appropriate deployment strategy.

  Let us go through the implementation of a couple of methods mentioned above. Since the book is about IoT Data Analytics using Python, covering containerization and orchestration, MLOps, and Cloud-based deployment are outside this chapter's scope. Fundamentally, the concepts of model deployment remain the same; learning the methods mentioned above and the subsequent implementation instructions will give you the confidence to adopt any other methods quickly.

Manual Deployment of ML Models

The first step for the manual deployment procedure is to develop a model and download the model artifacts as deployable and callable files and objects. Here is the Python code for implementing the first step:

```
import pandas as pd
import numpy as np
```

```
from sklearn.preprocessing import StandardScaler
from sklearn.ensemble import RandomForestClassifier
import pickle
import psycopg2
# Connect to datalake
conn = psycopg2.connect(
        host="localhost",
        database="IoTDataLake",
        user="postgres",
        password=""
    )
cur = conn.cursor()
# Query curated zone of the data lake for the wind turbine table and create a dataframe
cur.execute("SELECT * FROM curatedzone.c_external_wind_turbine_data")
wind_turbine_data = pd.DataFrame(cur.fetchall(), columns=['id', 'rtc', 'year', 'month', 'day', 'hour', 'minute',
 'temperature_100', 'temperature_120', 'temperature_80', 'wind_direction_100', 'wind_direction_120', 'wind_direction_80', 'wind_speed_100','wind_speed_120', 'wind_speed_80','pressure_200','pressure_100','pressure_0', 'power_output_80','power_output_100','power_output_120'])
# Define the threshold values for each parameter
thresholds = {'temperature_100': 25, 'pressure_100': 1100, 'wind_speed_100': 15, 'power_output_100': 2000}
# Create a new column 'Above_Threshold' in the training dataset based on the threshold values
wind_turbine_data['Above_Threshold'] = np.where((wind_turbine_data['temperature_100'] > thresholds['temperature_100']) |
                                                (wind_turbine_data['pressure_100'] > thresholds['pressure_100']) |
                                                (wind_turbine_data['wind_speed_100'] > thresholds['wind_speed_100']) |
                                                (wind_turbine_data['power_output_100'] > thresholds['power_output_100']),
                                                1, 0)
```

```
# Select the columns to use for modeling
features = ['temperature_100', 'pressure_100', 'wind_speed_100', 'power_output_100']
# Split the data into training and testing sets
train_data = wind_turbine_data.sample(frac=0.8, random_state=42)
test_data = wind_turbine_data.drop(train_data.index)
# Standardize the data
scaler = StandardScaler()
scaler.fit(train_data[features])
train_data_scaled = scaler.transform(train_data[features])
test_data_scaled = scaler.transform(test_data[features])
# Build the model
model = RandomForestClassifier(n_estimators=100, random_state=42)
model.fit(train_data_scaled, train_data['Above_Threshold'])
# Save the model as a pickle file
with open('alert_model.pkl', 'wb') as f:
    pickle.dump((model, scaler, thresholds), f)
```

This Python code implements the steps for saving a machine learning model file for edge deployment manually for edge analytics and prediction purposes. In the first few lines of the code, the necessary libraries are imported, including **Pandas**, **NumPy**, **scikit-learn 's StandardScaler**, and the **RandomForestClassifier** model. The Pickle library is also imported for saving the trained model. Then, a connection is established to a data lake stored in a PostgreSQL database.

The wind turbine data is queried from the data lake, and a Pandas DataFrame is created. The code then defines threshold values for four parameters, **temperature**, **pressure**, **wind speed**, and **power output**. Using these thresholds, a new column in the training data indicates whether each observation is above or below the threshold.

Next, the code selects the features to use for modeling and splits the data into training and testing sets. The training data is standardized using scikit-learn's **StandardScaler**.

Then, a Random Forest Classifier model is built using scikit-learn's **RandomForestClassifier**. The model is trained on the standardized training data and the earlier binary column.

Finally, the trained model, **StandardScaler**, and threshold values are saved as a pickle file named **'alert_model.pkl'** using the Pickle library's **dump()** method. This file can then be used for edge deployment on devices with limited computational resources, where the trained model can be used to classify new data and raise alerts if necessary.

The second step is to create a Python code to be deployed on the Edge device. The purpose of this Python code is to load the deployed model objects file in the pickle format and perform prediction for a given record. Save the following code as **call_function.py to transfer the file along with the model objects file (pickle file)**:

```
import pandas as pd
import pickle
# Load the model from the file
with open('alert_model.pkl', 'rb') as f:
    model, scaler, thresholds = pickle.load(f)
# Define a function to predict alerts based on the input data
def predict_threshold(df, columns):
    # Standardize the input data
    input_data_scaled = scaler.transform(df[columns])
    # Make predictions using the model
    predictions = model.predict(input_data_scaled)
    # Check if each prediction is above or below threshold
    alerts = []
    for i in range(len(predictions)):
        if predictions[i] == 1:
            alerts.append(f"Row {i}: Above threshold")
        else:
            alerts.append(f"Row {i}: Below threshold")
    return alerts
# Example usage
input_data = pd.DataFrame({'temperature_100': [20],
                           'pressure_100': [1000],
                           'wind_speed_100': [10],
                           'power_output_100': [1500]})
# Select the columns to use for modeling
features = ['temperature_100', 'pressure_100', 'wind_speed_100', 'pow-
er_output_100']
alerts = predict_threshold(input_data, features)
for alert in alerts:
    print(alert)
```

The third step is to create a folder called **models** on the edge device, as shown in *Figure 9.4*:

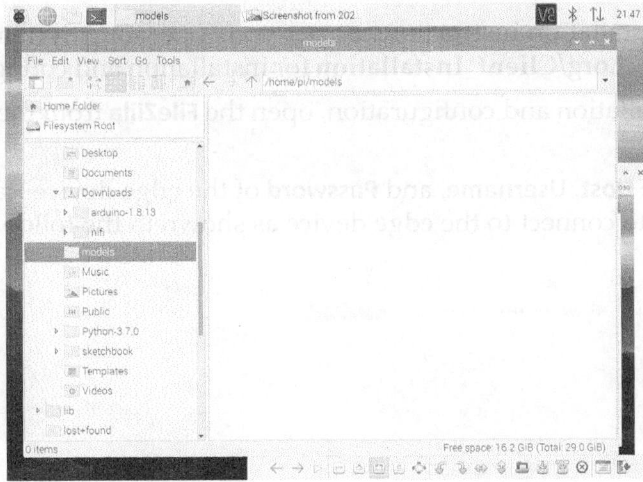

Figure 9.4: Create a folder on the edge device

The third step is configuring the necessary SFTP tool for transferring the model objects in the pickle file created above. Here are the steps for installing and performing manual transfer of the model file to the edge device:

1. Go to **https://filezilla-project.org/download.php?show_all=1**
2. .Below *Figure 9.5* shows the list of operating systems and the download links. Download the file as per your operating system

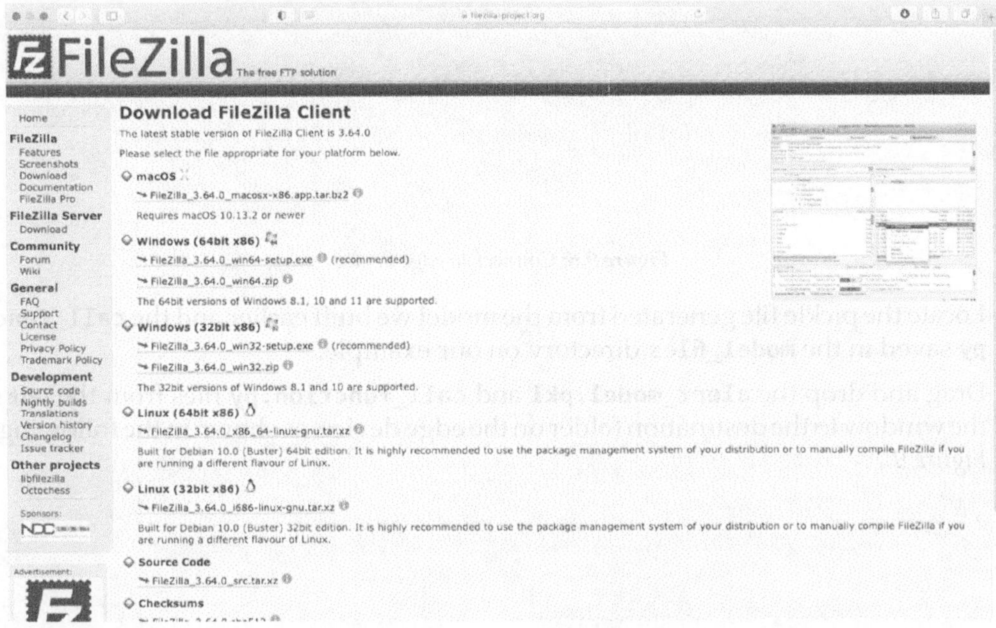

Figure 9.5: FileZilla download options

3. Follow the installation instructions as per your operating system. Refer **https://wiki.filezilla-project.org/Client_Installation** for installation and configuration instructions.
4. After the installation and configuration, open the **FileZiila** from the installed location on your computer.
5. Configure the **Host, Username**, and **Password** of the edge device Raspberry Pi, and click **Quickconnect** to connect to the edge device as shown in the following *Figure 9.6:*

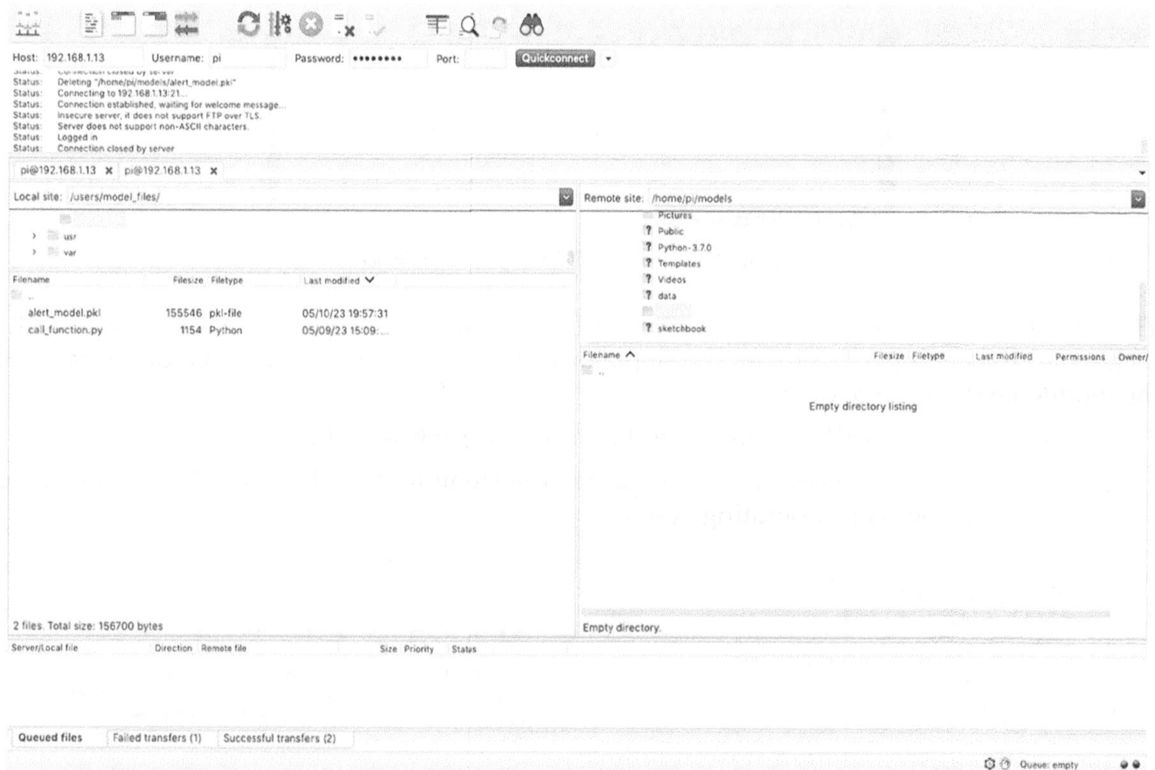

Figure 9.6: Connect to edge device

6. Locate the pickle file generated from the model we built earlier and the **`call_function.py`** saved in the **`model_files`** directory on our example.
7. Drag and drop the **`alert_model.pkl`** and **`call_function.py`** files from the left side of the window to the destination folder on the edge device, as shown in the following figure *Figure 9.7*:

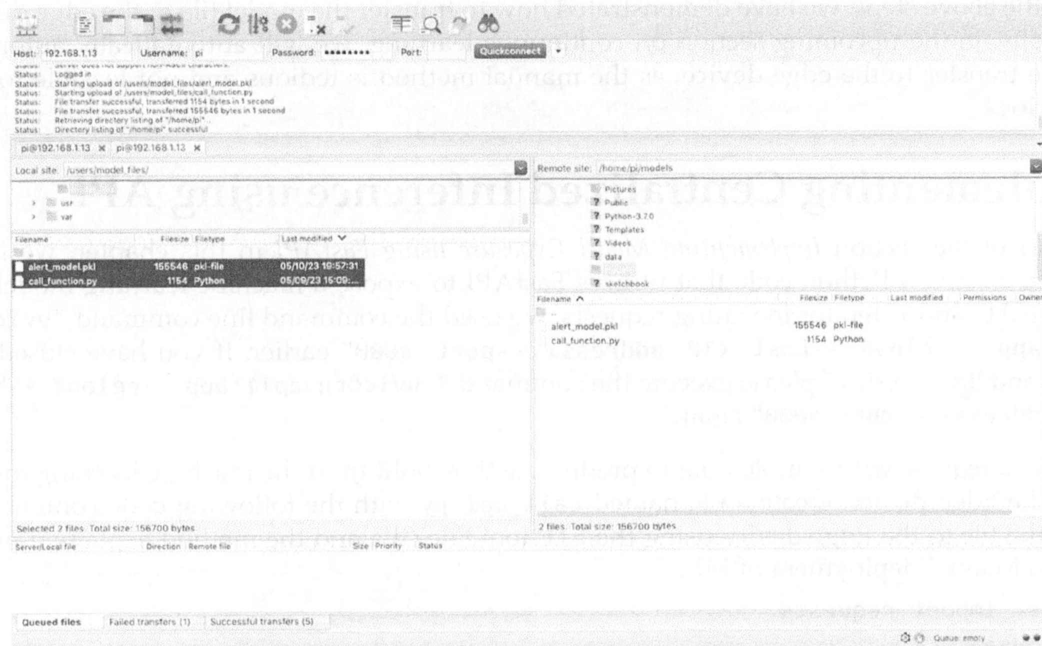

Figure 9.7: Transfer model and call_function files to edge

We have demonstrated how to manually transfer model files to the Edge device from the above steps.

8. After transferring the files to the edge device, we can invoke the model using **`call_function`**, as shown in *Figure 9.8*. Make sure that you have installed on Python libraries and the dependencies before executing the following command (see *Figure 9.8*):

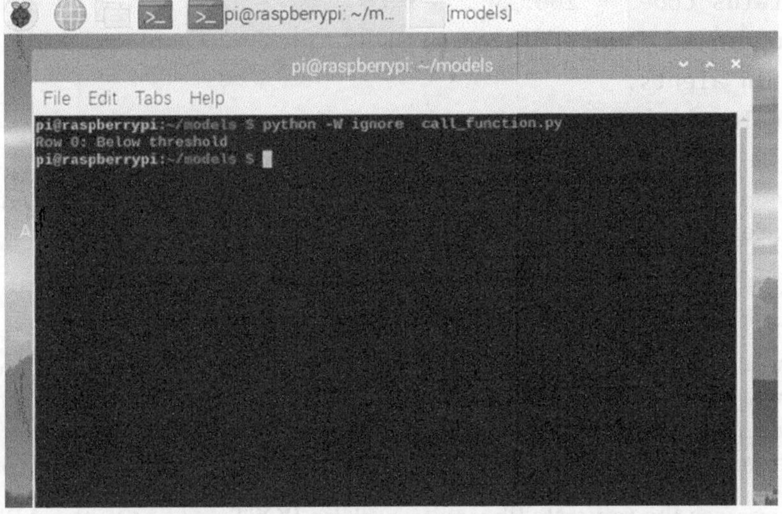

Figure 9.8: Executing the call_function from Edge Device

From the above steps, we have demonstrated how to transfer the model file to the edge device manually. In the upcoming section on continuous learning, we will automatically automate the file transfer to the edge device, as the manual method is tedious and not feasible for all scenarios.

Implementing Centralized Inference using API

As part of the section *Implementing Model Exposure using FastAPI* in this chapter, we have already created a Python code that utilizes FastAPI to expose a machine learning model. To run the API and listen for incoming requests, we used the command line command **"uvicorn api1:app --reload --host <IP address> --port 8000"** earlier. If you have closed the command line window, please execute the command **" uvicorn api1:app --reload --host <IP address> --port 8000"** again.

To send a request with sample data to predict the threshold from the machine learning model from the Edge device, create a file named **call_api.py** with the following code content and push the file to the Edge device using the FTP tool FileZilla and the method explained in the section Manual deployment of ML:

```
models."import requests
input_data = {
     'temperature_100 ': 20,
     'pressure_100 ': 1000,
     'wind_speed_100 ': 10,
     'power_output_100 ': 1500
}
response = requests.post( 'http://<IP address>:8000/predict ', json=input_data)
if response.status_code == 200:
    alerts = response.json()[ 'alerts ']
    for alert in alerts:
        print(alert)
else:
    print(f"Prediction failed with status code {response.status_code}:
    {response.text}")
```

Make sure that line#8 **response = requests.post('http://<IP address>:8000/predict ', json=input_data)** should be modified to your computer's IP address

The above Python program demonstrates how to use an API from an Edge device to make predictions using a machine learning model. First, the program defines a dictionary containing input data to be sent to the API listening on a centralized server or the cloud. This input data includes four parameters: temperature, pressure, wind speed, and power output.

The program then uses the requests library to make a POST request to the API URL. The json parameter is set to the input data dictionary and passed as the request payload.

If the API successfully returns a status code of 200, the program retrieves the alerts generated by the model and prints them to the console. If the API returns any other status code, the program prints an error message indicating the reason for the failure.

You can now execute the Python code from the Raspberry Pi, as shown in *Figure 9.9*:

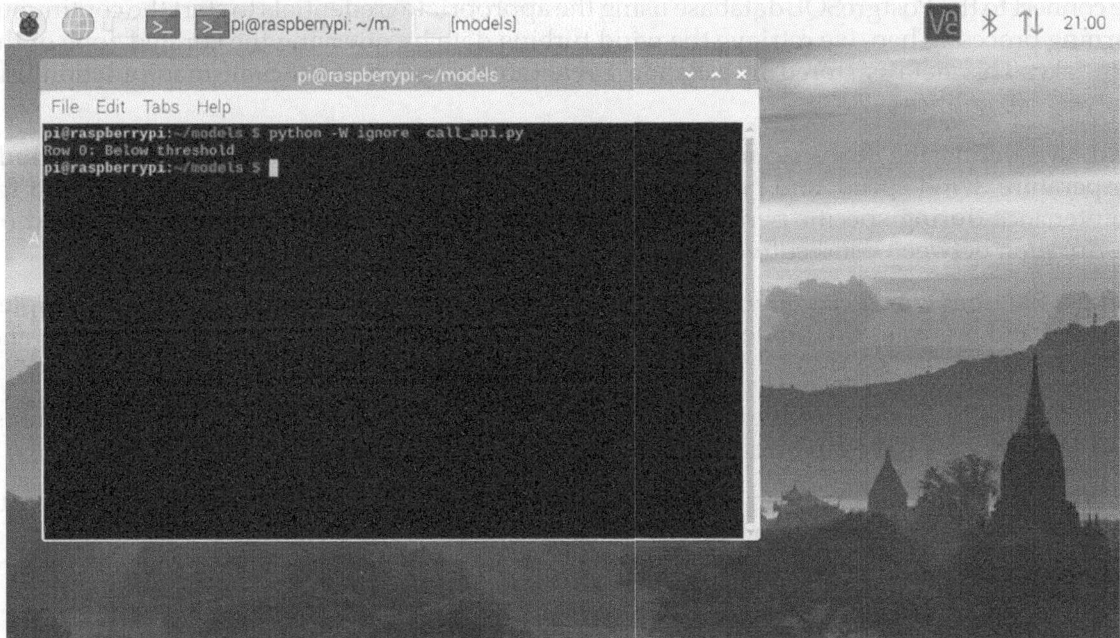

Figure 9.9: Executing the call_api from Edge Device

Concept of Continuous Learning

Continuous learning is a key concept in machine learning that allows models or systems to continually improve their performance by learning from new data or knowledge as it becomes available. It involves updating and refining the existing model, allowing it to improve its performance and make more accurate predictions or decisions. Continuous learning is crucial in dynamic environments where the underlying patterns in the data may change. The model can adapt to these changes by continuously learning, maintaining effectiveness, and providing better results.

There are several reasons why continuous learning is important. Firstly, it allows the model to be adaptable to evolving data. In situations where the data is constantly changing or arriving in real-time, continuous learning ensures that the model remains up-to-date and responsive to the latest information. Secondly, continuous learning improves the overall performance of the model. The model can refine its predictions or decisions by incorporating new data and feedback, increasing accuracy and effectiveness. Additionally, continuous learning enhances the scalability of the model. It can handle large and streaming datasets without requiring complete retraining, making it more efficient and practical.

Let us take an example of a wind turbine model to illustrate the concept of continuous learning. In this case, historical data from wind turbines, including sensor measurements like temperature, wind speed, and power output, is stored in a PostgreSQL database within an IoT Data Lake.

We connect to the PostgreSQL database using the appropriate credentials to start the continuous learning process. Then, we retrieve the wind turbine data by querying the curated zone of the data lake. This data is stored in a Panda DataFrame, providing efficient manipulation and analysis capabilities.

Next, we define the features and target variables for our model. These features include temperature, wind speed, and power output, while the target variable indicates the need for maintenance during specific periods. We determine the maintenance requirements based on the duration between consecutive data points.

Using a Random Forest classifier, a robust machine learning algorithm is suitable for complex datasets, and we train the model using the wind turbine data and the defined features and target variables.

After training the model, we save its state, which includes the learned patterns and relationships, to a file using the pickle module. This allows us to store the model for future use.

With the model saved, we can implement the continuous learning process. As new data becomes available from the wind turbines, we periodically update the model by retraining it with the newly acquired data. This ensures the model remains current and captures changes or patterns in the turbine's behavior.

By embracing continuous learning, the wind turbine model can adapt to evolving conditions, enhance its predictive accuracy, and optimize maintenance strategies. This approach enables the model to remain effective and relevant in dynamic environments where data and operating conditions may change over time.

Concept of Adaptive Learning

Adaptive learning is an advanced concept in machine learning that builds upon the foundation of continuous learning. While continuous learning focuses on updating and refining the existing model over time, adaptive learning takes the process further by actively adjusting the model's structure or parameters based on the changing data or knowledge.

In adaptive learning, the model learns from new data and adapts its internal representation or architecture better to accommodate the evolving patterns and dynamics in the data. This dynamic adjustment allows the model to capture and respond to changes in the underlying relationships between the input features and the target variable.

The importance of adaptive learning lies in its ability to improve the model's performance and predictive capabilities in complex and dynamic scenarios. By continuously adapting, the model can effectively handle non-stationary data, where the statistical properties of the data change over time. This is particularly relevant in real-time or streaming data applications, where the model needs to adapt to new information and make accurate predictions quickly.

Adaptive learning offers several advantages over static or fixed models. Firstly, it enables the model to maintain accuracy and relevance as the underlying data distribution evolves. This is crucial in domains where the relationships between variables are subject to frequent changes, such as financial markets, social media trends, or environmental conditions.

Adaptive learning enhances the model's adaptability to varying data conditions and distributions. It allows the model to automatically adjust its complexity or structure to handle different patterns or regimes in the data. This adaptability improves the model's robustness and generalization capabilities, making it more reliable in diverse environments.

In the context of the wind turbine model, adaptive learning can be applied to continuously update and refine the model's architecture or parameters as new data from the turbines become available. By monitoring the changing sensor measurements and power output, the model can dynamically adjust its internal representation to capture variations in the turbine's behavior over time.

For example, suppose the turbines' wind patterns or operating conditions change seasonally. In that case, the adaptive learning model can identify and adapt to these patterns, ensuring accurate power output and maintenance requirements predictions. The model can optimize maintenance strategies, improve energy efficiency, and minimize downtime by continuously adapting to evolving conditions.

Adaptive learning empowers machine learning models to continually adapt and learn from new data, enabling them to remain effective and relevant in dynamic and evolving environments. It is a powerful technique that enhances the model's performance, robustness, and adaptability, making it an essential approach for addressing complex real-world challenges.

Conclusion

This chapter explored using Python and FastAPI for Edge Analytics and Model Deployment. Edge Computing minimizes latency while improving response time. FastAPI helps overcome the challenges of deploying machine learning models on edge devices, such as limited resources.

The chapter provided a guide to installing and configuring FastAPI. It covered concepts like requests, responses, and endpoints, and readers learned how to make real-time predictions on data sourced from edge devices.

The chapter also introduced continuous and adaptive learning. Readers learned to incorporate new data and adapt models to changes in their environment or data distribution.

By the end of the chapter, readers had a deep understanding of edge analytics, IoT system simulators, model deployment using Python and FastAPI. They were equipped with the knowledge and tools to build and deploy machine learning models on edge devices, enabling real-time insights to optimize maintenance schedules, enhance machine performance, and reduce costs.

The next chapter covers various topics related to Edge Computing and Analytics, including the concepts of Edge Computing and Analytics, the data flow between edge devices and the cloud, and industry use cases for Edge Analytics. The chapter also introduced the basics of MicroPython, a popular programming language for microcontrollers, and explained how to build machine learning models for MicroPython. The chapter provided readers with a comprehensive understanding of Edge Computing with MicroPython and how it can be used to build powerful IoT applications with machine learning capabilities.

Points to Remember

Following are the key takeaways from this chapter:

- **Edge computing**: Process data closer to its source on edge devices to reduce latency and improve response times.
- Various IoT system simulators like `iFogSim`, COSSIM, `ns-3`, `NetSim`, `MiXiM` are available to simulate IoT scenarios.
- **Deploying ML models on edge devices**: Challenging due to limited resources like memory and processing power.
- **FastAPI**: Python library for creating web APIs for ML models, suitable for edge deployment.
- **Essential steps**: Install and configure FastAPI to build and deploy ML models on edge devices.
- **Edge device capabilities**: Raspberry Pi, BeagleBone Black, Intel NUC, and NVIDIA Jetson Nano provide computing power and flexibility for Edge Analytics.
- **FastAPI and ML deployment**: Use FastAPI to host and expose ML models on edge devices for real-time predictions.
- **Benefits of edge computing**: Reduced latency, improved data security, and privacy by performing analytics closer to the data source.
- Raspberry Pi and other edge devices support Python and ML deployment, making them compatible with hosting models.
- **Model deployment process**: Data preparation, training, serialization, deployment, and reuse tailored to specific use cases.
- **Deployment methods**: Manual copying of model files and centralized inference using API for local execution or server-based predictions.
- **Additional considerations**: MLOps, containerization, orchestration, and cloud-based deployment for automation, scalability, and advanced tools.
- **FastAPI advantages**: Fast development, automatic documentation generation, easy integration with Python libraries, and interactive documentation UI.
- **Continuous learning**: Update models with new data to adapt and maintain effectiveness in dynamic environments.
- **Adaptive learning**: Adjust model structure or parameters based on changing data or knowledge for improved performance in complex scenarios.
- **Enhancing model adaptability**: Adaptive learning improves robustness and generalization capabilities for varying data conditions.

Chapter 10

Understanding Edge Computing with MicroPython

Introduction

This chapter focuses on understanding Edge Computing and Analytics, exploring their advantages and role in real-time data processing, latency reduction, and reliability improvement. Additionally, we will discuss industry use cases that showcase the transformative power of Edge Analytics in various sectors, including healthcare, manufacturing, and transportation.

This chapter will also introduce MicroPython, a lightweight and efficient programming language for resource constrained IoT devices. We will cover its syntax, features, and capabilities and explore how it can be leveraged to build machine-learning models optimized for edge devices.

We will start by discussing the data flow from edge to cloud, including obtaining data from IoT sensors and sending the processed data to the cloud for further analytics.

In the final section of this chapter, we will guide you through building machine-learning models optimized for MicroPython. From development to deployment, we provide step-by-step instructions, enabling you to invoke machine learning models from the remote server on edge microcontroller devices without compromising accuracy or performance.

By the end of this chapter, you will have a comprehensive understanding of integrating MicroPython with edge computing and analytics. This knowledge will enable you to leverage the power of MicroPython to build efficient machine-learning models for resource-constrained IoT devices, driving innovation and unlocking the potential of connected devices.

Structure

In this chapter, we will cover the following topics:

- The Concepts of Edge Computing
- The Concepts of Edge Analytics
- Introduction to Edge Platform
- Data Flow from Edge to Cloud
- Use Cases for Edge Analytics
- MicroPython for Edge Computing
- Invoking ML Models using MicroPython

Objectives

Edge computing and Edge Analytics are two important concepts of **Internet of Things (IoT)**. Edge Computing refers to the processing of data closer to the source, while Edge Analytics refers to the analysis of data at the edge. This chapter provides a comprehensive overview of Edge Computing and Edge Analytics. It discusses the different edge platform ecosystems, such as EdgeX, KubeEdge, and OpenWhisk. It also covers the data flow from edge to cloud, and how to consume and store data on edge with PostgresSQL database on the Edge. The chapter also presents use cases for Edge Analytics in manufacturing, energy, healthcare, transportation, agriculture, retail, and smart cities. It introduces MicroPython for Edge Computing and covers its installation on NODEMCU ESP8266 and programming with Thonny IDE. Finally, it showcases invoking machine learning models on NODEMCU ESP8266 using MicroPython. By the end of the chapter, readers will have a solid understanding of Edge Computing, Edge Analytics, and MicroPython. They will be equipped to explore and implement Edge Analytics solutions for various industries.

Concepts of Edge Computing

We reviewed the basic concepts of Edge Computing in *Chapter 9, Model Deployment on Edge Devices*. This chapter will delve into advanced edge computing concepts, specifically focusing on data streaming from IoT devices to edge devices. We will explore how edge computing enables real-time data processing, data cleaning, transformation, analysis, and visualization, using practical examples from the wind turbine industry.

Imagine a scenario where multiple wind turbines are equipped with sensors that collect various data points such as wind speed, temperature, and power output. These sensors continuously generate data streams, which need to be processed and analyzed in real-time to ensure optimal performance and maintenance of the wind turbines.

To achieve this, we will leverage the power of edge computing. The sensors on the wind turbines will send the data streams to an edge device, which acts as a gateway for data processing and analysis. The edge device can be a powerful embedded system or a microcontroller capable of running edge computing tasks.

Once the data streams reach the edge device, it performs data cleaning and transformation operations to ensure data quality and consistency. This involves removing outliers, handling missing values, and performing necessary data preprocessing steps. By conducting these tasks at the edge, we reduce the reliance on cloud infrastructure and minimize latency, enabling real-time decision-making.

After the data cleaning and transformation processes, the edge device can perform advanced analytics on the data streams. For example, it can apply machine learning algorithms to detect anomalies in wind turbine performance or predict potential failures based on historical data. These analytics enable proactive maintenance, reducing downtime and optimizing energy production.

Furthermore, the edge device can generate meaningful dashboards and visualizations based on the analyzed data. These visualizations provide real-time insights into the performance of the wind turbines, allowing operators to monitor key metrics and make informed decisions regarding maintenance, operational adjustments, or power generation optimizations.

The edge device can also transmit the processed and analyzed data streams to the cloud to facilitate seamless integration with cloud services. This enables long-term storage, further analysis, and integration with enterprise systems or third-party applications.

Using the wind turbine sensors and data as an example, we will demonstrate how edge computing can enable data streaming, data cleaning, transformation, advanced analytics, and real-time visualization at the edge in the later part of this chapter.

Concepts of Edge Analytics

In this section, we will build on the foundation of Edge Computing and machine learning model deployment that we explored in *Chapter 9, Model Deployment on Edge Devices*. We will then explore edge analytics, which is a powerful tool that can be used to process data and derive insights at the edge, where the data is generated. This can lead to faster decision-making and improved performance.

Building upon our previous example of wind turbine data and the deployment of machine learning models on the Edge, we now delve into real-time analytics. By performing data processing and analysis directly on the edge device, we unlock the potential for immediate insights and faster decision-making.

One of the key advantages of real-time analytics at the edge is the ability to extract valuable insights without relying heavily on cloud infrastructure or continuous network connectivity. The machine learning models deployed on the edge device can process the incoming data streams from the wind turbine sensors in real time, allowing for immediate detection of anomalies, prediction of failures, and proactive maintenance actions.

With real-time analytics, operators can monitor the wind turbines' health and performance continuously. Any deviations from expected behavior, such as drops in power output, unusual temperature fluctuations, or irregular wind speed patterns, can be quickly detected and addressed. This proactive approach to maintenance minimizes downtime, optimizes energy production, and ultimately enhances the system's overall efficiency.

In addition, the edge device can generate real-time visualizations and dashboards, providing operators with a comprehensive view of wind turbine operations. These visualizations enable operators to monitor key performance metrics, track trends, and receive immediate alerts or alarms when critical events occur. With this real-time situational awareness, operators can make timely decisions and take appropriate actions to ensure optimal performance.

Moreover, real-time analytics at the edge enables faster response times to critical events. Instead of waiting for data to be transmitted to the cloud for processing and analysis, the edge device can immediately trigger predefined actions based on predefined thresholds or rules. This rapid response capability is crucial in scenarios where immediate actions can prevent equipment failures, mitigate risks, or optimize energy usage.

By leveraging the power of real-time analytics at the edge, operators can extract insights and make data-driven decisions with minimal latency. This approach reduces dependence on cloud infrastructure, enhances system resilience, and maximizes the efficiency of IoT applications in industries such as energy, manufacturing, and transportation.

As we continue this chapter, we will delve deeper into the techniques and methodologies for implementing real-time analytics using the wind turbine dataset. We will explore Python libraries and tools that enable edge devices to perform advanced analytics, visualize data in real time, and enable immediate decision-making.

Introduction to Edge Platform

In the realm of Edge Computing and Edge Analytics, the need for robust and scalable Edge platforms becomes paramount. These platforms provide a foundation for managing and orchestrating the complex tasks of processing, analyzing, and visualizing data at the edge. They offer a range of functionalities that enable seamless integration, efficient data processing, and effective management of Edge devices.

Let us go through a few of the widely used open-source Edge platforms here. These are only examples of the Edge platform available on the market. There are wide varieties of both open-source and commercial platforms available. The choice of the platform depends on the industry use case, complexity, and processing requirements:

- **EdgeX Foundry** is one of the popular Edge platform. It is an open-source framework designed specifically for Edge computing applications. EdgeX Foundry offers a comprehensive set of tools and services that simplify the development and deployment of Edge solutions. It provides a flexible architecture for easy integration with different Edge devices, protocols, and data sources. With EdgeX Foundry, developers can leverage pre-built components and microservices to streamline data ingestion, processing, and analytics workflows.

- **KubeEdge** is another notable Edge platform which leverages the power of Kubernetes to enable Edge computing capabilities. KubeEdge extends Kubernetes to Edge devices, creating a unified platform for managing cloud and Edge resources. It offers device management, data synchronization, and containerized application deployment features. With KubeEdge, operators can seamlessly distribute workloads across Edge devices, ensuring efficient data processing and real-time analytics closer to the data source.
- **OpenWhisk** is yet another popular option in the Edge computing landscape. It is a serverless computing platform that enables the execution of functions in response to events. OpenWhisk provides a flexible and scalable infrastructure for running functions at the Edge, allowing for rapid and event-driven data processing and analytics. With its event-driven architecture, OpenWhisk is particularly well-suited for scenarios where real-time analytics and immediate response to data events are crucial, such as wind turbine monitoring.

These edge platforms share common objectives in the context of edge computing and edge analytics. Firstly, they aim to bring computation and analytics closer to the data source, reducing latency and enabling real-time insights. By processing data at the Edge, these platforms minimize the need for constant data transmission to the cloud, reducing bandwidth requirements and ensuring timely decision-making.

Secondly, these platforms provide a unified and scalable infrastructure for managing Edge devices, data ingestion, and analytics workflows. They offer device discovery, provisioning, and management tools, enabling seamless integration with a wide range of edge devices and sensors. Additionally, they provide robust data processing capabilities, allowing for data cleansing, transformation, and advanced analytics tasks.

Lastly, these edge platforms emphasize the importance of interoperability and standardization. They adhere to open standards, enabling easy integration with existing systems and promoting collaboration within the edge computing ecosystem. This interoperability ensures compatibility with various devices, protocols, and data formats, enabling flexible, future-proof Edge deployments.

In the context of wind turbines, edge platforms like EdgeX Foundry, KubeEdge, and OpenWhisk can facilitate the implementation of Edge computing and Edge Analytics solutions. They provide the tools and frameworks to enable real-time data processing, advanced analytics, and visualization at the Edge. By leveraging these platforms, operators can monitor the health and performance of wind turbines, detect anomalies, optimize energy production, and improve overall operational efficiency.

As we progress through this chapter, we will delve into specific use cases and practical examples of using Python on IoT analytics. The main subject of this book is about utilizing Python for analyzing IoT data. While we will not cover the installation and configuration of Edge platforms in detail, we encourage readers to explore these platforms and their features independently.

Implementing Edge Analytics using Python

In the previous chapter, *Chapter 9, Model Deployment on Edge Devices,* we learned about deploying machine learning models on edge for prediction. The data flow we discussed focused on moving data from the cloud to the edge. We will delve into the data flow from IoT devices to the edge and then to the cloud. This data flow is widely adopted and crucial in any IoT implementation.

Initially, we will explore how to consume IoT device data using a simple and widely used protocol called **Message Queuing Telemetry Transport** (**MQTT**). **Original Equipment Manufacturer** (**OEM**) providers offer IoT devices that expose sensor data through industry-standard protocols like MQTT. This data can be consumed for reporting and analytical purposes. We will demonstrate using an edge device to perform basic edge analytics using MQTT messages from IoT devices.

From *Chapter 5, Designing Data Lake and Executing Data Transformation,* specifically in the **IoT Real-Time Data Streaming** section, we learned how to install and configure PostgresDB, create databases, and set up schemas. In the section *Building a Data Pipeline to the Raw Zone* in *Chapter 5,* we demonstrated how to implement real-time data streaming from MQTT topics using Python. We will follow a similar approach for the edge implementation discussed here.

Install PostgresDB on Edge:

The following are the steps that explains how to install PostgresDB on Raspberry Pi:

1. Open a terminal or SSH into your Raspberry Pi.
2. Update the package lists by running the following command:
   ```
   sudo apt update
   ```
3. Install `PostgreSQL` by running the following command:
   ```
   sudo apt install postgresql
   ```
4. Once the installation is complete, `PostgreSQL` should start automatically. You can verify the status by running the following command:
   ```
   sudo service postgresql status
   ```

Create database and schema:

Here are the steps to be followed for creating a database and schema in an Edge device Raspberry Pi:

1. Connect to the PostgreSQL server using the `psql` command as the postgres user:
   ```
   sudo -u postgres psql
   ```
2. Once you are connected to the PostgreSQL server, create a new database:
   ```
   CREATE DATABASE iot_database;
   ```
3. Switch to the newly created database:
   ```
   \c iot_database
   ```

4. Create a new schema within the database:

```
CREATE SCHEMA raw_data;
```

5. Verify that the database and schema have been created:

```
\l       -- Lists all databases
\dn      -- Lists all schemas within the current database
```

You should see the **`iot_database`** listed in the database list and the **`raw_data`** schema listed in the schema list.

Install MQTT broker:

To install an MQTT broker on Raspberry Pi, you can follow these steps to install the popular open-source MQTT broker called Mosquitto:

1. Update the package lists and upgrade the system packages:

```
sudo apt update
sudo apt upgrade
```

2. Install the Mosquitto MQTT broker and its command-line clients:

```
sudo apt install mosquitto mosquitto-clients
```

3. Start the Mosquitto service:

```
sudo systemctl start mosquitto
```

4. Enable the Mosquitto service to start on boot (optional):

```
sudo systemctl enable mosquitto
```

5. Verify that the Mosquitto MQTT broker is running (optional):

```
sudo systemctl status mosquitto
```

You should see the status of the Mosquitto service indicating that it is active and running.

You have successfully installed and started the Mosquitto MQTT broker on your Raspberry Pi with these steps. You can now use the MQTT broker to send and receive MQTT messages between your devices and applications.

NOTE: This ensures that the Mosquitto MQTT broker will automatically start whenever the Raspberry Pi boots up.

Simulate Data Using MQTT Broker

Here are the steps to simulate data using Python on the Edge device. These steps will help you to understand how IoT Devices will send the data to the MQTT Broker topic and how to consume the data on the edge for real-time analytics and store it on the edge device using Python.

In the section *Building a Data Pipeline to the Raw Zone* in *Chapter 5, Designing Data Lake and Executing Data Transformation,* we demonstrated how to implement real-time data streaming from MQTT topics using Python.

We will use the same Python example here:

```
import json
import random
import datetime
import time
import paho.mqtt.client as mqtt

# Function to generate simulated data
def generate_data():
    data = {}
    data['header'] = {}
    data['header']['asset_id'] = 'WT001',
    data['header']['serial_number'] = '12345'

    data['data'] = []
    current_time = datetime.datetime.now().replace(microsecond=0).isoformat()
    data_point = {}
    data_point['rtc'] = current_time
    data_point['temp'] = round(random.uniform(20, 30), 2)
    data_point['pressure'] = round(random.uniform(1000, 1100), 2)
    data_point['wind_speed'] = round(random.uniform(5, 15), 2)
    data_point['rpm'] = random.randint(1200, 1800)
    data_point['energy_output'] = random.randint(800, 1200)
    data['data'].append(data_point)
    return json.dumps(data)

# MQTT client setup
client = mqtt.Client()
client.connect("localhost", 1883)  # Connect to Mosquitto MQTT broker

# Main program loop to generate data every 1 second
while True:
    data = generate_data()
    print(data)
```

```
        client.publish("wind-turbine-data", data)
        time.sleep(1)
```

Copy the above python code with the file **simulate_data_on_edge.py** and save it on your local computer. Transfer this file to Raspberry Pi using **FileZilla**. The detailed step on transferring file to raspberry file using FileZilla is in the section *Manual deployment of ML models of Chapter 9, Model deployment on Edge devices.*

After transferring the file on the Raspberry Pi, you can start simulating data using the following command from the directory where you have transferred the file:

```
python simulate_data_on_edge.py
```

Here is the screenshot of the Raspberry Pi executing the data simulation code (see *Figure 10.1*):

Figure 10.1: *Data simulation on Edge*

Consume Data on Edge PostgresDB

Here is the Python code which reads the MQTT topic and inserts data into PostgresDB. Transfer the below code to the Raspberry Pi device and execute it from the location you have transferred:

```
import psycopg2
import paho.mqtt.client as mqtt
import json
# MQTT settings
mqtt_broker_address = "localhost"
mqtt_broker_port = 1883
mqtt_topic = "wind-turbine-data"
# PostgreSQL settings
db_host = "localhost"
db_port = 5432
db_name = "iot_database"
db_schema = "raw_data"
db_user = "postgres"
db_password = "postgres"
table_name = "raw_wind_turbine_data"
# Create the table if it doesn't exist
def create_table_if_not_exists(cursor):
    cursor.execute(f"""
        CREATE TABLE IF NOT EXISTS {db_schema}.{table_name} (
            id SERIAL PRIMARY KEY,
            asset_id varchar(20),
            rtc TIMESTAMP,
            temp DOUBLE PRECISION,
            pressure DOUBLE PRECISION,
            wind_speed DOUBLE PRECISION,
            rpm DOUBLE PRECISION,
            energy_output DOUBLE PRECISION
        );
    """)
    print(f"Table '{db_schema}.{table_name}' created or already exists.")
# PostgreSQL connection function
def connect_postgres():
    conn = psycopg2.connect(host=db_host, port=db_port, dbname=db_name,
                            user=db_user, password=db_password)
```

```
    return conn
# MQTT on_connect callback function
def on_connect(client, userdata, flags, rc):
    print("Connected to MQTT broker")
    client.subscribe(mqtt_topic)
# MQTT on_message callback function
def on_message(client, userdata, msg):
    # Extract the received message payload
    payload = msg.payload.decode("utf-8")
    try:
        data = json.loads(payload)
        # Extract the data fields from the payload
        asset_id = data['header']['asset_id'][0]
        rtc = data['data'][0]['rtc']
        temp = data['data'][0]['temp']
        pressure = data['data'][0]['pressure']
        wind_speed = data['data'][0]['wind_speed']
        rpm = data['data'][0]['rpm']
        energy_output = data['data'][0]['energy_output']
        conn = connect_postgres()
        cursor = conn.cursor()
        # Create the table if it doesn't exist
        create_table_if_not_exists(cursor)
        # Construct the SQL query
        sql_query = f"""
            INSERT INTO {db_schema}.{table_name} (
                asset_id, rtc, temp, pressure, wind_speed, rpm, energy_output
            )
            VALUES (%s, %s, %s, %s, %s, %s, %s);
        """
        data = (asset_id, rtc, temp, pressure, wind_speed, rpm, energy_output)
        # Execute the SQL query
        cursor.execute(sql_query, data)
```

```
        conn.commit()
        print(f"Inserted data: {payload}")
    except (Exception, psycopg2.Error) as error:
        print(f"Error while inserting data into PostgreSQL: {error}")
    finally:
        # Close the database connection
        if 'conn' in locals():
            cursor.close()
            conn.close()
            print("PostgreSQL connection closed")
# Create an MQTT client
mqtt_client = mqtt.Client()
# Set the MQTT callback functions
mqtt_client.on_connect = on_connect
mqtt_client.on_message = on_message
# Connect to the MQTT broker
mqtt_client.connect(mqtt_broker_address, mqtt_broker_port, 60)
# Start the MQTT client loop to continuously listen for messages
mqtt_client.loop_forever()
```

The above Python code demonstrates the integration of MQTT and PostgreSQL for capturing and storing wind turbine data. First, the code sets up the MQTT broker and PostgreSQL database configurations, including the address, port, topic, and PostgreSQL database connection details.

The **create_table_if_not_exists** function is defined to create the table named **"raw_wind_turbine_data"** in the **raw_data** schema of the **"iot_database"** if it does not already exist. The **on_connect** callback function is executed when the MQTT client successfully connects to the MQTT broker. It subscribes to the specified MQTT topic to receive messages.

The **on_message** callback function is executed whenever a new message is received on the subscribed MQTT topic. It extracts the payload from the received message and attempts to insert the payload data into the PostgreSQL database. Inside the try-except block, a connection is established with the PostgreSQL database using the provided details. The **create_table_if_not_exists** function is called to ensure the table exists before inserting data. The payload data is then inserted into the **raw_wind_turbine_data** table using an SQL query.

An error message is printed if any errors occur during the database operation. Finally, the database connection is closed.

The code continues by creating an MQTT client, setting the callback functions, and connecting to the MQTT broker. The **mqtt_client.loop_forever()** method starts the MQTT client loop, allowing it to continuously listen for incoming messages.

This code sets up an MQTT client to receive wind turbine data, inserts the received data into a PostgreSQL database table, and ensures the table exists before insertion. This enables the capture and storage of wind turbine data for further analysis and processing.

Send Data to Remote Server

Once the sensor data has been successfully inserted on the edge, we will now focus on sending it to the cloud or remote server. This is a critical requirement for any IoT Analytics implementation, as the data must be stored on a cloud or centralized server to perform analytics and machine learning tasks.

First, let us perform necessary configuration on the remote server for the PostgresDB. We will be using our PC or laptop for remote server role, where we have already installed PostgresDB as a part of *Chapter 5, Designing Data Lake and Executing Data Transformation:*

1. Create **raw_wind_turbine_data** table on the remote PostgresDB:

   The following SQL statement will create table in the PostgresDB. On your PC, execute the SQL statement to create the table:

   ```
   CREATE TABLE IF NOT EXISTS rawzone.raw_wind_turbine_data (
               id SERIAL PRIMARY KEY,
               asset_id varchar(20),
               rtc TIMESTAMP,
               temp DOUBLE PRECISION,
               pressure DOUBLE PRECISION,
               wind_speed DOUBLE PRECISION,
               rpm DOUBLE PRECISION,
               energy_output DOUBLE PRECISION
               );
   ```

2. Create **last_updated_table** table on the Edge device Raspberry Pi:

   The following SQL statement will create a table in the PostgresDB on your Raspberry Pi device:

   ```
   CREATE TABLE raw_data.last_updated_table (last_updated timestamp)
   INSERT INTO raw_data.last_updated_table (last_updated)
   VALUES('2023-06- 05 16:09:50')
   ```

3. Modify the Postgres configurations for remote connectivity. Connecting to the remote PostgresDB require following configuration file modifications:

   a. Locate the **pg_hba.conf** file on your PC's. The file is typically located in the data directory of your PostgreSQL installation. The exact path may vary depending on your operating system and PostgreSQL version.

   b. Open the **pg_hba.conf** file using a text editor.
   c. Add an entry that allows the specified host, user, and database combination to connect without SSL. The entry should specify the host, database, user, authentication method, and whether SSL is required. For example:
      i. `# Allow connections from the specified host to the specified database for the specified user`
      ii. `host    IoTDataLake    postgres    192.168.1.14/32    trust`

4. Here is the Python code on Edge, which sends the data to the cloud periodically and in batches:

```
import psycopg2
import psycopg2.extras
from datetime import datetime
import time
# Local PostgreSQL settings
local_db_host = "localhost"
local_db_port = 5432
local_db_name = "iot_database"
local_db_user = "postgres"
local_db_password = "postgres"
local_table_name = "raw_data.raw_wind_turbine_data"
# Remote PostgreSQL settings
remote_db_host = "192.168.1.8"
remote_db_port = 5432
remote_db_name = "IoTDataLake"
remote_db_user = "postgres"
remote_db_password = "postgres"
remote_table_name = "rawzone.raw_wind_turbine_data"
# Batch size and time interval for sending data to the remote server
batch_size = 100 # Number of records to send in each batch
time_interval = 60  # Time interval (in seconds) between each batch send
# Connect to the local database
local_conn = psycopg2.connect(host=local_db_host, port=local_db_port, dbname=local_db_name,
                              user=local_db_user, password=local_db_password)
```

```
local_cursor = local_conn.cursor(cursor_factory=psycopg2.extras.DictCursor)
# Connect to the remote database
remote_conn = psycopg2.connect(host=remote_db_host, port=remote_db_port, dbname=remote_db_name,
                               user=remote_db_user, password=remote_db_password)
remote_cursor = remote_conn.cursor()
# Query the last updated timestamp from the separate table
last_updated_query = "SELECT last_updated FROM last_updated_table LIMIT 1;"
while True:
    try:
        # Start a new transaction on the local and remote databases
        local_conn.rollback()
        remote_conn.rollback()
        # Execute the last updated query
        local_cursor.execute(last_updated_query)
        last_updated = local_cursor.fetchone()[0]
        # Construct the SQL query to fetch the data
        select_query = f"""
            SELECT * FROM {local_table_name}
            WHERE rtc > '{last_updated}'
            ORDER BY rtc ASC
            LIMIT {batch_size};
        """
        # Execute the select query to fetch the data
        local_cursor.execute(select_query)
        records = local_cursor.fetchall()
        if len(records) > 0:
            # Construct the SQL query to insert the records into the remote table
            insert_query = f"""
                INSERT INTO {remote_table_name} (id, asset_id, rtc, temp, pressure, wind_speed, rpm, energy_output)
```

```
                VALUES %s;
            """
            # Prepare the data for bulk insert
            data = [(record['id'], record['asset_id'], record['rtc'], record['temp'], record['pressure'],
                     record['wind_speed'], record['rpm'], record['energy_output']) for record in records]
            # Start a new transaction on the remote database
            remote_conn.autocommit = False
            # Execute the bulk insert query
            psycopg2.extras.execute_values(remote_cursor, insert_query, data)
            # Commit the changes to the remote database
            remote_conn.commit()
            # Restore autocommit mode on the remote database
            remote_conn.autocommit = True
            # Get the latest timestamp from the fetched records
            latest_timestamp = max([record['rtc'] for record in records])
            # Update the last updated timestamp in the separate table
            update_query = f"UPDATE last_updated_table SET last_updated = '{latest_timestamp}';"
            local_cursor.execute(update_query)
            local_conn.commit()
            print(f"Inserted {len(records)} records into the remote database.")
        # Wait for the specified time interval before fetching the next batch
        time.sleep(time_interval)
    except (Exception, psycopg2.Error) as error:
        print(f"Error occurred: {error}")
# Close the database connections
local_cursor.close()
local_conn.close()
remote_cursor.close()
remote_conn.close()
```

The above Python code establishes connections to a local PostgreSQL database on the Raspberry Pi and a remote PostgreSQL database on a cloud server or remote server. It aims to transfer data from the edge device to the remote server.

The code follows a continuous loop that queries the last updated timestamp from a separate table on the local database. It constructs a SQL query to fetch records from the local table with a timestamp greater than the last updated timestamp. The fetched records are then bulk inserted into the remote table using a parameterized query.

After the data transfer, the code updates the last updated timestamp in the separate table on the local database and waits for a specified time interval before fetching the next batch of records. In case of any errors, it prints the error message.

Once the loop is interrupted the code closes the database connections.

Overall, the code ensures continuous data transfer from the edge device to the remote server, periodically fetching and inserting records in batches based on the last updated timestamp.

Data Flow from Edge to Cloud

Here is a dataflow diagram from EdgeX foundry documentation explaining the end-to-end data flow from IoT Devices to the Cloud. This is the typical flow of data for any IoT implementation using Edge. We must understand the flow to build analytical solution suitable for Micro Controllers, Edge devices and the Cloud (see *Figure 10.2*):

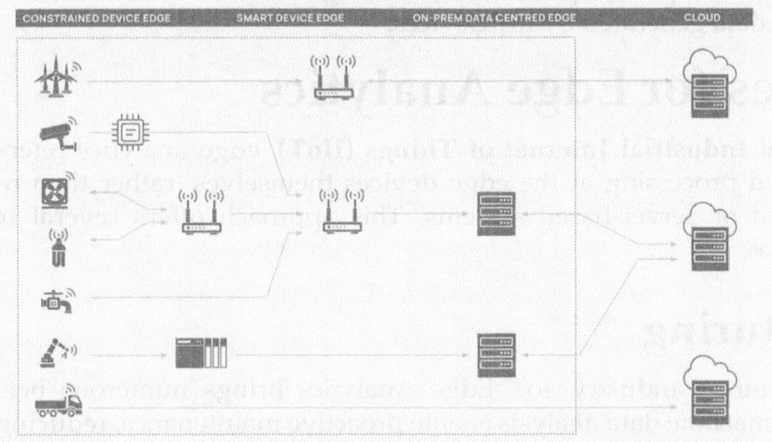

***Figure 10.2:** Dataflow from IoT to Cloud*

In IoT Analytics, the dataflow from IoT devices to the edge and then to the cloud involves a distributed and tiered architecture. This architecture allows for efficient data processing and analysis at different stages of the network.

At the initial stage, we have the IoT devices, often called **things**. These things can include sensors, controllers, and embedded devices that collect data from the physical world. These devices serve as the starting point for the dataflow.

Moving from the devices, the data is transmitted to the edge. The edge represents the intermediate layer between the devices and the cloud. Here, data processing and analysis take place near the data source. This proximity allows for real-time and localized decision-making, reducing latency and optimizing resource utilization.

Within the edge layer, various components can come into play. For example, **Programmable Logic Controllers (PLCs)**, gateways, or advanced sensors may host communication services and initial data processing capabilities. These components help aggregate, filter, and transform the raw data, making it more manageable and valuable for subsequent analysis.

Beyond the edge, the processed data is further transmitted to the cloud. The cloud represents a centralized and scalable infrastructure where advanced analytics, storage, and insights generation occur. By leveraging the cloud's computational power and storage capabilities, organizations can perform in-depth analysis, derive meaningful insights, and gain a broader perspective on the collected data.

This dataflow from IoT devices to the edge and the cloud allows for an efficient and effective approach to IoT Analytics. It enables localized decision-making at the edge, reducing the need for constant communication with the cloud and allowing for real-time responses. Meanwhile, the cloud is a centralized hub for extensive analysis, long-term storage, and higher-level insights generation.

By leveraging this distributed dataflow architecture, organizations can optimize their IoT Analytics processes, improve operational efficiency, and uncover valuable insights from the vast amounts of data generated by IoT devices.

Use Cases for Edge Analytics

In the context of **Industrial Internet of Things (IIoT)**, edge analytics refers to performing data analysis and processing at the edge devices themselves, rather than relying solely on centralized cloud or server-based systems. This approach offers several use cases across various industries.

Manufacturing

In the manufacturing industry, IoT Edge Analytics brings numerous benefits. Real-time monitoring and machine data analysis enable proactive maintenance, reducing downtime and optimizing production processes. For example, sensors embedded in machinery can collect data on temperature, vibration, and other parameters, which is then analyzed at the edge. By detecting anomalies and predicting failures in real-time, maintenance can be scheduled more efficiently, ensuring minimal disruption to production.

Furthermore, edge analytics enables the optimization of manufacturing processes. By analyzing data from various sensors, such as those monitoring machine performance, energy consumption, or quality control, manufacturers can identify areas for improvement. Insights gained from edge analytics can enhance productivity, reduce waste, and increase overall equipment effectiveness.

Energy and Utilities

In the Energy and Utilities sector, edge analytics plays a crucial role in enabling the transformation towards smarter grids and infrastructure. By analyzing data from sensors deployed throughout the power generation, transmission, and distribution systems, operators can gain real-time insights into system performance, faults, and anomalies. This information enables prompt decision-making and swift response to issues, ensuring grid reliability and stability.

Edge analytics also facilitates predictive maintenance of energy assets. Monitoring equipment conditions in real time and leveraging advanced analytics algorithms makes it possible to predict failures and schedule maintenance activities before breakdowns occur. This proactive approach reduces downtime, improves asset utilization, and enhances the overall operational efficiency of the energy infrastructure.

Healthcare

Edge analytics in the healthcare industry opens new possibilities for patient care, remote monitoring, and diagnostics. Wearable devices, medical sensors, and monitoring systems generate vast data that can be processed and analyzed at the edge. Real-time patient monitoring becomes feasible, allowing healthcare providers to remotely track vital signs, detect anomalies, and intervene promptly when necessary.

One key use case is the continuous monitoring of patients with chronic diseases. Edge devices collect data on vital signs, such as heart rate, blood pressure, and glucose levels, and apply analytics algorithms to identify patterns or abnormalities. If any critical condition is detected, alerts are sent to healthcare professionals, enabling timely interventions, and reducing the risk of complications.

Another use case is the analysis of medical imaging data at the edge. High-resolution images, such as MRIs or CT scans, can be processed locally, allowing for quicker analysis and diagnosis. Edge analytics can identify patterns indicative of diseases, enabling healthcare providers to make faster and more accurate decisions regarding patient's treatment plans.

Transportation and Logistics

Edge analytics improves operational efficiency, fleet management, and maintenance processes in the transportation and logistics industry. Organizations can optimize routes, reduce fuel consumption, and enhance overall logistics operations by analyzing data from vehicles, assets, and infrastructure in real-time.

For example, vehicle sensors can collect data on speed, fuel consumption, and engine performance. Edge analytics processes this data to provide real-time driver behavior and vehicle health insights. By monitoring and analyzing these parameters, organizations can identify areas for improvement, such as driver training programs or vehicle maintenance schedules.

Furthermore, edge analytics enables predictive maintenance in the transportation sector. Analyzing sensor data from vehicles can help detect early signs of equipment failure. Maintenance activities can then be scheduled proactively, reducing unplanned downtime, and minimizing operational disruptions.

Agriculture

In the agricultural industry, edge analytics enables precision farming practices. Farmers can gain valuable insights into crop health, soil conditions, and irrigation needs by analyzing data from sensors, weather stations, and satellite imagery.

For instance, soil moisture sensors can collect data on the water content in the soil. By analyzing this data at the edge, farmers can determine optimal irrigation schedules, ensuring that crops receive the right amount of water. This targeted approach to irrigation reduces water wastage, improves crop yields, and promotes sustainable farming practices.

Edge analytics also facilitates early detection of pests or diseases in crops. By analyzing data from sensors that monitor environmental conditions, such as temperature and humidity, farmers can identify patterns that indicate the presence of pests or diseases. Early detection allows for prompt intervention, reducing crop damage and minimizing the need for pesticides or other interventions.

Retail

In the retail industry, edge analytics offers opportunities for enhancing customer experience, optimizing operations, and enabling personalized marketing strategies. Retailers can make data-driven decisions and improve business outcomes by analyzing data from various sources, such as customer behavior, inventory levels, and sales patterns.

For example, edge analytics can analyze data from in-store sensors, such as footfall tracking devices or shelf sensors, to gain insights into customer behavior. This information helps retailers optimize store layouts, improve product placements, and enhance overall shopping experience.

Furthermore, by analyzing real-time data on inventory levels and customer demand, retailers can ensure optimal stock levels, reducing instances of stockouts or overstocking. This leads to improved operational efficiency, better customer satisfaction, and increased sales revenue.

Personalized marketing is another use case for edge analytics in retail. By analyzing customer data, such as purchase history or browsing behavior, retailers can deliver targeted promotions and recommendations to individual customers. This approach enhances customer engagement, increases cross-selling opportunities, and improves marketing effectiveness.

Smart cities

Edge analytics plays a vital role in realizing the vision of smart cities, where data-driven insights and intelligent decision-making improve the quality of life for citizens. By analyzing data from various IoT devices, sensors, and infrastructure systems, cities can optimize resource utilization, enhance public services, and improve sustainability.

One use case is traffic flow optimization. By analyzing real-time data from traffic sensors, GPS devices, and other sources, cities can gain insights into traffic patterns and congestion points. This information enables the implementation of intelligent traffic management systems, optimizing signal timings, and improving traffic flow.

Furthermore, edge analytics facilitates environmental monitoring and sustainability efforts in smart cities. Sensors that measure air quality, noise levels, or waste management parameters can collect data for analysis at the edge. By processing this data, cities can identify areas that require intervention, improve waste management practices, and reduce pollution levels.

Additionally, edge analytics enables public safety applications in smart cities. Real-time data from surveillance cameras, emergency response systems, and social media can be analyzed to detect anomalies, identify potential security threats, and enable prompt responses from law enforcement agencies.

MicroPython for Edge Computing

MicroPython is a lean and efficient implementation of the Python programming language designed specifically for microcontrollers and embedded systems. It is well-suited for edge computing, which involves processing data at or near the source rather than relying on centralized cloud services. Here is an overview of MicroPython for edge computing, including its benefits, use cases, and considerations:

Why MicroPython for Edge Computing

Here are the main reasons for choosing MicroPython for performing Edge Computing:

- **Simplified development:** MicroPython provides a familiar and easy-to-use programming language, allowing developers with Python experience to leverage their skills for edge computing projects. Its high-level syntax and extensive standard library simplify the development process and reduce the learning curve.
- **Memory efficiency:** MicroPython is optimized for memory-constrained devices. It offers a compact runtime environment, efficient memory management, and allows for fine-grained control over resource allocation. This makes it suitable for running low-power microcontrollers with limited memory and processing capabilities.
- **Fast prototyping:** MicroPython facilitates rapid prototyping by enabling quick iteration cycles. Its interactive shell allows developers to write and execute code directly on microcontrollers, making it ideal for testing and debugging in real-time.
- **Extensibility:** MicroPython supports hardware interfaces and provides modules for accessing various sensors, actuators, and communication protocols commonly used in edge computing scenarios. It can interact with peripheral devices like sensors, motors, and displays, enabling seamless integration into edge applications.

When to Choose MicroPython

MicroPython is particularly beneficial in the following scenarios:

- **Resource-constrained environments**: When dealing with edge devices with limited memory and processing power, MicroPython's efficiency and lightweight footprint make it an ideal choice. It allows for efficient execution of code on microcontrollers with constrained resources.
- **Rapid prototyping:** MicroPython's simplicity and interactivity make it suitable for quick experimentation and prototyping. It enables developers to iterate and test their ideas rapidly, facilitating the development of edge computing solutions.

The advantages of MicroPython are:

- Familiar and easy-to-use programming language for Python developers.
- Optimized for memory-constrained devices, making it suitable for edge computing.
- Supports a wide range of hardware interfaces and communication protocols.
- Rapid prototyping capabilities with an interactive shell for quick iteration.
- Enables seamless integration with peripheral devices commonly used in edge applications.

The disadvantages of MicroPython are:

- Limited access to low-level hardware features compared to languages like C/C++.
- Reduced execution speed compared to compiled languages may impact performance in certain use cases.
- Less mature ecosystem compared to other programming languages used in embedded systems.

An application example is MicroPython for wind turbine data.

In the context of wind turbine data, MicroPython can be utilized for edge computing tasks such as real-time monitoring, anomaly detection, and predictive maintenance. Here is an example scenario:

- **Data acquisition:** MicroPython can interface with sensors attached to wind turbines, collecting data on parameters like wind speed, rotor RPM, temperature, and energy output. This data is continuously monitored and processed at the edge.
- **Real-time analysis:** MicroPython algorithms running on the microcontroller can analyze the collected data in real-time. For instance, it can identify abnormal wind speed or temperature patterns that might indicate potential issues with turbine operation.
- **Anomaly detection:** MicroPython can use statistical analysis and machine learning techniques to detect anomalies in the collected data. It can compare the current data with historical patterns or predefined thresholds to identify deviations that require attention.

- **Predictive maintenance:** MicroPython can predict maintenance requirements and identify failures by analyzing sensor data at the edge. It can detect early signs of equipment degradation, enabling proactive maintenance scheduling to prevent costly breakdowns and optimize turbine performance.

In this example, MicroPython's memory efficiency, rapid prototyping capabilities, and support for hardware interfaces make it well-suited for implementing edge analytics on wind turbine data. Its ability to process data at the edge reduces latency, minimizes reliance on cloud connectivity, and enables timely decision-making for efficient wind turbine operation and maintenance.

Microcontrollers for MicroPython

Microcontrollers play a crucial role in IoT Analytics due to several key reasons.

Firstly, microcontrollers provide the hardware interface and connectivity options required for IoT devices to collect and process data. They often feature built-in sensors, analog-to-digital converters, and communication protocols such as Wi-Fi or Bluetooth, enabling seamless integration with various IoT devices and sensors.

Secondly, microcontrollers are designed to operate with low power consumption, making them ideal for battery powered IoT devices that need to run for extended periods without frequent recharging or maintenance. This energy efficiency ensures that IoT Analytics can be performed continuously without interruptions.

Furthermore, microcontrollers offer real-time processing capabilities, enabling on-the-spot data analysis and decision-making at the edge of the network. This is particularly valuable in scenarios where real-time or near-real-time insights are required for immediate actions, such as anomaly detection, predictive maintenance, or event-triggered responses.

In addition, microcontrollers are often cost-effective and compact, making them suitable for deploying IoT Analytics solutions at scale. Their small form factor allows integration into various devices, enabling data collection and analytics at the edge, closer to the data source.

Overall, microcontrollers provide the necessary hardware capabilities, power efficiency, real-time processing, and cost-effectiveness required for performing IoT Analytics. By leveraging microcontrollers, organizations can enable intelligent data processing, reduce data transmission costs, enhance data privacy and security, and derive valuable insights closer to the data source, leading to more efficient and responsive IoT Analytics solutions.

Here are some of the most widely used microcontroller boards for IIoT applications:

- **Raspberry Pi:** Raspberry Pi boards, such as Raspberry Pi 4 or Raspberry Pi Zero, are popular choices for IIoT due to their powerful processing capabilities, built-in connectivity options (like Wi-Fi, Bluetooth, and Ethernet), and support for various operating systems, including MicroPython.
- **ESP8266:** The ESP8266 is a low-cost Wi-Fi-enabled microcontroller board. It is widely used for IIoT projects due to its simplicity, low power consumption, and compatibility

with MicroPython. It offers built-in Wi-Fi connectivity, making it suitable for IoT applications that require wireless communication.

- **Arduino:** Arduino boards, such as Arduino Uno or Arduino Nano, are widely used in IIoT projects. They are known for their ease of use, large community support, and extensive range of compatible sensors and modules. Arduino boards can be programmed with Arduino IDE, which supports MicroPython as well.
- **BeagleBone Black:** BeagleBone Black is an open-source microcontroller board that offers extensive connectivity options, including Ethernet, USB, and HDMI. It has a more powerful processor compared to some other microcontrollers, making it suitable for complex IIoT applications.
- **Particle Photon:** Particle Photon is a compact Wi-Fi-enabled microcontroller board designed specifically for IoT applications. It provides a cloud-based development platform and supports MicroPython. Particle Photon offers built-in cloud connectivity, making it easy to integrate with IoT platforms and services.

These are just a few examples of widely used microcontroller boards for IIoT. Each board has its own features, capabilities, and community support, so the choice depends on the specific requirements of your IIoT project.

Installation and Configuration of MicroPython

The procedure for installing and configuring MicroPython varies depending on the microcontroller board you are using. In this case, we will take NODEMCU ESP8266 board as an example and walk you through its installation and configuration process.

Here are the steps to install and configure MicroPython on a NODEMCU ESP8266 board:

1. Download the MicroPython firmware.
2. Visit the official MicroPython website at **https://micropython.org/download/esp8266/**.
3. Scroll down to the **Firmware** section and download the latest stable firmware for ESP8266. Choose the appropriate version for your board.
4. Connect the NODEMCU ESP8266 board to your computer:
5. Use a micro-USB cable to connect the NODEMCU ESP8266 board to your computer.
6. Flash the MicroPython firmware:

   Install a tool for flashing firmware to the ESP8266 board. One popular tool is esptool.
7. Open a terminal or command prompt and install esptool using pip: pip install esptool.
8. Erase the flash memory of the board by running the following command: **`esptool.py --port /dev/ttyUSB0 erase_flash`** (replace **`/dev/ttyUSB0`** with the appropriate serial port of your board).
9. Flash the MicroPython firmware by running the following command: **`esptool.py --port /dev/ttyUSB0 --baud 460800 write_flash --flash_size=detect 0 path_to_firmware.bin`** (replace **`/dev/ttyUSB0`** with the appropriate serial port and **`path_to_firmware.bin`** with the path to the downloaded firmware file).
10. Verify the installation:

a. After the firmware is flashed, you can connect to the board's serial **Read-Eval-Print Loop** (**REPL**) to interact with it.

b. Use a terminal program (PuTTY, Minicom, or screen) and connect to the board's serial port (baud rate: 115200).

c. You should see the MicroPython prompt (>>>) indicating that the installation was successful.

11. Install Thonny IDE by following the instructions:

a. Visit the Thonny IDE official site **https://thonny.org** to download the latest version as required for your operating system. Let us go through the installation steps for windows operating system (see *Figure 10.3*):

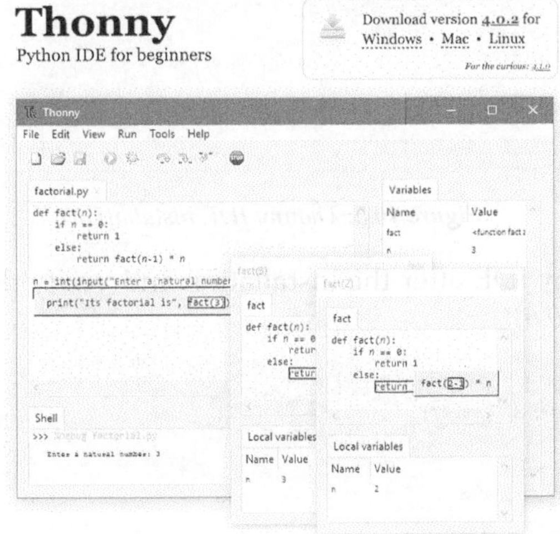

***Figure 10.3:** Thonny IDE download*

b. Go to the directory where your downloaded is saved on your local computer and double-click on the **.exe** file (see *Figure 10.4*):

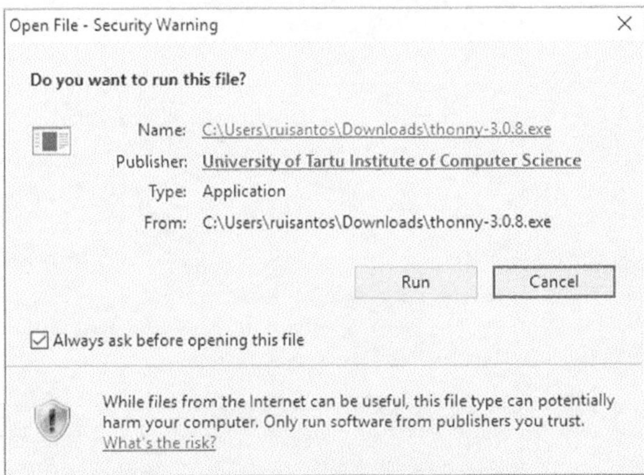

***Figure 10.4:** Thonny IDE installation1*

c. Click on **Next** to proceed further (see *Figure 10.5*):

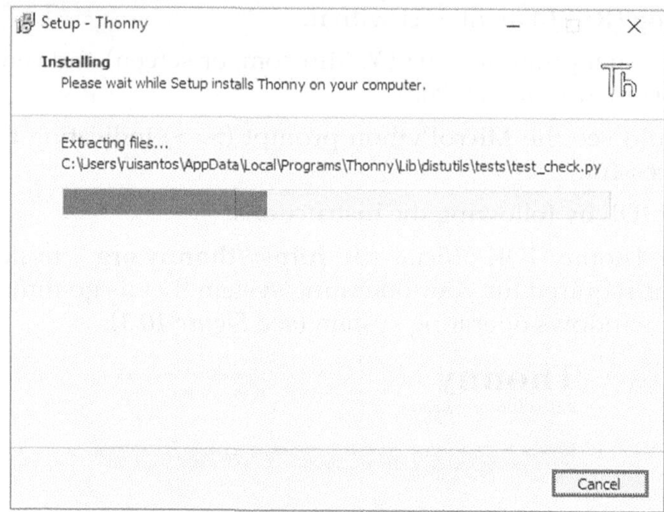

***Figure 10.5:** Thonny IDE installation2*

d. Open Thonny IDE after the installation and verify that installation is successful (see *Figure 10.6*):

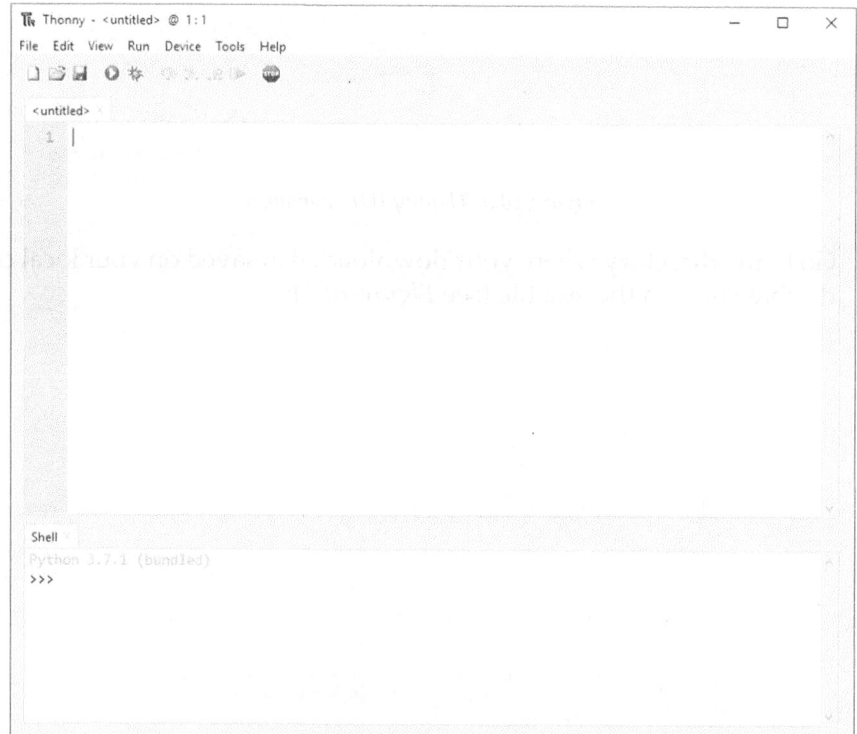

***Figure 10.6:** Thonny IDE verify installation*

12. **Write and execute MicroPython code:** Once connected to the IDE, you can write and execute MicroPython code directly on the NODEMCU ESP8266 board. This allows you to interact with the board's hardware peripherals and sensors.

Following the above steps, you can successfully install and configure MicroPython on a NODEMCU ESP8266 board, enabling you to program and utilize its features for IoT and IIoT applications. Next, we will show you how to perform programming on the microcontroller board NODEMCU ESP8266 using Thonny IDE.

Programming Microcontrollers using MicroPython

After installing MicroPython on the NODEMCU ESP8266 board and installed Thonny IDE on your PC or laptop, plugin the board on your PC or laptop USB drive and open the Thonny IDE and select the USB drive of the board as shown in the *Figure 10.7* from **Tools | Options** menu:

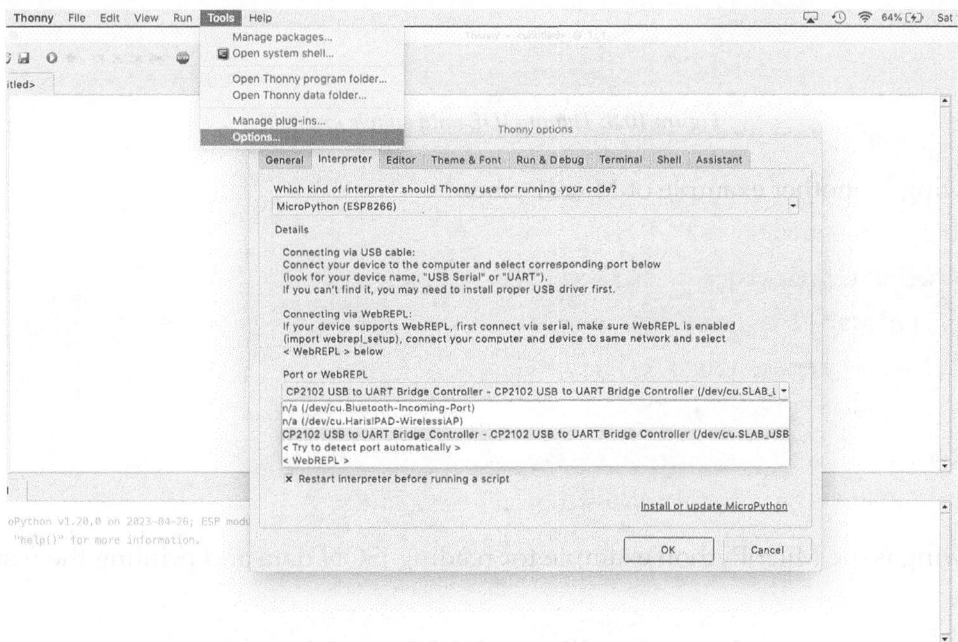

***Figure 10.7:** Thonny IDE select the USB port of ESP8266*

Now, we are ready to try some basic Python operations. Here is some basic programming you can try on the board using MicroPython:

```
1. print("Hello, World!")
```

Figure 10.8 is the screenshot of the Thonny IDE on how to perform Python programming:

***Figure 10.8:** Thonny IDE with simple example*

The following is another example of MicroPython:

```
wind_temperature = 25
if wind_temperature > 30:
    print("It's hot!")
elif wind_temperature < 15:
    print("It's cold!")
else:
    print("The wind temperature is moderate.")
```

The following is the MicroPython example for reading JSON data and printing the results:

```
import json
# Sample wind turbine data in JSON format
wind_turbine_data = '''
{
  "id": "WT001",
  "timestamp": "2023-05-17T12:30:00",
  "wind_speed": 15.2,
  "power_output": 1200.5,
  "temperature": 25.8
}
```

```
'''
# Parse the JSON data
data = json.loads(wind_turbine_data)
# Extract relevant data points
wind_speed = data["wind_speed"]
power_output = data["power_output"]
temperature = data["temperature"]
# Perform data analysis
average_power = power_output
max_wind_speed = wind_speed
min_temperature = temperature
# Print the results
print("Data Analysis Results:")
print("Average Power Output:", average_power)
print("Max Wind Speed:", max_wind_speed)
print("Min Temperature:", min_temperature)
```

The following is the MicroPython example for performing simple data analysis, calculating average, sum, maximum and minimum values based on given data:

```
import json
# Sample wind turbine data in JSON format
wind_turbine_data = '''
{
  "id": "WT001",
  "timestamp": "2023-05-17T12:30:00",
  "wind_speed": [14.5, 15.2, 16.8, 14.9, 17.2],
  "power_output": [1200.5, 1150.2, 1185.6, 1220.8, 1199.3],
  "temperature": [25.8, 26.3, 24.9, 27.1, 25.5]
}
'''
# Parse the JSON data
data = json.loads(wind_turbine_data)
# Extract relevant data points
wind_speed = data["wind_speed"]
power_output = data["power_output"]
temperature = data["temperature"]
```

```
# Perform data analysis
average_power = sum(power_output) / len(power_output)
max_wind_speed = max(wind_speed)
min_temperature = min(temperature)
# Calculate energy efficiency
energy_efficiency = sum(power_output) / sum(wind_speed)
# Print the results
print("Data Analysis Results:")
print("Average Power Output:", average_power)
print("Max Wind Speed:", max_wind_speed)
print("Min Temperature:", min_temperature)
print("Energy Efficiency:", energy_efficiency)
```

The following is the MicroPython example where the data is stored in a text file on the microcontroller board and later retrieved for performing statistical analysis:

```
import uio
# Define the wind turbine data
data = [
    (12.5, 350.2, 25.0),
    (11.8, 320.5, 24.5),
    (13.2, 380.1, 25.8),
    (10.6, 300.7, 23.2),
    (14.4, 400.9, 26.5)
]
# Open the file in write mode
with open("wind_turbine_data.txt", "w") as file:
    # Iterate over the data and write each entry to the file
    for entry in data:
        line = ",".join(str(value) for value in entry) + "\n"
        file.write(line)
print("Data written to the file.")
# Read wind turbine data from file
with open("wind_turbine_data.txt", "r") as file:
    data = file.readlines()
# Extract wind speed, power output, and temperature from data
wind_speed = []
power_output = []
```

```
temperature = []
for line in data:
    values = line.strip().split(",")
    wind_speed.append(float(values[0]))
    power_output.append(float(values[1]))
    temperature.append(float(values[2]))
# Calculate average power output
average_power = sum(power_output) / len(power_output)
# Calculate standard deviation of wind speed
mean_wind_speed = sum(wind_speed) / len(wind_speed)
std_deviation_wind_speed = (sum((x - mean_wind_speed) ** 2 for x in wind_speed) / len(wind_speed)) ** 0.5
# Calculate correlation between temperature and power output
mean_temperature = sum(temperature) / len(temperature)
covariance = sum((x - mean_temperature) * (y - average_power) for x, y in zip(temperature, power_output))
correlation_temp_power = covariance / ((sum((x - mean_temperature) ** 2 for x in temperature) * sum((y - average_power) ** 2 for y in power_output)) ** 0.5)
# Print the results
print("Advanced Analytics Results:")
print("Average Power Output:", average_power)
print("Standard Deviation of Wind Speed:", std_deviation_wind_speed)
print("Correlation between Temperature and Power Output:", correlation_temp_power)
```

Invoking ML Models using MicroPython

Performing machine learning tasks on microcontroller boards can be challenging due to several limitations. First, microcontrollers typically have limited computational power and memory, which can restrict the size and complexity of the machine-learning models that can be deployed. Machine learning algorithms often require significant computational resources, such as matrix operations and iterative processes, which may exceed the capabilities of microcontrollers.

Furthermore, microcontrollers usually lack dedicated hardware for accelerating machine learning tasks, such as specialized GPUs or TPUs. This can result in slower inference times and longer processing durations, making real-time or time-sensitive applications impractical.

Additionally, microcontrollers often have limited storage capacity, making it difficult to store large datasets or pre-trained models directly on the board. This can hinder the ability to perform complex machine-learning tasks that require extensive training data or large model files.

To overcome these limitations, a practical approach is to offload the machine learning tasks to a remote server or cloud-based infrastructure. By calling a FASTAPI or similar API from the microcontroller, the raw data can be transmitted to the server for processing and prediction. The server can leverage powerful hardware, ample storage, and scalable resources to execute sophisticated machine-learning algorithms efficiently. The results can then be returned to the microcontroller for further actions or display.

This approach enables microcontrollers to leverage the capabilities of more robust computing environments while preserving their lightweight and energy-efficient nature. It allows for flexible and scalable machine learning implementations by separating resource-intensive tasks from resource-constrained microcontrollers. Additionally, it enables seamless integration with cloud-based analytics platforms, facilitating data aggregation, model updates, and collaborative decision-making in IoT applications.

Let us explore how to invoke machine learning models running on the remote server from the microcontroller ESP8266 board. It is critical that we need to have Wi-Fi connectivity to perform these tasks.

First, we need to make sure that the FastAPI service we built in the previous chapter, *Chapter 9, Model Deployment on Edge Devices*, is running. We can do this by following the steps in the section **Expose models using FastAPI** in that chapter, especially the subsection **Implementing Model Exposure using FastAPI**.

Ensure that the python program given in this sub-section is saved as **`main.py`** and the **`alert_model.pkl`** file is saved in the same directory.

The next step is to execute the following Python program from the ESP8266 using Thonny IDE:

```
import urequests as requests
import network
# Connect to the WiFi network
ssid = "your_wifi_ssid"
password = "your_wifi_password"
wifi = network.WLAN(network.STA_IF)
wifi.active(True)
wifi.connect(ssid, password)
while not wifi.isconnected():
    pass
print("Connected to Wi-Fi")
print("IP address:", wifi.ifconfig()[0])
input_data = {
    'temperature_100': 20,
    'pressure_100': 1000,
    'wind_speed_100': 10,
```

```
    'power_output_100': 1500
}
response = requests.post('http://<your_ip_address>:8000/predict', json=input_data)
if response.status_code == 200:
    alerts = response.json()['alerts']
    for alert in alerts:
        print(alert)
else:
    print(f"Prediction failed with status code {response.status_code}: {response.text}")
# Disconnect from the WiFi network
wifi.disconnect()
```

The above Python program connects an ESP8266 board (such as NODEMCU) to a Wi-Fi network and sends a JSON payload to a remote server for prediction using a REST API.

To use the program, the user needs to modify the values of **`your_wifi_ssid`**, **`your_wifi_password`**, and **`<your_ip_address>`** with their actual Wi-Fi network name (SSID), Wi-Fi password and the IP address of the remote server respectively.

The program starts by importing the required modules, including **urequests** for making HTTP requests and **network** for connecting to the Wi-Fi network.

Next, the program connects to the Wi-Fi network using the provided SSID and password. It waits until the connection is established and prints the IP address assigned to the board.

The **`input_data`** dictionary contains the values for different parameters related to the wind turbine (For example, temperature, pressure, wind speed, and power output). These values can be modified as needed.

The program makes a POST request to the remote server's URL with the JSON payload containing the input data. It expects a response with the predicted alerts in JSON format.

If the response status code is 200 (indicating a successful request), the program retrieves the alerts from the response JSON and prints them. Otherwise, it prints an error message indicating the failure and the response status code.

Finally, the program disconnects from the Wi-Fi network before terminating.

NOTE: It is important to ensure that the ESP8266 board is properly connected to the Wi-Fi network and the remote server is running and accessible at the specified IP address.

Conclusion

In conclusion, this chapter introduced edge computing and edge analytics. We explored edge platforms, data flow from the edge to the cloud, and use cases of edge analytics in various industries. We also delved into MicroPython for edge computing and how to invoke machine learning models from the NODEMCU ESP8266 board.

The next chapter will delve into an end-to-end case study using a dataset of Vehicle CAN data from the Cadillac CT6 Super Cruise On-road Data. We will apply the concepts we have learned throughout the book to perform IoT Data Analytics, incorporating vehicle CAN data and information from a sensor array to gain insights from the dataset. By exploring this comprehensive case study, we will solidify our understanding of IoT Data Analytics and further enhance our skills in handling real-world IoT data.

Points to Remember

Following are the key takeaways from this chapter:

- The concepts of edge computing and edge analytics were introduced, highlighting their significance in processing data closer to the source and extracting real-time insights.
- An introduction was provided to popular edge platforms, including EdgeX Platform, KubeEdge, and OpenWhisk, which enable seamless deployment and management of edge applications.
- The data flow from edge to the cloud was explained, and a detailed Python implementation was presented. This implementation demonstrated the process of collecting wind turbine data on a Raspberry Pi, pushing it to an MQTT broker topic, and consuming and storing the data on edge using an Edge PostgresSQL database. The data was also periodically sent to a remote or cloud server.
- Use cases for edge analytics were explored across various industries, such as manufacturing, energy and utilities, healthcare, transportation and logistics, agriculture, retail, and smart cities. These examples showcased edge analytics's practical applications and benefits in each industry.
- MicroPython for edge computing was introduced, highlighting its suitability for resource-constrained microcontroller boards. The advantages, disadvantages, and installation or configuration process of MicroPython on NODEMCU ESP8266 microcontroller boards were discussed. Additionally, the usage of the Thonny IDE for MicroPython programming was explained, along with basic examples, including data analytics.
- The process of invoking machine learning models using MicroPython was demonstrated. Specifically, the example showcased how a machine learning model developed for wind turbine data analysis, as discussed in *Chapter 9, Model Deployment on Edge Devices,* could be invoked from a NODEMCU ESP8266 board. The model was exposed via FASTAPI on a remote server.

CHAPTER 11

IoT Analytics for Self-driving Vehicles

Introduction

In this last chapter of our book, *IoT Data Analytics using Python*, we will explore a comprehensive end-to-end case study on self-driving vehicles. We will analyze a rich dataset gathered from a 2019 Cadillac CT6 equipped with Super Cruise technology.

The dataset includes over 60 individual drives, covering more than 1,000 miles, predominantly collected during highway driving. It includes vehicle data, Lidar information, and camera data obtained from a vehicle-mounted sensor array.

Our objective is to use IoT Data Analytics to extract valuable insights from this dataset, providing a deeper understanding of self-driving vehicle behavior and performance. We will follow the **Cross Industry Standard Process for Data Mining** (**CRISP-DM**) framework to guide us in uncovering meaningful knowledge.

Join us as we embark on this journey of leveraging IoT Data Analytics for self-driving vehicles. Through our analysis, we aim to transform raw data into actionable insights, driving us closer to a safer and more efficient future on the roads.

Structure

In this chapter, we will cover the following topics:

- CRISP-DM Framework

- Business Understanding of Self-Driving Vehicles
- Data Collection and Understanding
- Data Preparation and Feature Engineering
- Modeling and Evaluation
- Deployment of Machine Learning Models

Objectives

The objective of this chapter is to apply a case study to recollect and apply the learnings from the concepts we discussed so far in this book. The chapter conducts a comprehensive case study on self-driving vehicle dynamics using a dataset of 60 individual drives. The chapter follows the CRISP-DM framework to apply IoT Data Analytics techniques to extract meaningful insights from the dataset. The chapter explores various attributes of the dataset, including vehicle CAN data, Lidar information, and RIDAR data, to uncover hidden patterns and predictive models that can enhance our understanding of self-driving vehicle dynamics.

CRISP-DM Framework

We learned about approaching data science projects using the CRISP-DM framework in *Chapter 2, Up and Running with Data Analytics Fundamentals*.

The CRISP-DM framework consists of six iterative steps:

1. **Business understanding:** We will understand the business requirements and domain knowledge.
2. **Data understanding:** We will explore the data and understand its characteristics.
3. **Data preparation:** We will clean and prepare the data for analysis.
4. **Modeling:** We will build and evaluate machine learning models.
5. **Evaluation:** We will evaluate the performance of the models.
6. **Deployment:** We will deploy the models into production.

We will explore each step-in detail, starting from comprehending the business requirements and domain knowledge, conducting exploratory data analysis, preprocessing the data, performing feature engineering, applying machine learning techniques, and finally, deploying our trained model.

We will be using a dataset from the U.S. Department of Energy, Office of Energy Efficiency and Renewable Energy on Self-driving vehicles and demonstrate how to use the CRISP-DM framework to perform data analysis to obtain insights for the business requirements. Let us now follow each step of the CRISP-DM framework. Each of the following sections provides on how to approach a given business problem.

Business Understanding of Self-driving Vehicles

Before delving into the data analysis problem at hand, it is crucial to gain a comprehensive understanding of the business domain, the technologies involved, and the challenges associated with it. Therefore, let us begin by exploring the fundamental concepts of self-driving vehicles.

Self-driving vehicles, also known as autonomous vehicles, have emerged as a game-changing innovation in the transportation industry. Enabled by the convergence of the **Industrial Internet of Things (IIoT)**, advanced sensors, and IoT Analytics, self-driving vehicles hold immense importance and significance in shaping the future of transportation.

The key significance of self-driving vehicles lies in their potential to revolutionize road safety, efficiency, and convenience. By leveraging a comprehensive array of sensors such as Lidar, radar, and cameras, these vehicles can perceive their surroundings with unprecedented precision and accuracy. This enables them to make real-time decisions, navigate complex traffic scenarios, and prevent collisions, ultimately enhancing overall safety on the roads.

The social and economic impacts of self-driving vehicles are far-reaching. Improved safety features can significantly reduce accidents and save countless lives. Additionally, self-driving vehicles have the potential to optimize transportation logistics, alleviate traffic congestion, and reduce fuel consumption, leading to economic savings and environmental benefits.

The advantages of self-driving vehicles include enhanced mobility for individuals with disabilities, reduced driver fatigue, and increased productivity during travel. Moreover, self-driving vehicles can transform industries like ridesharing and freight transportation, opening new business models and opportunities for innovation.

However, self-driving vehicles also come with certain limitations and challenges. Technological advancements are still required to ensure the reliability and robustness of self-driving systems in all driving conditions. Legal and regulatory frameworks need to be established to address liability and responsibility in case of accidents or malfunctions. Additionally, privacy and cybersecurity concerns must be addressed to protect against potential data breaches and malicious attacks.

In conclusion, self-driving vehicles represent a significant paradigm shift in transportation technology. Through the convergence of IIoT, sensors, and IoT Analytics, they offer transformative benefits in terms of safety, efficiency, and convenience. While challenges and limitations exist, continued research, development, and collaboration among industry stakeholders will pave the way for a future where self-driving vehicles become an integral part of our transportation ecosystem.

Technologies Behind Self-driving Vehicles

Self-driving vehicles employ a variety of advanced technologies, sensors, protocols, communication technologies, devices, storage, analytics, and algorithms to operate autonomously. Let us explore each of these aspects in detail.

The following are basic technologies for self-driving vehicles:

- **Artificial Intelligence (AI) and Machine Learning:** AI algorithms play a crucial role in enabling self-driving vehicles to perceive and interpret their surroundings, make decisions, and learn from their experiences.
- **Computer vision:** Computer vision systems utilize cameras and image processing techniques to identify and understand objects, road signs, traffic lights, pedestrians, and other relevant visual cues.
- **Sensor fusion:** Sensor fusion combines data from multiple sensors such as cameras, **Light Detection and Ranging (Lidar)**, radar, and ultrasonic sensors to obtain a comprehensive and accurate understanding of the vehicle's environment.
- **GPS and Localization: Global Positioning System (GPS)** provides precise location information, while localization algorithms enable the vehicle to determine its position relative to the surrounding environment.

Sensors installed on a self-driving vehicle:

- **Lidar:** Lidar sensors use laser beams to measure distances, creating a detailed 3D map of the vehicle's surroundings. They are particularly effective in detecting objects and capturing high-resolution spatial data.
- **Radar:** Radar sensors use radio waves to detect and track objects, providing information on their speed, distance, and relative motion.
- **Cameras:** Cameras capture visual data, allowing the vehicle's computer system to analyze and interpret the environment in real time.
- **Ultrasonic sensors:** Ultrasonic sensors use sound waves to detect objects near the vehicle, assisting in parking and low-speed maneuvering.

Protocols and communication technologies:

- **Controller Area Network (CAN):** CAN is a common communication protocol used in vehicles to transmit data between various components and sensors.
- **Ethernet:** Ethernet is increasingly being adopted in self-driving vehicles for high-speed and reliable communication between onboard systems.
- **Dedicated Short-Range Communications (DSRC):** DSRC is a wireless communication technology specifically designed for **vehicle-to-vehicle (V2V)** and **vehicle-to-infrastructure (V2I)** communication, enabling real-time data exchange for safety and traffic management.

Devices and storage:

- **Onboard computers:** Self-driving vehicles are equipped with powerful onboard computers capable of processing vast amounts of sensor data, running AI algorithms, and making real-time decisions.
- **Solid-State Drives (SSD):** SSDs provide fast and reliable storage for storing and retrieving data in self-driving vehicles, facilitating efficient data access and processing.

Analytics and algorithms:

- **Sensor data processing:** Advanced algorithms are used to process sensor data, extract relevant information, and generate a coherent representation of the vehicle's surroundings.
- **Perception and object recognition:** AI algorithms analyze sensor data to identify and classify objects, including other vehicles, pedestrians, cyclists, and road infrastructure.
- **Path planning and decision-making:** Algorithms determine the optimal path and trajectory for the vehicle based on sensor data, traffic conditions, and predefined rules, ensuring safe and efficient navigation.
- **Machine learning and deep learning:** Machine learning and deep learning techniques are employed to enhance the vehicle's perception capabilities, improve decision-making, and adapt to changing environments.

It is important to note that the specific technologies, sensors, protocols, and algorithms used may vary among different self-driving vehicle manufacturers and research projects. Ongoing advancements in these areas continue to drive the development and refinement of self-driving vehicle technologies.

Data Challenges from Self-driving Vehicles

Dealing with data from self-driving vehicles poses several challenges that need to be effectively addressed. These challenges include:

- **Data volume:** Self-driving vehicles generate massive amounts of data from multiple sensors, resulting in high-volume data streams. To handle this challenge, scalable storage and processing systems are required, such as distributed computing frameworks and cloud infrastructure.
- **Data variety:** Self-driving vehicles rely on various sensors, such as cameras, LiDAR, radar, and GPS, which generate data in different formats and structures. Managing and integrating these diverse data types require data integration techniques, including data mapping, transformation, and alignment.
- **Data velocity:** Real-time decision-making is critical for self-driving vehicles to navigate and respond to their environment. Processing and analyzing data streams in real-time demand high-speed data ingestion, stream processing frameworks, and low-latency analytics capabilities.
- **Data quality:** Ensuring the accuracy and reliability of the data is crucial for the performance and safety of self-driving vehicles. However, sensor noise, calibration issues, environmental factors, and data transmission errors can introduce inaccuracies. Data quality assurance techniques, such as data validation, error detection, and outlier removal, should be employed.
- **Data privacy and security:** Self-driving vehicles collect sensitive information, including location data, images, and personal data of passengers. Protecting data privacy and ensuring data security from potential cyber threats are significant concerns. Encryption,

access controls, secure data transmission protocols, and privacy-preserving techniques need to be implemented.

Business Requirements

After understanding the business domain, business landscape, and challenges, it is important to understand business requirements before attempting to perform analysis on the data. Here are the key requirements that come from the customer on the self-driving vehicle business:

- **Anomaly detection:** Identify abnormal behavior or malfunctions in self-driving vehicles by analyzing the sensor data. Detecting anomalies can help in proactively identifying potential issues and ensuring the safety and reliability of the vehicles.
- **Performance optimization:** Analyze the sensor data to optimize the performance of self-driving vehicles. This can involve analyzing the accelerator pedal position, braking activity, engine speed, torque, and throttle position to improve fuel efficiency, reduce wear and tear, and enhance overall vehicle performance.
- **Behavior analysis:** Study the behavior of self-driving vehicles by analyzing the sensor data. This can involve analyzing the vehicle's response to different road conditions, traffic situations, and driver inputs. Understanding the behavior can help in improving autonomous driving algorithms, enhancing vehicle control, and ensuring passenger comfort and safety.
- **Traffic analysis:** Utilize the Lidar and camera data from the sensor array to analyze the traffic surrounding the self-driving vehicles. This analysis can provide valuable insights into traffic patterns, congestion levels, and potential hazards. It can help in developing intelligent traffic management systems and optimizing routes for autonomous vehicles.
- **Predictive maintenance:** Analyze the vehicle CAN data to predict maintenance needs and optimize maintenance schedules. By monitoring sensor data related to engine performance, tire pressure, battery health, etc., it is possible to predict when maintenance or repairs may be required. This can help in reducing breakdown time, optimizing maintenance costs, and ensuring the longevity of the vehicles.
- **Safety analysis:** Use the sensor data to analyze safety-related aspects of self-driving vehicles. This can involve evaluating the effectiveness of the autonomous driving algorithms, assessing the vehicle's response to different scenarios, and identifying potential safety risks. The analysis can contribute to the improvement of safety measures and the development of robust autonomous driving systems.

Of course, the dataset we get may not be able to provide a solution for all these above-mentioned requirements. But discussing with the stakeholders on the business requirement to finalize the requirements is critical for any successful implementation.

Data Collection and Understanding

The dataset we will be using for our case study is obtained from:

`Livewire Data Platform (LDP). ld-cav-functionality/cadillac-ct6. Maintained by Livewire Data Platform for U.S. Department of Energy, Office of Energy Efficiency and Renewable Energy. DOI: 10.15483/1922210. Accessed: 04 Jun 2023`

Here are the steps to obtain the dataset from the Livewire data platform:

1. From your browser, navigate to **https://livewire.energy.gov/register** and register with your details to create an account, as shown in *Figure 11.1*:

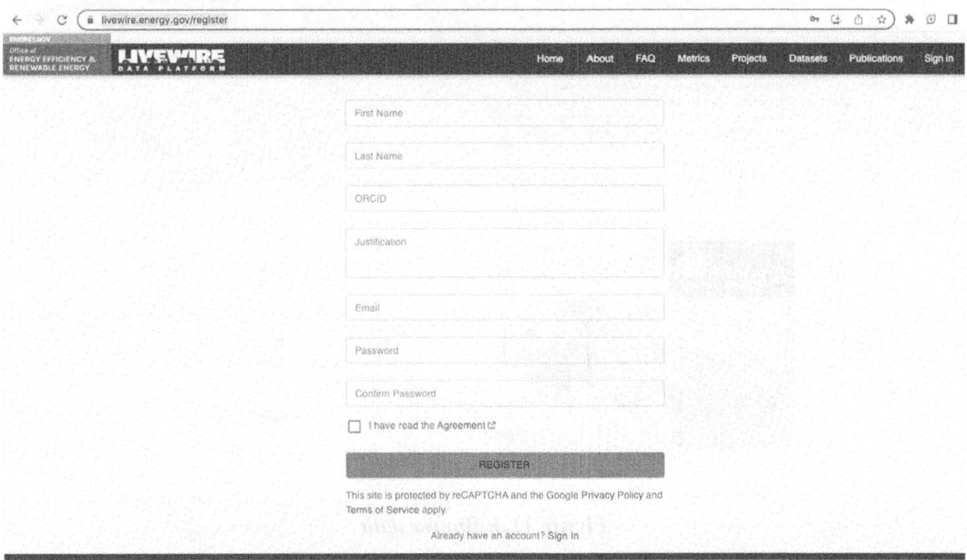

***Figure 11.1:** Register to download the dataset*

2. Check your inbox to verify your email account. You will be receiving an email similar to the one shown in *Figure 11.2*. Click on the **Verify Email Address** button on the email:

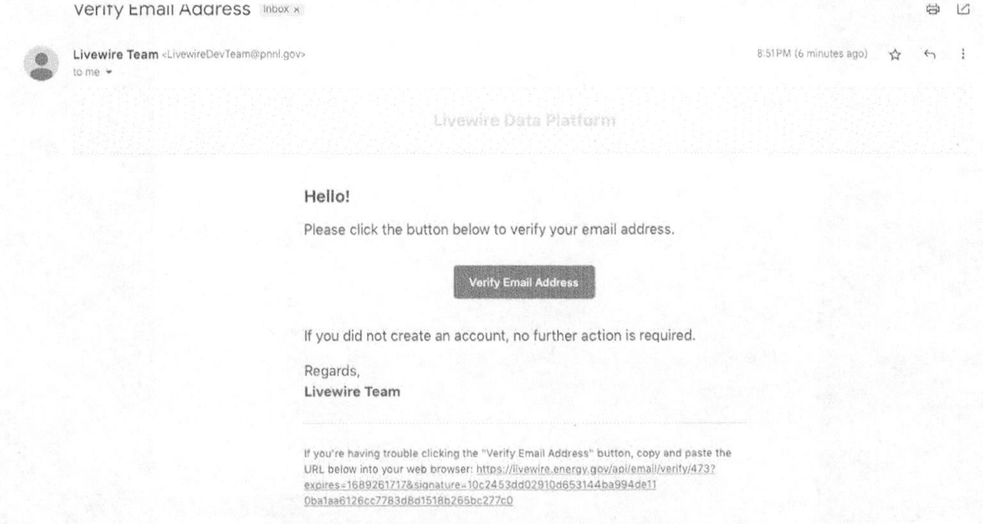

***Figure 11.2:** Verification of the registration*

3. After a successful verification and Sign-in, go to the link **https://livewire.energy.gov/ds/ld-cav-functionality/cadillac-ct6** and click on the **Browse Data** button as shown in *Figure 11.3*:

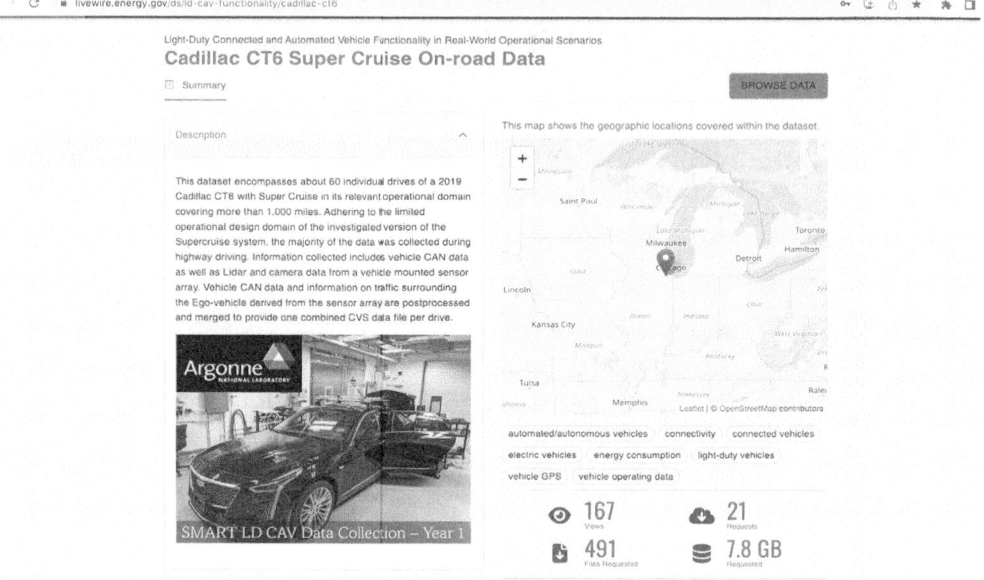

***Figure 11.3:** Browse data*

4. Click on the **Zip** button as shown in *Figure 11.4*:

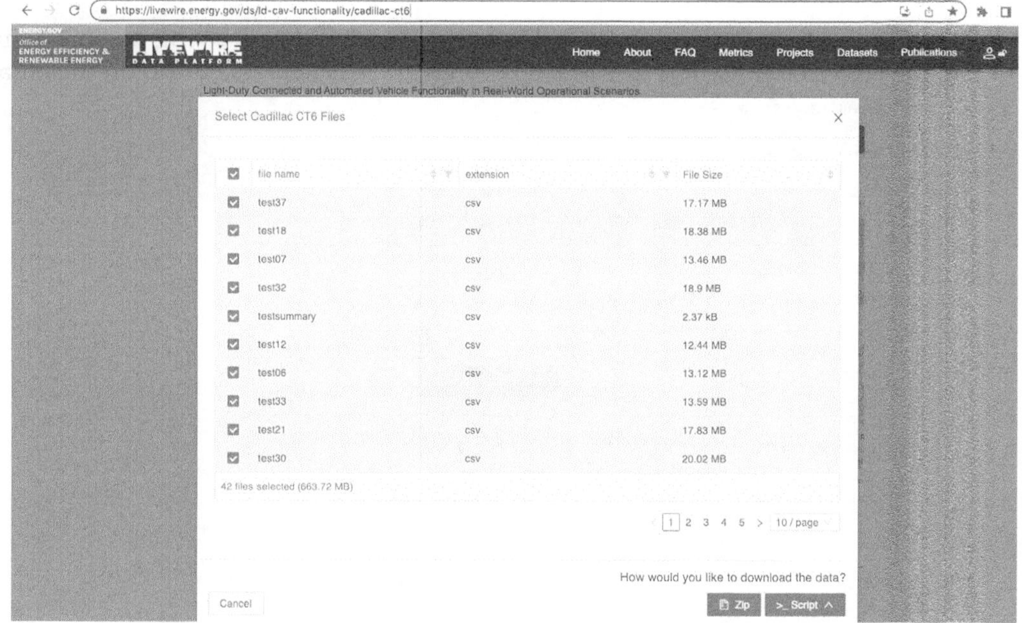

***Figure 11.4:** Download the zip file*

The above steps will download the datasets on your computer's default download location. We will proceed to perform data processing and integration in the next section.

Data Understanding

In the CRISP-DM framework, data understanding is typically the initial step in the data mining process, where we explore and familiarize ourselves with the collected data. We will examine the data's structure, content, and quality, identify relevant attributes, and gain initial insights into its characteristics. This understanding of the data serves as a foundation for making informed decisions during the subsequent Data Preparation stage.

Here is the Python code which aims to check the common and unique structures of datasets within a zip file which is downloaded above from **https://livewire.energy.gov/ds/ld-cav-functionality/cadillac-ct6**:

```
import os
import zipfile
import pandas as pd
# Specify the path to the zip file
zip_file_path = 'Downloads/cadillac-ct6.zip'
# Specify the directory to extract the zip contents
extract_dir = './vehicle_data'
# Create the extraction directory if it doesn't exist
os.makedirs(extract_dir, exist_ok=True)
# Extract the zip file
with zipfile.ZipFile(zip_file_path, 'r') as zip_ref:
    zip_ref.extractall(extract_dir)
extract_dir = './vehicle_data/cadillac-ct6'
# Get a list of all CSV files in the extraction directory
csv_files = [f for f in os.listdir(extract_dir) if f.endswith('.csv')]
# Initialize a dictionary to store the file structures
file_structures = {}
# Iterate through each CSV file
for csv_file in csv_files:
    file_path = os.path.join(extract_dir, csv_file)
    print(f"CSV File: {csv_file}")
    # Try different encodings until the file can be successfully read
    encodings = ['utf-8', 'latin-1']
```

```
    successful_read = False
    for encoding in encodings:
        try:
            # Read the CSV file into a DataFrame
            df = pd.read_csv(file_path, encoding=encoding)
            successful_read = True
            break
        except UnicodeDecodeError:
            continue
    if successful_read:
        # Get the structure of the DataFrame
        structure = df.dtypes.to_dict()
        # Check if the structure already exists in the dictionary
        for key, value in file_structures.items():
            if value == structure:
                print(f"Structure similar to: {key}")
                break
        else:
            print("Unique structure")
        # Add the structure to the dictionary
        file_structures[csv_file] = structure
        print(f"Columns: {df.columns.tolist()}")
    else:
        print("Unable to read the file.")
    print()
```

The above Python code is used for checking the common and unique structures of datasets within a zip file.

Here is the detailed walkthrough of the above Python code:

1. The code begins by specifying the path to the zip file and the directory to extract its contents. It also creates the extraction directory if it does not exist.
2. The zip file is then extracted to the specified extraction directory.
3. A list of all CSV files in the extraction directory is obtained.
4. A dictionary called **file_structures** is initialized to store the structures of the CSV files.

5. The code iterates through each CSV file in the list.
6. For each CSV file, it attempts to read the file using different encodings (utf-8 and Latin-1) until it can be successfully read. This is done to handle potential Unicode decoding errors.
7. If the file is successfully read, the code determines the structure of the DataFrame by accessing the data types of each column.
8. The code then checks if the structure already exists in the **`file_structures`** dictionary. If a matching structure is found, it prints **`Structure similar to`**: followed by the file with the matching structure. If the structure is unique, it prints **`Unique structure`**.
9. The structure of the current CSV file is added to the **`file_structures`** dictionary.
10. Finally, the code prints the columns of the DataFrame and moves on to the next CSV file.
11. If a CSV file cannot be read successfully, the code prints **`Unable to read the file`**.
12. The process continues until all CSV files have been processed.

The result of the above code shows that all the CSV files contained in the zip file have similar structures except for **`cadillac-ct6.signaldescription.csv`** and **`cadillac-ct6.testsummary.csv`**. Now, we can merge all the files which are common structures.

Let us merge the files except for **`cadillac-ct6.signaldescription.csv`** and **`cadillac-ct6.testsummary.csv`**:

```
import os
import zipfile
import pandas as pd
# Specify the path to the zip file
zip_file_path = 'Downloads/cadillac-ct6.zip'
# Specify the directory to extract the zip contents
extract_dir = './vehicle_data'
# Create the extraction directory if it doesn't exist
os.makedirs(extract_dir, exist_ok=True)
# Extract the zip file
with zipfile.ZipFile(zip_file_path, 'r') as zip_ref:
    zip_ref.extractall(extract_dir)
extract_dir = './vehicle_data/cadillac-ct6'
# Get a list of all CSV files in the extraction directory
csv_files = [f for f in os.listdir(extract_dir) if f.endswith('.csv')]
# Exclude specific files from merging
exclude_files = ['cadillac-ct6.testsummary.csv', 'cadillac-ct6.signalde-
```

```
    scription.csv']
csv_files = [f for f in csv_files if f not in exclude_files]
# Initialize an empty DataFrame to store the merged data
merged_data = pd.DataFrame()
# Merge the CSV files into a single DataFrame
for i, csv_file in enumerate(csv_files):
    file_path = os.path.join(extract_dir, csv_file)
    df = pd.read_csv(file_path)
    # Generate Vehicle ID for each CSV file
    v_id = f"V{i+1:03d}"
    df.insert(0, 'V_ID', v_id)  # Insert V_ID as the first column
    merged_data = pd.concat([merged_data, df])
# Reset the index of the merged DataFrame
merged_data.reset_index(drop=True, inplace=True)
# Save the merged data to a CSV file
output_file = 'vehicle_dataset.csv'
merged_data.to_csv(output_file, index=False)
# Print the location of the saved file
print(f"Final CSV dataset saved as {output_file}")
```

The above Python code merges all the CSV files inside the zip file except two CSV files that do not have a common structure (**cadillac-ct6.signaldescription.csv** and **cadillac-ct6.testsummary.csv**). The final CSV file is saved as **vehicle_dataset.csv**.

The file **cadillac-ct6.signaldescription.csv** contains a description of each column of the self-driving vehicle data we downloaded earlier in this section.

The file **cadillac-ct6.testsummary.csv** contains a test summary of forty individual drives which generated the 40 different CSV files. We merged all these forty files to create one dataset file for our analysis. We also created a new column **V_ID** to identify each unique trip from each of the CSV files. This will help in the analysis of each trip in comparison with another trip.

In addition, these two files give you an understanding of the dataset. It is always important to create a data dictionary to document key features of the dataset such as data quality summary, error summary, missing data, and about each column in the dataset, it is datatype, unit, and description.

You can download the documentation of the dataset we just downloaded from **https://livewire.energy.gov/api/datasets/ld-cav-functionality/cadillac-ct6/files/dictionary-ld-cav-functionality.cadillac-ct6.pdf**.

And you can understand how the technology of self-driving vehicles works is explained here: **https://www.cadillac.com/ownership/vehicle-technology/super-cruise**

It contains all important aspects of the dataset to understand the dataset. You need to prepare a similar document for any project you get involved in the industry. This type of documentation is the key first step in approaching any data science project, especially using the CRISP-DM framework.

Let us understand the data through simple **Exploratory Data Analysis** (**EDA**) on the dataset we created above.

Exploratory Data Analysis

Exploratory Data Analysis is a crucial step in the data analysis process that involves investigating and understanding the data. EDA aims to discover patterns, relationships, and trends within the dataset to gain insights and inform subsequent analysis.

The following Python program shows some basic details of the dataset, such as the total number of columns and datatypes of each column and some basic statistics of each column:

```
import pandas as pd
# Specify the path to the final dataset
dataset_path = 'vehicle_dataset.csv'
# Read the dataset into a DataFrame
dataset = pd.read_csv(dataset_path)
# Get the number of columns in the dataset
num_columns = len(dataset.columns)
print("Number of columns:", num_columns)
print("***********************************")
# Get data types of the columns
column_data_types = dataset.dtypes
print("Columns and their data types:")
for column, data_type in column_data_types.items():
    print(f"{column}: {data_type}")
print("***********************************")
# Get data types of the columns
column_data_types = dataset.dtypes
data_type_counts = column_data_types.value_counts()
print("Data type counts:")
for data_type, count in data_type_counts.items():
```

```
    print(f"{data_type}: {count}")
print("**********************************")
# Perform basic analysis on the columns
dataset_description = dataset.describe()
print("Dataset description:")
print(dataset_description)
print("**********************************")
# Display the top 10 rows of the dataset
top_10_rows = dataset.head(10)
print("Top 10 rows of the dataset:")
print(top_10_rows)
print("**********************************")
```

The above Python program provides us with some basic but important information about the dataset. We have 133 columns in the dataset, and there are 99 columns, which are float64 datatype, 26 columns with int64 datatype, and 8 object types.

The next important analysis is to find how many columns contain missing values. Here is the Python code which prints the list of columns with the percentage of NULL values:

```
import pandas as pd
# Specify the path to the final dataset
dataset_path = 'vehicle_dataset.csv'
# Read the dataset into a DataFrame
dataset = pd.read_csv(dataset_path)
# Get the percentage of empty or NaN rows for each column
empty_percentages = dataset.isnull().mean() * 100
# Filter columns with non-zero percentage of NULL values
non_zero_columns = empty_percentages[empty_percentages > 0]
# Sort the non-zero columns by the percentage of NULL values in descending order
sorted_columns = non_zero_columns.sort_values(ascending=False)
# Display the columns with their corresponding empty percentages in descending order
print("Columns with a non-zero percentage of NULL values in descending order:")
for column, percentage in sorted_columns.iteritems():
    print(f"{column}: {percentage:.2f}%")
```

The above python code shows 45 columns with some percentage of NULL values. Following is the full output of the above program with the percentage of NULL presence:

```
Columns with a non-zero percentage of NULL values in descending order:
LID_Same2|Distance y (m): 96.96%
LID_Same2|Distance x (m): 96.96%
LID_Same2|ID: 96.96%
LKASVehicleSpeed|ASCMLKASteeringCmd|HS CAN (kph): 91.01%
LKASteeringCmd: 91.01%
LKASMode|ASCMLKASteeringCmd|HS CAN: 91.01%
LID_Right2|Distance y (m): 87.74%
LID_Right2|Distance x (m): 87.74%
LID_Right2|ID: 87.74%
LID_Left2|ID: 79.63%
LID_Left2|Distance y (m): 79.63%
LID_Left2|Distance x (m): 79.63%
LID_Right1|Distance x (m): 67.34%
LID_Right1|ID: 67.34%
LID_Right1|Distance y (m): 67.34%
RAD_Same2|Acceleration (m/s2): 63.01%
RAD_Same2|Lat_Velocity (m/s): 63.01%
RAD_Same2|Long_Velocity (m/s): 63.01%
RAD_Same2|Distance y (m): 63.01%
RAD_Same2|Distance x (m): 63.01%
RAD_Same2|Track ID: 63.01%
LID_Right-1|ID: 62.57%
LID_Right-1|Distance y (m): 62.57%
LID_Right-1|Distance x (m): 62.57%
LID_Same1|Distance y (m): 58.81%
LID_Same1|Distance x (m): 58.81%
LID_Same1|ID: 58.81%
LID_Left1|Distance y (m): 38.13%
LID_Left1|ID: 38.13%
LID_Left1|Distance x (m): 38.13%
LID_Same-1|ID: 36.79%
```

```
LID_Same-1|Distance x (m): 36.79%
LID_Same-1|Distance y (m): 36.79%
RAD_Same1|Acceleration (m/s2): 36.14%
RAD_Same1|Lat_Velocity (m/s): 36.14%
RAD_Same1|Long_Velocity (m/s): 36.14%
RAD_Same1|Distance y (m): 36.14%
RAD_Same1|Distance x (m): 36.14%
RAD_Same1|Track ID: 36.14%
LID_Left-1|Distance x (m): 31.40%
LID_Left-1|Distance y (m): 31.40%
LID_Left-1|ID: 31.40%
LKASteeringCmd|ASCMLKASteeringCmd|HS CAN2: 8.99%
LKASVehicleSpeed (kph): 8.99%
LKASMode: 8.99%
```

The above list clearly shows that we can have 30% as the cut-off for removing all the columns which contain a significant number of NULL values. Using these columns will have a significant impact on our analysis, as any imputation technique will lead us to a biased result.

The next step is to perform univariate, bivariate, and multivariate analyses. Here is an example of a univariate analysis of the dataset for the selected columns:

```
import pandas as pd
import matplotlib.pyplot as plt
# Read the dataset into a DataFrame
dataset = pd.read_csv('vehicle_dataset.csv')
# Specify the columns for univariate analysis
columns = ['VehicleSpeed (mph)','ActVehAccel (m/s^2)', 'EngSpd (rpm)', 'GasPedalAndAcc',
           'InstFuelConsmpRate (ltrs/hr)', 'LKASVehicleSpeed (kph)',
           'VehOdo (km)']
# Perform univariate analysis for each column
for column in columns:
    # Print column name
    print(f"Column: {column}")

    # Get column data
```

```
    column_data = dataset[column]

    # Basic statistics
    print("Basic Statistics:")
    print(column_data.describe())
    print()

    # Histogram
    plt.figure()
    column_data.hist(bins=20)
    plt.xlabel(column)
    plt.ylabel("Frequency")
    plt.title("Histogram")
    plt.show()

    # Box plot
    plt.figure()
    column_data.plot(kind='box')
    plt.ylabel(column)
    plt.title("Box Plot")
    plt.show()
    print("************************************")
```

The above Python program shows the distribution of data using frequency and histogram diagrams.

Here is an example of performing bivariate analysis. The example shows the relationship between Brake Pedal Position **(% full)** and Engine Speed **(rpm)** in self-driving vehicles. A high Engine Speed with a full Brake Pedal Position indicates sudden braking. When the Brake Pedal Position is low, the vehicle maintains speed or accelerates. A high Brake Pedal Position suggests deceleration or emergency stops. If data points show high Engine Speed and full Brake Pedal Position, it signifies sudden braking events. Context and other variables should be considered for a complete analysis of vehicle operation.

```
import pandas as pd
import seaborn as sns
import matplotlib.pyplot as plt
# Read the dataset into a DataFrame
```

```
dataset = pd.read_csv('vehicle_dataset.csv')
plt.scatter(dataset['BrkPdlPos (% full)'], dataset['EngSpd (rpm)'])
plt.xlabel('BrkPdlPos (% full)')
plt.ylabel('EngSpd (rpm)')
plt.title('BrkPdlPos (% full) vs. EngSpd (rpm)')
plt.show()
```

Similarly, we can perform multivariate analysis to understand the dataset and its attributes.

Now, let us move on with the data preparation steps, which include feature selection.

Data Preparation and Feature Engineering

The data preparation stage is concerned with transforming the collected data into a format suitable for analysis. It involves several critical tasks, such as data cleaning, integration, transformation, and reduction. Data cleaning entails handling missing values, outliers, and inconsistencies to ensure data quality. Data reduction techniques may be applied to reduce dimensionality and eliminate redundant or irrelevant attributes. The data preparation stage ensures that the data is accurate, complete, and formatted correctly for analysis.

Feature engineering is typically a part of the data preparation stage in the CRISP-DM framework. Feature engineering involves transforming and manipulating the existing variables (features) in the dataset to create new, more informative features that can improve the performance of the predictive models.

During the data preparation stage, after the initial understanding of the data, cleaning and preprocessing steps are performed to handle missing values, outliers, and inconsistencies. Feature engineering is then carried out to create new features or modify existing ones based on domain knowledge, statistical techniques, or data transformations.

Feature engineering techniques may include:

- **Creating interaction terms**: Combining two or more existing features to capture interactions or relationships that can be important for the analysis.
- **Extracting date/time features**: Breaking down date/time variables into components like year, month, day, or hour, which can reveal temporal patterns or seasonality.
- **Encoding categorical variables**: Converting categorical variables into numerical representations that can be used by machine learning algorithms. This can involve techniques like one-hot encoding, label encoding, or target encoding.
- **Feature scaling or normalization**: Rescaling variables to a common scale to prevent certain features from dominating the analysis due to their larger values.

The methods and approaches of feature engineering differ based on the business problem and our solution approach. We may not always need to follow all these above-mentioned methods. We will go through simple data cleaning and feature engineering steps in the following sections.

Data Cleaning

We have observed from the previous section that there are multiple columns with more than 30% missing values. Let us remove the columns from our analysis using Python:

```
import pandas as pd
# Specify the path to the final dataset
dataset_path = 'vehicle_dataset.csv'
# Read the dataset into a DataFrame
dataset = pd.read_csv(dataset_path)
# Get the percentage of empty or NaN rows for each column
empty_percentages = dataset.isnull().mean() * 100
# Filter columns with more than 30% NULL values
filtered_columns = empty_percentages[empty_percentages > 30]
filtered_columns_names = filtered_columns.index
# Print the number of columns filtered
num_filtered_columns = len(filtered_columns)
print("Number of columns filtered:", num_filtered_columns)
# Print the names of the filtered columns
print("Columns filtered based on percentage of empty values:")
for column in filtered_columns_names:
    print(column)
# Filter the dataset to keep only the non-empty columns
dataset_filtered = dataset.drop(filtered_columns_names, axis=1)
# Save the filtered dataset to a CSV file
output_path = 'vehicle_dataset_final.csv'
dataset_filtered.to_csv(output_path, index=False)
# Print the total number of columns in the filtered dataset
num_columns_filtered = len(dataset_filtered.columns)
print("Number of columns in the filtered dataset:", num_columns_filtered)
# Display the new dataset's columns
print("Columns in the filtered dataset:")
for column in dataset_filtered.columns:
    print(column)
```

This above Python program reads a dataset from a CSV file and performs data filtering based on the percentage of empty or NaN values in each column. It calculates the percentage of empty values for each column and filters out the columns with more than 30% empty values. The program then prints the number of columns filtered and the names of the filtered columns.

Next, the program removes the 42 filtered columns from the dataset, creating a new filtered dataset. It saves the filtered dataset to a new CSV file.

Finally, the program prints 91 as the total number of columns in the filtered dataset and displays the names of the columns in the filtered dataset.

Data Pre-processing

We have the following columns, which are still having some empty values. We need to handle them before moving to a feature engineer. Here (see *Table 11.1*) are the columns with empty values of 8.99%:

Column Name	Percentage of empty rows
LKASMode	8.99%
LKASteeringCmd I ASCMLKASteeringCmd I HS	8.99%
LKASVehicleSpeed (kph)	8.99%

***Table 11.1:** Columns with empty values*

Feature Engineering

The approach for feature engineering depends on the business problem we solve through the dataset. Understanding the dataset in the context of business is critical to perform feature engineering for model building in the later stage.

The **vehicle_dataset_final.csv** we have is already filtered for non-empty columns. Now when we look at the dataset from the problem statement of predicting Lane Keeping of the self-driving vehicle, the following features are the key determining lane keeping for self-driving vehicles, from our understanding of the dataset:

1. Non-empty Column Names from the dataset:
2. LKASMode
3. LKASVehicleSpeed (kph)
4. LKASteeringCmd|ASCMLKASteeringCmd|HS CAN2
5. LnQltyCnfdncLvlLft (%)
6. LnQltyCnfdncLvlRght (%)
7. LnMrkrTypLft
8. LnMrkrTypRght

9. LnSenseDistToLLnEdge (m)
10. LnSnsDistToRLnEdge (m)
11. LnSnsLatVRelToLftMrkg (m/s)
12. LnSnsLatVRelToRgtMrkg (m/s)
13. LnSnsLnCrvtrLft (1/m)
14. LnSnsCrvtGrdntLft (1/rad/s)
15. LnSnsLnCrvtrRght (1/m)
16. LnSnsCrvtGrdntRt (1/rad/s)
17. LnSnsTngtOfHdngLnLft (m/m)
18. LnSnsTngtOfHdngLnRt (m/m)
19. LnPrvwDstncLft (m)
20. LnPrvwDstncRght (m)
21. LnMrkg3LnQltyConfLvl (%)
22. LnMrkg3LnMrkrTyp
23. LnMrkg3LnSnsLnDst (m)
24. LnMrkg3LnSnsLnCrvt (1/m)
25. LnMrkg3LnSnsLnCrvtGrad (1/(m*sec))
26. LnMrkg3LnSnsLnHdngTngt (m/m)
27. LnMrkg3LnPrvwDst (m)
28. LnMrkg4LnQltyConfLvl (%)
29. LnMrkg4LnMrkrTyp
30. LnMrkg4LnSnsLnDst (m)
31. LnMrkg4LnSnsLnCrvt (1/m)
32. LnMrkg4LnSnsLnCrvtGrad (1/(m*sec))
33. LnMrkg4LnSnsLnHdngTngt (m/m)
34. LnMrkg4LnPrvwDst (m)

Let us now use these features to perform analysis on feature importance using Python programming:

```
import pandas as pd
from sklearn.ensemble import RandomForestRegressor
import matplotlib.pyplot as plt
# Read the dataset into a DataFrame
dataset = pd.read_csv('vehicle_dataset_final.csv')
# Select the relevant features and target variable
```

```
features = ['LKASMode', 'LKASVehicleSpeed (kph)', 'LKASteeringCmd|ASCM-
LKASteeringCmd|HS CAN2', 'LnQltyCnfdncLvlLft (%)', 'LnQltyCnfdncLvlRght
(%)', 'LnMrkrTypLft', 'LnMrkrTypRght',
            'LnSenseDistToLLnEdge (m)', 'LnSnsDistToRLnEdge (m)', 'Ln-
SnsLatVRelToLftMrkg (m/s)', 'LnSnsLatVRelToRgtMrkg (m/s)', 'LnSnsLn-
CrvtrLft (1/m)', 'LnSnsCrvtGrdntLft (1/rad/s)',
            'LnSnsLnCrvtrRght (1/m)', 'LnSnsCrvtGrdntRt (1/rad/s)', 'Ln-
SnsTngtOfHdngLnLft (m/m)', 'LnSnsTngtOfHdngLnRt (m/m)', 'LnPrvwDstncLft
(m)', 'LnPrvwDstncRght (m)',
            'LnMrkg3LnQltyConfLvl (%)', 'LnMrkg3LnMrkrTyp', 'LnMrkg3Ln-
SnsLnCrvt (1/m)', 'LnMrkg3LnSnsLnCrvtGrad (1/(m*sec))', 'LnMrkg3LnSnsLn-
HdngTngt (m/m)', 'LnMrkg3LnPrvwDst (m)']
target = 'LnMrkg3LnSnsLnDst (m)'
# Extract the selected features and target variable from the dataset
X = dataset[features]
y = dataset[target]
# Convert the string columns to numerical using one-hot encoding
X_encoded = pd.get_dummies(X, columns=['LKASMode'])
# Create a Random Forest Regression model
model = RandomForestRegressor()
# Fit the model to the encoded data
model.fit(X_encoded, y)
# Get feature importances
feature_importances = model.feature_importances_
# Create a DataFrame with feature importances
importance_df = pd.DataFrame({'Feature': X_encoded.columns, 'Importance':
feature_importances})
# Sort the DataFrame by importance (descending order)
importance_df = importance_df.sort_values('Importance', ascending=False)
# Plot the feature importances
plt.figure(figsize=(10, 6))
plt.barh(importance_df['Feature'], importance_df['Importance'])
plt.xlabel('Feature Importance')
plt.ylabel('Features')
plt.title('Feature Importances')
plt.show()
```

```
# Print the top important features
print("Top Important Features:")
print(importance_df)
```

Below is the output of the above Python program, which shows the importance of features from the given list (see *Figure 11.5*):

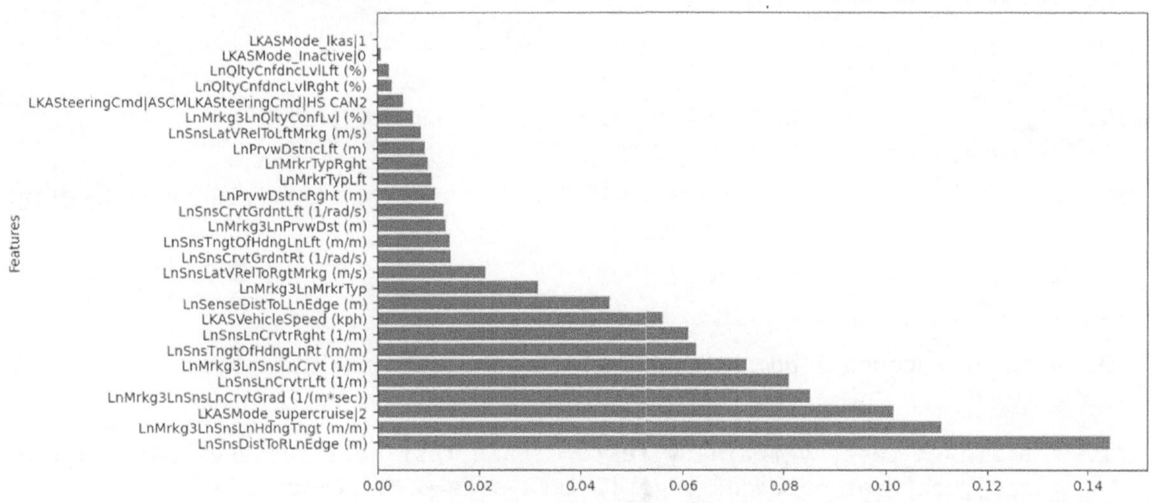

***Figure 11.5:** Feature Importance*

Let us try to build the machine learning model for predicting lane keeping using these features.

Modeling and Evaluation

Here is the model we built using the selected features, which shows accuracy as well:

```
import pandas as pd
from sklearn.model_selection import train_test_split
from sklearn.ensemble import RandomForestRegressor
from sklearn.metrics import mean_squared_error, r2_score
import pickle
import matplotlib.pyplot as plt
# Read the dataset into a DataFrame
dataset = pd.read_csv('vehicle_dataset_final.csv')
# Select the relevant features and target variable
features = ['LKASVehicleSpeed (kph)', 'LKASteeringCmd|ASCMLKASteering-
Cmd|HS CAN2','LnQltyCnfdncLvlLft (%)', 'LnQltyCnfdncLvlRght (%)', 'Ln-
MrkrTypLft', 'LnMrkrTypRght',
```

```
            'LnSenseDistToLLnEdge (m)', 'LnSnsDistToRLnEdge (m)', 'LnSnsLatVRelToLftMrkg (m/s)',
            'LnSnsLatVRelToRgtMrkg (m/s)', 'LnSnsLnCrvtrLft (1/m)', 'LnSnsCrvtGrdntLft (1/rad/s)',
            'LnSnsLnCrvtrRght (1/m)', 'LnSnsCrvtGrdntRt (1/rad/s)', 'LnSnsTngtOfHdngLnLft (m/m)',
            'LnSnsTngtOfHdngLnRt (m/m)', 'LnPrvwDstncLft (m)', 'LnPrvwDstncRght (m)',
            'LnMrkg3LnQltyConfLvl (%)', 'LnMrkg3LnMrkrTyp', 'LnMrkg3LnSnsLnCrvt (1/m)',
            'LnMrkg3LnSnsLnCrvtGrad (1/(m*sec))', 'LnMrkg3LnSnsLnHdngTngt (m/m)', 'LnMrkg3LnPrvwDst (m)']
target = 'LnMrkg3LnSnsLnDst (m)'
# Perform one-hot encoding for 'LKASMode'
dataset_encoded = pd.get_dummies(dataset, columns=['LKASMode'])
# Split the data into training and testing sets
X_train, X_test, y_train, y_test = train_test_split(dataset_encoded[features], dataset_encoded[target], test_size=0.2, random_state=42)
# Create a Random Forest Regression model
model = RandomForestRegressor()
# Train the model
model.fit(X_train, y_train)
# Make predictions on the test set
y_pred = model.predict(X_test)
# Evaluate the model's performance using mean squared error and R-squared score
mse = mean_squared_error(y_test, y_pred)
r2 = r2_score(y_test, y_pred)
print("Mean Squared Error:", mse)
print("R-squared Score:", r2)
# Save the model as a pickle file
with open('lane_prediction.pkl', 'wb') as file:
    pickle.dump(model, file)
# Plot the actual vs predicted values
plt.scatter(y_test, y_pred, color='blue', label='Actual vs Predicted')
plt.plot([y_test.min(), y_test.max()], [y_test.min(), y_test.max()], col-
```

```
or='red', linestyle='--', label='Perfect Prediction')
plt.xlabel('Actual Values')
plt.ylabel('Predicted Values')
plt.title('Actual vs Predicted Values')
plt.legend()
plt.show()
```

After training the machine learning model on the dataset, we evaluated its performance and obtained insightful results. The model file, **`lane_prediction.pkl`**, is saved in the working directory. The accuracy metrics demonstrate the effectiveness of the model in predicting lane behavior. The Mean Squared Error, with a value of 0.03986051099919496, indicates the average squared difference between the actual and predicted values, reflecting the model's precision. Additionally, the R-squared Score of 0.9728002128061396 signifies the proportion of the variance in the dependent variable that is captured by the model. These results highlight the model's strong predictive capabilities and its ability to accurately analyze and anticipate lane behavior. *Figure 11.6* shows the actual and predicted values with a perfect prediction drawn. This clearly shows the accuracy of the model we built (see *Figure 11.6*):

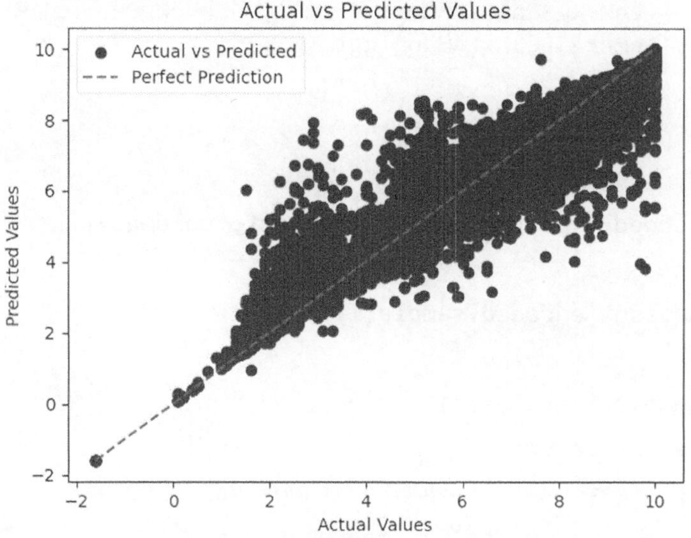

Figure 11.6: *Actual vs. Predicted*

Here is the Python code which validates the ML model using some sample data from the dataset:

```
import pandas as pd
from sklearn.ensemble import RandomForestRegressor
import pickle
```

```
# Read the dataset into a DataFrame
dataset = pd.read_csv('vehicle_dataset_final.csv')
# Select the relevant features and target variable
features = ['LKASVehicleSpeed (kph)', 'LKASteeringCmd|ASCMLKASteeringCmd|HS CAN2', 'LnQltyCnfdncLvlLft (%)',
            'LnQltyCnfdncLvlRght (%)', 'LnMrkrTypLft', 'LnMrkrTypRght', 'LnSenseDistToLLnEdge (m)',
            'LnSnsDistToRLnEdge (m)', 'LnSnsLatVRelToLftMrkg (m/s)', 'LnSnsLatVRelToRgtMrkg (m/s)',
            'LnSnsLnCrvtrLft (1/m)', 'LnSnsCrvtGrdntLft (1/rad/s)', 'LnSnsLnCrvtrRght (1/m)',
            'LnSnsCrvtGrdntRt (1/rad/s)', 'LnSnsTngtOfHdngLnLft (m/m)', 'LnSnsTngtOfHdngLnRt (m/m)',
            'LnPrvwDstncLft (m)', 'LnPrvwDstncRght (m)', 'LnMrkg3LnQltyConfLvl (%)', 'LnMrkg3LnMrkrTyp',
            'LnMrkg3LnSnsLnCrvt (1/m)', 'LnMrkg3LnSnsLnCrvtGrad (1/(m*sec))', 'LnMrkg3LnSnsLnHdngTngt (m/m)',
            'LnMrkg3LnPrvwDst (m)']
target = 'LnMrkg3LnSnsLnDst (m)'
# Perform one-hot encoding for 'LKASMode'
dataset_encoded = pd.get_dummies(dataset, columns=['LKASMode'])
# Get a sample value from the dataset
sample = dataset_encoded.sample(1)
# Print the sample value for features
print("\nSample Features:")
for feature in features:
    print(f"{feature}: {sample[feature].values[0]}")
# Load the trained model from the pickle file
with open('lane_prediction.pkl', 'rb') as file:
    model = pickle.load(file)
# Prepare new sample data
new_sample = {}
for feature in features:
    new_sample[feature] = sample[feature].values[0]
# Convert new sample data to DataFrame
```

```
new_sample_df = pd.DataFrame(new_sample, index=[0])
# Get the actual value from the dataset
actual_value = sample[target].values[0]
# Make predictions using the trained model
predicted_value = model.predict(new_sample_df)
# Print the actual and predicted values
print("\nActual Value:")
print(actual_value)
print("\nPredicted Value:")
print(predicted_value[0])
```

Here is the output of the above Python program:

Features with sample value:

LKASVehicleSpeed (kph): 87.6

LKASteeringCmd|ASCMLKASteeringCmd|HS CAN2: 3.0

LnQltyCnfdncLvlLft (%): 100.0

LnQltyCnfdncLvlRght (%): 100.0

LnMrkrTypLft: 2

LnMrkrTypRght: 1

LnSenseDistToLLnEdge (m): 1.85

LnSnsDistToRLnEdge (m): 1.35

LnSnsLatVRelToLftMrkg (m/s): -0.06

LnSnsLatVRelToRgtMrkg (m/s): 0.1

LnSnsLnCrvtrLft (1/m): -0.000135326

LnSnsCrvtGrdntLft (1/rad/s): -4.768e-07

LnSnsLnCrvtrRght (1/m): 7.8146e-05

LnSnsCrvtGrdntRt (1/rad/s): 1.788e-07

LnSnsTngtOfHdngLnLft (m/m): 0.002

LnSnsTngtOfHdngLnRt (m/m): -0.004

LnPrvwDstncLft (m): 40.0

LnPrvwDstncRght (m): 40.0

```
LnMrkg3LnQltyConfLvl (%): 100.0

LnMrkg3LnMrkrTyp: 2

LnMrkg3LnSnsLnCrvt (1/m): -0.000105783

LnMrkg3LnSnsLnCrvtGrad (1/(m*sec)): -2.9204e-06

LnMrkg3LnSnsLnHdngTngt (m/m): -0.004

LnMrkg3LnPrvwDst (m): 30.0
```

Actual and predicted values:

```
Actual Value: 4.8

Predicted Value: 4.841
```

Deployment of Machine Learning Models

In *Chapter 10, Understanding Edge Computing with MicroPython,* and *Chapter 9, Model Deployment on Edge Devices,* we covered the topic of how to deploy machine learning models on the Edge. In chapter *Chapter 5, Designing Data Lake and Executing Data Transformation,* we learned how to build a data pipeline for real-time streaming. We will apply the concepts here to perform streaming of Self-driving vehicle data to a **Message Queuing Telemetry Transport (MQTT)** topic and read the MQTT message to perform prediction using the model built above. Make sure that you have installed Mosquitto MQTT broker and started the service. Also, make sure that you have installed the **paho-mqtt** Python package installed.

Here is the Python code which publishes the data to an MQTT topic from the given dataset:

```
import pandas as pd
import paho.mqtt.client as mqtt
import time
import json
# Read the dataset into a DataFrame
dataset = pd.read_csv('vehicle_dataset_final.csv')
# Select the relevant features
features = ['LKASVehicleSpeed (kph)', 'LKASteeringCmd|ASCMLKASteeringCmd|HS CAN2', 'LnQltyCnfdncLvlLft (%)',
            'LnQltyCnfdncLvlRght (%)', 'LnMrkrTypLft', 'LnMrkrTypRght', 'LnSenseDistToLLnEdge (m)',
            'LnSnsDistToRLnEdge (m)', 'LnSnsLatVRelToLftMrkg (m/s)', 'LnSnsLatVRelToRgtMrkg (m/s)',
            'LnSnsLnCrvtrLft (1/m)', 'LnSnsCrvtGrdntLft (1/rad/s)', 'Ln-
```

```
SnsLnCrvtrRght (1/m)',
            'LnSnsCrvtGrdntRt (1/rad/s)', 'LnSnsTngtOfHdngLnLft (m/m)',
'LnSnsTngtOfHdngLnRt (m/m)',
            'LnPrvwDstncLft (m)', 'LnPrvwDstncRght (m)', 'LnMrkg3LnQlty-
ConfLvl (%)', 'LnMrkg3LnMrkrTyp',
            'LnMrkg3LnSnsLnCrvt (1/m)', 'LnMrkg3LnSnsLnCrvtGrad (1/
(m*sec))', 'LnMrkg3LnSnsLnHdngTngt (m/m)',
            'LnMrkg3LnPrvwDst (m)', 'Autoware Time', 'V_ID', 'LKASMode']
# Convert DataFrame row to JSON
def convert_row_to_json(row):
    data = row[features].to_dict()
    return json.dumps(data)
# Publish a JSON message to MQTT broker
def publish_to_mqtt(client, json_data):
    client.publish("vehicle_data", json_data)
# Connect to the MQTT broker
client = mqtt.Client()
client.connect("localhost", 1883, 60)
# Publish each row to the "vehicle_data" topic
for _, row in dataset.iterrows():
    json_data = convert_row_to_json(row)
    publish_to_mqtt(client, json_data)
    print("Published:", json_data)
    time.sleep(1)  # Wait for 1 second before publishing the next row
# Disconnect from the MQTT broker
client.disconnect()
```

Now, we can subscribe to the MQTT topic **vehicle_data** to read the data and perform the prediction of Lane Keeping using the machine learning model built earlier and saved in the local computer as a pickle file. Here is the Python program to predict the Lane Keeping of self-driving vehicles using real-time streaming of data:

```
import paho.mqtt.client as mqtt
import pandas as pd
import pickle
import json
# Load the trained model from the pickle file
with open('lane_prediction.pkl', 'rb') as file:
```

```python
    model = pickle.load(file)
    print("Loaded model for prediction")
# MQTT on_connect event handler
def on_connect(client, userdata, flags, rc):
    print("Connected to MQTT broker")
    # Subscribe to the "vehicle_data" topic
    client.subscribe("vehicle_data")
# MQTT on_message event handler
def on_message(client, userdata, msg):
    # Print the received message
    data_dict = json.loads(msg.payload.decode('utf-8'))
    data = pd.DataFrame(data_dict, index=[0])
    print("Data from the input stream:",data)
    # Select the relevant features
    features = ['LKASVehicleSpeed (kph)', 'LKASteeringCmd|ASCMLKASteeringCmd|HS CAN2', 'LnQltyCnfdncLvlLft (%)',
                'LnQltyCnfdncLvlRght (%)', 'LnMrkrTypLft', 'LnMrkrTypRght', 'LnSenseDistToLLnEdge (m)',
                'LnSnsDistToRLnEdge (m)', 'LnSnsLatVRelToLftMrkg (m/s)', 'LnSnsLatVRelToRgtMrkg (m/s)',
                'LnSnsLnCrvtrLft (1/m)', 'LnSnsCrvtGrdntLft (1/rad/s)', 'LnSnsLnCrvtrRght (1/m)',
                'LnSnsCrvtGrdntRt (1/rad/s)', 'LnSnsTngtOfHdngLnLft (m/m)', 'LnSnsTngtOfHdngLnRt (m/m)',
                'LnPrvwDstncLft (m)', 'LnPrvwDstncRght (m)', 'LnMrkg3LnQltyConfLvl (%)', 'LnMrkg3LnMrkrTyp',
                'LnMrkg3LnSnsLnCrvt (1/m)', 'LnMrkg3LnSnsLnCrvtGrad (1/(m*sec))', 'LnMrkg3LnSnsLnHdngTngt (m/m)',
                'LnMrkg3LnPrvwDst (m)']
    # Perform one-hot encoding for 'LKASMode'
    data_encoded = pd.get_dummies(data, columns=['LKASMode'])
    # Perform predictions using the trained model
    predicted_value = model.predict(data_encoded[features])
    rounded_predicted_value = round(predicted_value[0], 2)
    print("Predicted Value:", rounded_predicted_value)
```

```
# Connect to the MQTT broker
client = mqtt.Client()
client.on_connect = on_connect
client.on_message = on_message
client.connect("localhost", 1883, 60)
# Start the MQTT loop
client.loop_forever()
```

The above Python program demonstrates the integration of the MQTT messaging protocol with a machine-learning model for real-time prediction. The program begins by loading a trained model from a pickle file. Upon successful loading, it establishes a connection with an MQTT broker and subscribes to the **`vehicle_data`** topic.

When a new message is received on the subscribed topic, the **`on_message`** event handler is triggered. The received message, which is in JSON format, is decoded and converted into a Pandas DataFrame. Relevant features are selected from the DataFrame, and one-hot encoding is performed on the **`'LKASMode'`** column.

Next, the trained model is used to make predictions on the encoded data, and the predicted value is obtained. The predicted value is then rounded to two decimal places. Finally, the program prints the received data, as well as the rounded predicted value.

The program utilizes the Paho MQTT client library for establishing MQTT connectivity and the Pandas library for data manipulation. It showcases how MQTT can be leveraged to receive real-time data, apply machine learning predictions, and provide feedback accordingly.

Conclusion

In conclusion, this chapter delves into a comprehensive case study on self-driving vehicle dynamics using IoT Analytics. By analyzing a dataset of over 60 individual drives from a 2019 Cadillac CT6, valuable insights are extracted about self-driving vehicle behavior and performance. The CRISP-DM framework serves as a guide throughout the analysis, from understanding the business requirements to deploying machine learning models.

The chapter explores various aspects of the dataset, including vehicle data, Lidar information, and CAN data, which provide crucial information about the vehicle's surroundings, behavior, and operational parameters. Through the application of IoT Data Analytics techniques using Python, hidden patterns, correlations, and predictive models are uncovered, contributing to a better understanding of self-driving vehicle dynamics.

The discussed topics include the CRISP-DM framework, business understanding of self-driving vehicles, data collection and understanding, data preparation and feature engineering, modeling and evaluation, and deployment of machine learning models. Each step is explained in detail, showcasing how to approach the given business problem, and demonstrating the practical implementation of machine learning models for Lane Keeping predictions using real-time data from an MQTT broker.

By leveraging IoT Data Analytics methods, CRISP-DM framework and Python, this chapter paves the way for a safer and more efficient future on the roads, offering insights that can enhance the performance and reliability of self-driving vehicles.

Points to Remember

Following are the key takeaways from this chapter:

- The chapter focuses on a comprehensive end-to-end case study on self-driving vehicles using IoT Data Analytics methods and framework.
- A rich dataset from a 2019 Cadillac CT6 equipped with Super Cruise technology is analyzed, including vehicle data, Lidar information, and CAN data.
- The CRISP-DM framework is followed to uncover meaningful knowledge.
- The chapter covers topics such as the CRISP-DM framework, business understanding of self-driving vehicles, data collection and understanding, data preparation and feature engineering, modeling and evaluation, and deployment of machine learning models.
- The objective is to extract valuable insights about self-driving vehicle behavior and performance from the dataset.
- Python and MQTT are used for data analysis and real-time prediction.

Index

L

M